Endorsements from a variety of perspectives:

This is the most impactful and life-changing book project for me since I worked with Josh McDowell on *Right from Wrong* and wrote the *Truth Matters* curriculum for Lifeway. Thanks for writing this.

--**Dr. Larry Keefauver**, award winning best-selling author, ghostwriter and editor for works including Gary Smalley and John Maxwell

-----

The book *Seduced?* is exceptional in research, brilliant in reasoning, and convincing in its conclusions. Matthews has successfully reached back into history and drawn lines of thought up to the immediate present! A tremendous accomplishment! It brings into focus overriding themes of humanity. It is like turning the corner on a cornfield and seeing the rows line up. Thank you for writing it. *Seduced?* is a vital, necessary book to warn a historically illiterate generation of what lies ahead if society does not urgently have a course correction back to the eternal principles upon which America, and Western Civilization were built.

--**William J. Federer**, President of Amerisearch, Inc., American Minute, national radio and television host, and best-selling author of over twenty books and other resources with over one million sales

-----

We are in the midst of a seismic semantic revolution in which words are being systematically hijacked by a global coup d'état determined to overthrow the Judeo-Christian foundations of Western culture and civilization. In *Seduced?* D. K. Matthews offers a remarkably thorough and much-needed antidote to what may well be the ultimate battle for the future. This is a must-read!

--**Hank Hanegraaff**, President of the Christian Research Institute, best-selling author, national radio host, and author of *Truth Matters, Life Matters More: The Unexpected Beauty of an Authentic Christian Life*

Here's an important and timely work from an esteemed scholar at America's most important Wesleyan institution. Persons of faith and all persons committed to liberty of conscience will resonate with this work.

--**Mark Tooley**, President of Institute on Religion and Democracy, Editor of *Providence: A Journal of Christianity & American Foreign Policy*, author

-----

Matthews offers our society a thorough and much-needed reminder of two facts: first, "words mean things" and have consequences for church and culture, and second, "those who cannot remember the past are condemned to repeat it." If we are to have a future of faith and freedom, we'd better familiarize ourselves with what really has come before.

--**Dr. Daryl Diddle**, Pastor, Denominational Conference Superintendent

SEDUCED?

SEDUCED?

Shameless Spin, Weaponized Words, Polarization, Tribalism, and the Impending Disintegration of Faith and Culture

D. K. Matthews

LIBERTY HILL PUBLISHING

SEDUCED?
Shameless Spin, Weaponized Words, Polarization, Tribalism, and the Impending Disintegration of Faith and Culture

Liberty Hill Publishing
2301 Lucien Way #415
Maitland, FL 32751
407.339.4217
www.libertyhillpublishing.com

© 2020 by D. K. Matthews

Author Web Site and Blogs: doctord.org. PO Box 1398
Nicholasville, Kentucky 40356
Editorial director: Larry Keefauver, M.Div., D.Min.
www.doctorlarry.org

Printed in the United States of America.

ISBN-13: 978-1-6305-0333-8

DEDICATION

This work is dedicated to my father, Dr. Harold Matthews, my mother, Carlene Matthews, and my gracious wife, Dr. Carol Matthews. My father taught and modeled the verity that words really matter—for time and eternity. He read voraciously, and spoke and wrote deliberately, thoughtfully, precisely, painstakingly, meticulously, and with excellence. His semantic shoes cannot be filled by this work. My mother used words to encourage and support everyone, even during the darkest days of her twilight years, and bring much joy and comfort to family, friends, and countless individuals at multiple churches. She also taught us the joy of words set to music and the many celebratory words of Christmas. My wife contributed regularly to the cultural discernment and dialog that birthed this work, engaged in some editorial work, and, as always, sacrificially provided the Christlike inspiration and support requisite for such a project. I would be remiss not to express gratitude to Divine Providence. Completing multiple books in a few years amidst the extreme demands of work and the health issues and passing of many close loved ones was, humanly speaking, impossible. But as the words of Scripture remind us, "With God all things are possible" (Matthew 19:26). *Soli Deo Gloria.*

*For valiant, culturally and intellectually engaged
pastors, priests, rabbis,*

*and Judeo-Christian leaders who are sacrificially
standing in the gap*

*as civilization equivocates, stammers,
and staggers into the future.*

TABLE OF CONTENTS

"I believe there are more instances of the abridgment of the freedom of the people by gradual and silent encroachments of those in power than by violent and sudden usurpations."
James Madison

"Once a government is committed to the principle of silencing the voice of opposition, it has only one way to go, and that is down the path of increasingly repressive measures, until it becomes a source of terror to all its citizens and creates a country where everyone lives in fear."
Harry S. Truman

"Whoever would overthrow the liberty of a nation must begin by subduing the freeness of speech."
Benjamin Franklin

"Religious liberty might be supposed to mean that everybody is free to discuss religion. In practice [today] it means that hardly anybody is allowed to mention it."
G. K. Chesterton

"Just because something isn't a lie does not mean that it isn't deceptive. A liar knows that he is a liar, but one who speaks mere portions of truth in order to deceive is a craftsman of destruction."
Criss Jami

"American Millennials are far more likely than older generations to say the government should be able to prevent people from saying offensive statements . . .."
Pew Research Center

"Morality is always derivative. It stems from one's worldview."
Nancy Pearcey

"Having a Christian worldview means being utterly convinced that biblical principles are not only true but also work better in the grit and grime of the real world."
Nancy Pearcey

"A Republic must either preserve its Virtue or lose its Liberty"
John Witherspoon (President of the College of New Jersey/ Princeton, signer of the *Declaration of Independence*, professor of twelve members of the Continental Congress and nine of the writers of the Constitution, including James Madison)[1]

"Western societies, both in Europe and the U.S., are in an 'ABC moment' (Anything but Christianity). They are turning against the Jewish and Christian faiths that have made them what they are, and attempting to replace them with varieties of post-Christian secularism and other philosophies. Needless to say, the universities, which are some of the most powerful institutions in the modern world, grew out of directly Christian origins, so this is a fateful problem both for Christians and for the West at large. At best, the Christian faith is now regarded as purely private and irrelevant to academic thought. At worst, Christians are dismissed as 'faith-heads,' with beliefs that are untrue, irrational, reactionary, bigoted and on the wrong side of history."
Os Guinness

"If I could have entertained the slightest apprehension that the Constitution framed by the Convention, where I had the honor to preside, might possibly endanger the religious rights of any ecclesiastical Society, certainly I would never have placed my signature to it."
George Washington (1789)

"While just government protects all in their religious rights, true religion affords to government its surest support."
George Washington (1789)

Preface

PRELIMINARY EVIDENCE OF AN EMERGING AND ALTERNATE SEMANTIC UNIVERSE?

The genesis of this book is the accelerating verbal or semantic seduction fueling our cultural, ecclesial, and political polarization, tribalism, and crises.[2] Our public conversation is increasingly coarse and unhinged. The palpable toxicity of the present moment relative to political, academic, entertainment, and media discourse is inevitable given the cultural death of truth and the rudderless, relativistic, and tribalistic balkanization of communication.

The aroma of irresolvable conflict, verbal warfare and decay is ubiquitous. Should anyone be surprised at the consequences of over two generations of post-truth and anti-biblical indoctrination? Have we not educated and trained our political and media actors well to lead this rush toward fragmentation? Need we be surprised at the words and actions of those schooled by our shapeshifting colleges and universities—or echo chamber "multiversities"—that now populate the key positions of political and cultural leadership?[3]

The first draft of this book was completed in 2017. Subsequent culturally polarizing events, however, have only confirmed the core question of *Seduced?* and made the decision easy to bypass the slow pace of traditional academic publishing. Theologian and philosopher Carl F. H. Henry inquired more than a generation ago if we were living in the midst of a burgeoning "crisis of word," "truth," and "authority" as we drifted toward the "twilight of a great civilization." This crisis is now acute and exigent.

Of course, even the once aspirational term of civilization is controversial today and has been redefined by some as inherently oppressive, imperialist, and triumphalist (see Chapter 1). For many today, disillusioned by failed utopian or totalizing crusades, being civilized is now a vice, just as being bad is now good—as reflected in Icona Pop's (2012) double platinum "*I don't care*, I love it!"

This work also emerges from decades of interaction with students, faculty, the religiously uncommitted and unchurched, as well as leaders of religious communities. As is the case with morality and truth, words are now pervasively and opportunistically defined, re-defined, and utilized in a relativistic and sometimes weaponized fashion. Meaning and communication are "in the eyes of the beholder."

Today the beholder is the individual and/or the tribe, and no appeal is possible to a shared higher standard since the very existence of such a norm is now shrouded under the gathering cloud of widespread suspicion. And many ironically use words to affirm with Nietzsche the fact that "there are no facts," the truth that "there is no truth," and that we have "only interpretations" and "a mobile army of metaphors." Is it any wonder that we are living in an age where truth has been replaced with militant, tribalistic advocacy and the ethically vacuous will to have power over others?

Contemporary and Alternative Verbal Realities

As we approach historic and watershed moments and political decisions in the American context, is it fair to say that we have now fully traversed through a cosmic wormhole, or something akin to C. S. Lewis's wardrobe, and into another dimension? In this new reality verbal battles are raging, shameless political advocacy and spin rule the day, and words and phrases such as those in the following table are defined or redefined by each individual or warring tribe — even *within* many churches, synagogues, temples, and denominations.

Compassion	Convict	Democracy
Felon	Freedom	Freedom of choice
Freedom of speech	Femininity	Gender
God	Heaven	Inclusion
Infanticide	Jesus	"Judge not lest you be judged" (Judgmentalism)
Marriage	Masculinity	My body, My choice
Patriotism	Salvation	Social justice
The American experiment	Tolerance	Truth

Alternate Semantic Realities Refuted in Scripture

Word theft is not new and has emerged within faith communities many times over the course of multiple centuries. Chapter 4 will detail and discuss how the Apostle Paul, in just a few brief statements (2 Corinthians 11), challenged seven seductive definitions of key biblical terms. Paul countered these false definitions:

1. Another "Jesus"
2. A different "spirit" (*pneuma*, a term which Paul also uses in the classic passage on the Holy Spirit found in 2 Corinthians 3:17)
3. A different "gospel"
4. False "apostles"
5. Deceitful "workers"
6. A seductive "angel"
7. "Servants" of unrighteousness (rather than righteousness)

Paul had to expose these and many other pseudo-definitions and defend and restore the true definitions and beliefs in the church in order to preserve the church. Paul's task of preserving correct theological definitions within his faith community will be referred to in this work as semantic (verbal) polemics. Gently and respectfully making a reasoned or persuasive defense of right definitions, beliefs, and practice with those outside of our faith communities is known as apologetics (1 Peter 3:15). *Seduced?* is a book on the urgent nature of utilizing semantic apologetics and polemics today amidst our confused and verbally chaotic culture. For those especially concerned about semantic seduction in Jewish and Christian faith communities, see Chapters 3 and 4.

Cultural Wars and Losses

This work properly and intentionally focuses on the globally and digitally influential American and English language context, and it seems that everyone, regardless of political orientation, is accusing everyone else of fake news, spin, lies, and alternative fact universes. And we clearly have no workable or agreed-upon means for evaluating such allegations or defining key terms. We have lost our plumb line.

The United States Supreme Court's 5-4 Obergefell redefinition of marriage, which was also ultimately a redefinition of gender, language, and the human body, was yet another wave of a tsunami eroding the breakwaters of authentic Judeo-Christian influence on many faith communities, communication, civilization, cultural stability, and moral sanity.

Many religious conservatives have defined this erosion or cultural drifting somewhat simplistically, or in a rather atomistic fashion, and expressed concern about these perceived milestones of civilizational drift:

1. The removal of prayer, Judeo-Christian values, and God-talk from public education and the quest for a more perfect union
2. The attempts to remove affirmations of trust in and obedience to God from coinage and cultural artifacts
3. The Ten Commandments being removed from public buildings after decades and centuries of influence, approval, inspiration, and appreciation

4. The vanishing moral and ethical parameters and codes for entertainment and media
5. The boycotting or cancellation of contracts with businesses rooted in traditional biblical and Baptist values (such as Chick-fil-A),[4] and the perceived accommodation and caving under anti-Christian pressure when such businesses no longer support organizations such as the Salvation Army or the Fellowship of Christian Athletes
6. The accelerating eradication of the core Judeo-Christian worldview beliefs and moral framework from major cultural centers of power and influence (education, law, entertainment, media, and politics)
7. The increasing marginalization or even harassment of Judeo-Christian faith communities in an escalating "ABC" (anything but Christian) relativistic culture[5]

These watershed events are of varied import and the significance and proper response to such notable historical turning points are debated, even within faith communities. *However, the seductive banishment of biblical and Judeo-Christian influence from the entire American lexicon has far more profound and long-term implications and consequences for the health of faith communities, culture, law, and civilization than any single cultural loss or trend.*

The implications and consequences emerge from our definitions of terms, how we speak, how we communicate, how we utilize and apply words, how we interpret reality and controversial issues, how our terms interface with and define each other, and how we select and characterize the cultural norms of the emerging post Judeo-Christian verbal or semantic universe(s). And these seven illustrative watershed events and cultural losses just reviewed are, in large measure, symptoms of foundationless communication and verbal decay.

The rampant verbal seduction today is in many respects the diseased root that is producing the cancerous and decaying cultural fruit. This should be no surprise to Judeo-Christian faith communities centered in the personal Word and the inspired words that create, prescribe, characterize, and determine their identity and mission.

The verbally seductive redefinition of our entire vocabulary is redefining the future. This verbal or semantic trend is culturally virulent and is also taking place, as critically and previously noted, *within* our churches, synagogues, and temples. And the future of faith communities is the future of the world.

As core civilizational terms all morph and invert in relation to each other, the pages of history are being written or rewritten. Some of these authors of present and future history have themselves been seduced, while other seductive sirens deftly, intentionally, and covertly shape and lead the leaders and the masses. The willful seducers are not unaware of the seismic power of redefined and reformulated words.

Such verbal manipulation is often pronounced or conspicuous among certain political groups and ideological movements, especially those who have abandoned any normative conception of truth, but word theft is an equal opportunity employer regardless of political orientation. This work will repeatedly document and assess how some perspectives actually provide sanction for shameless and manipulative spin and deception, since no ultimate standard for truth exists. Yet it must be emphasized that departures from Judeo-Christian-influenced communication also include the tone and spirit of our civilizational and cultural dialog and debate.

Cultural Engagement, Integrity, Apologetic and Polemic Tone

Some who employ or trumpet Judeo-Christian beliefs, language, values, and terminology seem to lack in Judeo-Christian tone and virtue. Character, integrity, proper word usage, core values, and tone all matter for those who pursue "gentleness and reverence" (1 Peter 3:15) when dealing with fellow believers, critics, opponents, and especially skeptics and those who do not share the assumptions of our faith communities.

- "A gentle answer turns away wrath, But a harsh word stirs up anger." (Proverbs 15:1)

- "A soothing tongue is a tree of life, But perversion in it crushes the spirit." (Proverbs 15:4)
- "A hot-tempered man [or person, NIV] stirs up strife, But the slow to anger calms a dispute." (Proverbs 5:18)
- "The wise in heart are called discerning, and gracious words promote instruction." (Proverbs 16:21)
- "Gracious words are a honeycomb, sweet to the soul and healing to the bones." (Proverbs 16:24)
- And "sanctify Christ as Lord in your hearts, always being ready to make a defense to everyone who asks you to give an account for the hope that is in you, yet with gentleness and reverence." (1 Peter 3:15)

Corrections, rebukes, and prophetic warnings can be biblical and appropriate. Nathan challenged David, Moses rebuked Pharaoh, Paul corrected Peter, and Jesus fully exposed the heart motives and hypocrisy of the Pharisees. We must discern and judge but not judge hypocritically (Matthew 7:1-6), and our motive must be rooted in authentic love, holiness, and justice. Rebukes must be biblical in nature and should typically be a last resort, and those outside our circle of faith must be approached by a loving community with prophetic grace, gentleness, reverence, persuasive and well-prepared arguments, *agape*, and winsomeness.

Some today defend Judeo-Christian beliefs while simultaneously subverting Judeo-Christian values by their words, tone, and unbiblical character deficiencies. And others, in the name of "gentleness and reverence," parasite off of the sacrifices of others in the cultural trenches, contribute very little to influencing civilization, and avoid taking a costly stand for anything. Faith communities today are awash in both cheap grace and unattractive or tenuous grace.

What is clear is that the verbal or semantic center no longer holds in this fledgling and unstable chaotic universe. A snapshot list of well-known news stories and case studies less than a decade after Obergefell's macro-redefinition of civilization's fundamental family unit and pillar (marriage) is revealing, instructive, and should serve as a helpful preface to this work.[6] This list should also provide preliminary evidence for the central problem and question addressed in this book, which is are we being *Seduced?*

Twenty-Two Illustrative and Semantic Case Studies

1. Politicians on the left and right repeatedly accuse each other of *treason* with little attempt to define the term, its history, or its relationship to the United States Constitution—much less define appropriate standards of proof and conviction.[7] It is far more than a shared definition of marriage that is vanishing. We can't agree on correct definitions of treason, impeachment, freedom of speech, the establishment of religion, the American experiment, democracy, socialism, social justice, compassion, racism, morality, Christian, God, Jesus, salvation, heaven, or hell.

2. *Toy Story 4* and the latest version of *The Lion King* are accused of being "racist" in spite of the significant involvement of Beyoncé, James Earl Jones, and Chiwetel Ejiofor.

3. *Madonna* proclaims that her definition of "Jesus" would certainly support the choice of abortion, as she attempts to reconcile her passionate pro-choice spirituality with her Roman Catholic background, the teaching of the Pope, and her interpretation of the Bible. Multiple millennia of unique Jewish and Christian (including Roman Catholic) opposition to abortion and infanticide are either unknown or viewed as irrelevant to her personal definition of piety, spirituality, and Christianity or her advocacy for abortion. Madonna also "prays" like an evangelical with her team members prior to concerts where she engages in less than Roman Catholic behavior.

4. Similarly, in the current cultural context of verbal manipulation and tribalistic warfare, *Lady Gaga*, while performing in Vegas, felt most comfortable lecturing the Vice President as follows: "You are the worst representation of what it means to be a 'Christian.'"
   a. Why attack Pence? The reason was because Pence's wife works at a school that affirms a traditional and

biblical view of marriage. Hence, if a Christian affirms biblical morality, then they are not properly defined as an authentic Christian. Lady Gaga explained: "I am a 'Christian' woman, and what I do know about Christianity is that we bear no prejudice [other than against biblical Christians and organizations with traditional views] and everybody is welcome [except for traditionalists, because we are "inclusive"]. So you can take all that disgrace, Mr. Pence, and can look yourself in the mirror and you will find it right there."[8]

    b. Much could be asked, such as whether inclusion includes religious devotees who shroud their women in oppressive subjection, or if inclusion includes Stalinists who exterminated millions. The main point here, however, is how freely, in contrast to less than just a generation prior, terms such as Christian, marriage, human sexuality, love, inclusion, and disgrace are all simultaneously, organically, and shamelessly being redefined via new verbal or semantic universes. Lady Gaga is, for many, the heroine of the conflict and the "Christian" Pence clearly is the pseudo-Christian villain in such cultural stories and semantic narratives. Lady Gaga is probably very sincerely outraged, but she also has very likely been culturally and verbally seduced via her elitist bubble and celebrity echo chamber.

5. Such verbal seduction is evident and prevalent, as illustrated by the San Francisco Board of Supervisors, which as of late summer 2019 had passed a nonbinding resolution removing terms such as *convicts, felons, prisoners, juvenile delinquents, and inmates* from criminal justice semantics and replacing the terms with alternative terms and definitions such as *"justice-involved" persons* or young persons with "justice system involvement."

    a. Justice-involved could be viewed by some as referring to a social justice advocate.

  b. Substance abuser language was likewise softened. Why? The older terms, such as felon or substance abuser, it was argued, are not "inclusive" and support institutionalized "racism."[9]

  c. This illustration demonstrates how semantics is also connected to eschatology or future-visions. Verbal seduction can alter the present and create the future, just as with the redefinition of marriage.

  d. To be clear, truly just, compassionate, and redemptive treatment of criminals is welcomed from a Judeo-Christian perspective. Many Christians and Jews have been leaders in criminal justice reform and prison ministry (e.g., Chuck Colson). However, introducing more linguistic and moral ambiguity into criminal justice semantics, and the crushed worlds of victims, may be less than helpful, just, inclusive, or compassionate.

6. Meanwhile, in other areas of the American context, legal debates rage relative to criminalizing the actions of *pro-life medical staff* and doctors who refuse to participate in abortion procedures. Should abortion be defined as a choice and medical procedure, or the ending of a life? And this militant push to criminalize faith takes place just as increasing numbers of states attempt to turn back *Roe v. Wade*. Some red and blue states seem to be partially seceding from the Union either on abortion or on sanctuary cities.

7. A British woman, affirming that "gender" and "marriage" can only be defined by each individual, may portend the subjective logic of the American future when proclaiming that she is an *"objectum sexual."* In her semantic world she proclaims that she is attracted to and falls in love with inanimate objects and desires to marry her antique chandelier named Lumière.

  a. While this *objectum sexual* illustration is a bit extreme and may be publicity driven, it certainly underscores the *reductio ad absurdum* potential of a world without a linguistic or semantic plumb line in an era that is progressively embracing any self-chosen or tribal definition of "marriage" and "gender"—not to mention "love."

b. The cultural trending is simultaneously to reject binary gender norms and traditional marriage. Given the new ethical norms, or lack thereof, how can this new verbal universe possibly sustain opposition to voluntary, consensual polygamy? How can "marriage" ever be limited to the very Judeo-Christian conception of monogamy? Supreme Court justices have even asked such questions. The UK also recently banned advertisements that portray any gender stereotypes, such as emotionally tender or nurturing females or courageous males. Verbal redefinitions redefine reality.

8. World-class athletes not only challenge specific politicians or policies today, which certainly could be appropriate at times, but some now also curse the *White House* itself and denigrate the flag of *Betsy Ross*—while also claiming to be the true American "patriots."

9. Feminist athletes battle with transgender and formerly male athletes who claim to be "women" and whose presence and athletic victories are becoming conspicuous in female *sporting events* (see Chapter 1).

10. City leaders have now reversed their position in Minnesota, but initially they discontinued the practice of reciting the *Pledge of Allegiance* in order to be more "inclusive." The escalating calls for the banning of the *Pledge* from public and governmental, tax-funded meetings has added a new nuance to the definition of terms and ideologies such as patriotism, inclusivism, multiculturalism, post-colonialism, and antiracism.

11. The definitional distinction between "legal and illegal immigration" has almost completely been eradicated in much contemporary political and media discourse, and the verbal shift to "undocumented" was clearly intentional and allegedly "inclusive," "multicultural," and "compassionate."

Recently at a gathering of evangelical academic leaders, a major conservative evangelical thought leader seemed to mimic the political echo chamber of many media outlets and define anyone with sincere ethical and policy differences concerning open borders, or border security, or illegal immigration, with the term "*anti-immigrant*." And of course such "anti-immigrants" are unbiblical and lack compassion. Perhaps this use of "anti-immigrant" was unintentional, but the impression left was clear. Opponents of illegal immigration, by implication, are anti-immigrant, xenophobic, and bigoted. Also see case study and news story # 22 below in this Preface.

12. The governor of a major state amped up and anted up the universal health care debate and cost by going far beyond the prior definition of "universal."

    a. The debate used to revolve around whether all American *citizens* should be covered by the "right" of "universal" health care, but this governor subtly or brazenly redefined "universal" to include health care for all noncitizens: "If you [truly] believe in universal health care, you [must then] believe in *universal health care*." To do otherwise would compromise love, compassion, inclusion, and social justice.

    b. So universal now apparently means everyone within the nation's borders. But why stop there since we are being "compassionate" and "universal"? If universal means universal, then why not have American tax dollars subsidize the "universal" health care of everyone in this hemisphere? If we are going to play word games in the name of "social justice" and "compassion," then let's really be "compassionate" and do this right and truly think borderless and big. Why quibble over whether the business model for such health care is coherent and sustainable if one is sincerely committed to "social justice"? Little attention is being given to the detail, pseudo-math, practicability, and implications of the business model of such universal health care even if applied within the borders of one country.

13. In a similar vein, "biblical and/or compassionate social justice" is ever being identified with unsustainable freebies and handouts that would literally jeopardize both the domestic and global economies and cast millions if not billions into economic stagnation, poverty, and potential international instability. Such economic chaos was experienced and witnessed broadly in the twentieth century in the wake of multiple utopian movements.

    a. One recent presidential candidate promised somewhere in the neighborhood of an additional $90 trillion in U.S. budget deficits and handouts to achieve such ill-defined "social justice."[10] Even if the total is half that amount, such a business model is alarming for those who truly understand and care about the poor and properly defined justice.

    b. And this trillion-dollar deficit politician is not alone in covertly equating fiscal irresponsibility and probable economic chaos with compassion and the identification with the poor or the working class—as we recklessly rush toward quadrillion-dollar deficits.[11] Whether such promises amount to political prostitution or naïve idealism, the grave consequences are the same, regardless of whether such untenable budgetary promises emerge from the political left, right, or middle, and regardless of whether the bulk of the expenditures go to defense or entitlements.

    c. The definition of compassion and the desire to "spread the wealth around" is more than suspect if the proposed compassionate business model fails to engage in careful fiscal analysis that is mindful that, in the American context,

        • "the top 50 percent of all taxpayers paid 97 percent of all individual income taxes, while the bottom 50 percent paid the remaining 3 percent."

- "the top 1 percent paid a greater share of individual income taxes (37.3 percent) than the bottom 90 percent combined (30.5 percent)."[12]

  Even if these figures are not entirely accurate, it is reflective of important business model assumptions that must be rigorously analyzed and taken into account relative to sustainable and coherent compassion. Is a reckless "credit card" debt style compassion that mortgages the future of our posterity legitimately referred to as compassionate justice (see Chapter 7)?

14. By the way, for many occupying the same state and verbal universe as the pro-universal or "truly universal" health care governor referenced previously in item #12, the former enthusiasm for and attendance at *Fourth of July* celebrations and parades has now been replaced in some locales with like passion for *Gay Pride* parades and festivities. At least according to Rod Dreher, the Fourth of July celebration arguably has been redefined and replaced in our culture:

    Pride [the ideology and the parade] has become exactly ... a civil religion [or even a reflection of the emerging new civil religion or even church-state religion and neo-theocracy]. What began as a rebellion against bourgeois sexual and social norms based in Christianity has now displaced those norms, and been completely absorbed by the *civitas* [the politically organized community] . . .. The photos of Boy Scouts marching in the parade, of law enforcement, of all the top politicians, and of Bud Light Pride ads — this is exactly what the Fourth of July was when I [Rod Dreher] was a kid.[13]

15. Yet these daily headlines reveal that there is much more under assault than red state morality or political orientation in this escalating verbal conflict. It is far more than

conservative political values or traditional Judeo-Christian convictions that are under assault.

    a. Even the progressive and blue state Speaker of the House, known for complaining that the opposition political party is seeking to "make America white again," is implicitly if not explicitly accused of the *racist* singling out of women of color by progressive members of her own party. The Speaker dared to question the rationality of the *"social justice"* policies and tactics of junior members of the House.

    b. Another relatively progressive presidential candidate was accused by a fellow blue state presidential candidate and good friend and colleague of his own party for being implicitly racist due to differences over dated and contemporary desegregation policies and implementation. In addition, two of the most progressive or liberal presidential candidates have accused each other of shameless lying within the context of one campaign accusing the other of blatant sexism.

    c. Politically progressive Bill Maher was threatened with a boycott because he dared to question the wisdom of boycotting Israel, and he was, therefore, declared as "racist" relative to Palestinians. Seemingly everyone is a racist in our new semantic universe.

    d. The cultural dialog seems to be fraying and decaying toward historic incivility and outrage, akin to the Civil War or Revolutionary War eras. *However, there is one major difference between then and now. We increasingly have no shared plumb line for judging and meliorating the conversation.* Hence, much is at risk due to these verbal redefinitions.

16. Victor Davis Hanson created his own list of illustrations of a fraying civilization, including the seeming lack of any norm by which to define normative *morality* and debate and judge the *morality of countries or civilizations*: "As Barack

Obama once bluntly put it, America is only exceptional in relative terms, given that citizens of Greece and the United Kingdom believe their own countries are just as exceptional. In other words, *there is no absolute standard to judge a nation's excellence* [or cultural assumptions]."[14] In other words, beliefs are totally subjective. Hence, "patriotism" and the "American experiment" are matters of personal or cultural preference and definition rather than definable or measurable by and grounded in any knowable, shared or eternal principles (especially see Chapters 2, 3 and 9). Such macro-verbal redefinitions have massive implications. The point at this juncture is not to align with Hanson and defend American exceptionalism but to highlight the absence of a norm or plumb line to guide our definitions and usage of terms or our normed reflection on the morality of countries or civilizations.

17. Greg Lukianoff and Jonathan Haidt highlight one consequence of this endless verbal seduction and pseudo-sensitivity emanating from higher education.

    a. For example, they applaud the progressive political gains relative to the "*safety*" of children in the late twentieth century. Yet they also lament that "gradually, in the [postmodern or ultramodern] twenty-first century, on some college campuses, the meaning [and definition] of 'safety' underwent a process of 'concept creep' and expanded to include '*emotional* safety.'" Especially see Chapter 6 for definitions and explanations of postmodernism and ultramodern syncretism, including an assessment of the ten commandments of postmodernism. In the American context today, we are currently suffering through ultramodern syncretistic impeachment hearings.

    b. As an example, in 2014, Oberlin College posted guidelines for faculty, urging them to use trigger warnings to "show students that you care about their safety." The authors argue that what the "safety" memo was "really telling its faculty was: show students that you care about their *feelings*."

c. Hence, in *The Coddling of the American Mind*, Lucianoff and Haidt argue that via verbal seduction the concept of physical "safety," a very legitimate concern, has morphed into irrational hypersensitivity about emotional "safety." They conclude, "A culture that allows the concept [or definition] of 'safety' to creep so far that it equates emotional discomfort with physical danger is a culture that encourages people to systematically protect one another from the very experiences embedded in daily life that they need in order to become strong and healthy."[15]

d. Perhaps this verbal morphing is the soil out of which the widely covered and successful multimillion-dollar lawsuit against Oberlin College emerged (see Chapter 2).

18. In the critical area of faith communities and religious higher education, Union Theological Seminary has so redefined Judeo-Christian "prayer," how Union is supposedly "grounded in the Christian faith," and the seminary's view of God and repentance, that it now views as a legitimate option this recent worship service in Union's chapel: "In worship, our community confessed the harm we've done to plants, speaking directly in repentance."

a. Here, via this *praying to plants* scandal, we arguably have five heresies or departures from biblical and orthodox Judeo-Christian beliefs in this one brief and just-quoted sentence about praying to plants: *the redefinition of God, the redefinition of prayer, the redefinition of repentance, the neo-pantheistic redefinition of plants, and the redefinition of salvation.* Union was founded by Judeo-Christian Presbyterians in the early nineteenth century and long ago moved away from orthodox oversight or beliefs. Yet this bastion of progressive thought was

graced less than one hundred years ago by the presence of biblically influenced and historic scholars
such as Dietrich Bonhoeffer and Reinhold Niebuhr
who, because of their Christian convictions, would
not tolerate the deification of anything less than the
transcendent, personal God who created all things.
Hence, Bonhoeffer, Niebuhr, and we might include
Karl Barth, all opposed the Hitler movement for
theological, biblical, and Judeo-Christian reasons.
Deifying or praying to Hitler—or plants—is idolatrous. How far we have fallen *inside* of our faith
communities.

b. The school claims still to be in orbit of its "Christian"
tradition, even "grounded in the Christian tradition,"
while learning from other faiths, pursuing "social
justice" and praying and confessing sins to plants
in a chapel service. Predictably, Union defended
this truth and religious relativism by appealing
to that very same relativism and pluralism, rather
than moving toward intellectual honesty by simply
acknowledging their departure from any authentic
grounding in the Christian tradition. Union's web
site countered, "This [prayers to plants] is just
one expression of worship here at Union. Union
Theological Seminary is grounded in the Christian
tradition, and at the same time deeply committed
to inter-religious engagement [inclusion]. Union's
daily chapel is, by design, a place where people
from all the wondrous faith traditions at Union
can express their beliefs. And, given the incredible
diversity of our community, that means worship
looks different every day!"[16]

c. The religion of Union sounds more like polytheism than monotheism (especially see Chapter
6). Retaining the long ago vacated, or redefined,
and essentially abandoned symbols and terms of
the Judeo-Christian faith at Union hardly amounts

to a meaningful grounding in the Christian tradition. "Christian" has been redefined but retained for unbiblical and non-theological reasons, if not for the seductive attempt to continue to appear as a "Christian" seminary to assist with branding, enrollment, and fundraising. Why not just admit they are a post-biblical, post-Christian, multi-faith religious seminary? Why not just admit that they espouse a new post-Christian religion? Countless seminaries, Christian institutions of higher learning, and Jewish institutes of religion—typically launched and funded by very orthodox religious faith communities—have radically redefined or abandoned their "Judeo-Christian" heritage some time ago. This has been the oft-repeated pattern and drift, including the history of many colonial nurseries of piety (e.g., Harvard, Yale, or Princeton).

19. On the popular culture front, the 2019 responses to the Bible-believing "Christian" on the *Bachelorette* were telling.

    a. The Christian's concern that the bachelorette's sleeping with multiple partners *during the show and search for a spouse* might interfere with the future of their budding relationship was strongly condemned by many television hosts and their audiences. The "Christian," who certainly could have been more tactful and less naïve, was unmercifully vilified as "judgmental" not only by the bachelorette star but also subsequently by the talk show host moral "experts" and their entire and raucous studio audiences. On one show, a large picture of the "judgmental" Christian was revealed only to be covered by a large "X" as the crowd and hosts erupted in gladiatorial games style jubilation. No concerns surfaced about the treatment of the "Christian," or the behavior of the bachelorette, who was defined as "virtuous" because freely chosen fornication and relations with multiple partners—and a passionate and "judgmental" response to the courting Christian's concerns—were viewed as "tolerant" and "nonjudgmental."

b. The bachelorette was the virtuous heroine and the Christian was the unvirtuous villain. Again, this evangelical Christian bachelor could have been better coached on how to navigate such a public forum, but the response to the Christian reflected the militant moral relativism and gathering anti-Christian winds and semantics of this present generation.

c. This case study also illustrates how, in many respects, that the term *Christian,* which used to refer to the principled and religious virtuous person, has been redefined and covertly applied to the individual not biblically grounded, and vice versa. In other words, what we used to mean by "Christian," as a positive statement about one's faith-based character, is now applied to the individual who flaunts biblical morality and takes a stand against judgmental, hateful, intolerant, and non-inclusive "Christians."

d. This is a significant and most consequential verbal shell game shift. For some today, even pro-life Mother Teresa is defined as the villain and not the "saint." She was portrayed as *"Hell's Angel"* according to a British television program, and referred to as "a fanatic, a fundamentalist, and a fraud" by atheist Christopher Hitchens.[17]

e. As many have pointed out, good is now bad, bad is now good, crazy is now sane, sane is now crazy, cool is now post-biblical, and biblical is now uncool. For those who are philosophers, it is evident that Nietzsche's prophesied transvaluation or inversion of values *and* words is in full bloom.

20. An unsuccessful and losing presidential candidate, perhaps partially in jest relative to running for office again, recently redefined the concepts of winning or beating an opponent in an election by proclaiming that she could defeat or beat

their presidential opponent "again." This claim was made even though the candidate clearly had lost the electoral vote in the prior contest and did not occupy the White House, "again." So this unsuccessful candidate is rejecting the electoral college system and completely redefining the normal meaning of terms and concepts such as winning, victory, beating an opponent, and election results. Hopefully this was only intended as humor, but in the media it was framed as an actual redefinition of who "won" the election.

21. Relative to the promethean (or slippery) and opportunistic redefinition of "social justice," those who have touted themselves as social justice warriors, such as Nike, the NBA, or Lebron James, are now accused of social injustice by many social justice advocates for their fiscal opportunism and enabling of Chinese oppression.

   a. In 2019 the Hong Kong protesters who were risking everything reacted with stunned anger to James, even setting on fire the jersey of this self-proclaimed social justice warrior. The *Detroit Free Press*, hardly a bastion of conservative thought, was rather direct: "It's hard to imagine James being more tone-deaf. Or hypocritical. Or, frankly, selfish himself." Shawn Windsor, writing for the *Free Press* summarized the situation with James as follows by quoting James: "'I [Lebron] get to sit up here and talk about social injustice,' he said, responding to comments from Fox News' Laura Ingraham in 2018, a right-wing opinion-maker who didn't like James's description of President Trump as 'laughable' and 'scary.'" Windsor then again quoted Lebron: "'We will definitely not shut up and dribble,' James promised. And he hasn't."

   b. Windsor concluded, "Which is why his [Lebron's] words Monday night felt like a gut punch to so many who've admired his dedication to social justice, when he told Houston Rockets general manager Daryl Morey [who had supported the Hong Kong protesters] to do what Ingraham once told him: Shut up ... and build your team."[18] To be fair to some in the NBA, basketball star and luminary Shaquille O'Neal recently defended Daryl Morey's right to free speech and opposition to Chinese oppression.

c. This NBA case study may well reflect the well-known argument found in chapter 7 of this work that, for some, and more and more frequently for many, "social justice" has now been redefined as "just us." "Social justice" is chic, *avant-garde*, and also rudderless. And true social justice is abandoned at whim for personal, tribal, or fiscal reasons.

22. Such word definitions and redefinitions, and the death of meaningful communication, might impact the very future of free speech.

a. The more progressive or liberal media outlet CNN has reported, "You can now be fined up to 250,000 if you call someone an 'illegal alien' in New York City." These new social justice guidelines from New York's Commission on Human Rights, which also "ban discrimination based on . . . English proficiency," do clarify that the potential $250,000 fine is "based on a discriminatory motive." This is a rather difficult determination that will, of course, be decided by those likely predisposed to the assumptions that led to such verbal or semantic redefinitions in the first place.[19]

b. As a point of reference, *Merriam-Webster*, *Cambridge*, the IRS, ICE, and Homeland Security all essentially concur on the definition and concept of an illegal alien. An alien is someone who is "not a citizen of the United States," and an illegal alien is a "foreign person who is living in a country without having official permission to live there, or someone who lives or works in another country when they do not have the legal right to do this." DHS also equates "immigrant" with "permanent resident alien" rather than conflating "legal immigrant" and "illegal immigrant" and opportunistically obscuring the question of legal status.

c. Even the IRS, much criticized by conservatives as harboring an anti-conservative agenda, defines an "undocumented alien" as one who "entered the United States *illegally* without the proper authorization and documents, or who entered the United States legally and has since violated the terms of his or her visa or overstayed the time limit. An undocumented alien is deportable if apprehended."[20]

d. Hence, the popular euphemism today of the "*undocumented* immigrant or alien," which is used to replace "illegal immigrant or alien" and soften or cloak concerns about legality, is actually premised upon an official definition of undocumented that assumes the very concept of an illegal alien. *In other words, undocumented technically or literally means illegal.*

e. Perhaps that is why some advocates for sanctuary cities and illegal immigration have now shifted their ambiguous semantics from undocumented aliens to "new Americans."[21]

f. This discussion is illustrative of the verbal games of the present generation. Undocumented alien or immigrant arguably means illegal alien but some attempt to spin terms like undocumented or immigrant in order to shroud the question of legality — including Michelle Obama.[22]

g. Would it not be far more helpful simply to maintain the distinction between legal and illegal immigration and then, for those supporting illegal immigration, either argue for the morality of civil disobedience or pursue a legal remedy and attempt to decriminalize illegal immigration via legislation — and/or simply press for legal and open borders? Such an approach would seem to reflect enhanced verbal or semantic integrity and constructive public discourse.

h. Perhaps an even better alternative exists in an early form in the *Evangelical Call for Restitution-Based Immigration Reform.* This statement seeks to synthesize these principles: the biblical faithful are frequently aliens, sojourners, slaves, and outsiders; the biblical faithful are called to be welcoming of and compassionate to the strangers in their midst; the biblical faithful are called to compassionate justice that respects law, order, borders, and social impact; and the biblical faithful should advocate for compassion and appropriate accountability for illegal immigration, both relative to the actions of illegal immigrants and the systems, individuals, and groups that contribute to or enable the legal and illegal immigration crisis. Legal immigration reform is the focus rather than subversion or virtue-signaling. This statement reflects some questionable assumptions and needs further refinement, but it at least serves as a more transparent, honest, and balanced approach to the current legal and illegal immigration crises.[23]

i. In any event, fining folks $250,000 for referring to someone as an "illegal alien," while also attempting to discern and determine intent and motive, would seem to reflect the present, chaotic, militant, and tribalistic alternate reality we have now entered that was referenced at the beginning of this Preface. Should not such proposals at least be carefully vetted as yet another potential and imminent threat to free speech?

This list is a miniscule sampling of relevant news stories and semantic and cultural morphing. Every major area of culture and civilization—politics, entertainment, music and the arts, media and news, law, and social media—has reached the crisis point of a verbal impasse or outright semantic conflict.

Religiously and Politically Conservative Target Audience

The examples just provided intentionally seek to find resonance with religiously and politically moderate to conservative faith communities which will serve as the target audience of this book. Hence, the endorsements sought out for this work were primarily religiously and politically conservative or moderate leaders involved in media ministry and faith communities, in order to connect with and hopefully impact that important and influential sub-culture. Within the context of dialog with this target audience, a key reason for this work is to make the case for preferable definitions of terms that can shape and enhance church, synagogue, and culture—starting with the conservative/moderate American faith communities. Other diversity endorsements sought out were agreed to but not received by the publishing deadline. The preferable definitions of terms suggested in this work should be on the discussion table at the very center of the marketplace of ideas as culture evolves in a post Judeo-Christian direction. These definitions are arguably much more consistent with and generative of the authentic and original American experiment in responsible freedom than the cultural lexicon that dominates education, media, and entertainment today. If this work had a different and more politically and religiously progressive target audience, other examples and case studies would have been provided. The argument and structure of the book would have been greatly modified in order to persuade progressives that a semantic crisis is upon us, civilization is adrift, and that an appropriate semantic response is needed to ensure future religious and political flourishing. The author is very cognizant of the kinds of examples more politically progressive or politically liberal advocates would identify, but the semantic thesis of this work should stand regardless of one's political or social perspective. Words rule.

Many of those who are more politically conservative in the American context sense that such case studies reflect how the political left is rushing toward the marginalization, harassment, or even criminalization of those espousing the original American experiment and biblically-based Judeo-Christian beliefs and practice. Alarmist or not, they view the political left as seeking to eradicate Judeo-Christian culture, the Judeo-Christian memory, Judeo-Christian influenced terminology, and the authentic Judeo-Christian influenced American experiment from Western civilization. This book will carefully assess that concern.

Perhaps even more disturbing to these conservatives is that they see the political left as now seductively wrapping themselves in the flag of a redefined "patriotism" and the cross of a Judeo-Christian "spirituality." When the American Speaker of the House repeatedly and publicly trumpets how she prays for her chief political opponent, and she and other presidential candidates known for opposing traditional biblical morality quote Scripture to justify an unbiblical ethos (like abortion), conservatives sense that verbal seduction is well underway. Condescending virtue-signaling and spiritual-signaling is certainly evident in such statements. These traditionalists observe that both within faith communities and in political discourse the selective, opportunistic, and distorted use of the Bible by political and religious leaders has moved out of the orbit of authentic Judeo-Christian values and the actual meaning of their sacred writ.

It is now "biblical" and "compassionate," for example, to redefine marriage and gender. One presidential candidate growing in popularity has used Scripture to justify homosexual marriage and homosexual ordination, and another has used the Bible to condemn any opposition to open borders or illegal immigration as lacking in Christian compassion and being unbiblical and sub-Christian. The traditionalists and red state faith communities sense that "biblical social justice" is now being redefined and used to subvert the actual teachings of the Bible on legion moral issues, including justice issues.

The nontraditionalists, it is argued, known for undermining biblical values and the original American experiment, are progressively and shamelessly trying to wrap themselves in the flag, cross, true spirituality, and Scripture. They are, therefore, now claiming and redefining the biblical, Judeo-Christian semantic or verbal universe. Conservatives see this as reminiscent of the eighteenth century when some used Scripture to justify slavery, or the nineteenth century when classical liberal Christian theology rede-fined virtually every key theological term, or the twentieth cen-tury when supporters of Hitler referred to him as the "Messiah." Indeed, schoolchildren referred to Hitler as the Messiah, and the Nazi movement referred to itself by utilizing the biblical concept of the kingdom: The Third *Reich* (Kingdom).

Yes, both (or all) sides of the political aisle misuse words and stray from constructive tone and discourse. Political conservatives are accused of touting biblical values like compassion while sup-porting social injustice, maintaining privilege and power, practicing exclusion, and supporting indecent and unscrupulous politicians. Yet even if all of these allegations are true, this work should present more than sufficient evidence that, at least in the American context, what is known as the political left is the ideological orientation from which emerges most of the full-scale assaults on Judeo-Christian values and biblical faith communities.

Nevertheless, as these traditionalists desperately seek to respond to the perceived onslaught and find or support presidential and polit-ical candidates who are more biblically "pro-faith" and "pro-family," critics contend that these conservatives have redefined "pro-faith" and "pro-family" out of existence. How? It is claimed that these con-servatives have missed the mark by aligning their faith and them-selves with candidates who fall far short of emulating the biblical values of faith and family and who undermine the compassionate American experiment by failing to welcome outsiders. In order to court political favor or protection, it is argued, such conservatives are enabling very public vices such as vulgarity, sexism, racism, xenophobia, misogyny, and the abuse of political power.

While most American evangelicals are politically "red state," evangelical leadership is often just as polarized and tribalistic as the general culture. Prominent American evangelicals such as Robert Jeffress and Mark Labberton truly seem to inhabit alter-nate verbal or semantic universes relative to "truth," "evangelical," "Scripture," and "justice" (see especially Chapter 3).

Jeffress acknowledges that his preferred presidential candidate is no "choir boy" but affirms that on the balance his candidate is more supportive and protective of biblical values and American evangelicalism than the alternatives. Labberton, apparently representing "woke" evangelicalism, affirms that the preferred candidate of Jeffress is in bed with malevolent and systemic racism and misogyny, and that we should not be surprised to hear crowds chanting slogans such as, "Send them back, send them back" to those who are different. *Christianity Today* (via Mark Galli) aligns more with Labberton and believes that "Trump Should Be Removed from Office" (December 19, 2019) for immorality and the abuse of power. Jeffress and countless evangelical leaders, including Franklin Graham and Cissie Graham Lynch, have condemned *Christianity Today's* op-ed. Are the only remaining options today for American evangelicals the cultural engagement models of Labberton, Jeffress, disengaged pietism, populism, crude nationalism, democratic socialism, or, perhaps, Rod Dreher's neo-monastic Benedict Option (see especially Chapters 1 and 3)?

Many religious leaders on the religious and political right *and left* in America are asking, "How can millions of Americans and countless Judeo-Christian faith communities be so utterly confused and deluded concerning the implications of their faith for politics?" In this work presidential politics, therefore, will serve as one case study and window into the soul of faith communities and their usage and definition of key terms (including their lexicon or semantics of cultural engagement).

Especially see Chapter 3, but what is certain is that faith communities, including evangelical leaders, are often extremely polarized. With such intense conflicts not everyone can be right, so countless cultural leaders and the masses are being seduced. Someone is getting things really, really, wrong. Hopefully, someone is getting things largely right or will get things right in the future.

Systemic Semantic Seduction

The biblical "angel of light" principle may have relevance if properly applied to the current context. Paul warns believers in 2 Corinthians (11:14), "Even Satan disguises himself as an angel of light." If we apply this principle to the current verbal hostilities, this does not mean that everyone who seduces is demonic or that everyone who has been seduced has been directly seduced or possessed by the dark side. The applicable part of this analogous principle is consistent with Scripture and *The Screwtape Letters* (1942) of C. S. Lewis. Something that looks good, pure (light), or even angelic (via terms and aspirations such as compassion, freedom, or justice) can, in reality, be employed in a fashion that is terribly destructive to individuals, faith communities, and nations. In principle, millions could advocate for what they affirm or even sincerely believe is a noble or biblical cause when, in fact, they have been deceived.

Millions have been seduced as we approach a civilizational watershed and navigate the current cultural crisis.

Given the intensity of these tribal conflicts, what is certain is that if normative truth exists and can be known and shared, then everyone can't be right and someone, or most everyone, is getting it wrong. Hence, a sizable proportion of the populace has been intellectually, emotionally, and verbally seduced.

What is certain is that a verbal revolution is underway or nearly complete. What is certain is that words partially define each other and the redefinition of one word powerfully ripples through the verbal universe and our communal reality and dynamics. What is certain is that the redefinition of one word redefines other words, and the definition of a single word often mutates under the influence of its semantic relatives.

For example, the redefinition of marriage is part of this verbal revolution, evolution, devolution, or metamorphosis. The traditional definition of marriage, embraced for millennia, is now viewed by most civilizational centers of power as a false definition of marriage. And this new definition of marriage is also inseparably related to the new and allegedly noble definitions or pseudo-definitions of terms such as:

- Inclusion
- Tolerance
- Love
- Compassion or biblical compassion

- Social justice or biblical social justice
- Multiculturalism
- Diversity
- Truth
- Morality
- Judgmental
- Legalistic
- Family
- Nonbinary gender identity
- Sexual preference or orientation
- Discrimination
- Establishment of religion
- Educational neutrality
- Patriotic
- American experiment
- Civilization

In other words, the definition of marriage is organically and systemically connected to and influenced by the definition of all of these terms, and vice versa. Or, stated conversely, one who affirms traditional marriage—now viewed as the false definition of marriage—is characterized as the following: non-inclusive, homophobic, intolerant, unloving, hateful, opposed to compassionate social justice, against diversity, legalistic, discriminatory, uneducated or ignorant, lacking a grasp of truth and ethics, xenophobic, trying to establish a religion or theocracy, unpatriotic, un-American, destructive of "neutral" public education, cancerous to higher education, and disruptive of the noble quest for civilization. And this pejorative list is only briefly illustrative and not exhaustive.

Word definitions clearly function together as potent and fluid clusters, families, or interconnected verbal universes, and the Judeo-Christian influence on these civilizational verbal pillars is waning and the pillars are crumbling in many quarters of the globe. This verbal revolution is redefining the future, the very nature of Judeo-Christian faith communities, and the very nature of the American experiment.

This work affirms that much of the cultural and civilizational problem is related to the seductive abuse of words (corrupt semantics) and our groundless attempt to pursue and navigate the journey to a more perfect union and the common good without a shared norm or standard for measuring accurate and truthful discourse. And the norm tested and proved for centuries is now vanishing on the horizon at the approaching sunset of a formerly and progressively free and spiritually flourishing civilization (see the Introduction and Chapter 1).

We are floundering and flailing in a postmodern verbal quagmire. This work will define postmodernity, replace the term with a more accurate descriptor of the contemporary situation (especially see Chapter 6 on ultramodern syncretism), and diagnose our pathological context and moment in history while proffering a prescription for cultural recovery and authentic human and cultural advance.

We are communicating constantly via words; consequently, every day the currency of words devalues. Thoughtful individuals of various religious and political perspectives now ask if God and truth are dead. Numerous pundits and presidents complain about fake news or folks who simply "make stuff up," use verbal manipulation, and tell endless falsehoods. This book asks if our core convictions concerning God, truth, words, free speech, or any meaningful definition of the Judeo-Christian faith, America, or civilization are gravely ill and headed toward life support. This book also contends that there are potential solutions to the current verbal impasse and civilizational crisis.

For additional information and to gift this book to pastors, Christian leaders, teachers, family members, students, friends, and cultural leaders, please visit *doctord.org* and join the movement to influence the present and future in the dawning light of the New Creation.

THE IMPERILED FUTURE OF WORDS, COMMUNICATION, UNDERSTANDING, AND CIVILIZATION

I think there's a lot more people concerned about being precisely, factually, and *semantically* correct than about being morally right.
[Semantics refers to the definitions and usage of words; emphasis added]
— Representative Alexandria Ocasio-Cortez
(January 6, 2019, *60 Minutes*)

A soft side to the meaning of [this] post-truth [term and age] suggests that objective facts are less influential in shaping public opinion than are appeals to emotion and personal belief. But the hard meaning of the word [post-truth] is that in this culture we willfully and justifiably convey something false because it accomplishes a personal or end goal: the end justifies the means, which do not need

to justify themselves. Once we remove God and decide instead to play God, truth gives way to fiction. It used to be said, "If a Cretan tells you all Cretans are liars, can you believe him [or her]?" ... *With the death of truth, the unique capability of Homo sapiens [created in the image of God] for abstract reasoning and language is now taken to the morgue and all language is meaningless.* Indeed, we have so extinguished the light of truth in our halls of learning that it is possible for a Harvard student to say, "I can believe anything I want, so long as I don't claim it to be true."
—Ravi Zacharias, "Think Again: Timeless Words"[24]

I fear that in every elected office, members will obtain an influence by noise and not sense. By meanness, not greatness. By ignorance, not learning. By contracted hearts, not large souls.... There must be decency and respect.
—John Adams[25]

Welcome to the seductive verbal age, or nightmare, of ultramodern syncretism, where endlessly redefined words are mere manipulative tools of power, and the utilization of any normative conception of truth to redeem this verbal opportunism is dismissed as yet another power grab—even *within* many faith communities. The contours of this present *Zeitgeist* (spirit of the times), less than accurately referred to by some as postmodern, will be explored and assessed.

Given the dominance of moral relativism and the rejection of words as fallible but imperfect means of arriving at some form of shared truth, should there really be any consternation at the present verbal cacophony of words, meaning, and values? Are we surprised at the resulting ecclesial and educational drift, shameless spin, scurrilous accusations, proliferating deceit, polarization, and tribalism? Is it any surprise that a verbal civil war is raging? *Is it possible that our faith communities and Judeo-Christian influenced civilization, which are symbiotically related, are now at risk of centrifugal disintegration?*

Philosophers, linguists, and literary scholars could provide a healing salve to the present cultural pathologies, but unfortunately many of these academics are often the primary bearers of the relativistic verbal pathogens. Ultimately, for meaning to have meaning, for words to serve as words and not weapons, and for individuals and civilizations to flourish freely, spiritually, and fiscally, terms and communication desperately need realignment with a normative plumb line!

Loss of the Cultural Plumb Line

For centuries in the American context that cultural plumb line was viewed as self-evident divinely grounded truths and moral imperatives, discoverable by God-given reason and/or experimentation, plus an underlying, supportive, indispensable, and foundational Judeo-Christian culture and spirit. This culture was largely framed and influenced by Judeo-Christian assumptions about core convictions such as truth, revelation, knowledge, reality, morality, God, and the future, including the afterlife. This civilization was permeated with and guided by what was believed to be divinely revealed Scripture, centered in the very Word or Logos of God. Hence, the shared and publicly accessible and proclaimed truths and norms guiding the experiment emanated from two primary, interfacing, and allied sources: key Enlightenment convictions and divine revelation centered in a personal, authoritative, and written Word.[26] And it is upon the stable foundation of this dominant plumb line duality (Enlightenment thought and Logocentric kingdomcentrism) that other influences (e.g., indigenous, Spanish, African, and what Michael Novak refers to as *The Spirit of Democratic Capitalism*) contributed to the emerging American experiment.

As will be argued throughout this work, this plumb line observation in no way suggests that we should go backward or forward to a theocracy, church-state union, or a naïve and unrefined conception of simplistically reviving Christendom. We should neither unqualifiedly celebrate the demise of Christendom nor attempt to naively revive theocratic or misguided versions of Christendom. Indeed, these Enlightenment and biblical influences mitigate against and aggressively negate both a Christian theocracy *and* a secular, relativistic, and syncretistic democratic republic.

While tensions sometimes existed between these two primary sources ("Word-centric" or Logocentric culture and the Enlightenment), the American experiment crafted a novel synthesis between the two. Enlightenment thought, which emphasized themes such as the quest for truth by reason, scientific verification and experimentation, toleration, and civilizational progress, paradoxically drank from the Judeo-Christian fountain while seeking to purify the stream. Enlightenment thinkers varied, but even those more critical of traditional Judeo-Christian religion presupposed many Judeo-Christian assumptions about human nature, reality, knowledge, truth, and the future—sometimes unconsciously.

On the eve of the birth of the American experiment, the Judeo-Christian inspired First Great Awakening led by Jonathan Edwards and George Whitefield (and the Wesleys and Whitefield in England and America) countered many of the excesses of the Enlightenment and assisted with unifying the colonies. Like two leaves swirling around each other in the fresh colonial era winds of change, both Logocentric and Enlightenment cultures informed, challenged, and nurtured each other while birthing a novel and inclusive vision of the future—the "more perfect union" of the Constitution. As will be argued in this work, the "more perfect union" is a Judeo-Christian influenced view of the future (eschatology), rooted in Judeo-Christian theological assumptions (e.g., human nature or theological anthropology).

The fount of this Judeo-Christian culture nurturing the experiment was, of course, centuries of reflection on the Judeo-Christian heritage and experience, the journey through historical and cultural transitions, the Renaissance, Reformation, and Enlightenment, biblically influenced assumptions and moral precepts, biblically influenced affections, and a biblically influenced vision of the future. This resulting and shining "city set on a hill" vision (Matthew 5:14), referenced by countless pivotal leaders, such as the Puritan John Winthrop, John F. Kennedy, Ronald Reagan, and Barack Obama, reflected this underlying and optimistic future-vision (or eschatology) forged at the confluence of these two powerful, cultural Judeo-Christian and Enlightenment rivers.

Enlightenment eschatology, just like Marxist eschatology, had a parasitical relationship to Judeo-Christian eschatology. The difference is that Marxist eschatology was overtly heretical in relationship to Christianity, whereas the Enlightenment eschatology was more synthetic and attempted in some respects to enhance Christian eschatology. What was the resulting American experiment and future-vision? A "more [but less than] perfect union" that would audaciously seek to serve as an illuminating "city set on a hill"!

Hence, civilization and language were significantly kingdomcentric, and Logos-centered or Logocentric. The Logos was the king of the normative semantic kingdom. The historical evidence for significant Logocentric influence on the American experiment and culture, along with the influence of Enlightenment ideals, which were, as noted, impacted by Logocentric influence, is irrefutable and will be addressed in multiple chapters (especially see Chapter 3).[27] This book specifically rejects the false dichotomy that either the American experiment was or should be a theocracy or it was or should be a secular and direct democracy; both of these models are disastrous relative to understanding the past or charting a more perfect future (also see Chapter 3).

This work rejects these distortions and disjunctive emphases:

- That the Enlightenment was totally opposed to—and not somewhat parasitical upon—everything Judeo-Christian
- That all affirmations by the Enlightenment and modernity were wrong
- That because some Enlightenment thinkers like Voltaire passionately attacked traditional Christianity therefore all Enlightenment influenced thinkers rejected the Judeo-Christian perspective largely or entirely—and rejected virtually all Judeo-Christian assumptions
- That all of the founders of the American experiment, or even the most influential founders, can be simplistically categorized as either post-Christian Deists or orthodox conservative Christians

Critics will predictably and redundantly argue that the American experiment was rooted only, or primarily, in Deistic or Enlightenment thought and not rooted in Judeo-Christian values. Deism typically affirmed that God created the universe but is no longer directly involved in the world—this is the famous clock-maker vision of God and God's relationship to the creation. In addition to this criticism being historically false (see especially Chapters 3 and 9), the argument is loaded with false dichotomies.

First, while Deistic thought certainly rejected some core Christian convictions, Deism was also birthed from Christian soil and retained many Christian assumptions about reality (e.g., there is one God, God is the creator, morality exists and can be known, the world can be redeemed, and individuals will be held account-able in the next life). Those who completely polarize Deism and Christianity are philosophically and theologically uninformed. Deism and Christianity have far more in common than Deism and atheistic Nihilism, or Deism and the New Age movement.

As noted, the Enlightenment intellectual movement both reacted to and was influenced by Christian thought. Many Enlightenment emphases constructively interfaced with Judeo-Christian assump-tions and teachings, such as toleration (in orbit of "do unto others" and *agape* love), or the possibility of and quest for shared norma-tive truth. Deism not only has far more in common with Judeo-Christian core values than the New Age movement, but Deism also has more in common with Judeo-Christian thought than other worl-dviews such as atheism, polytheism, relativistic postmodernism, or nihilism. This commonality with Judeo-Christian theology includes the nature of human nature and the nature of human thought.

Second, Deistic and Enlightenment thinkers were not mono-lithic. John Locke's writings were central to and practically plagia-rized by the *Declaration of Independence*, and he affirmed rational supernaturalism, meaning he selectively embraced key tenets of Enlightenment thought *and* traditional Christianity. Locke in some ways served as a bridge between Christianity and the Enlightenment (especially see Chapters 5 and 9). Locke affirmed the reality of rev-elation, miracles, and resurrection as truths above, but not contrary to, reason.

Third, Enlightenment thought and Judeo-Christian thought were *both* very influential on the birth of the American experiment, and both created a functional and cultural plumb line consensus for law, culture, semantics, values, political thought and political experimentation. Indeed, the historical evidence is conclusive that Judeo-Christian influence was culturally and longitudinally more significant than Deism. Scripture influenced everything, including personal names and city names, and the majority of the signers of the Declaration were primarily identifiable as Christians and not Deists, with most being biblically oriented or orthodox Christians. Many were directly or indirectly influenced by the First Great Awakening. Not many cities or individuals were named after Deists like Voltaire, yet Scriptural influence was absolutely pervasive for centuries in every area of American culture and thought.

Historical revisionists truly strain a gnat when trying to cover up this Judeo-Christian dimension of multiple centuries of faith influenced leaders, law, politics, literature, education, abolitionism, social reform, art, music, and especially the American imagination and affections. This influence is well known, easily established, and even can be seen in the common practice of naming children, such as "Abraham" Lincoln, or the countless cities named after biblical cities or prefaced by "Saint."

The evidence of Judeo-Christian influence is mammoth and even includes two speeches for the ages, the famous "I have a Dream" and "I've Been to the Mountaintop" proclamations of the nation's most celebrated civil rights advocate, Martin Luther King, Jr. M. L. King's famous words were laced with explicit biblical allusions, assumptions, and values, including the quest for a city set on a hill "promised land." These speeches should be required reading for anyone truly seeking to understand the profoundly religious nature of the American experiment, even in the midst of the 1960s cultural revolution. Only seductive historical revisionists would dare to discount the incalculable, monumental, historic and historical influence and impact of Judeo-Christian assumptions on the very warp and woof of the American experiment—and that in no way discounts the simultaneous impact of the Enlightenment (especially see Chapters 2, 3, 4, and 9).

Hence, to sum up, the semantic plumb line is not the Logos or the Bible, or the Enlightenment beliefs per se, though from a Judeo-Christian perspective the Logos is the ultimate source of the cultural plumb line revealed through holy writ, reason, conscience, creation, history, and experience. When religious and political conservatives suggest that we need the country to get back to the Bible they are partially correct, but it is a bit more profound and complex than that. When progressives argue that the American constitutional experiment was not a biblical theocracy they are right, but their attempt to eradicate the biblical dynamic from the experiment is shallow and based in false assumptions and historical misinformation.

The civilizational plumb line is the hybridized Logocentric and Enlightenment influenced assumptions and culture of the American experiment, and the Logocentric influence was clearly primary. *The only true and proper usage of words is influenced by, grounded in, and aligned with the personal Word and the inspired, authoritative, written Word.* If this influence is removed or replaced with the unstable formula of syncretistic relativism, or any other "ism," the civilizational experiment inevitably fragments or stagnates as the cultural glue dissolves over time. The country may persist in name only, even as the experiment is on life support or even post-mortem.

The loss of this plumb line has created civilizational vertigo. It is one thing to have shared standards of truth and then debate and marshal evidence as to who is departing from such standards, or who is engaging in hypocrisy in relation to the shared standards. It is quite another thing to be debating ethical issues, core values, the meaning of terms, and the future of civilization without any shared and normative standard(s) whatsoever. There seems to be no semantic adult in the room capable of restoring orderly and constructive public discourse.

We have lost true north on our journey toward a more perfect civilization. An eternally grounded, fecund, and stable plumb line has been replaced with a phantom plumb line and multiple tribalistic and individualistic plumb lines. An inspiring vision of the future has been replaced with an escalating verbal civil war and semantic balkanization. And the cold civil war is heating up with occasional outbreaks of violence. Intense periods of verbal and physical conflict are not entirely new in American history, but the postmodern, relativistic, and anti-Judeo-Christian context is unprecedented and treacherous.

The Enlightenment (or modernity) had enormous flaws, such as its occasional worship of reason (rationalism) or science (scientism). Its definition of "toleration" was sometimes used to intolerantly suppress or oppress the less enlightened and the religious, and its vision of "progress" was at times used to trample on others while chasing a utopian or nearly utopian future. One of the strengths of the original American experiment is that it reflected a guarded optimism concerning the future, the more perfect union, rather than the blood-soaked utopianisms of the French Revolution, Nazi ideology, and Stalinist communism. Human attempts at perfect unions inevitably deliver the tragic opposite.

A fair assessment of modernity is instructive in our so-called postmodern age. Most movements are built on something that is believable, socially, existentially, and psychologically relevant, and that contains at least a few half-truths. The Czar in Russia and the exploitation in Cuba were corrupt, yet the subsequent revolutions that promised heaven delivered hell for many.

Likewise, postmodernism is correct that words, even religious words, are slippery and sometimes used to cover up hidden agendas, manipulate, and oppress—even when used by traditionalists. Yet many variants of postmodernity today seem to be blind to their own abuse of words and power. We are very influenced by our contexts or tribes, but postmodern moral relativism and tribalism are not only toxic to nations and families, extreme postmodernity itself is blatantly self-contradictory when passionately suggesting that everyone is hopelessly mired in subjectivity—except, of course, for the postmodern elites who possess the secret "truth" about the relativity of truth and morality. Extreme postmodernism functions as a neo-Gnosticism or secret knowledge cult, which may explain affinities between postmodernity and the New Age movement.

The world was seduced by modernism, and I have colleagues who are still stuck in the assumptions of the Enlightenment. I have other colleagues who have swallowed in whole the hook, line, and sinker of postmodern assumptions. The biblical and Judeo-Christian resources should prophetically critique, and affirm when possible, the various elements of all cultural, sociological, historical, and intellectual movements. Our communal and cultural history has seen the West traversing from the worship of reason to and through the rejection of reason. Both extremes are dangerous to civilization, and core Judeo-Christian convictions, such the image of God in humanity and the radical sinfulness of humanity, provide a balanced alternative.

The vanishing and guiding plumb line horizon is, at the core, the Judeo-Christian-Enlightenment birthed semantic universe. This universe is a constellation or family of words, phrases, and terms that are symbiotically or organically defined by other terms. This plumb line was guided by the values, assumptions, and deep heart affections that underlie and nurture this semantic universe.

This authoritative, potent, fertile, fluid, nimble, and stabilizing cultural and semantic plumb line, hammered out over centuries of profound reflection, debate, sacrifice, and historical experience, is the only legitimate hope for our continued journey toward a more perfect union and city set on a hill. The authentic American experiment will not survive the shift to an alternative semantic universe.

Every culture and subculture or tribe has the equivalent of a biblical Ten Commandments. The core commandments often birth many more commandments and precepts and are enforced by cultural liturgies, cultural allegiances, cultural or subcultural condemnations, and even the force of law and the criminalization of speech and behavior. Some commandments are more welcoming to diverse views, freedom of speech, and freedom of association than others. The commandments emerge from and norm the semantic or verbal universe, just as the Ten Commandments normed the American experiment. The vanishing Judeo-Christian plumb line includes the replacement of the biblical Ten Commandments with tribalistic alternatives.

We will therefore explore whether key questions that scholars and journalists have been discussing for well over a century are directly connected to each other and coming to fruition with the present cultural and semantic chaos—and the seemingly escalating outrage. Perhaps these questions, asked separately over many decades, are simply pieces of a larger cultural mega-trend (especially see Chapter 2).

- *Is God Dead* in our culture?
- *Is Truth Dead* in our culture?
- *Are Words Dead or Dying?*
- *Is Free Speech Dead or Dying?*
- *Is America, or the authentic American Experiment, Dead or Dying?*

This work emphasizes that any civilization lacking shared and normative truths is ultimately unsustainable and tottering on the precipice, and this work will provide evidence of how Judeo-Christian influence on words and culture has provided cultural stability while grounding, meliorating, and continuously renewing a tolerant and flourishing experiment in civilization. Hence, the semantic task of this work is ultimately theological in nature.

The usefulness of this work is to empower and equip theologians, religious leaders, linguists, and philosophers, as well as lay Christians, to flesh out the immense, specific, and nuanced implications of the words they use.

This book seeks to directly address religious leaders, while also providing relevant and useful information for informed laity and especially for those who have experienced higher education. The substantial endnotes and parenthetical definitions attempt to serve as a bridge between multiple audiences by exploring at least some of the academic or scholarly questions that will necessarily emerge while also keeping the book accessible to nonspecialists. As will be noted at the end of this introduction, the hope is that laity will both engage with this work and place a copy of this book in the hands of every teachable religious leader. Academic specialists will find that this book is intentionally written at the popular level at many points. Nonspecialists or popular readers will find that this book does at times address specialized or academic issues, terms, and concepts that simply can't be ignored due to the current cultural and ecclesial crises, yet some of that material has been moved to the endnotes and appendices. Hopefully all audiences can contribute to and benefit from the discussion.

The semantic task of this work is most urgent, for we have clearly planted our civilizational feet firmly in the mid-air of conflicting, hostile, and self-destructive verbal or semantic universes, and we need to return to the reality of Logocentric discourse rooted in absolute or normative truth (*amet*).[28] In order to navigate a culture with our feet and communication firmly planted in mid-air, you may wish to take a quick detour at this juncture and skim Chapter 5 to understand a proper definition of truth further.

At this point in the dialog, let's view this broadly applicable concept of truth, ultimately rooted in the eternal Logos, as *normative truth*, meaning that there is a divinely revealed and knowable norm and standard. This standard serves as a plumb line for measuring and framing all words, communication, and claims to what is true, real, and moral. This norm is accessible and not cloistered among the elect or the elites. And, most importantly, this standard yields relevant and applicable *knowledge* to serve as a cultural guide and plumb line.

This normative measuring rod counters all the pervasive claims that truth and ethics are always or merely personal or cultural preferences. The norm is accessible via reason, our affections, and conscience because we are all created in God's image. This norm is accessible via supernatural revelation because we are fallen and in need of God's revelatory redemption (see Romans chapters 1 and 2). For the philosophers reading this work, no attempt is being made to defend or resurrect simplistic Enlightenment, Cartesian, or modernistic conceptions of reason or absolute truth—yet normative biblical truth will be affirmed, explored, explained, and connected to the idea of shared semantic and cultural truth—the critics of normative and shared truth notwithstanding.

Normative truth (see Chapter 5) is illustrated and affirmed throughout the Old and New Testament Scriptures, with one classic expression found in Galatians (1:8) from the Apostle Paul: "But even if we, or an angel from heaven, should preach to you a gospel [the good news of how to be saved] contrary to what we have preached to you, he is to be [or "let them be", NIV] accursed!" Paul was explicit that the gospel teaching, proclamation, and the way of salvation were not matters of mere personal preference, but firm or full convictions of revealed, normative, accessible, clear, preached, published, understood, and shared truth and knowledge (1 Thessalonians 1:5).

Words, truth, and definitions matter and are of temporal and eternal importance. Whether one believes that Paul was right or wrong on his normative definition of gospel truth and its temporal and eternal consequences, Paul repeatedly affirmed and assumed normative truth, beliefs, and morality even while operating in a cross-cultural, syncretistic, and largely relativistic context. As a Jewish scholar and leader trained under Gamaliel (Acts 22:3), he was uncompromising in affirming the existence and knowability of such normative truth and ethics. Some measure of truth and morality were clearly accessible to all (Romans chapters 1 and 2; Acts chapter 17), such that all were accountable to God.

Paul even makes a verbal distinction between the true God and a "so-called" god, and between the one true Triune God and the verbal seduction and deception of the "man of lawlessness" who falsely presents or displays "himself as being God" (2 Thessalonians 2:3–4). This illustration is perhaps the ultimate example of the angel of light principle—that many will be seduced on a grand scale. The biblical literature and mindset affirms and assumes normative truth, truth as a basis of accountability for all, and affirms and assumes that some word definitions are true or more true and some are largely or entirely seductive and false. The accurate meaning of words is not in the eyes of the beholder.

For Paul, the pervasive conviction repeated thousands of times in various ways throughout Scripture that God had spoken authoritatively, such as "Thus says the Lord" (Jeremiah 6:16), was not viewed as a contextualized personal or cultural preference. If Paul is right, truth and morality commitments in Scripture are not akin to choosing a salad dressing or a favorite car. As many have noted, the Ten Commandments are not the ten suggestions and they have incalculable implications for culture, law, and civilization.[29]

Regardless of the challenges of clarifying and articulating "truth" in our relativistic and postmodern age, Scripture affirms that normative truth exists, it has been revealed through God's actions *and words*, and some core truths can be "clearly" perceived and understood by all (Romans 1:20). Hence, all are without excuse relative to ethics and basic knowledge concerning reality, and this normative revealed truth serves as the basis and ultimate source for shared self-evident truths. This normative truth serves as a plumb line or measuring rod for all personal and cultural claims to truth, morality, word definitions, and visions of a more perfect kingdom or union. We all have our personal and cultural stories, and we have become a bit obsessed with "our" stories, but Scripture gives us the normative, transcendent, and Epic Story.[30]

This discussion of truth and words is rooted in my personal experience. I am a theologian who did his doctoral work in religion (theology), with a minor in political science. My specialization focused on the interface between theology and cultural engagement. I came to faith out of a posture of extreme skepticism, and what only can be described as a largely postmodern or ultramodern mind-set—well before such terms as postmodernism were fully in vogue.

I am intimately familiar with virtually all, and used to embrace many of, the flawed arguments against shared and normative truth and Judeo-Christian values. As an unbeliever at a Christian college, I debated friends, professors, chapel speakers, and my future wife. A friend at college encouraged me to be quiet lest I get dismissed from the Christian school. He asked something like, "You do know, duh, that this is a Christian college, right?" My best recollection is that he lovingly encouraged me to "shut up."

My memory of this season of life is that I was relatively polite but outspoken and somewhat dismissive of faith, the Bible, and repressive Christian ethics. Jesus and the Christian faith were viewed as little more than manufactured mythological terms and concepts, on the order of the Easter bunny or many of the unhistorical stories of the ancient Greek fables. Without knowing it, I truly breathed the post-Christian, postmodern, and relativistic spirit of our age.

After finding faith, my background, educational training, career, and experience led me to study and teach most every theology and philosophy class in the university, including apologetics and ethics courses.[31] I have been involved with, supervised, and assessed countless apologetic encounters with skeptics. I have creatively made the case for Judeo-Christian beliefs and values, and guided such apologetic assignments for multiple decades. I served as a nontraditional chaplain to a demographic with a high percentage of unchurched and nontraditional or post-traditional collegians.

The discipline of apologetics is rooted in a Greek term referring to a legal defense (*apologia*), word, justification, account, or a speech defending an action, oneself, or one's point of view (1 Peter 3:15; also see below in this introduction). I have engaged with students of diverse backgrounds and demographics at the academic and pastoral counseling level. This interaction was a tremendously positive experience, and the students most graciously awarded me with many teaching awards. Yet I also remember one class, and fortunately only one class, where my gentle evangelism was received by many with typical relativistic opprobrium and distaste for the alleged imposition of truth.

Because of my background, I've spent hours after class, in my office, in the student center, dorms, with youth groups, or at places such as Tim Hortons in loving but passionate dialog with those who have been educated to have suspicion concerning faith and truth claims. These students are immersed in a culture that increasingly redefines and weaponizes words in pursuit of a redefined "America" liberated from Judeo-Christian influence, and a "Christianity" liberated from historic, orthodox, biblical, and Christian beliefs and morality.

I remember in one class where a "Christian" student was most animated about how the concept of a Christian worldview (a system of core beliefs) was oppressive and not inclusive—even though we were studying and assessing countless worldviews.[32] I even role played the perspective of representative worldviews and challenged Christian students in such classes to respond to non-Christian arguments. I remember impersonating a major Deist in one class and the nihilist Nietzsche in another. This negative reaction to the pursuit of truth took place in a traditional class at a *conservative* Christian university. The student affirmed that comparing and contrasting worldviews in view of the pursuit and love of wisdom in a Christian philosophy or theology class was non-inclusive and oppressive; the class should be abolished or completely overhauled since no correct worldview can or should be determined. The quest for truth itself was, by definition, if I heard the student correctly, non-inclusive and manipulative. One observation after years of teaching is that many parents and pastors are relatively clueless about what their high school and college students *really* believe.

"Philosophy" is a term that literally means the love and pursuit of wisdom or truth,[33] but for this student it seemed that philosophical and theological inquiry was merely the pursuit of Christian power and control over others. I related very well with that student, as with virtually all skeptics who were drawn to a former and recovering skeptic, but the dialog reflected how pervasive this mindset was becoming in culture and the American evangelical church, only a few years into the new millennium. Indeed, one professor colleague in an evangelical Christian college some years later suggested that the very idea that the Christian faith had fixed core beliefs and values that could be favorably compared and contrasted with other perspectives amounted to using the Christian worldview as a "billy club."

Christian beliefs, it was argued, should be viewed as fluid, indeterminate, and other perspectives and religions likely had as much or more to contribute to the spiritual quest as historic Christian orthodoxy (right belief). We can share our story, but there is no Story. Besides, all beliefs are culturally bound and thus comparing and contrasting the strengths and weaknesses of belief systems amounts to cultural totalitarianism.

Less than a decade after these representative interactions, we are now fully navigating a new semantic universe or verbal multiverse. Everything is being redefined and relativized. It is the conviction of this work that unless Judeo-Christian religious leaders and educators take the lead on lovingly, patiently, and systematically redeeming the use of words, then Judeo-Christian communities of faith and civilization will continue to drift and disintegrate, including American evangelicalism, Roman Catholicism, and biblical Judaism.

The priority or focus of this work is the Judeo-Christian faith communities—especially churches, synagogues, denominations, religious organizations, movements, parachurch organizations, and institutions of education. Let's launch this semantic reformation in our own back yard.

The contention of this work is that if nothing changes we will eventually, fully, and finally move almost entirely out of the orbit and influence of biblical beliefs and ethics and stagger or free fall into the future. While some of my evangelical colleagues almost seem giddy about the prospect of going back to the days of persecution and the catacombs, neighbor love would suggest that such perverse delight is unbiblical and misguided.

Biblical convictions are likely to be ever marginalized, if not criminalized, apart from a semantic or verbal reformation under the Word of God. To hold to biblical precepts today, according to many critics and verbal opportunists, means that one is homophobic, intolerant, bigoted, racist, oppressive, and lacks compassion or any commitment to social justice—and many of these opportunists wear clerical garb. Word theft and spin are not new, but the postmodern or ultramodern pandemic is now fully upon us.

As noted, this work makes no attempt to reanimate "Christendom" (especially see Chapters 3 and 6), in the sense of an established religion, a theocracy, or any kind of church state union. Just as with the debate about the nature of the original American experiment, some simplistically present a false dichotomy of only two choices. Either we accept that Christendom (an established Christian religion, which is the history of many European states) has collapsed and we have lost the culture wars in America, or we try to revive an established religion, church-state union, or theocracy.

There are other options worthy of exploring, including Michael Novak's model of a Trinitarian influenced culture and civilization (especially see Chapters 2, 7, and 9). In addition, conflating the historical experience and theology of European church-state unions with the voluntarist religious ethos of the American experiment and Trinitarian balanced power framework of the Constitution is intellectually irresponsible (especially see Chapters 2 and 3). America, and the outlandish experiment to be a unique "City set on a hill," was and is peculiar and largely singular.

I recommend that you, the reader, quickly overview Appendix A, which is filled with proposed definitions of terms and words and refer to it as needed as you read this book. By doing so, you will more clearly understand what I am writing and have a biblically influenced and research based tool for examining the personal biases and denotations many have relative to the seminal terms used throughout this work. Religious leaders would do well to utilize the appendices in teaching, preaching (subtly and creatively grafted into multiple sermons), instruction, and formal catechesis.

It is especially important that religious leaders provide specific, term by term instruction within faith communities on the definitions of theological, ethical, and contemporary words and phrases such as God, Jesus, sin, salvation, truth, right and wrong, knowledge, love, compassion, social justice, gender, masculinity, femininity, marriage, and love. All terms are being redefined today, even in communities of faith, and especially in academic and popular culture.

Unfortunately, the church often follows the culture. Such redefinitions fundamentally and eventually alter individuals, communities, culture, church and state. Word definitions truly transform and create present and future ecclesial and cultural reality, sometimes for ill, and sometimes for the good.

Semantic seduction is seemingly ubiquitous—it is everywhere and would require multiple volumes to document and assess. This work will focus on the verbal seduction and case studies in these historical contexts and faith communities:

- The *New Testament era* faith communities (first century) that were being seduced by various heresies attempting to redefine the faith via the redefinition of core terms

- The faith communities of the *Early Church era* and the *era of Augustine* that were being seduced from within and semantically assaulted from without
- The Judeo-Christian faith communities seduced by modernism from within and without, especially from the *nineteenth century to the present*
- The *contemporary twentieth and twenty-first century* Judeo-Christian faith communities being seduced today from within and without by relativism, ultramodern syncretism, and pseudo-compassion and pseudo-justice
- The youthful or upcoming and *next generations and the emerging and digitized global culture* being endlessly seduced by the power centers of culture

It will be repeatedly argued that the *future of Judeo-Christian faith communities is the focus of this text and the primary determiner of the future course of culture and civilization.* So goes the faith communities so goes the civilization. Polemics (preserving right beliefs and definitions inside our faith communities) must precede and guide apologetics (making the gracious, respectful, creatively engaged, and persuasive case for Judeo-Christian belief and practice with those outside of our faith communities).

A few preliminary historical examples of verbal seduction will suffice for now, and will be explored in greater detail throughout this work. In the New Testament era of the first century the early Christian church countered the seductive corruption of key terms and beliefs, but also borrowed, polished, and utilized terms in common, religious, legal, or scholarly usage for kingdom advance. The New Testament rejects numerous seductive verbal redefinitions. Here are five examples:

1. *Christ* was being redefined as a non-physical spirit and/or his humanity was denied or deemphasized (1 John 1:1–3; 1 John 4:1–3; John 1:14; Colossians 2:8–10)
2. The *gospel* was being redefined by legalists (Galatians 1:6–9)
3. The Lord's Supper or *Eucharist* was being recast and redefined in Corinth by the Corinthian Christians (1 Corinthians

11:20)—those practicing the Eucharist were actually practicing something else based on this redefinition (Paul tells
the Corinthians that "it is not the Lord's Supper you eat")
4. The definition of an *apostle* was repeatedly being corrupted
(2 Corinthians 11:13)
5. The bodily *resurrection* of Christ was being distorted,
denied, or marginalized (1 Corinthians 15)

From the biblical perspective, the redefining and redeployment
of terms is acceptable if aligned with divinely revealed and normative truth. Such helpful and properly deployed first-century terms
included logos, redemption, justification, *apologia*, slave, pris-
oner, and love—to name but a few. Words, and ultimately much
of civilization, were brought into some measure of alignment or
re-alignment with the Word or Logos and new forms of civilization
emerged across the globe. Faith communities led the way.

Love became rooted in Christlike agape, and the gladiatorial
games, infanticide, abortion, and pederasty diminished or disap-
peared. The sacredness of human life began to emerge as a core
value. Homicide rates fell in subsequent centuries. Women eventually were redefined as more than chattel. Those in the orbit of
the Logos viewed it as utterly inconceivable that infanticide or the
choice to destroy an unborn child could be viewed either as a legitimate choice or as pro-family—much less loving, compassionate,
or good for society. The unborn child, as with John the Baptist and
Jesus, was not viewed as a part of the mother's body but as a sacred
person and gift of God (see Luke chapters 1–2). This pro-life ethic
dominated faith communities and much of Judeo-Christian influenced culture well into the twentieth century. Civilization, including
the term civilization itself, became largely Logocentric influenced
over the course of centuries. Words are powerful and create reality,
and either echo or distort and corrupt the generative intent of the
Creator and Logos and the ultimate creator of language itself. "And
God said, let there be...."

In the first few centuries after the New Testament era church,
those seeking to marginalize or destroy Christian influence redefined numerous Christian terms such as the Lord's Supper or

Eucharist as "cannibalism." Gnosticism (a diverse ancient movement with some parallels to the contemporary New Age movement) was also redefining or corrupting virtually every Judeo-Christian term or belief, including Christ and Satan, and trying to do so inside of faith communities, over the course of multiple centuries. The early church responded with semantic apologetics and polemics to these endless verbal distortions.

After Nicaea, St. Augustine, in the *City of God*, responded to many verbal distortions that blamed Christians for undermining citizenship and precipitating the decline and fall of the Roman Empire. Augustine addressed pagan distortions concerning terms and concepts such as evil, creation, time, sin, free will, foreknowledge, patriotic citizenship, and Christian ethics.

Indeed, in many respects the history of the Christian church in the first five centuries after Christ was a history of Gnostics, Neo-Platonists, Hellenists, Docetists, and Ebionites seeking to redefine core Judeo-Christian words, phrases, key terms, concepts, beliefs, and ethics from inside of the Church. And in some respects, the emergence of what is now referred to as orthodox Christian beliefs, shared by many branches of Christianity, was in response to these internal and external attempts at seduction. Is it any wonder that some of the most pointed controversies in church history revolved around a single word or letter of the alphabet? Words and semantics rule and define the future for churches and civilizations.

In more recent centuries, even within the church and the synagogue, religious leaders who have left behind Judeo-Christian orthodoxy have tried to retain their positions and influence within religious communities by redefining core terms. For example, in many Christian churches and denominations the miraculous and bodily resurrection of Christ has been rejected then redefined as Christ living on in his followers or in the preaching of his disciples. The deity of Christ has been redefined as the merely human Jesus having a high level of God-consciousness or serving as a merely human pipe-line to God. The actual and supernatural return of Christ has been denied and redefined as good eventually winning out over evil—yet the seducers will affirm they still believe in "the return of Christ." Indeed, as with the early church era, the movements known as Deism, Latitudinarianism, and classical liberal theology all proffered semantic and theological redefinitions of the faith.

And these Christian church or denominational leaders invariably still claim to believe in and preach the resurrection, Deity, and return of Christ. When challenged they respond, "I believe in the resurrection, I just interpret it differently than you do, so what is the problem?" They remained and still remain "in" the "church" or "synagogue" as ecclesial or denominational and religious leaders, including serving as bishops in many denominations. Church and synagogue are placed in quotation marks because in some of these religious bodies church and synagogue have been almost entirely redefined in an unbiblical fashion. This type of semantic seduction is taking place with virtually all words in and outside of religious communities, including the definition of marriage in the church. A colleague of mine studied at a Hebrew university under atheistic rabbis! To what degree is a synagogue led by an atheistic rabbi still a "synagogue"? Please also refer to the discussion of Union Seminary in the Preface.

The proper response to this word equivocation within religious communities is called semantic polemics. In the Christian tradition, polemics responds to theological and verbal distortions coming from those within the church and apologetics responds to all challenges to the faith, and typically focusing on arguments that emerge from those outside of the church. The first priority for religious communities, and the first priority of this book, is to employ semantic apologetics and polemics in service of strengthening religious communities. To modify a statement of John Paul II, the future of religious communities and families is also the future of the nation and the world.

To summarize, illustrate, and expand briefly upon our discussion, and this repetition should be helpful to the reader, this work emphasizes case studies and verbal seductions and distortions that have been utilized in the attempt to improperly redefine central Judeo-Christian concepts. These redefinitions seek to modernize or postmodernize the faith and "liberate" religious communities,

22

the church, and culture from Logocentric influence (especially see Chapters 3, 4, and 9):

1. **In Scripture:** The Genesis creation narrative and the Pauline literature both rejected attempts to redefine core Logocentric terms such as "you shall die," gospel, Jesus, apostle, circumcision, and wisdom.

2. **In the early church and Augustine:** Non-Logocentric and semantic attempts to literally destroy the church from within or without were many and included the attempt to redefine terms such as the Lord's supper (Eucharist), love feasts, the greeting of a holy kiss, atheism, and patriotism. Pagan critics taught that the Eucharist was a cannibalistic service, and even "Christ" was redefined by the Gnostic "Christian" heretics during this time period in a non-Hebraic fashion.

3. **In the era of contemporary theology:** Since at least the eighteenth century virtually *every* orthodox theological and biblical term and concept has been seductively redefined, often by religious leaders themselves, in order to conform religious belief and practice to the assumptions of some variant of modernity and postmodernity (Christ, resurrection, sin, the return of Christ, marriage, compassion, etc.). These distortions amount to a semantic coup within faith communities and a virtual redefinition of the nature of Judeo-Christian churches, synagogues, denominations, and religious movements. As intentionally noted many times, this book believes that the first priority in responding to this semantic challenge is to address the verbal decay *within* the religious communities.

4. **In contemporary culture:** Similarly, building on these assessments from the past, the major emphasis of this work is that core terms shaping the future are now being divorced from Logocentric and biblical influence in order to marginalize, privatize, ghettoize, or criminalize Judeo-Christian values, practice, and influence. Such terms include civilization, truth, faith, compassion, marriage, social justice, tolerance, love, inclusivism, patriotism, and multiculturalism.

Ocasio-Cortez and Trump Controversies as Symptoms

Today, the communication process is rapidly drifting from the plumb line influence of the Logos, or any shared norm whatsoever, via an onslaught of just such seductive semantics. No attempt will be made to divine the full meaning and context of Ocasio-Cortez's recent quote from the beginning of this introduction where she affirmed: "I think there's a lot more people concerned about being precisely, factually, and semantically correct than about being morally right." However, this statement seems to reflect a growing cultural trend, often reflected in public discourse, political discourse by multiple political parties and perspectives, countless recent surveys, and even in classrooms that I have taught.

This cultural mega-trend suggests that advocacy for political or ethical positions no longer requires divine sanction, meticulous and accurate research, authentic facts, sound reasoning, or the careful and proper use of words (semantics). Subsequent comments by Ocasio-Cortez include these claims: that the world will end in just over a decade; tearful comments that motherhood is now a bittersweet dream; that billionaire status should be prohibited and their money should be forcibly redistributed; that the nation has a healthcare crisis because folks in Alabama can't get access to medical care for "ringworm"; that the "punch a cop" movement has legitimacy; and that American Immigration and Customs Enforcement (ICE) is operating "concentration camps" on the southern border and forcing detainees to drink "toilet water."[34] In the American semantic context, "concentration camps" clearly conjures up memories of the Nazi death camps or the Soviet Gulag, especially since she attached the phrase "never again" to her concentration camp reference. She also has enthusiastically joined the attack on the electoral college, even posting a video of non-populated areas of the country to illustrate why some states (yes, in a republic) should have their electoral power largely divested or transferred. Ocasio-Cortez also has advocated for "prison abolition" and again made reference to the forced drinking of toilet water in prison. Such statements would seem to confirm a postmodern and ethically emotivist interpretation of Ocasio-Cortez's militant political advocacy.

Regardless of how to interpret Ocasio-Cortez or other liberationists, and we should all hope for their maturing, this postmodern, relativistic, and emotivist political advocacy is seemingly omnipresent. Emotivists reject any norm for truth and ethics, so ethical and value statements are simply emotional assertions and preferences—even though they may defensively defend their belief in truth and norms for pragmatic rather than philosophical (epistemological or ontological) reasons. For emotivists, "I think murder is wrong" is placed in the same ethical category as "I like pistachio ice cream." Today, terms and phrases like concentration camps, "Heil Hitler," and treason are passionately asserted and thrown around by leaders of multiple political parties with reckless abandon.

Countless media sources and news agencies are tracking what they describe as the dangerous, numerous, and constant lies or distortions of President Donald Trump. Such "Pinocchio" lists are endless, and such fact checking, or Pinocchio awards, and allegations of falsehood against Presidents and presidential candidates are not entirely new. Such tracking and allegations took place with the Clintons, Obama, and during both of the Bush presidencies.[35] However, the intensity of the debate and nature and documentation of the allegations today seem unprecedented in recent history.

There is a new wind blowing that has ushered in much semantic fog and significantly decreased visibility. The Trump and Ocasio-Cortez controversies and eruptions are symptoms of a deeper tectonic magnitude semantic and philosophical shift. In the American context, our culture used to assume the existence of a plumb line of truth and a measuring rod for morality. The modernists appealed to reason and/or science as the plumb line and downplayed or rejected divine revelation. The Judeo-Christian leaders appealed, typically, to reason and revelation. A plumb line of sorts existed. Yes, politicians were known for falsehoods, stretching the truth, or lies, but the assumption was that they had *departed* from or violated a shared standard of truth—they were liars, hypocrites, charlatans or worse.

Perhaps it was sometime during the administration of President Bill Clinton, arguably our first largely postmodern President, that the cloud of suspicion concerning the very existence and knowability of some form of normative truth became public and palpable at the level of popular culture, media, and presidential politics. The semantic maneuvering relative to terms and phrases such as "it depends on what the meaning of the word is is," or the definition of "sexual relations with that woman," suggested that the post-modern shift many decades' prior in universities across the globe was now becoming the new and public normal. Thoroughly post-modern Billy, no disrespect intended, had seemingly taken polit-ical and legal posturing to a new level. This shift in many sectors of society, especially in entertainment, seemed to move far beyond opportunistic spin or creative lawyering and towards the eclipse of a shared and normative conception of the truth.

Today, the 1990s in America seem much closer in orbit to the Judeo-Christian plumb line than our present civilizational gyra-tions. The actions and words of politicians, left and right, are symp-toms of something deeper, historic, and much more profound than political gamesmanship.

It is not the purpose of this work to engage in the analysis or endorsement of political candidates. Politicians will come and go. Suffice it to say that we have reached a point where lesser evil calculations are often necessary relative to such reflection. Comprehensive and hierarchical rankings of the costs and benefits of candidates, political parties, and policies are increasingly essen-tial. Some issues are more important than others, and some may legitimately be disqualifiers of some candidates. Robust, compre-hensive, and integrated assessments that move beyond a select and preferred few issues would seem to be a moral imperative amidst the thickening semantic fog.

The seeming increase of narcissistic candidates is concerning. A healthy ego is likely a prerequisite for the rough and tumble of politics, but something seems psychologically awry and possibly unprecedented with multiple political leaders as we ramp up to the next decade of American politics. Twitter and social media culture has, for many, only amped up this narcissistic culture.

Enthusiastic support for politicians is a necessary part of the democratic political process, yet those within the Judeo-Christian orb must never confuse a transient political agenda or leader with the eternal kingdom of God or the coming Messiah. However, shrewd discernment between options is needful, including assessing how representative religious leaders like Mark Labberton and Robert Jeffress are responding to presidential politics (especially see Chapter 3), or assessing the pronouncements of the young liberationists like Ocasio-Cortez.

A Civilization in Crisis

Hence, the passionate and often heated debates concerning the truth, falsity, accuracy, or impact of public statements by contemporary politicians will not be resolved in this work. As noted, this escalating verbal civil war is symptomatic. It is hard to resist the conclusion that our civilization is in crisis and increasingly rudderless.

The social glue that bound our diversity in unity together is dissolving. *E Pluribus Unum* has become "out of the many comes shameless tribalism." The acidic and corrosive impact of semantic theft and the death of truth is escalating social fragmentation and tribalistic polarization. Yes, technology and sociological realities have contributed, but the ideological and verbal shifts seem to be fueling much of this and driving where all this will lead. The underlying cancer producing the current caustic discourse will outlive any specific politician, and apart from a cure the prognosis for a flourishing future is less than hopeful.

This book "cuts both ways" relative to semantic warfare. Some of the more philosophically oriented and trained spokespersons in the American context tend not only to freely manipulate facts and words, but many have aligned with the postmodern tendency to see all words as hopelessly slippery if not meaningless. Hence, it is a two-front war today, combatting both truth relativism and shameless spin or verbal seduction. Nevertheless, many of us in more philosophically and politically conservative communities resonate at times with the concern that within our own communities some conservative leaders manipulate religious language, faith, references to God or God's will, God's blessings, spirituality, and even manipulate the Bible as a smokescreen for ulterior motives such as power, money, control, and unethical behavior. The focus of this book is on how Judeo-Christian beliefs, values, and ethics are under verbal assault, but the methodology of this book cuts both ways. In other words, the political and religious left and right stand under the plumb line of truth and the moral imperatives of truthful and constructive communication.

This semantic chaos in culture is inevitable since neither reason nor revelation are viewed as normative plumb lines, and passionate or even militant advocacy for one's tribe or cause is sufficient since normative truth is beyond our grasp. The mantras are "express yourself" emotionally, fight for your tribe, or simply a "whatever works" pragmatism. Therefore, it is suggested, go ahead and shamelessly advocate for political change, with no normative or shared standard for determining truth, facts, or the proper definition of terms. We are all speaking very different languages.

We have arrived again at the confusion of languages at the Tower of Babel—the sequel—yet there is no place left to which we can scatter and worship our tribal gods in isolation. Should we be astonished that public discourse has become so frustrating, conflictual, and heated? We are subtly taught that we must vanquish the other gods in order to protect and prosper self or tribe.

Are we perplexed that outrage, hate, and violence seem so near the surface? Is it any wonder that many believe that the unabashed use of power and manipulation, rather than elections, persuasion, truth, discourse, and debate, remain the only possible means for resolving disagreements? Why dialog when you can silence and shame others into submission to your tribe? Besides, who is to say which tribe should rule? Perhaps the fit will survive—for a season?

Properly defining and consistently using terms is truly challenging, including in this work, but in many quarters we are utterly failing to even attempt to communicate and dialog. We are often not even trying to dialog. Words are used as weapons.

We seem rather distant from the age when core civilizational documents, dialog, definitions, and convictions required at least some grounding in the sacred and shared affirmation that "we hold these truths," from the Creator and Nature's God, "to be self-evident" norms.

Has no one noticed that, in our relativistic post-truth age, that shameless spin, fake news, alternative facts, "virtuous" lies, and moral relativism are accelerating at unprecedented levels? Does no one see the connection between the public school and university "education" of at least three generations in postmodern relativism and syncretism and everyone accusing everyone else today of deceit and alternative fact universes—or that many claim that all words and statements are really truth-less smokescreens for manipulative power? Are we missing the connection between seductive education and seduced and seducing politicians and governmental bureaucrats? Are we surprised when an American Speaker of the House states that she rejects the "facts" of a Cabinet member, and the Cabinet member responds by saying that "these are not my facts but *the* facts"?

We are no longer just debating the facts or terms; we are now arguing over the essential nature and possibility of any facts, truth, or meaningful communication whatsoever, including the very possibility of civil discourse and civilization. Nietzsche is well known for predicting that the cultural death of God would result in the twentieth century being the bloodiest century in history, and that the death of God would eventually eclipse the meaningfulness of all words and the very meaning of meaning. Nietzsche paradoxically affirmed the truth that there is no normative truth. Recall the insightful quote from Ravi Zacharias at the beginning of this introduction: "With the death of truth, the unique capability of Homo sapiens [created in God's image] for abstract reasoning and language is now taken to the morgue and all language is meaningless."

Is it not quite troubling that we no longer can agree on the proper definitions of virtually any key terms and values—often even inside of the church? Are we surprised that political groups with radically different agendas all claim to be "pro-family" today?[36]

In America, Judeo-Christian-influenced conceptions of freedom of speech and freedom of religion clearly birthed and allowed for the constitutional possibility of unfolding and tolerant religious and political diversity; such inclusion, properly defined, emerged over decades and centuries.

These Judeo-Christian-influenced conceptions of freedom also approved of public Judeo-Christian-influenced architecture, monuments, Presidential decrees, publications, coinage, the public display of Judeo-Christian Scripture, official days of prayer and fasting, and endless cultural artifacts. Judeo-Christian norms even influenced and undergirded many of the countless public, biblical, and religious based arguments against slavery. Consider the broad nineteenth century usage of Harriet Beecher Stowe's *Uncle Tom's Cabin* or Lincoln's religiously based addresses supporting abolitionism.

Judeo-Christian influence was a key wellspring for a shared understanding of political and cultural toleration, including the possibility and limits of "toleration," and our common life together. Does it not almost seem more than absurd and disingenuous today to redefine terms like pro-faith, freedom of speech, and freedom of religion, and then use those verbal redefinitions to advance arguments to eradicate Judeo-Christian influence from the very civilization birthed in large measure by Judeo-Christian values? The picture above is a graphic portrayal of what it means to be seduced. "Pro-family" does and should not exist in a semantic vacuum.

Semantic Clusters and Universes

Words function within families of words or semantic clusters. This is similar to the principle that many are familiar with known as interpreting the Bible by the Bible.

Biblical words and passages are to be better or more fully understood and defined, in part, by finding their meaning and definition in reference not only to contemporary usage but also to other biblical passages and word usages (semantics). For example, the Logos doctrine in John chapter one is better understood by relating it to the personalized doctrine of divine wisdom in Proverbs and the creation narrative of Genesis, as well as the word usage and definitions in the gospel of John. That is why John 1:1 intentionally echoes Genesis with "in the beginning." The tree of life references in Revelation are better understood as a fulfillment of Genesis and defined in reference to the tree of life references in Genesis. Scripture interprets Scripture. Jesus constantly referred to the Old Testament in his teaching to ground, define, and illustrate his ministry and key affirmations. In philosophical terms, individual terms should not be interpreted in an unconnected or atomistic fashion but instead treated in a more systemic, relational, or organic manner.

Hence, for nearly two thousand years in Judeo-Christian-influenced Western civilization the concept of "pro-family" was defined as heterosexual and monogamous. Likewise, for some two millennia the concept of the sacredness of life or "pro-life," fully situated in the Judeo-Christian semantic universe, meant a rejection of infanticide, abortion, and the cheapening of innocent life via the brutal gladiatorial games.[37] Long live Telemachus. Indeed, abortion was deemed by the Judeo-Christian community to be just another form—a "speedier" means (Tertullian, AD 210)—of infanticide.

Until roughly the twentieth century in the American context, feminism was almost universally pro-life, pro-monogamy, and pro-heterosexual marriage, and all of these core values were considered to be appropriately patriotic. In America this Judeo-Christian framed culture was believed to be part of the advancing or dawning kingdom rule of God, and patriotism was viewed as at least potentially and simultaneously non-idolatrous *and* pro-American.

Nineteenth century Judeo-Christian-influenced feminism viewed abortion, slavery, and gender discrimination as part of a unified family of sub-Christian practices, terms, values, and beliefs and most oppressive—and especially oppressive to women, including abortion. These practices, such as slavery, were even considered to be justifiable reasons for God to judge America (see *Uncle Tom's Cabin*, especially the last section, or see Lincoln's addresses referenced in Chapter 3).

We live in an amazing time when outrage is expected and encouraged over endless social justice causes, or conditions at the border, or mass shootings, or even saving endangered species. Even if all of these causes are truly just, the lack of outrage concerning roughly 300,000 to 800,000 abortions per year (or multiple thousands per day),[38] and sixty million legal abortions since 1973, raises serious questions, at least from a Judeo-Christian perspective, about whether compassion, or well-informed compassion, is the motivating factor for some of these other causes. Such questions are especially pertinent when the abortion data is suggestive of black genocide along with the fact that most abortions are of females. Being dismissive of the hundreds of thousands of unborn even based on the premise that choice is God hardly reflects erring on the side of compassion and justice for those with no voice, potential life, or life with great potential.

Terms cluster together and define each other. Hence, redefining "pro-choice" as patriotic, "pro-family," or "pro-woman" reflects more than just a few word redefinitions. The semantic ground is shifting, and we are being propelled by many, often intentionally, into a new semantic universe.

The seduced and the seducers are subtly redefining and recreating reality and civilization—post-Logos. Because words, definitions, assumptions, and values cluster together into families or semantic universes, the accomplished lawyers on the Supreme Court often land on 5-4 decisions on historic issues that define our nation, culture, and future. The Court often can't agree even on the truly big rocks of civilization. Even 7-2 decisions are troubling and seemingly perplexing on such core, fundamental, and historic decisions. The Supreme Court divisions cannot simply be explained by legal precedents, or faulty logic, or personality differences, or legal competencies, or legal deficiencies, or sociological contexts. Simply put, the justices often inhabit different semantic universes and they are speaking different languages (especially see Chapter 2 on the Supreme Court). Congressional tribalism is even more evident.

It is arguable that in the American context we are fully moving into a verbal or sematic civil war. Every term is now a hill to secure or take. The definition of concepts like "social justice" dominoes or radiates throughout the verbal universe and organically reshapes other words as well as the entire semantic universe. Commitment to inclusion for many entails the rejection of biblical morality.

The verbal universe guides our individual and collective passions and actions. Words matter and they are immensely powerful. Each word is precious and potent. Each word is a watershed or linchpin or barometer or fulcrum of culture and the very future of civilization.

To illustrate further the familial nature of how words function, some even go so far as to defend the erection of satanic monuments (Baphomet) on public property in America (e.g., the Arkansas and Illinois state capitol buildings)—most ironically in the name of "freedom of speech" or the "non-establishment" clause of the Constitution (especially see Chapter 9 on these topics).[39] The "American Experiment," "Democracy" and "separation of church and state" are also redefined such that public school students access to the Satanic Temple website is morally and legally equated with website access to Jewish and Christian organizations.

Values and terms have been inverted. Pro-choice is redefined as pro-family and pro-faith, and religious freedom and tolerance are redefined as tribute to Satan and the relativization or eradication of biblical influence. Jesus and Satan are relativized, and the latter is considered by some to be more publicly virtuous than the former. And all are to accept this relativism in the name of religious neutrality. In the Illinois State Capitol, yet another satanic statue was erected, and arrogantly defined as a "Snaketivity," to counter Christian symbols during the official national holiday season of Christmas that celebrates the nativity. By way of simple reminder, Christmas, not Santa Claus or Satan, is a national holiday—and declared to be such by the great liberator, Ulysses S. Grant, who was only marginally Methodist.[40]

This satanic image, artwork, and inscription, on full display at the Illinois State Capitol, redefined the serpent and the apple as good, or even very good. The tragic fall of humanity releasing untold pain, incalculable suffering, torture, and murder was recast as a metaphor for knowledge and progress. This artwork referred not to Christ as the greatest Christmas gift, but instead viewed the satanic seduction in the garden and the words of Satan as "knowledge" and "the greatest gift." Satan is the heroic metaphor, human rebellion is a virtue, and the Old Testament Creator is the villain.

Words are powerful, word definitions rule, and they also redefine synagogue, church, civilization, and generate the future. As noted, today it is good to be bad and bad to be good. Nietzsche's well-known project of the transvaluation or inversion of Judeo-Christian values, and therefore the seductive morphing of words, is well underway. Have we traversed the cosmic wormhole? Truly all is at stake.

Shameless Spin

Yes, as noted above in this introduction, those on both the political right and left engage in shameless spin—which should be expected in view of universal and fallen human nature. Most on the religious and political right have observed conservative leaders, or family members, or employers, engaging in shameless spin and dishonesty baptized in pseudo-spirituality. God, Jesus, God's will, prayer, love, or the leading of the Spirit are used to cover up base motives, unethical practices, and manipulation.

Similarly, when political conservatives engage in spin to justify unbiblical attitudes and actions such as racism or sexism, the root problem involves spiritual blindness, a hard heart, inconsistency, and hypocrisy. When political liberals engage in such spin the root problem also emerges from our fallen nature and a lack of virtue, but it also may involve two additional key factors for some on the left: (1) the intent to move away from authentic biblical and Judeo-Christian influence; and (2) the conviction that words are ultimately disconnected from normative truth and therefore mere means of power and personal or tribal advocacy. *In other words, some at least believe that there is really nothing wrong with using words deceitfully.* Perhaps this explains much in Hollywood and the nation's capitol. Hence, deceitful spin typically falls into one or more of these categories:

1. **Intentional and shameless spin** by those who know better, which amounts to hypocrisy,
2. **Unintentional spin or false beliefs** affirmed by those who have been seduced, or
3. **Relativistic or postmodern spin** by those who view spin and deceit as justifiable since there is ultimately no moral or semantic north star.

Spin has now reached pandemic proportions in our relativistic age. Is anyone really asking the deep questions as to why? Many simply believe that saying anything is justifiable since there is no norm for truth or morality. Say anything to advocate for yourself or your tribe. Make things up if it advances your personal, political, or tribal cause or "truth." Regardless of the counter-evidence even from very liberal and progressive judicial system investigations, some continue to claim, without any qualification whatsoever, that Michael Brown was murdered—and they seemingly have no shame even if they are a candidate for the presidency of the United States. There seems to be no moral compass to assess spin. Spin is in and spin is all there is. Not only has relativism taught us that history and justice are in the eye of the beholder, but now many believe or feel that truth and facts are in the eye of the beholder.

One presidential candidate in Iowa, apparently via a blunder, may nevertheless have unintentionally summed up the spirit of our age: "We choose 'truth' over facts." Truth is what the individual or tribe believes it is, and trumps facts. Today truth is fluid, chosen, and quickly created, not sacrificially discovered, diligently researched and cherished. Besides, in an age of spin, where spin is unavoidable, facts are often met with suspicion, for in this relativistic age all facts are also viewed as part of someone's manipulative spin narrative. Facts are not facts, and they are even despised in some quarters. Everything is spin so go for it. All facts are a matter of interpretation anyhow. Welcome to the ultramodern relativistic world of incoherent syncretism!

The shameless political and media discourse that can be observed daily well illustrates the emerging and rudderless semantic universe. Lying is no longer lying; it may well be virtuous. The political right and left are both equal opportunity employers for those who have abandoned the plumb line. Today, dishonesty and verbal seduction are viewed as moral (a just cause) or amoral (because a norm for truth does not exist or can't be known). Lies are told as if there is a moral compass, a just cause, or as if normative morality exists in order to persuade and manipulate.

Many of the seducers, however, are either agnostic or covertly nihilistic concerning normative truth and morality. They are also progressively nihilistic concerning semantics. Many of our "finest" universities and "creative" cultural guides have birthed and sustained a generation lacking a cultivated sense of conscience. The culture as a whole is beginning to exhibit the characteristics of sociopathy.

This book will ask the deep questions as to why we are in this quagmire and proffer heuristic answers for how to navigate the present crisis. Unfortunately, the contemporary political left often has a passionate and central ideology most desirous of eradicating Judeo-Christian influence from civilization in the name of "progress," and premised upon an unconstitutionally redefined concept of freedom or a confused understanding of the non-establishment of religion clause. Or they at least want to redefine Judeo-Christian influence, the American experiment, and then wrap themselves in flag, cross, and spirituality. These issues will be addressed in multiple chapters.

As many have noted, freedom of religion does not mean freedom from religion, and for centuries America even cherished and promoted Judeo-Christian religious and moral cultural influence and viewed such influence as both eminently constitutional and the key or principal support of democracy and true freedom in America. Tax benefits for clergy and non-profits, now under assault in the media and the courts, would be illustrative.

Many on the contemporary political left desire to establish their powerful, manipulative, and sometimes oppressive post or anti-Christian ideology and relativistic worldview that, frankly, functions like the very oppressive and fundamentalist religions they claim to despise. And their target is no longer the mere fundamental transformation of the state; they are now also pursuing the fundamental transformation and control, or at least redefinition, of the church and religious communities of faith. As noted, phase one of this redefinition of the church is the redefinition of biblical words and concepts like basic biblical beliefs, and values, including the following: judging others (Matthew 7:1–2), compassion (Colossians 3:12), love, salvation, inclusion (Galatians 3:28), marriage, male, female, and social justice. Phase two, already well under way, is radically to morph law and culture.

Yes, the dark and bitter experiences of those who have been oppressed, persecuted, marginalized, enslaved, and degraded by authentic phobias, bigotry, racism, sexism, or any form of dark supremacism must be empathetically identified with by those calling for a return to and creative future application and enhancement of Judeo-Christian values. Such evil behaviors must be passionately called out and condemned by biblically influenced religious communities. Yet such prophetic and loving condemnation is only effective and biblical when properly defined with appropriate terms and shrewdly utilized with tactful frequency.

As I write these words, America is celebrating Martin Luther King, Jr. Day. I tragically recall that I have heard too many on the religious right making crass racist jokes or comments such as "Martin Lucifer King"—either due to bigotry, or sometimes when reacting to what they sense is manipulation by the contemporary political left. I have even observed some tragically and intentionally using racist terms, not because they regularly did so, but simply to challenge what they perceive as an increasingly controlling and oppressive culture.

One such individual using racist terms was also a staunch supporter of a minority candidate for President and other diversity political and cultural leaders! This individual and others of a similar mind even shared campaign materials supportive of an African-American politician. They seemed to be far more concerned about ideology and what they viewed as pathological subcultures than genetics or skin color or ethnic origin. Indeed, they had invested significant philanthropic dollars in nonwhite regions of Africa.

The seeming escalation of racist comments and racist allegations is a very destructive and self-perpetuating cycle. When "ist" and "ism" allegations are recklessly employed or overused the terms become background noise, vapid, unnecessarily provoking, and easily dismissed as "the boy or girl who cried wolf." When unbiblical "ist" and "ism" comments are made, whether emanating from a toxic and bigoted subculture or merely to provoke or give push back to those constantly leveling allegations or racism, the vicious cycle continues and only degrades further. As noted, the methodology in this book "cuts both ways," and both groups should cower in shame at the abuse of language.

Many "ism" and "ist" allegations are losing their effectiveness and becoming verbal static, such as the recent acrimonious verbal assault claiming that Chick-fil-A is an "industrial, white supremacist, imperialist, capitalist" cult that should be banned from access to a major university.[41] Chick-fil-A, now the third largest fast-food company, has been growing even while under near constant assault and threats of boycott across the nation (and globe) for its traditional Judeo-Christian values—attacks taking place in the name of "social justice," "freedom," and "inclusion," questionably defined. Support for Judeo-Christian and biblical conceptions of marriage are now deemed as non-inclusive, bigoted, and hateful. Nearly a dozen universities, such as Purdue and Kansas (KU), have seen efforts to boycott the company, along with boycotts by cities and airports in the United States and beyond.

The concerns with Chick-fil-A are endless, such as donations to anti-gay groups (apparently this refers to any group that supports traditional conceptions of marriage, like the Salvation Army); the "closed on Sunday" non-inclusive and bigoted theocratic policy which attempts to fulfill their vision of honoring God and helping employees; or Chick-fil-A's own statements over the years supporting traditional conceptions of marriage. It will be instructive to see if Chick-fil-A's policy changes regarding donations to groups such as the Salvation Army will soften opposition. The problem for Chic-fil-A is that the opposition to this fast food provider was broader and deeper than specific donations, and by caving to pressure from the critics Chic-fil-A effectively now has enabled those who strive to ban or silence traditional Judeo-Christian businesses and, eventually, faith groups and parachurch organizations.

Judeo-Christian organizations supportive of traditional hetero-sexual marriage should be aware that even Chick-fil-A's attempts to mollify its critics by altering actions, public statements, and policies have thus far had little impact on the critics. The critics simply detest the company's traditional Judeo-Christian and Baptist heritage, former or current values, and former or current definition of marriage. This very same vitriol could easily be applied to other less known organizations, individuals, or religious groups.

Traditional Judeo-Christian values, beliefs, and practices will eventually be criminalized if this current trajectory continues, which is another reason why religious leaders need to lead on semantic apologetics and polemics. Such condemnations of Chick-fil-A reek of yet another form of elitism, supremacism, and will ultimately undermine legitimate efforts to marginalize authentic and evil "isms" and reform, sustain, and enhance a more perfect union.[42]

The future of Chick-fil-A may be a bellwether or canary in the mine shaft relative to the future of Judeo-Christian faith communities and Judeo-Christian influenced businesses. As with any organization, leaders change over time and spokespersons sometimes excel and sometimes fall short when managing public perceptions. Regardless of public relations, perhaps the fundamental question for a free society is whether this Atlanta based organization's donations to charity, Baptist subculture and history, traditional Judeo-Christian values, view of marriage, view of gender, and view of the family should be met with vitriolic boycotts or criminalization. And has Chick-fil-A responded appropriately to date and will its discontinuation of specific donations negatively impact freedom of religion and freedom of speech?

IT IS A GREAT TIME FOR FROSTED KEY LIME
closed sunday

Irresolvable Conflicts and the Vanishing Plumb Line

Trying to resolve conflicts over such flash points—such as marriage, gender identity, transgender athletes, feminism versus non-binary and subjective choice gender norms, Chick-fil-A, Christmas as a national holiday, multiculturalism, "In God We Trust" coinage, the sculpted frieze of the Ten Commandments in the Supreme Court building, or inclusion—without the north star of a cultural and civilizational plumb line is beyond futile. Mediating disputes between seemingly infinite protected and victimized classes eventually unravels, for such groups demand rights and protections that rob other groups of their rights and protections.

The conflicts are irresolvable apart from shared and normative conceptions of truth, noble values, a noble vision, and a shared language or semantic universe. The challenge still is daunting even with a shared *telos*. Yet apart from such norms, what remains is tribal warfare, shameless spin, and the relativistic use of power. What remains is a civilization built on sand.

How can we possibly determine if traditional foster care organizations should be shut down if they hold to traditional religious values or a traditional view of marriage? Should LBGTQ foster care organizations receive public funding? How about Roman Catholic or evangelical faith based organizations? Nearly half a million children are seeking homes. Should the Salvation Army be condemned, and lose its tax-exempt status, along with all such religious organizations?

To what degree should massive Islamic immigration and culture be allowed to reshape the law and culture of democracies? Even progressive Europe and the appeal to "European values" can't seem to mediate that festering dispute. The FAA (Federal Aviation Administration) is now investigating Chick-fil-A's exclusion at multiple airports.[43] The Little Sisters of the Poor won a Supreme Court case in 2016 and they are not required to supply the week after pill, but one precedent rarely resolves all similar conflicts and the basis of the decision seemed to be that the government had other ways of providing the abortifacient to the public. The Supreme Court decision was far less than a rebirth of Judeo-Christian religious freedom. The Little Sisters of the Poor are not likely out of the legal woods.

Legal precedents are helpful but not determinative of future legislation, especially as the Judeo-Christian semantic universe decays (see Chapter 1 concerning the Supreme Court's sometimes philosophically confused and foundationless and cryptic decision-making). In one state legislation makes abortion more restrictive, and in another state the legislature gives a "standing ovation for a bill that, among other things, removed requirements that infants born during abortion procedures receive legal protection as persons." Claims of conservative infanticide hysteria notwithstanding, a governor in another state attempting to clarify whether he did in fact endorse infanticide muddied the waters further by stating that "babies determined to have 'severe deformities' or be 'nonviable' would be delivered, 'kept comfortable,' and 'resuscitated if that's what the mother and the family desired, and then a discussion would ensue between the physicians and the mother.'"[44] Pro-choice news agencies (e.g., CNN) reported the same exact words from this governor:

[Third trimester abortions are] done in cases where there may be severe deformities. "There may be a fetus that's nonviable. So in this particular example, if a mother is in labor, I can tell you exactly what would happen," Northam, a pediatric neurosurgeon, told Washington radio station WTOP. "The infant would be delivered. The infant would be kept comfortable. The infant would be resuscitated if that's what the mother and the family desired. And then a discussion would ensue between the physicians and the mother."[45]

The attempt to resolve such core value conflicts apart from a shared semantic universe and plumb line is a will-o'-the-wisp and a perfect recipe for verbal civil war and escalating tribalism, if not worse. In contrast, a Logocentric plumb line clothed in *agape* love can and has assisted with mediating such disputes and providing a healthy context for authentic toleration and inclusion, robust dialog, collaboration, consensus building, valuing life and minorities, democratic processes, plus human and civilizational flourishing. Even with the plumb line there are challenges, but without the plumb line disintegration, fragmentation, balkanization, or tyranny may obtain sooner rather than later. When culture and civilizations have irreconcilable differences and conflicts of interest without a default value system and method for reconciliation and adjudication the only remaining default may well be the use or abuse of power.

A Truly Inclusive and More Perfect Union Experiment

To be crystal clear, this book project is absolutely committed to values such as compassion, social justice, toleration, freedom of religion, freedom of speech, and inclusion—properly defined. The bitter experience of non-inclusion or exclusion must be kept before us. This work is absolutely committed to countering and condemning evils such as racism, sexism, homophobia, and xenophobia—properly defined. Indeed, exposing the false definitions of key terms related to social justice, inclusion, and freedom and preserving the authentic concepts actually demonstrate a greater and more long term commitment to freedom and justice than social justice pandering and patronizing. A sustainable more perfect union can only be built on authentic justice, toleration, inclusion, and compassion.

The difference between properly defining a concept like social justice or religious freedom and making the case for how to best implement social just or religious freedom cannot be overemphasized. The definition of a term like social justice and the means or application of that term certainly overlap but should be somewhat separate or discreet.

For example, advocates from different political perspectives should seek, as much as is possible, a common and non-question-begging definition of biblical social justice. Such a definition may synthesize biblical teachings (e.g., Amos 5, the Sermon on the Mount and other synoptic material) on justice and the key emphases of the most credible theories of social justice. Then the fair dialog or debate can ensue about the best means of implementing or achieving social justice.

If social justice is defined as socialism, communism, Rawlsian justice, or capitalism, in advance of the dialog, then the dialog becomes insincere and unproductive. The dialog today is frequently question-begging, conflictual, and inherently provoking. The implication is that "If you believe in social justice, then you must agree with me on the best means for achieving social justice."

We desperately need honest debates on such matters today in order to restore some measure of civil discourse and at least a somewhat collaborative quest for a more perfect union. For example, let's have open dialog concerning whether some version of socialism or Michael Novak's Trinitarian democratic capitalism best achieve social justice. Let's admit that some who disagree with us are sincerely committed to biblical social justice, and that the disagreement is at least in part over the means and not the goal of a just and compassionate social order. This dialogical template could greatly assist the common good relative to the vitriolic and accusatory nature of border security and immigration debates.

This work is focusing on taking the first steps toward reclaiming a constructive and ameliorative cultural lexicon, yet once that task is well underway it will be important to remember that properly defining justice or toleration is only one dimension of kingdom advance. Pastor Bryan Loritts has aptly noted that toleration, improperly defined, is a "spineless, low ethic" and that tolerant indifference enables racism and falls far short of passionate and constructive cultural and ecclesial engagement. The same could be said of the term inclusion. Biblical, sacrificial, *agape*, and overflowing Christ-like love of every tribe and tongue and people and nation is the higher, eschatological, and doxological standard and *telos* (Revelation 5). Sound semantics is the foundational, generative, and creative medium within which we must passionately pursue the true future of God's kingdom—already.

The proper definitions of words and phrases must be influenced and shaped by Logocentrism and kingdomcentrism (not the pursuit of a theocracy but language and values influenced by the biblical vision of a just and inviting kingdom). Proper word usage requires sound reasoning, clear communication, real evidence, actual news, historical and cultural analysis, rigorous ethical reflection, the quest for the common good, and much, much common sense.

Biblical love or *agape* far more effectively and longitudinally grounds and counters countless evil "isms" than endless "anti-ist" opportunistic, utopian, and ambiguously defined ideologies. "Anti-ist" ideologies can't fill the heart with divinely enabled overflowing love, and too often fill the hearts of the ideological crusaders with hate and yet another form of non-inclusive oppression. Too often in higher education, law, or popular culture, for example, "inclusivity" means excluding those with Judeo-Christian or biblical convictions. Inclusion today certainly does not include some 300,000 – 800,000 unborn without a voice that are destroyed each year in America alone. Inclusion often does not include businesses that seek to live consistently with what they perceive as biblical values.

Amazingly, even within faith communities and Judeo-Christian organizations the seductively promethean term and ideology of inclusivism has often replaced a much more ecclesially and culturally potent means and dynamic supportive of authentic and biblical compassion and social justice. *Agape* love or "biblical inclusion" far better grounds, frames, and addresses the sometimes legitimate concerns of those battling the bitter toxicity of legitimate and oppressive non-inclusivism. Biblical agape or biblical inclusion also properly frames the endless controversies related to sexual ethics.

Agape is servant love, tough love, normed love, sacrificial love, and it seeks out the lost sheep, touches the leper, elevates the marginalized, abolishes false racial distinctions, identifies with the oppressed in Egypt and Rome, involves cosmic *kenosis* (Philippians 2), requires "no greater love" (John 15:13), and is exemplified by the forsakenness and forgiveness of Calvary's cross.

> Love is patient, love is kind and is not jealous; love does not brag and is not arrogant, does not act unbecomingly; it does not seek its own, is not provoked, does not take into account a wrong suffered, does not rejoice in unrighteousness, but rejoices with the truth; bears all things, believes all things, hopes all things, endures all things. (1 Corinthians 13:4–7)

Indeed, "faith, hope, love, abide these three; but the greatest of these is love" (1 Corinthians 13:13).

Perhaps more importantly, in an increasingly hateful, polarized, and tribalisitc era, why would Judeo-Christian faith communities adopt inclusive semantics over *agape* semantics? Given the fallen human condition, authentic inclusion is simply not definable, achievable, or sustainable apart from a heart transformation by grace through faith. The hardness of the human heart is at the core of unbiblical exclusion, so the cure must include open heart surgery (Ezekiel 36:26). At a minimum, faith communities should always qualify inclusion semantics via the ethical north star, true source, and spiritual living water of kenotic *agape* (Philippians chapter 2).

Such love, for example, patiently and sacrificially liberates rather than enables the alcoholic. Such love shrewdly counsels the unfaithful spouse seeking wholeness. Such love prayerfully, sacrificially, and wisely reaches out to the poor and homeless with support, assistance, *and* accountability, as modeled by the relief efforts documented in Marvin Olaskey's *The Tragedy of American Compassion.*[46] True compassion employs shrewd strategy, tactics, and sound theology and biblical assumptions concerning how to transform human nature and constructively impact the larger social context and civilizational system.

In any event, it is clear that semantic filters and caution are lacking today amidst the haze of relativistic and tribalistic postmodernity or ultramodernity. Indeed, the utilization of such filters and proper definitions actually would demonstrate a shrewd, long-term, and much, much deeper and authentic commitment to biblical social justice. We live in tempestuous times amidst an age of outrage and tribalism, at least in part, because we live in an age of foundationless and tempestuous semantics.

At times communities of faith have failed, yet biblically influenced communities should lead, and often have led the way, in prophetically condemning true "hate-isms" such as racism and sexism, while also advancing correct conceptions of "isms," as well as concepts such as toleration and inclusion. Unless allegations of racism or sexism are used with integrity and wisdom, such allegations actually backfire and cheapen the value and potency of such terms and critiques. And if such terms are not properly defined they easily lend themselves to yet another form of supremacism or elitism, where anyone who disagrees is an evil "ist," which is ever the cultural trajectory today.

Indeed, a new racism or new sexism of the contemporary political left is gathering momentum in culture and the academy. Some three decades ago the French scholar Etienne Balibar, on the social and political left, used the term neo-racism in a specific manner in the European context to condemn covert or hidden racism.[47] Yet, in the American context, the concepts and terms of neo-racism, neo-sexism, and countless other "neo-isms" are especially applicable to the contemporary political left today.

Martin Luther King, Jr. famously provided the monumental definition of and parameters for racism properly defined: "I have a dream that my four little children will one day live in a nation where they will *not be judged by the color of their skin but by the content of their character*." Neo-racism and neo-sexism allege that those with a certain skin color or gender or social position are inevitably, unavoidably, or inherently racist or sexist. This is the radical postmodern idea that one is not just influenced by one's context—news flash, we all are to one degree or another—but that one is essentially *determined* by their context and can't possibly escape or transcend their "ist" conditioning. Of course these postmodernists embarrassingly contradict themselves. If we can't escape our tribe or context or conditioning, then certainly these postmodern elitists also can't escape their biases and prejudices and hence their moral outrage is nothing more than a personal or tribal preference.

If there is no plumb line, then there is no basis for principled outrage. This variety of postmodernism that is obsessed with making allegations of racism is just another form of race-baiting and virtue signaling and amounts to racist tribalism on steroids. While racial and gender differences cannot be entirely ignored when pursuing justice, King clearly condemns, in principle, this emerging American neo-racism and neo-sexism. For neo-racists and neo-sexists, factors such as skin color, gender, and social status are the very basis for neo-discrimination, silencing dissent, making false accusations, and engaging in defamatory spin, class envy, hate, and even violence—all under the guise of social justice, compassion, and anti-discrimination. For King, influenced by Scripture and Gandhi, love and truthfulness were viewed as absolutely essential to pursing the dream of an enduring and just civilization.

Those suggesting that we cannot escape our context or prejudices should consider what it would be like to tell that to the Germans who sacrificed their lives opposing Hitler, or the white abolitionists who also gave the ultimate gift while battling slavery. Tell that to Bonhoeffer. Tell that to Catherine of Alexander, or Magdalene of Nagasaki. Tell that to the loved ones of Kayla Mueller or Sophie Scholl.

Interestingly, neo-racist and neo-sexist groups are at times strikingly and functionally similar to the very racist groups they despise most, such as the KKK, relative to psychological orientation, mindset, tribalistic obsession with racial differences, groupthink, and lockstep conformity.

"White makes right" and "non-white makes right"
are both racist and culturally toxic.

The commitment to combat racism and advocate for social justice should not "become a new excuse for prejudice."[48] Subsequent to many revolutions for "the workers," for "the people," or for the *"Volk,"* the people have often been imprisoned or exterminated by the liberators. In like manner, the word theft, misuse, and dilution of important terms like racism, sexism, and inclusion will be addressed throughout this work in order to avoid such calamitous seductions of the past.

A genuine more perfect union is also truly inclusive, in contrast to numberless and tribalistic pseudo-inclusive future-visions today. The term inclusion is not a silver bullet and does not and cannot stand alone. It is part of an organic system and family of values and terms. Do inclusion advocates truly want to include all beliefs, values, practices, and groups, including those that they deem not to be inclusive? Should inclusion advocates exclude their own inclusion movements if such movements exclude other groups? The suggestion that inclusion includes everyone who defines inclusion like "we" do is less than persuasive or sound and less than virtuous. The answer to what is properly inclusive and supportive of a more perfect union presupposes a semantic universe, and this work argues that the Judeo-Christian semantic universe fosters authentic, compassionate inclusion, political freedom, and human flourishing.

Inclusion "in the eye of the beholder" is culturally destructive and potentially if not inexorably oppressive. Inclusion improperly or relativistically defined subverts the worthy goal of inclusion.

Indeed, inclusion and tribalism cannot coexist logically or sociologically. Over time, inclusion ideology untethered from biblical moorings and *agape* becomes politically and legally enforced inclusion. And enforced inclusion easily becomes a form of militant tribalism that ultimately devours gracious, Judeo-Christian-influenced inclusion and *agape*.

Even more directly related to this work, many terms like inclusion are now redefined and re-employed as battering rams to smash and eradicate the Judeo-Christian foundations for and influence on culture and civilization. Words can be used for good or evil. Words can be used to combat social injustice or, in the name of social justice and compassion, used to justify social injustice, animosity, and anti-religious bigotry.

Perhaps the recent and sad case of Oberlin College illustrates such pseudo-justice, or Trojan Horse justice (see Chapter 2), or 'just us" justice, or, simply put, unjust justice? "An Ohio jury awarded a local bakery $33 million in punitive damages, on top of $11 million in compensation, because college officials were involved in student [justice] protests that accused the store of racism in a shoplifting incident."[49] If the jury got this right, the true racists and religious bigots were not the bakery owners, but the self-righteous "social justice" students and employees of Oberlin College. Time will tell, and the damages awarded have been reduced in the name of "free speech," then restored then again appealed, but the case is potentially illustrative. Not everything parading as compassionate social justice necessarily is compassionate or just or biblical.

Apologetics, Polemics, and Semantics — Plus Tone and Attitude

Those who love religious freedom and human and cultural thriving will pay great attention to the use and meaning of words (*semantics*), and the preservation of authentic Scriptural faith within religious communities (*polemics*). Truth and freedom lovers will also energetically attend to the loving and persuasive advocacy for and defense of Judeo-Christian beliefs, practices, values, and words in the broader marketplace of ideas (*apologetics*; 1 Peter 3:15 and Acts 17). **Polemics, semantics, and apologetics all intersect at the crossroads of the future for the church, culture, and civilization.** This book is a preliminary and heuristic project in *semantic polemics and apologetics*.

Semantic apologetics and polemics can play a crucial role in the journey back to the enhanced Judeo-Christian-influenced future of a more perfect union.

The tone, motive, careful preparation, and attitude guiding semantic apologetics and polemics are as important as the desperate need for semantic precision and refinement. This work does and *should* passionately and respectfully advance an argument—that is the nature of works in apologetics and polemics (e.g., *Contra Celsum*, *Against Apion*, *Contra Julian*, *Apology*, *City of God*, *Evidence That Demands a Verdict*, *Scaling the Secular City*, *Mere Christianity*). Yet those utilizing this book in personal and public dialog should conform their hearts and minds and affections to five core principles of biblical apologetics and polemics:

1. Gentleness (1 Peter 3:15)
2. Extreme reverence (φόβου) and respect for the critics of biblical faith (1 Peter 3:15), like unto the respect owed to a ruler in the ancient world
3. Speaking the truth in love (Ephesians 4:15)
4. Irenic tone (Hebrews 12:14)
5. Intensive preparation for apologetic and polemic encounters analogous to a legal defense or *apologia* (1 Peter 3:15) that anticipates objections and winsomely persuades

The proper response to youthful and energetic Ocasio-Cortez's quote is not hateful scorn, if she indeed is illustrating the contemporary and emotivist disconnect between political advocacy and truth We can depart from Judeo-Christian semantics both via definitions and tone or attitude. It is hard to know the full motivation underlying such comments from Ocasio-Cortez or other militants apart from robust and patient dialog.

A better and loving response to this seeming polarization of truth and morality might be simply to ask if those on the political right also need not pay careful attention to being "precisely, factually, and semantically correct," as Ocasio-Cortez put it, if they already *know* they are "morally right"? This type of response gently emphasizes the urgent need for a semantic plumb line today, the shared quest for normative truth, and hopefully opens a dialog with growing numbers of such youthful socialists and liberationists—and many others. It is also critical to remember that many of these reckless social justice warriors in politics and the media are products of a sometimes rather indoctrinating tax-funded educational system.

God loves words. Judeo-Christian religions resonate concerning the critical importance of words, the direct connection between wisdom, understanding and words, and the centrality of the Logos or Word doctrine and person. Christianity especially embraces the Logos as Wisdom revealed through words (Proverbs), the Logos as the person of Christ (John 1), the Christ or Logos as the rabbi who taught with authoritative words and actions, and the Triune Logos as the very wellspring and foundation for the normative words of Scripture (John 6:63; Romans 3:2; 2 Timothy 3:14–17). Paul's words in 2 Timothy once served as a core assumption of the church and Judeo-Christian influenced culture:

> You, however, continue in the things you have learned and become convinced of, knowing from whom you have learned *them*, and that from childhood you have known the sacred writings which are able to give you the wisdom that leads to salvation through faith which is in Christ Jesus. All Scripture is inspired by God and profitable for teaching, for reproof, for correction, for training in righteousness; so that the man [servant, NIV] of God may be adequate, equipped for every good work.

This shared plumb line shaped our culture, guided our law, influenced the very structure of our government, inspired our art, culture, music, and even our letters to loved ones to and from the battlefields of the world when history tottered in the balance. This north star influenced war-time secret codes, and named our cities, our children, and even many of our American heroes. This plumb line guided much public and private education (e.g., the early nineteenth century *McGuffey Readers* supported by Harriet Beecher Stowe) and *was* the air we breathed; indeed, it served as the very warp and woof of the experiment in our arduous and unending journey toward a more perfect civilization.

God loves the human quest for semantic clarity and truthfulness. God reveals normative truth through words to guide the quest. Jeremiah chapter one emphasizes the following: the "words of Jeremiah"; the "word of the Lord" that came to Jeremiah; that

Jeremiah was told to "say whatever I [YHWH] command you;" the very touching of Jeremiah's mouth so that he might accurately speak for God; and that "I [YHWH] have put my words in your mouth."

The God of Scripture is the God who acts, the God who speaks *through words*, and the God who interprets his actions, words, and the entire redemptive journey—from paradise lost to paradise regained—through authoritative and inspired words. "Thus says the Lord" appears countless times throughout the Old Testament, and the New Testament affirms that "God, after He spoke long ago to the fathers in the prophets in many portions and in many ways, in these last days has spoken to us in His Son, whom He appointed heir of all things, through whom also He [the Logos, John 1:3] made the world [all things and words]" (Hebrews 1:1–2). Hebrews also repeatedly introduces quotes from the Old Testament with some verbal equivalent of "God says" or "God said."

Words can reveal truth or they can deceive and harm. The biblical books of Proverbs, James, and the words of Jesus in the Gospels make very strong statements concerning the abuse of the tongue and the power of words to seduce, harm, or heal. The tongue is seemingly uncontrollable, likened to a small fire that starts a forest fire, blesses and curses, destroys or heals others, and "A soothing tongue is a tree of life, but perversion in it crushes the spirit" (Proverbs 15:4). Jesus predictably unearthed the very core of this issue when observing that "out of the abundance of the heart" the mouth speaks (Luke 6:45).

Words, tone, attitude, intent, and the verbal impact on others all have monumental and real world consequences. Unfortunately, Washington D.C., Hollywood, the judiciary, the ivory tower, the media, and growing numbers of religious leaders increasingly turn to other norms for semantics, truth, tone, ethics, our common life, and often shamelessly and seductively redefine our semantic pillars and therefore redefine our shared reality.

As a civilization we are being deceived—daily. As noted, some of the seducers have themselves been deceived. Some seducers are simply and intentionally post-Christian or anti-Christian. Postmodernists who are post-Christian, and out of the orbit of the Logos, often don't hesitate to redefine words because they partially and inconsistently believe that all words are ultimately meaningless and mere tools of power and manipulation, so why not shapeshift words for the sake of one's tribe or cause? Logocentric light and communication are urgently needed to pierce this growing and shadowy haze. *The Logocentric and linguistic Judeo-Christian substrata grounding and guiding our more perfect union is vanishing and we are morphing toward the age of fragmentation and antichrist.*

In reference to the deceptive and satanic images discussed previously in this chapter, the Logocentric truth is that the fall of humanity was a cosmic and catastrophic tragedy reaping untold suffering and evil—and the serpent in Genesis is *not* the metaphporical hero of history. The serpent is the villain who tried to redefine God's words with "has God said" (Genesis 3:1–7) and who endlessly deceives. As C. S. Lewis illustrates in *The Screwtape Letters*, the villain of history is the master of word and thought deception. The power centers of civilization now advocate for and rush rather recklessly toward rudderless communication, semantic toxicity, and ecclesial and cultural decay.

Hence, Judeo-Christian leaders could provide historic direction for a Logocentric semantic renaissance capable of fostering a preferable tomorrow for all, beginning with semantic renewal in our religious communities. In the face of the death of words and meaning, the healing influence of the Logos is the key to the resurrection of liberating words and our grand experiment in forming more perfect civilizational unions that advance true freedom and true human flourishing. This work, admittedly a developing theological proposal, desires to make an incisive contribution to this large project.

If the argument is persuasive concerning how church and culture are being verbally seduced, the hope is that the reader would request that every teachable pastor, priest, rabbi, and religious leader frequently and enthusiastically lead on semantic apologetics and polemics as our civilization equivocates, stammers, and staggers into a fragmenting and precarious future.[50]

Chapter 1

Civilization After the Death of Words

Heaven and earth will pass away, but My words will not pass away.
— Matthew 24:35

The difference between the right word and the almost-right word is the difference between lightning and the lightning bug.
— Mark Twain

Words. The right ones used in the right way can be powerful. But in today's world I'm afraid a lot of people use a lot of words to produce merely a lot of noise.
— Josh McDowell

Beloved, while I was making every effort to write you about our common salvation, I felt the necessity to write to you appealing that you **contend earnestly for the faith which was once for all handed down to the saints.**[51]
— Jude, verse 3

> *Let no one deceive you with empty words, for because of these things the wrath of God comes upon the sons of disobedience.*
> —*Ephesians 5:6*

> *First of all, then, I urge that entreaties and prayers, petitions and thanksgivings, be made on behalf of all men, for kings and all who are in authority, so that we may lead a tranquil and quiet life in all godliness and dignity.*
> —1 Timothy 2:1–2

> Indeed the safest road to Hell is the gradual one – the gentle slope, soft underfoot, without sudden turnings, without milestones, without signposts.
> —C. S. Lewis, *The Screwtape Letters*

> *Righteousness exalts a nation, But sin is a disgrace to any people.*
> —Proverbs 14:34

Shifting Sands

Sadly, we live in the dawn or high noon of the age of shameless spin, fake news, uncivil advocacy, the eclipse of truth, and the seductive redefinition of core concepts undergirding civilization. This is the age of the demotion of noble, shining, and sustaining ethical principles to mere personal or cultural preferences. Our civilization equivocates, stammers, and staggers into uncharted and treacherous territory.

The intentional, systematic and detailed clarification and reclamation of the "meaning of meaning" and the "meaning of words" is long overdue.

Today we cannot agree, even in many houses of worship, on the definition of terms and phrases like marriage, social justice, compassion, inclusion, male, female, transgender or intersex.

Selina Soule, an also ran in the 2018 Connecticut 100-meter State Open high school final, unwittingly highlighted yet another cultural contradiction and early warning tremor emanating from the underlying verbal and civilizational fault line charting the future of Western civilization. Commenting on the state mandated transgender entries into track and field events, Selena protested, then backpedaled: "I think it's unfair to the girls who work really hard to do well and qualify for Opens and New Englands.... These girls, they're just coming in and beating everyone. I have no problem with them wanting to be a girl." In other words, it is perfectly acceptable to redefine the terms "male and female" (Genesis 5:2) based on personal preference, but it is not an acceptable personal preference to have to compete against such a personal preference.[52]

Ethical pronouncements after the decline of Judeo-Christian influence and the death of normative meaning and words are inevitably and inherently self-stultifying or self-refuting. How can a mere personal or cultural preference be an authoritative standard, and if such norms don't exist how can civilization mediate between conflicting personal and cultural or sub-cultural preferences? Mob rule? A political *Leviathan o*r King? Social media votes? "Majority Rule" as in the episode of the same name from the television show *The Orville*? We've come a long way from when the state had to bow in reverence and gratitude to divinely sanctioned, revealed, and self-evident truths—and even agreed to do so as part of the social contract. Are we progressive or actually regressive today?

Cam Smith summarizes this illustrative Connecticut gender norm conflict, which is not particularly a conflict between cultural so-called progressives and cultural conservatives, but more fundamentally it is *between* progressives attempting to reposition the Republic on the shifting sands of a post Judeo-Christian world: "For the second straight year, a small group of transgender athletes dominated their respective events at the girl's track and field state championships in Connecticut. Apparently, the second time through the ringer for some fellow competitors was too much, with parents of those athletes now stepping forward to try to ban those transgender athletes from competing as females."[53] Even Martina Navratilova, though gaining empathy for the plight of transgender athletes, remains skeptical of the fairness of such competition, which points to the irresolvable nature of many conflicts.[54]

Attempts to move beyond this dilemma within the framework of Connecticut law will likely involve discussions of possibly requiring terms or time periods for the hormone therapy for transgender athletes, or required surgery, prior to competing. How long? What surgery? Who decides? Clarity and consensus will be challenging now that the terms male and female are defined based on the relativisitc perceptions of the eye of the beholder.

This work will document that this verbal confusion and theft is not new, though it is proliferating. Even in the first century the apostle Paul was forced to engage in verbal or semantic analysis, when referring to "so-called" gods (2 Thessalonians 2:4) or "what is falsely called 'knowledge'" (1 Timothy 6:20), in contrast to "sound words" and doctrine (1 Timothy 6:3). Indeed, Chapter 4 documents how Paul divests many "so-called" terms of their false meanings (e.g., gospel), then redeems them and restores them to their true and intended and Logocentric meaning to protect the church and advance the mission of God in the world. As noted in the preface, Paul presupposes the relevance of the "angel of light" principle (2 Corinthians 11:14), that darkness steals and redefines the biblical terms of light in order to shamelessly seduce and corrupt the church and civilization.

Self-Devouring (and So-Called) Progressivism

This Connecticut case is just one of many illustrations of the self-devouring nature of the post Judeo-Christian "progressive" cultural trend—and the grave consequences of the post Judeo-Christian redefinition and usage of words and terms (semantics).[55] I will begin this analysis with the American context—after all, that is my context, I know it best, and such an influential culture deserves attention. Then I will move to more digital and global implications in subsequent chapters.

This work will document that virtually all significant terms are being impacted as with the Connecticut case, including terms like "social justice." However, in a culture more than forgetful of its precious spiritual heritage and that now seeks to find ultimate and spiritual fulfillment through gender and sexuality, such controversial gender-related issues seem to be constantly before us. Perhaps advocates of various gender causes are waging the losing battle of trying to elevate human sexuality and romantic love to what Paul Tillich referred to as an "ultimate concern."

Duke Divinity School at Duke University, known for its progressive posture on many theological and ethical issues, recently experienced tumult and protests as progressives complained that Duke was not sufficiently progressive on LBGTQ+ issues.[56] The Dean of the theologically progressive school was interrupted during an annual address. The Duke case is an illustration of self-devouring progressivism or liberalism. Once the biblical and Judeo-Christian norm is abandoned, no real or sustainable norm remains to evaluate such matters or to define key terms. The will to have power over others is often the only option for settling disputes.

This insecure foundation or norm, and the self-devouring nature of post Judeo-Christian progressive culture, is also illustrated by the conflict between European feminists and the LGBT advocates who reject binary definitions of gender. Gender is increasingly viewed as a spectrum by many, subjectively determined (see the Preface for an extreme example), and the older categories of gay, straight, and feminist, it is argued, need to be replaced with advocacy for all fluid and self-chosen experiences on the spectrum.

Gender and sexuality are matters of subjective choice or personal preference. Feminism, it is argued, reinforces binary conceptions of gender and is therefore oppressive to the + in LBGTQ+.[57] Needless to say, defining "male and female" (Genesis 5:2) in Judeo-Christian terms is a non-starter for those leading such conversations today. Even Harvard University, according to the *Chronicle of Higher Education* (January, 2019), is struggling with this self-devouring impulse, as Harvard's abolition of all-male clubs has also eradicated women's groups devoted to gender-exclusive spaces supportive of progressive feminist causes.[58] The rejection of normative truth and morality inevitably contributes to irresolvable conflicts and tribalism.

Chapter 2 will assess the "Masterpiece Cake Baker versus the Colorado Civil Rights Commission" case where the Supreme Court, in a 5-4 decision, sided with the cake baker primarily due to the lack of neutrality and possible prejudice of the Colorado Commission—yet with no reference to a normative definition of marriage. Once again we must note the 5-4 decision that supports the thesis of this book—that we have a Supreme Court operating largely without a true north star or shared semantic universe relative to resolving core civilizational principles and definitions. Legal precedent hardly can resolve all judicial cases. Any reference to the proper definition of marriage as a basis for deciding the case was likely precluded because of the 2015 precedent of Obergefell v. Hodges which legalized gay marriage and which legally redefined marriage.

While certainly deferring to the legal experts on the details and nuances of legal matters and decisions, especially at the level of the highest court in the land, it seems that the theological, historical, and philosophical naiveté and confusion of some Supreme Court members suggesting that there is no norm or precedent in the American context for a proper definition of marriage is striking—and perhaps even shameful if intellectual honesty matters. Common law, culture, history, civilizational assumptions, the *Reynolds v. United States* 1878 unanimous Supreme Court decision rejecting bigamy and polygamy, all expose the true origin of these current cultural winds.

Many Supreme Court members seem to be suffering from historical, theologically liberal, philosophical, and postmodern historical myopia and amnesia; hopefully this is unintentional. Some justices seem obsessed and enamored with contemporary perspectives and intellectual fads most inconsistent with the actual American experiment, and quite willing to abandon that experiment for a more contemporary European alternative that rests on a different, philosophical, cultural, and civilizational foundation.

Indeed, one dissenting justice on the Obergefell v. Hodges case, Justice Alito (joined by two other justices), overtly discussed this "postmodern" word spin, plus the semantic and historical gyrations and verbal equivocation required to redefine marriage. Justice Alito rebuked this semantic smuggling:

> The Constitution says nothing about a right to same-sex marriage, but the Court holds that the term "liberty" in the Due Process Clause of the Fourteenth Amendment encompasses this right. Our Nation was founded upon the principle that every person has the unalienable right to liberty, but *liberty is a term of many meanings*. For classical liberals, it may include economic rights now limited by government regulation. For social democrats, it may include the right to a variety of government benefits. **For today's majority, it has a distinctively *postmodern meaning.*** To prevent five unelected Justices from imposing their personal vision of liberty upon the American people, the Court has held that "liberty" under the Due Process Clause should be understood to protect only those rights that are "deeply rooted in this Nation's history and tradition." Washington v. Glucksberg, 521 U. S. 701, 720–721 (1997). And it is beyond dispute that the right to same-sex marriage is not among those rights.[59]

It should be observed that Justice Alito is properly engaging in semantic analysis prior to reaching his conclusion concerning the heterosexual norm that should have guided this decision:

> For today's majority, it does not matter that the right to same-sex marriage lacks deep roots or even that it is contrary to long-established tradition. The Justices in the majority claim the authority to confer constitutional protection upon that right simply because they believe [based on postmodern and post Judeo-Christian assumptions] that it is fundamental.

The term "marriage" was well rooted in the rich and stable soil of Judeo-Christian influenced civilization for centuries. The definition of marriage has changed not because of reason, law, or precedent—indeed the unanimous 1878 precedent of *Reynolds v. United States* assumed the legitimacy of a heterosexual monogamous benchmark. Same-sex marriage is only an option because the Judeo-Christian assumptions and pillars have been replaced with post Judeo-Christian, secular, pluralistic, and relativistic alternatives. In other words, terms like "marriage" and "gender" have been redefined by uprooting them and replanting them in the shifting sands of secularity (falsely viewed as non-religious and neutral), syncretistic post-Christian spirituality, as well as pluralism and relativism (affirming that all beliefs are mere personal preferences and/or are of equal value relative to sustaining civilization).

Perhaps what is deeply troubling about all of this is that the nearly split decision uncovers a terminal disease in the Supreme Court and among contemporary cultural leaders. One must ask, "a split decision on the definition of marriage in America, really?" The justices supportive of the redefinition of marriage in *Obergefell* are either knowingly subverting semantics, law, relevant history, theology, philosophy, culture, and legal precedent, or they are seemingly clueless and seduced regarding their own post Judeo-Christian and postmodern myopia and semantic theft. Either they are blindly enraptured by contemporary intellectual fads or they are intellectually dishonest and intentionally removing the pillars of Judeo-Christian influence from within and beneath our civilization. They are redefining the American experiment. These are the only two alternatives—naiveté or subversion. They are far too intelligent and informed to overlook the pervasive Judeo-Christian assumptions of the American experiment, especially as they pass by the fresco of the Ten Commandments in their own building.

Equally troubling is the reality that these postmodern majority justices in *Obergefell* have seemingly learned nothing from a core tenet of the very postmodernity that is guiding their semantic redefinitions—the core postmodern assumption that bias and prejudice in such or all decisions are difficult or impossible to transcend. The majority postmodern or ultramodern influenced justices supporting the redefinition of marriage presented their arguments as naïve modernists who seem to believe that legal objectivity on this contentious historic case is relatively simple and uncomplicated. The majority seemed utterly clueless concerning their own postmodern prejudice, bias, semantic or verbal equivocations, and their manipulation of words and position as a means of asserting power.

And in spite of warnings by the dissenting justices, the majority did not accept the obvious implications of this decision—that the legalization of same sex marriage is yet another watershed historical moment moving our civilization via a quantum leap toward the eventual marginalization and criminalization of Judeo-Christian belief and practice. Whatever one thinks about the egalitarianism versus complementarianism debate on the role of women in the church, the legal pursuit of the criminalization of complementarianism in Holland is one of countless examples that provide a foretaste of the American future.[60] It is simply a matter of time, apart from God's grace, the work of the Spirit, and a more effective apologetic and polemic response by religious communities, until it is not merely complementarianism but core biblical views on marriage, gender, and human sexuality that will be oppressed. That is the future of our children and children's children unless this generation steps up to the semantic, apologetic, and polemic plate.

Isn't it ironic that Judeo-Christian influenced terms like *liberty*, *freedom*, and *toleration*—terms that framed the American experiment—are now being redefined to eradicate Judeo-Christian influence on civilization and end the original Judeo-Christian influenced American experiment? Such parasitism is terminal. The emerging "America" may bear little resemblance to the "America" of the original American experiment.

The fact that so many of these civilization-defining Supreme Court decisions have been narrow 5-4 decisions helps to substantiate the thesis of this book. Semantic equivocation and manipulation are being used to subvert Judeo-Christian influenced civilization. Such close votes on core issues also point to the emerging and relativistic cultural chaos. Whatever opinion one holds on the recent Kavanaugh appointment and hearing, the heated and shameless verbal warfare vividly illustrated a nation divided at the most fundamental level.

Relativism can sustain temporary but not long-term alliances, as is becoming more and more clear from the self-devouring nature of the contemporary social experiment in radical and so-called progressivism. Word definitions are largely dependent on the definitions of other terms and organic families of terms (semantic universes), and these families of terms are laden with theological and philosophical assumptions concerning truth (or the lack thereof), reality, values, and ethics. In the American context, "marriage" and "gender" will largely be defined based on the family of terms (semantic universe) from which they emerge or in which they are placed or contextualized. Terms nourish and sustain and help to define each other. For example, for progressives the terms inclusion and marriage are symbiotic. Inclusion implies acceptance of same-sex marriage.

Relative to Judeo-Christian influenced civilization, Christ and the apostles "turned the world upside down" (Acts 17:6), in part, via a new semantic universe. This cosmic inversion, or more properly this setting the world and words upright, eventually touched virtually every term, including the naming of cities and children, and the very concept and term and vision for civilization itself. The pursuit of a more perfect civilization became inseparable from Judeo-Christian assumptions about the future, truth, reality, and morality—at least until the eighteenth century in Europe and roughly until the twentieth century in America.

Hence, within these broader considerations I am arguing that redefining marriage or gender as indeterminate personal preference or cultural preference in the American context lacks scholarly integrity and amounts to word theft or semantic fraud. The current Supreme Court is swimming in at least two if not multiple semantic universes. The resulting nearly split decisions and confusion are inevitable and point to irresolvable conflicts after the death of the original intent of the constellation of words that framed the nation's birth. We have lost true north for our journey to the more perfect union.

Spin, Polemics, and Apologetics

Redefining terms and narratives to gain advantage, sometimes called "spin" or "fake news," is not new, though perhaps it is now becoming an epidemic or even a pandemic in Western civilization. The ancient Greek Sophists were widely known and criticized (e.g., by Aristotle) for their ability to manipulate phrases and rhetoric and seemingly prove or disprove any argument. Aristotle believed that logic could counter such unprincipled rhetoric and restore logical dialog. Modernism shared much of Aristotle's hope and assumption about the quest for truth until modernism began to fragment in the twentieth century and devoured its own logic, rationality, and scientific objectivity.

In biblical times, as noted previously and documented in Chapter 4 of this book, the apostle Paul had to counter the false definitions of Jesus, gospel, apostle, circumcision, and wisdom that were corrupting the church. The crafty "hath God said" of Genesis (chapter 3, KJV), is viewed by Paul in 2 Corinthians 11 as underlying the seductive redefinitions of the "gospel" and "apostle" that were threatening the Corinthian church. The implication is that the fall of humanity was directly related to and caused by the verbal or semantic theft utilized by the serpent in the garden. The serpent brings the false word and words. The Messianic seed of the woman brings the true Word and words.

As noted in the Introduction, this Pauline defense of orthodox (right beliefs and practices) terms inside of the church is known as *polemics*. The defense of or advocacy for right beliefs and practices within the broader culture is known as *apologetics* (1 Peter 3:15).

In the eighteenth and nineteenth centuries in the West, those abandoning historical or biblical Christian beliefs and accommodating to modern thought virtually redefined every key Christian term and doctrine used in the church—God, Trinity, Jesus, salvation, sin, resurrection, and even the return of Christ. This redefinition took place *inside* of the church and synagogue. Orthodox faith disintegrated and continues to disintegrate, and is often led by the so-called leaders, pastors, superintendents, and bishops of the faith. The laity are often reluctant to depart from "the faith which was once for all handed down to the saints" (Jude, verse 3). The biblical material is permeated with various types of polemics, including semantic polemics (see John and 1 John concerning the redefining of Christ; Galatians concerning the redefining the gospel; and especially see Chapter 3 of this work).

In addition, the seductive assault on core beliefs and terms from outside of faith communities especially since the 18th century was pervasive and intense. Some thought that they could save Christianity in a sometimes hostile modern world by redefining it — this is a lesson to be learned for those of us living in a postmodern age. The Trinity was viewed as an absurdity by modernists, and the resurrection of Christ, if not Christ's actual historicity, was viewed by the modern mind as being in conflict with historical evidence.

An ordained professor and dear relative who fell prey to this modernist assault from outside the church, and this semantic shift within the church, was crystal clear that he had changed his views just after World War II and rejected belief in the Judeo-Christian God (monotheism) and embraced the belief that all is God (pantheism). Yet he continued to serve in the church and as a "Christian" professor at a denominational school for his entire life, but at his passing his instructions were to decline a Christian funeral in the church. Words and ideas have consequences. This relative attended Wheaton College in Illinois, and apparently taught a class there which included Billy Graham — and he said that he flunked Billy Graham! He then went to Boston for his PhD, redefined his faith and married a Unitarian.

During those contentious nineteenth and twentieth century conflicts between orthodox Judeo-Christian beliefs and modernity, some utilized polemics and apologetics to challenge this modernistic version of Christianity in and outside of the church. Others retreated from culture and focused on charting the end of the world. Still others turned to experiential, emotional, or personal truth rather than appropriately responding to these verbal redefinitions — such as the challenge by some liberal theologians who viewed Jesus' resurrection as nothing more than the rising of Jesus in the hearts and faith of his followers. Jesus did not actually rise from dead, and certainly did not rise physically, it was argued.

However, no problem, the liberals asserted, as we still believe in and preach the resurrection of Christ. Perhaps it was a spiritual resurrection, or perhaps Christ lives on in the faith of his disciples.

The simplistic and ineffective answer by many conservatives to those providing historical evidence that Jesus never lived or rose from the grave was, "You ask me how I know He lives? He lives within my heart." For a variety of reasons, many older and major Christian denominations, and many Jewish scholars, simply accommodated to this modernistic historic semantic and philosophical shift that undermined orthodox beliefs. Many communities of faith retreated into separatism and/or experientialism. Many, but not all, within Roman Catholic and Orthodox traditions have often held their ground on historically orthodox theology.

Lawyers and politicians have been regularly identified from time immemorial with the manipulation of words, including a well-known President and lawyer who quibbled over the "what the definition of *is* is." Abraham Lincoln's "Emancipation Proclamation," including his use of the term emancipation, and his attempts to liberate the slaves and preserve the union was described as "despotism" by some in his day: "President Lincoln's Government seems to have exercised its ingenuity to dispel any such delusion. Its acts demonstrate clearly that the purpose is to subjugate us, confiscate our property, and emancipate our slaves. To attain this end, the plainest provisions of the Constitution have been disregarded. It has been superseded by the most *odious despotism*."[61] What terms best describe Lincoln? In the nineteenth century some viewed Lincoln as the great emancipator and others viewed him as the odious despot? Someone was engaging in semantic deception.

Or, of perhaps more recent historic significance relative to verbal deception, "On Oct. 6, 1939, Adolf Hitler returned from touring the trampled city of Warsaw to address the Reichstag. He was ready to do something surprising: ask the world for *peace*."[62] Of course his "peace" was the reassertion of German hegemony and power in the world, especially Europe, after German decline subsequent to World War 1 and the Versailles Treaty.

The key to such "word theft" is equivocation.

Britain and France wanted a just peace that would see the end of German expansion and a restoration of European stability and a balance of power. Hitler wanted a *pax Germanica* where Hitler would rule much or all in Europe and beyond—Hitler was intentionally equivocating on the meaning of the term peace desired by the Allies. The Allies were being played by semantic equivocation. Hitler's point was that if he got his way, there would be peace. The Marx brothers famously used satire to uncover Hitler's true desire for peace—a piece of Czechoslovakia, a piece of Poland, France, and numerous other countries.

Hence, word *theft* and verbal *spin* are not new. Yet it in a postmodern or ultramodern context, academic and cultural leaders often affirm that truth is relative, or a matter of personal or cultural perspective, or that perhaps truth in any normative sense is dead, and that words are simply tools or means of gaining power. Words are not true or accurate, they are just "means" to assert self-interest or tribal interests. This dark and shifting semantic shadow hovers over the nation, entertainment, media, education, law, and even recent Supreme Court and congressional deliberations.

Public education often functions as an aggressive—and supposedly neutral—secular religion in terms of training students in this type of perspective and relativistic advocacy. It is argued that words have no defined meaning and are subject to change as needed. Culture and civilization, it is suggested, have no norm by which to determine the accuracy or appropriateness of word definitions like truth, gender, marriage, God, social justice, inclusion, America, patriotism, or morality. Surely the present situation qualifies as a verbal or semantic crisis.

Humans—or should we say persons—are fallen and have always used verbal maneuvers to inappropriately gain advantage. Hence, Scripture proclaims "Thou shalt not bear false witness." (Exodus 20:16, KJV) The Judeo-Christian plumb line has largely vanished in Europe and is under assault in America. And, directly related to the shift away from Judeo-Christian assumptions, contemporary culture is now framing ethics, value, meaning, and truth in terms of relativistic personal or cultural preferences. It is also within this surreal context that many cultural leaders, including

Supreme Court members, are attempting to resolve vexing legal and moral dilemmas and connect law to culture.

In this age of spin and fake news, where the left accuses the right and the right accuses the left of the same verbal fraud, those committed to Judeo-Christian influence will want to be intentional and systematic about preserving and advocating for sound word definitions and usages. When possible, an irenic tone is much preferred to avoid additional defensiveness and polarization, yet progress and consensus are unlikely if we continue to drift further out of orbit from the Logos. Faith communities that bury their heads in the sand eventually will be buried by that very same sand.

Semantic polemics and apologetics have arguably never been more essential to the mission of those seeking to advance Judeo-Christian influence and impact. By way of analogy, there have always been those who break the speed limits, ignore stop signs, drive outside of the lines, or engage in reckless behavior that harms others. Also, there have always been opportunistic verbal spin, semantic theft, semantic ambiguity, legal verbal maneuvering, and hollow political promises. The problem today is the verbal equivalent of the abolition of the motor vehicles guide and rules—the rules are no more, the center of culture has vanished, and many are celebrating. We are being told we can't evaluate statements or terms by reason or Scripture anymore, as both are being marginalized or discarded entirely. Or we are told that reason and Scripture are oppressive. We must lovingly, forcibly, and aggressively challenge this trend.

Militant advocacy for many social causes now uses words not to *conform* to truth or reality, or discover truth, but simply to *create* a new reality that gives more power to individuals or groups. This is viewed as moral, *whatever "moral" means,* because the claim is to empower those who have been dominated by Judeo-Christian influenced culture.

Words are now viewed as "a means to power," not vehicles of truth. In other words, terms such as truth, justice, and equality, for some, are not being utilized with the assumption that such universal principles even exist.

Truth, justice, and equality are truth, justice, and equality *for me* or *for us*. This work will argue what many have observed, that justice is now increasingly no more than "just us." Yes, justice has been just us previously, but we used to have a shared vantage point from which to reject such glorified personal or tribal narcissism— that vantage point or plumb line was Logocentric reason, Scripture, and the Logos influenced semantic universe.

Hence, language, beliefs, and convictions are used to gain power and move others to action. This degrading of communication via opportunistic verbal equivocation should be concerning to those who identify with both the political left and the political right. For those who believe that shared norms still exist for truth and ethics, statements of advocacy need to be judged and unpacked based on evidence and Judeo-Christian framed assumptions about reality.

When potential presidential candidate and Senator Elizabeth Warren, in 2018, called for her followers to "save this democracy," such phrases need to be unpacked. Yes, this is a critique of the current political majority in at least two branches of government, but what exactly is the vision to save the democracy or save "democracy itself"?[63]

Which democracy is being saved? Are we saving a democracy largely consistent with the original American experiment, or one more consistent with European democratic socialism—at least based on the European nations that have not returned to a large measure of free enterprise in order to survive? Saving America is often a conservative theme, as witnessed by the Reagan and Trump shared campaign slogan of "[Let's] Make America Great Again." Warren's appeal has these unclear tones of conservativism that might assist with a national run for President and a broader appeal. However, is she really suggesting a conservative agenda that preserves the original American experiment, or simply equivocating for opportunistic political gain? Does she want to save or redefine democracy? Is her preferred future republican democracy or direct democracy? She might find better ways to articulate what is likely her main point, that the current President's perceived abuse of power is a threat to democracy. Yet has she considered that her proposals also pose another kind of threat?

When candidate and President Donald Trump employs the Reagan campaign phrase of "Make America Great Again," this much criticized phrase and vision also needs to be unpacked. We must ask,

- *If the phrase appeals to those who believe that America is drifting from its original vision or Judeo-Christian foundation, which period of American history does Trump want to revive?*

- *Is his vision identical with Reagan, or how does it differ from how Reagan and other presidential candidates (the Clintons, George H. and George W. Bush) utilized the phrase? Is the phrase, as Bill Clinton (who ironically used the phrase) put it, a "dog whistle" for racism, or a sincere appeal to renew and revive the original American experiment? Why is it so scandalous today to refer to making America great again (MAGA) when this phrase was utilized without such extreme opprobrium in prior presidential campaigns (Bill Clinton, Hillary Clinton)?*

- *Is his implementation of this vision and leadership style for accomplishing this vision similar to or markedly different from Reagan?*

- *Where does his domestic and foreign policy differ with Reagan, for better or worse?*

- *How is his communication style contributing to or detracting from his vision, civil discourse, the possibility of shared norms for truth and justice, shared norms for ethics, and the long-term flourishing of civilization?*

- *Is Trump referring to a specific time period in American history, or simply the key concepts and assumptions of the original American experiment, or both?*

- *Are there elements of America's past practices that he is willing to denounce, or at least argue are inconsistent with the core and original American vision?*

Politicians like Warren and Trump will always seek to move the masses and the political barometer, but semantic analysis, a thoughtful political process, a media return to journalistic integrity, true religious leaders, and an informed citizenry will push these candidates beyond spin and equivocation. Semantic pressure is needed to move our leaders toward verbal precision and at least some shared norm for truth, justice, and the more perfect way of the American experiment!

Some who see themselves as deeply spiritual may see this conversation as being too political and miss the point of this discussion entirely. How we use words and conduct our political activities touches on the very nature of authentic spirituality, truth, justice, ethics, and basic decency. Culture greatly influences the church and synagogue, so to ignore culture is to ignore the health and vitality of the church and synagogue. It bears directly on the nature and future of civilization, Judeo-Christian influence on culture and civilization, and the fate and well-being of our children and children's children. It directly impacts whether our children's children will be criminalized for practicing a faith that was applauded just two centuries prior. It directly impacts on whether our posterity will find faithful biblical teaching in our houses of worship.

Scripture, including the command to love one's neighbor, requires due diligence regarding semantic polemics and apologetics. If we care we will dare to challenge word and communication abuse. For those in the Christian tradition, with a firm commitment to the Word or Logos who created all things including words, and who breathed the very words of Scripture,[64] and who claimed to be the "way, and the truth, and the life,"[65] attention to word usage is critically essential. Such passionate attention to words is our Word-centric DNA.

For our culture this is ultimately a question of truth—and not just modernistic or Enlightenment conceptions of truth. Does any shared norm for truth exist—and there are more options than just modernistic or rationalistic "truth—that can judge this pandemic of opportunistic verbal spin and warfare?

Indeed, educators, pastors, rabbis, priests, and parents need to be as intentional about training the next generation in proper semantics as the surrounding culture and public educational centers are at advocating for post Judeo-Christian definitions and usages of terms. Universities are now obsessed with training future leaders concerning their view that correct speech is post Judeo-Christian speech. Pastors, priests, and rabbis should lead the way in guiding their flocks through the many future-defining words and phrases of our day, such as marriage, gender, social justice, inclusivism, compassion, democracy, freedom, multiculturalism, and America. Even Islamic religious leaders should resonate with this collaborative semantic mission which can employ and involve many faiths.

Public education, birthed by Judeo-Christian influence and assumptions, often functions as a loosely organized but activist religion that often seeks to uproot Judeo-Christian influence from culture, education, communication, and words.[66] In some educational quarters, free speech by advocates of Judeo-Christian values is met with suppression or hostility.[67] American tax dollars are funding a public education that sometimes targets the very destruction of the Judeo-Christian influenced original American experiment. Public education often leads the way on defining, redefining, or creating new terms and words that assist with reshaping the cultural landscape. This mega-trend is cyclone strength, and only the foolish would think that faith communities will not be greatly impacted.

Lee Bolinger, President of Columbia University, makes a valiant attempt at suggesting that free speech is possibly healthier in higher education than in many or any other sectors of society. There is no crisis on campus and free speech is doing just fine, he argues. His flawed evidence? Universities are more "hospitable venues for open debate than the nation as a whole." Why? Because most college students favor an "open learning environment" and because most universities invite speakers of differing perspectives. Of course that argument misses the point entirely—the problem in such universities is that the vast majority of faculty and administrators, verified by and repeated via countless surveys, are ideologically progressive and largely uniform in rejecting conservative religious and political perspectives. Additionally, while granting that some institutions of higher education do invite diverse views, including token conservatives, that pales in comparison to

the speakers invited who reinforce the values of the majority professors and administrators. A few conservative speakers get a few
hours with a few students per year, whereas the classrooms, on-line
environments, and cumulative academic culture inevitably will
have a more significant impact on future leaders. This is a complex
debate, and many try to deemphasize the impact on students while
admitting that political liberals rule the universities.[68] However, if
there is anything we have learned from postmodernity, with all its
flaws, it is that the idea that professors and out-of-class educators
will teach without allowing their biases and prejudices to influence
students is more than naïve.

Graduates of such educational institutions continue to shape
the future of church and state. Is it any surprise that the Judeo-
Christian voice is often muted or marginalized in major sectors of
society, such as media, education, law, and entertainment? Given
the pivotal role of education in training the citizenry, influencing
future leaders in civilizational centers of power, and therefore the
shaping of the future, semantic apologetics and polemics are especially needful today. And semantic polemics and apologetics are
absolutely inseparable.

Polemics, Apologetics, and *Viva La* Church and Civilization

C. S. Lewis warned, "Civilization is a rarity,[69] attained with difficulty and easily lost."[70] The current and often seductively covert
global semantic[71] conflict that will write the words and pages of
future history has thus far wreaked havoc on communities of faith,
and on Judeo-Christian attempts to influence and meliorate twenty-first-century civilization. These global word wars[72] continue
to lay siege to the orthodox church, the academy (including the
Christian academy), culture, and civilization. In many quarters the
loss or virtual loss of the cultural war in America and the West
is freely acknowledged, especially in view of the previously referenced semantic redefinition of "marriage" in America (2015).
This redefinition was viewed by many as a historic and cultural
watershed.[73]

What is taking place in the West and America relative to the redefinition of terms and the reshaping of culture and civilization is far more than legalizing practices once unacceptable to Judeo-Christian influenced civilization. It is not a mere slippery slope argument to consider the prospect that the long game for this seismic shift includes the incremental criminalization of Judeo-Christian words, values, beliefs, and practices. Current trajectories suggest that it is not alarmist to ask if biblical convictions and practices will be oppressed or even criminalized in this century in America. Many argue that such is already well underway in Europe and many areas of American life.

At the publicly funded University of Minnesota, in the summer of 2018, it was reported that a new gender identity policy was under consideration known as the "Pronoun Rule." "All students, faculty, and staff would have the right to be addressed by whatever pronoun is preferred—he, she, 'ze'" or an alternative. "And everyone from professors to classmates would be expected to call them by the right words or risk potential disciplinary action, up to firing or expulsion."[74] This policy may or may not have been adopted or modified, but it demonstrates, along with recent cases regarding gender and marriage, that in America we have moved way beyond slippery slope speculation. We are on many levels emulating post-Christian Canadian and European culture. The cultural trajectories in Europe would seem to confirm this view of the post Judeo-Christian or anti-Christian game plan in America.

If one assumes that Judeo-Christian apologetics not only strengthens the faithful but also assists with evangelism,[75] discipleship, and positively impacts future civilization and core cultural assumptions, then, regardless of the current state of America or any civilization, much is at stake across the digitally connected globe relative to countering these semantic distortions and providing more accurate semantic alternatives. Indeed, the very term for and concept of "civilization" itself has morphed in some quarters from being an aspirational term, or something desired, to being an *exasperational* term, representing oppression or a failed and antiquated quest.

This vision or aspiration for "civilization," and the very term itself, was birthed in recent centuries by Logos influenced culture and history. Logocentric culture produced Logos-influenced civilization, which birthed and defined the very concept of civilization within a Logocentric family or universe of terms. Yes, some nations established versions of Christendom that included State-Church unions. Some of these nations modified the nature of the union and freedom over time. Yet, and this is a classic example of semantic equivocation, not all "Christendoms" are created equal.

In the American religiously voluntarist context it was less of a formalized union and more of an originating and undergirding influence on assumptions and culture. Christendom in America was very different than other instantiations of Christendom. Hence, the simplistic suggestion and hasty generalization that Christendom has collapsed everywhere is opportunistic, misleading, a self-fulfilling prophecy, and a threat to continued healthy Judeo-Christian influence on culture. Celebrating the death of Christendom, as if Christendom is monolithic, reflects sloppy scholarship and adversely impacts strategic planning for the mission of faith communities and organizations.

In any event, today our post-Logos culture is increasingly at war with Logos influenced or Logocentric civilization. Nevertheless, while the semantic war is a harsh reality—and many are at war with evangelical orthodoxy and its influence and the Judeo-Christian lexicon of terms, or even the memory of Judeo-Christian influence—the biblical response and apologetic tone must reflect gentleness and reverence and speak the truth in love.[76]

Shapeshifting word definitions are ceaselessly being used to short-circuit Christian commitment to and influence on civilization. And to modify Plato slightly, the civilization that forgets to tell its story (accurately and precisely with words) will most certainly perish.

Can the trajectory of these global word wars be altered, so that semantic intentions and cultural impact are exposed? The primary goal of this book is to make the case for the determined, forceful, intentional, systemic, and systematic enhancement of making critical semantic distinctions such that Judeo-Christian influence on ecclesial and public discourse, culture, and civilization is enhanced. This desired outcome presupposes cultural and philosophical hermeneutics but is much broader in scope.

Specifically, semantic polemics and apologetics should be aggressively harnessed for the civilizational task.[77] Evangelicals,[78] Roman Catholics, Orthodox Christians, and biblically focused Judeo-Christian believers of all stripes need empowerment relative to making creative and critical semantic distinctions. Likewise, those not actively engaged in a religious community but committed to core Judeo-Christian values as social glue for our common life and vision together also need semantic assistance. Training is desperately needed in how to use the powerful tool of verbal communication such that Judeo-Christian influence on future public discourse, culture, and civilization is maximized.

During the heyday of the intense assault by modernism on Christian orthodoxy just referenced,[79] the orthodox apologetic and polemic response seemed to move primarily in three directions:

1. a retreat into anti-intellectualism, separatism, eschatological escapism, and/or emotionalism and experientialism;
2. vigorous challenges to the modernist *conclusions* and argumentation; and,
3. well-articulated polemics (e.g., J. Gresham Machen, *Christianity and Liberalism*) that made the case that the cultural accommodations of modernist or liberal *Christian* theology had so altered Christian thought that the liberal theological product was essentially a different and new religion.

Concerning the third option, Machen's suggestion was that a new and different religion was now *inside* of the walls of the church and Judeo-Christian faith communities. John Wesley made a similar argument in the eighteenth century concerning liberal or latitudinarian "Christianity" within the Church of England. He argued that Islam had more in common with Christianity than post-biblical liberal Christianity.

What is difficult to locate in this multi-century response to modernism is concise, didactic, detailed, point by point (or term by term) responses and refutations to the modernist semantic distortions and word theft. Such a response was needed to better equip pastors, priests, and laity to challenge the seductive modernist challenge in and outside of the church (see Tables 3.1, 4.1, and 4.2).[80] This project offers just such semantic tools for the contemporary post-modern or ultramodern syncretistic context, and the increasingly manifold semantic, philosophical, and hermeneutical challenges in the age of modernity and postmodernity.

This book and the semantic distinctions within it, including appendix A, are admittedly a heuristic. The tables presented in this work, including the appendices, especially are offered as explor-atory tools to assist historically orthodox pastors, rabbis, educators, leaders, and laity in launching or assisting with this apologetic and polemic task.

The hundreds of thousands of pastors, rabbis, religion majors, seminary students, religious leaders, college graduates, and self- or college-educated parents committed to promoting these shared values should be able to comprehend and use most of the material in this work in training current generations and the next generation.

The difficulty level of this work is not as great as reading assignments that undergraduate religion and philosophy majors have comprehended for over two decades in my classrooms. Given the gale force of the cultural winds, and the escalating and unfore-seen conflicts, such training should take on the form of systematic instruction or catechesis.

This needed, critical, urgent, and systematic instruction needs to at least include and address the following questions:

1. What is the nature and function of families of terms or semantic universes?
2. How do these families of terms influence and define each other and function as an organic reality?
3. How do these semantic universes shape and influence indi-viduals, culture, civilization, and the future?

However, at the core of such instruction and an understanding of these questions is instruction on the actual terms themselves. For example, such instruction will compare and contrast the Judeo-Christian and the contemporary post Judeo-Christian defi-nitions and usages of terms, some of which have been referenced previously, like male and female, marriage, social justice, inclusion, multiculturalism, freedom of choice, Christian nation, patriotism, God, Jesus, America, white privilege, micro-aggression, compassion, tolerance, civilization, establishment of religion, colonialism, gender identity, sexual orientation, sexism, racism, family, homophobia, and extremist. And this list is far from a complete or exhaustive list!

The repetition of these terms in this book is most intentional in order to chart the nature of effective instruction—plus repetition is the key to learning. Based on classroom experiences with countless students, it is indispensable that those being instructed (catechumens) grasp the big picture of the semantic universe, and gain the ability to compare and contrast such specific terms biblically, especially the ethically and theologically based terms.

In this age of postmodern or ultramodern syncretistic word spinning and fake news, careful attention to the fruit (the words and their definitions) and the root (the semantic universes and undergirding philosophical and theological assumptions) is imperative for those wanting to preserve or advance Judeo-Christian influence and mission in church, culture, synagogue, and state. This worthy and urgent task is the goal of semantic polemics and apologetics.

Judeo-Christian religious groups, families, and individuals are now living amidst an often-hostile environment, where the major power centers—law, entertainment, education, media, and overall culture—function as a syncretistic and pluralistic uncivil civil religion. The powerful unity of this uncivil religion of relativism and pluralism seems to revolve around removing every possible remaining Judeo-Christian influence on civilization and language, including "Christmas." Within this context, careful instruction in how words—virtually all words—are being used to remake reality is timely.

The current situation is like the mission field, where missionaries and their families must master the language, culture, beliefs, practices, and civilizational assumptions in order to be effective. Just because the words sound or look familiar in the American context (e.g., freedom, justice, liberty, marriage) does not mean that we are all speaking the same language. Tree bark and a dog's bark are not one and the same.

Pausing to Overview Subsequent Chapters

Chapter 2 essentially throws down the gauntlet concerning what is at stake in this discussion. Can any civilization flourish in any meaningful sense—or hold together, or even survive, much less avoid hostility, Balkanization, or even armed conflict—if not built on a bedrock of shared word definitions and usages that can endure and unite? Is there a **plumb line** or civilizational glue that can hold us together and preserve essential unity with diversity?

Chapter 3 explores the contemporary relevance of semantic apologetics and polemics and the value of cultural and intellectual engagement when many are now proclaiming that evangelicals and orthodox Christians have lost the cultural war in Europe and America. Table 3.1 illustrates how the **early church** engaged in semantic apologetics amidst extreme cultural marginalization and persecution and draws lessons for today.

Chapter 4 gleans insights from Scripture and from the **nineteenth century classical liberal assault** on historic biblical orthodoxy concerning how semantic distortions have often undermined Judeo-Christian values and the orthodox and biblical Christian mission. Table 4.2 documents this semantic theft and provides biblical, apologetic, and polemic responses.

Chapters 5 and 6 contend that the death of truth also leads to the death of meaning and communication, resulting in shameless spin, militant advocacy, and "polybabble" (as defined in Chapter 5). It is argued that Logocentric culture and semantics—words grounded in or at least influenced by the Word—are being replaced with **hyper-polytheistic culture and polybabble**. The emerging conflict and cacophony that threaten civilization is accelerated by ephemeral word definitions and usage.

Chapter 7 illustrates the current semantic quagmire via **analyzing representative key issues and terms** regarding Christian influence on civilization—**especially justice and compassion.**

This chapter evidences and explains how both church and state are being seduced by word games and shameless spin.

Chapter 8 demonstrates how a more civilized approach to the quest for an aspirational civilization, namely dialogical semantics, is being replaced with **semantic terrorism** due to the vanishing of kingdom-centric and Logocentric culture, values, and communication.

Chapter 9 reinforces and contends that semantic analysis must recognize and clearly articulate that individual terms are part of larger semantic tapestries or clusters—**semantic universes** are organic and symbiotic families of words. Chapter 9 also reviews, presents, and reflects upon many contested terms and clusters and illustrates how such semantic tapestries utilized today in public discourse reduce to a shameless or seductive attempt to gain personal or tribalistic power. This work argues that the meaning and usage of virtually all words are impacted by shifting between semantic universes, so the numerous terms discussed in the work and the appendices are truly and only illustrative and not comprehensive or encyclopedic. As noted already in this chapter, the emerging comparative lexical work is preliminary and a heuristic.

Chapter 10 recommends **the way forward** and, as noted, appendix A provides a **preliminary Lexicon** for this discussion. Appendix B addresses illustrative and **possible objections** to this apologetic and polemic primer.

It should be noted that some repetition between chapters is intentional in view of how today's readers selectively read only portions of books. The repetition should assist with understanding and learning the content, and also allow the reader to meaningfully review chapters without re-reading the entire text. However, important nuances will be missed apart from a thorough reading of every chapter.

Addressing This Essential Theological Task

The magnitude of the civilizational challenge is great. Some will retreat into the escapism of giving up on the world that God so loved before God does and chart the end prematurely. This approach has been wrong on predicting the future for centuries and has likely contributed via self-fulfilling prophecies to present challenges.

For example, in the Christian tradition, every generation since the first generation of Christians has believed that it was the last generation. Historical evidence is irrefutable—we have been terribly wrong when predicting the end or the antichrist, fatalism is fatal to the church and cultural impact, some Christians have courageously turned the tide on cultural decay, and our vision of the future greatly determines our actual future. Billy Graham used to say something like "we must prepare as if we will be here for the next 1,000 years, but also live as if Christ could return tomorrow." Dietrich Bonhoeffer made a similar and even more profound statement.[81]

Others may avoid predicting the end of the world prematurely, yet take a less direct, though intentional, and neo-engaged approach similar to the cultural engagement model introduced in Chapter 3—such as the Benedict option. Much of the direct engagement on such volatile issues, it is argued, no matter how well-intended, often reignites the flames of the lost cultural war, adds to the cultural losses, and gives Christianity a bad name. This "Benedict Opt" thesis and related ideas will be clarified and discussed further in Chapter 3. A few preliminary comments are, however, in order concerning the Benedict option.

Those influenced by the Benedict option or Hauerwasian approaches to culture often argue that the best cultural strategy is just to "be" the church and disengage from or at least de-prioritize the directly engaged culture wars. There is a half-truth embedded in such models. Those who put their faith in political victories or the outcome of elections and culture wars will forever be disappointed, disillusioned, and tactless cultural engagement often backfires. The passion of such purist or neo-purist groups is to be commended, and the concern about the how of cultural engagement is legitimate and worthy of dialog. This model of cultural engagement is a new or neo-engagement model that prioritizes being the church and tries to avoid cultural war and conflict. The argument for this model is a half-truth.

This work argues, however, that such explicit or implicit retreatism ultimately compromises neighbor love and produces civilizational parasites who benefit from the great sacrifices of those striving in the trenches (amidst constant criticism from all sides) to make a better future, including a better future for the children and grandchildren of the parasites.

Even assuming that the substance of the *Benedict Option* is sound, and the author (Rod Dreher) goes to great pains not to encourage surrender or cultural retreat, the umbrella concept (Benedict Option) and cultural engagement model comes across as monastic or neo-monastic. The last thing Judeo-Christian faith communities need to adopt today, while the authentic American experiment literally hangs in the balance, is a monastic moniker, vision, and mission—even if Dreher is contending for a new kind of engaged monasticism. The "Benedict Option" is disastrous messaging at this point in history. As previously noted, the American context is unique and different from the European or other post-Christendom contexts—as my European friends endlessly remind me. The European experiment in Christendom is effectively over and has been dead for quite some time in most every country and community—save places like Vatican City. The true American experiment still shows occasional and hopeful signs of life.

Some of my colleagues understandably criticize culturally or politically engaged evangelicals, especially those who are rather brazen, while also parasitizing the economic and political freedoms secured or preserved by some of these Christians. Such freedom and benefits are in part due to the sacrifices of others engaged in difficult and daily legal and cultural trenches where they are literally under assault, no matter how gentle and compassionate they present themselves or their cultural, legal, and educational cases.

Scripture is clear that those who do everything right can be persecuted. Only a sappy and unbiblical moralism would suggest otherwise. Judeo-Christian cultural engagement has misfired at times, however, and contributed to the problem by speaking half-truths divorced from a spirit of gentleness, compassion, reverence, wisdom, and love. Loving engagement with the world is the way forward. Let's be more directly loving, not less directly engaged.

Let's be a loving and compassionate city set on a hill with an exemplary and alternative community, but let's not be surprised if opponents storm the hill and tear down the fortifications. Dreher's Benedict Option argument serves as a well-intended and needed corrective. Nevertheless, I fear that if the Benedict option moniker or Hauerwasian model defines the future of American faith communities, then it will also destroy vital and biblical faith, practice, cultural impact, and it may contribute to the loss of freedom of religion and freedom of speech. The same can be said of tactless civilizational engagement by conservative faith communities.

Some of my colleagues have retreated in another fashion by resignedly accepting the reality that words are slippery and that there is not much that can be done to slow the semantic avalanche. There is nothing particularly newsworthy about the fact that words are slippery—this has been evident to philosophers since the fifth century B.C. or earlier.

The point here, and the challenge, is to conform words and language, as much as is possible, to the divine perspective—inasmuch as we can grasp and communicate such truth. Just as with the more perfect union we are not chasing absolute semantic perfection. And believing in the norm of absolute truth does not mean we claim always to possess absolute truth; instead, we view such normative truth as graciously revealed and humbly pursued. In a world of postmodern and ultramodern syncretistic word spin attention to the accuracy and truthfulness of words and word usage is essential for those seeking to advance kingdom values. Even if the culture can no longer be impacted in America, which is the context of this work, the task remains of keeping religious communities faithful. Additionally, God is at work outside of the American context; some of the greatest expansions of Judeo-Christian movements are in other parts of the globe. Biblically faithful and Spirit-led and creative faith communities will have a global impact, but that faithfulness hinges upon semantic apologetics and polemics.

This work, then, as noted in the introduction, is more theological and ethical in nature and written by a theologian, with a PhD minor in political philosophy, with years of experience teaching theology, philosophy, polemics, apologetics, and cultural and intellectual engagement. Experts in philosophy and philosophical linguistics and semantics will approach this discussion, as would be appropriate, very differently and in a more specialized manner. They also could move the dialog to the next level in academia.

What is known as worldview analysis, which focuses on comparing and contrasting major categories of belief between worldviews like atheism, Deism, and monotheism, will assist but is not the focus of this work for three reasons:

- First, as will be noted in the next chapter, this analysis will emphasize more than overtly religious beliefs and major categories of beliefs. Beliefs *and* passions are reshaping all words and our entire semantic universe, which then refashions the church and culture. Beliefs, passions, and words are all inextricably bound together.
- Second, this work focuses on language and communication as a whole and the specific usages and definitions of countless terms, not just on major categories of belief or major terms as with worldview analysis.
- Third, and absolutely critical to this project, is the grunt work of reflection on how terms define and interpret other terms and create cultural momentum and overt or covert norms. These families of terms or semantic universes shape church and state, and the assumptions of state. These terms also gain momentum in relation to each other and modify, shape, or nuance worldview, philosophical, and religious beliefs. The relationship between worldviews and semantic universes is analogous to the "chicken and the egg," but this work is suggesting that the semantic universe may be more impactful and relevant to current cultural and political dynamics.

This work rejects the rather dated thesis that worldview belief systems and/or ideology are/is driving and singularly responsible for the pervasive cultural drift and accelerating moral/cultural relativism. That dated thesis rests on what I would refer to as the modernistic professor fallacy—that professors propagate ideas in the academy that relentlessly and inevitably control culture and civilization. There is much to be said for the argument that education shapes culture, but cultural change is much more complex than such a simplistic and intellectual interpretation. Sociology, historical conditions (e.g., the psychology and sociology of the Versailles treaty after World War I), and even what we love or desire, all play essential roles. Social media is interjecting a very strong "from the ground up" influence on culture, even though it is also true that education and media influence social media.

The preliminary evidence reviewed in this work suggests that the heart of the battle for the future is not worldview analysis, politics, or law, even while fully granting each of these realities their civilizational importance. The heart of the battle for the future that connects all of these realities and more will take place in the fluid and ubiquitous semantic domain. This should not be surprising to the people of the Word.

Perhaps this is why Scripture emphasizes the Word and revealed words. Perhaps this is why the Jews, for centuries, meticulously and slavishly copied, checked, and double checked each word, jot and tittle (Matthew 5:18): "For truly I say to you, until heaven and earth pass away, not the smallest letter or stroke shall pass from the Law until all is accomplished." Perhaps this is why the biblical book of Isaiah was essentially unchanged after nearly a millennium of copying and recopying the text based on a comparison of the Dead Sea Scrolls with the Masoretic text.

The other dimension of the professor fallacy is the idea that the way individuals determine their core beliefs and practices is by reflecting on the big questions of life as if they are a neutral professor sitting in an ivory tower exploring all the options logically, objectively, and carefully prior to adopting a belief system, ideology, philosophy, worldview, or ethical posture. This book is suggesting that the dynamic and interdependent nature of cultures, subcultures, cultural passions and fads, semantic universes, and historical context are much more formative.

The reality is that there are multiple, and difficult to quantify, influencers on culture and civilization, and they often exist in the aforementioned "chicken and egg" relationships. This work, by way of analogy, views semantics as akin to the unseen tapestry and interconnections of the unified space-time continuum. Just as the galaxies seem to be interconnected and influence each other by unseen and hard to detect forces or structures, so are the elements of our community life connected by semantics. The organic or systemic nature of semantics interlinks all of the distinct verbal influencers on time and history.

The Word created and spoke into existence the universe, the reality of culture, and the universe of words, and then spoke redemptively into the fallen universe, a universe through which the kingdom of God can be approximated, realized, or rejected. In recent decades in the American context words are becoming the quantum field, for lack of a better analogy, that unifies, advances, and approximates the kingdom of darkness.

Regardless, what is needed presently is not more worldview arguments or specialized philosophical or linguistic analysis of words and word families or semantic universes. What is urgent is a general, preliminary, and especially *theological* unpacking of contemporary word usage—as civilization morphs and rots—and the provision of biblical and *theological* direction for this watershed cultural conversation and moment. Semantic usage and semantic universes rule culture and civilization, and at the deeper level of culture theology or religiously held convictions and assumptions generate these semantic universes.

Paul Tillich's theology was often flawed, but he got it largely right with his famous and oft-quoted observation that "religion is the substance of culture, [and] culture is the form of religion." Our words or semantics reveal the reality and health of our cultural and civilizational soul. At the core of culture and civilization is our communal spirit or soul. And, to apply a passage of Scripture in a non-individualistic fashion, "out of the abundance of the heart" (Luke 6:45) culture and civilization speaks.

Words and proper word usages are ultimately rooted in the Word, or Logos, who is the very agent of creation and communication. Words and meaningful communication are grounded in the doctrine of creation and the image of God. We are fallen creatures created in God's image who can, sometimes, through a glass darkly (1 Corinthians 13:12), and sometimes with great

confidence (2 Timothy 1:12), understand and communicate with
God and others and be communicated with by God through words.
The image of God, our fallen nature, and the grace and revelation
of God are the context in which we interpret and utilize terms. If
we get it right, we can use words to build or preserve civilization
and advance God's kingdom. God created words and the humans
that employ words.

Hence, the idea that just any semantic universe will do to guide
civilization runs contrary to Scripture, common sense, and the evidence of history. Were Stalin's or Pol Pot's semantic universes morally equivalent to all others? How about Hitler's "kingdomcentric"
Third Reich (or "kingdom")?

Our goal, then, is to conform words, terms, definitions and
concepts, as much as possible, to the divine perspective. Prior to
the new heaven and earth this will be in an approximate fashion.

*Our theological words and language should be Logocentric — in
the overt and intentional theological sense of conforming communication, as much as possible in this present age, to the influence and vantage point of the Logos.*

This Logocentrism is broader than a simplistic view of agreeing
with the Logos or the divine perspective, or of using the right words
to merely get to heaven or properly communicate with or pray
to the Logos. Logocentric or Word-centric language is ultimately
kingdom-centric, profoundly philosophical and theological, and
all terms are intentionally integrated and defined in reference to
each other. Logocentrism includes a semantic universe, family, or
constellation of terms. And Logocentric language is relevant to and
touches everything in culture and creation.

The kingdom was central to all that the Christ the Logos taught
and did, and hence language should conform to the created intent
of the cosmic and global kingdom of God that is in-breaking into
our world already, and which will someday envelope the entire
created order. Words must increasingly conform to that which
accurately describes, creates, and communicates the entirety of
the kingdom future-vision for culture, history, law, relationships,

science, art, civilization, and the wholeness of the divine creation and consummation. The renewal of all things already underway is aided and guided by words, and that same Spirit-actualized renewal also births and refines words. This vision then must be formulated and clarified concerning what is and is not appropriate and attainable within law and culture in the present age, prior to Paradise regained. My recent publication written for pastors and scholars, *A Theology of Cross and Kingdom* (Pickwick), addresses what is and is not attainable for civilizations prior to the next phase of God's cosmic redemption.

Therefore, words are future-oriented or eschatological at their core, and an indispensable dimension of the dawning New Creation. The semantic universe of the New Creation, when the kingdoms of this world become the kingdom of the Logos, is the norm to be approximated in a fallen world, and the only norm that will truly enhance civilization as we look forward to that Great Day.

Ask Yourself or Your Group

- *How do you agree or disagree with the author's definition of Truth and Logos?*
- *Why does the author believe that our civilization is now being built on shifting and unstable sands?*
- *What does it mean to describe Progressivism as "self-devouring"?*
- *Was Hitler's Third Reich Kingdomcentric? Logocentric? What is the meaning of "Reich"?*
- *What is the difference between Polemics and Apologetics, and which is most important today?*

Chapter 2

Bedrock Words that Endure or Ephemeral Words that Divide?

> *The law of the LORD is perfect, refreshing the soul.*
> *The statutes of the LORD are trustworthy, making wise*
> *the simple.*
> —Psalm 19:7

> *The grass withers, the flower fades, But the word of our God*
> *stands forever.*
> —Isaiah 40:8

> *For truly I say to you, until heaven and earth pass away, not*
> *the smallest letter or stroke shall pass from the Law until all is*
> *accomplished.*
> —Matthew 5:17

More is sacrificed by defecting from the truth of revelation than simply the truth about God and man and the world; loss of the truth and Word of God plunges into darkness the very truth of truth, the meaning of meaning, and even the significance of language. To sever the concerns of reason and life from the

revelation of God as the final ground and source of truth and the good accommodates and accelerates the contemporary drift to nihilism. It is not merely Christianity that stands or falls with the reality of revelation. To avert a nihilistic loss of enduring truth and good, only the recovery of revelation will suffice.
—Carl F. H. Henry (*God, Revelation, and Authority*, Volume 1)

The Winds of War

As our verbal and cultural conflicts increasingly escalate toward something akin to nineteenth-century Pre-Civil War animus, learning from the past may prove useful. In the American context (in the summer of 2018), nearly one-third of Americans believed that America was headed toward another civil war—and "soon."[82] Regardless, and there are likely many other nearly toxic alternatives than armed conflict, it is evident that a historic and future-defining political and verbal civil war is well underway.

And while the outrage or vitriol associated with the Civil and Revolutionary wars was intense, today's outrage is increasingly accelerated or proliferated by the lack of a semantic plumb line. Just imagine a sequel to the American Civil War with the presence of new, technological warfare, and the increasing absence of any moral framework.

Perhaps an illustration from the movie career of film star great Greta Garbo will provide one telling illustration of the nature of the current and escalating civil and verbal polarization and seduction. In 1939, Greta Garbo portrayed Ninotchka Yakushova, a Stoic, devout, and militant communist sent to Paris by the drab and brutal Bolshevik regime to complete an unfinished mission and retrieve backsliding *comrades* seduced by capitalistic Paris.[83] Garbo's script, written just as Hitler and Stalin were moving toward a non-aggression pact on the eve of World War II, depicted Ninotchka as a carping social justice advocate, swift to articulate all of the observed *social injustice* of the decadent West. Ninontchka's uncompromising advocacy for *justice* for the workers, for equality, and for the people was dramatized and satirized as passionate—yet terribly misguided and lifeless.

Nearly eighty years after Garbo's first major comedy portrayed social justice as inept justice, or even as perilous pseudo-justice, orthodox Christians, Jews, and the general culture are still terribly and progressively divided on the meaning and definition of key terms and phrases like compassionate social justice. Such terms, for many, define an important dimension of the mission of faith communities and nations. Such key words certainly define much of political discourse and debate. In many religious circles today, social justice is a nonnegotiable moral imperative and even a basis for shaming.

Similarly, contemporary definitions and usages of interdependent terms like justice, compassion, truth, family, marriage, faith, colonialism, multiculturalism, diversity, inclusion, gender, tolerance, love, judgmentalism, legalism, the establishment of religion, freedom of religion, free speech, and homophobia — to name only a few — seem especially fluid and opportunistic in recent decades. The confused usage of these terms appears to be the fruit or symptom of something much, much deeper and interconnected. And the definitions often seem to serve personal or tribal interests.

In a classic, heated, and illustrative conflict in the present decade, Glenn Beck defined "social justice" as a seductive code word for Nazism or communism and encouraged believers to leave churches or movements that advocate for this kind of social justice. Jim Wallis of the *Sojourners'* self-proclaimed social justice movement responded by telling Beck's evangelical[84] listeners to turn the dial and place Beck's show in the same category as Howard Stern's pornographic broadcasts.[85] For both individuals, true and biblical spirituality, compassion, and justice are associated with rather conflicting definitions and meanings. Indeed, for Beck and Wallis, being a genuine and caring *Christian* embarks one on very different pilgrimages. Beck and Wallis, and many contemporaries, inhabit alternate verbal or semantic universes.

The Trojan Horse of Social Justice

When I was coursing my way through my PhD program, with a minor in political science (mainly political philosophy), I encountered myriad conceptions of justice and social justice, from the ancient Greeks to the present. Justice was to be debated, not assumed, and question-begging arguments—"if you love justice then you agree with me"—were to be avoided at all costs. Social justice was viewed as best achieved by direct democracy, or representative and republican democracy, or democratic socialism, or socialistic communism, or economic democracy, or anarchy, or benevolent divine right theory, or Rawlsian justice, or countless other variants. Unfortunately, today, as will be noted later, many people attempt to silence this healthy debate by invoking, often in the name of Scripture, the social justice, biblical justice, or compassionate justice trump cards.

Social justice or compassionate social justice is appealed to in order to bypass careful reflection and employ something analogous to cloture in Congress. The fair debate concerning what actually constitutes compassionate social justice prematurely ends. The unfaithful are then stigmatized or even silenced, especially in an age of resurgent socialism.

The implication of this guilting seems to be the following: "This is about compassionate social justi*ce*, so of course you love Jesus and follow the Bible and agree with me." *Sojourners* magazine, on the political left, proudly claims to stand for social justice, and frequently, if not incessantly and loudly, self-identifies as the true prophetic voice for lovers of biblical, evangelical, social justice. Communism (Ninotchka's ideology), as previously noted, claimed to be implementing social justice *for the people* and the working class—often by any means necessary. On the political right, one of the most legally influential movements in contemporary America is the American Center for Law and Justice or ACLJ. The ACLJ has justice in their name and frequently makes arguments for what is perceived to be right and just, but they seem, at least anecdotally, to avoid the frequent "we represent true social justice" self-defining practiced by the *Sojourners* movement. These two groups almost always disagree (e.g., responding to presidential policy and decisions, or economic issues). A *Sojourner's* magazine contributor has even asked if the current Trump era[86] qualifies as a "Bonhoeffer Moment."[87] Bonhoeffer, of course, was involved in an assassination plot on Hitler, though this contributor eschews violence.

Many or most desire to be aligned with social justice, biblical justice, or biblical compassion. The unresolved and central question, however, is who best aligns with genuine compassion and authentic biblical justice.

Rather than being defended with transparency and open dialog concerning options, social justice can be utilized as a Trojan horse and a sacred cow to seduce and manipulate. "If you agree with social justice, compassion, and inclusion, then you must support homosexual marriage and ordination." Perhaps it would be helpful to have the argument about what constitutes social justice, and what are the norms, at least as often as the term is utilized to condemn, advocate, fundraise, or proselytize. Such open discussion would make it much easier for diverse social and political groups to find much needed consensus on challenging flagrant injustice and devastating exclusion.

Those considering social justice options, especially in the church and academy, certainly have the moral right to learn about theories, definitions and applications. Much is at stake. Indeed, this work later affirms that the definition of compassionate social justice may well chart much of the future of Christian orthodoxy, evangelical orthodoxy—and civilization.[88] Sincere wisdom-seekers on the religious and political left and right should sense the importance and value of semantic analysis and clarity, even if the arguments of this work are only partially accepted.

As this work was being finalized with the publisher, Noah Rothman released a relevant book concerning social justice that has implications for semantic apologetics and polemics.[89] Regardless of whether one agrees with all of Rothman's points, his work clearly demonstrates that the definition of social justice defines much of the national conversation and our communal ethics.

Rothman argues, "Identity politics is not limited to any one political party or socioeconomic class. Many of those who have embraced the philosophy that animates the most militant practitioners of identity politics may not even recognize the trap into which they have fallen"—or, stated differently, how they have been verbally seduced, captured, and even enraptured.[90] Rothman observes, "On a cosmetic level, social justice is a noble pursuit—one perfectly in keeping with the American political tradition. In practice, though, it has been corrupted, perhaps beyond the point of redemption." This is because it often "steals from its enthusiasts a sense of charity, forces them to compete for victim status, and in the end to wallow in self-pity."[91] Devotees are turned into "imperious hall monitors. It demands that they judge others not on their individual merit but on their group identity. And it insists that its champions abandon the traditions of Anglo-American common law and the foundational principles of Western jurisprudence—the bedrocks of civilization—in service to arbitrary, capricious, and ultimately unsatisfying vengeance."[92]

Hence, "the first step toward untangling this mess is to embrace a paradigmatic shift. The successful [social justice and] civil rights movements of the mid-twentieth century were effective not because they were bitter and vengeful and violent, but because they held tight to the Founders' ideals. Indeed, these movements seemed to exemplify those ideals far more fully than their opponents did."[93] Rothman adds this warning:

> Nations exist only as long as their citizens are committed to their preservation. Systems implode when those who believe in their purpose and rectitude are outnumbered by the cynical, disengaged, and exhausted. The tipping point is nowhere near, but it may be coming. That's especially true if America's responsible and historically literate citizens—both Republican and Democratic—do nothing to protest injustice committed in the name of tackling injustice.[94]

Rothman's work is a quick read, but as I was absorbing the key points for a possible summary it occurred to me that it might be helpful to rely on another scholar's brief review and assessment of Rothman's new publication. I recently ran across a review of Rothman's *Unjust*, and the reviewer, Graham Hillard, while unaware of the semantic thesis of this book or my Trojan Horse argument, succinctly explained Rothman's perspective and confirmed many of the arguments of *Seduced*. This extensive quotation on social justice semantics is helpful and revealing [©2020 *National Review*, used with permission]:

> Rothman ... has assembled ... the most complete record of the social-justice movement's offenses against reason (and justice) that readers are likely to find. Subscribers to this magazine will recognize much of the rotten fruit that Rothman gathers but will be stunned anew by the sheer weight of the harvest. Conservatives approaching the book with only a vague sense of the problem may well leave it in a state of panic.
>
> Because the fact is that public life in this nation is now almost completely dominated by "the antisocial dogmas that underlie ideological social justice," to borrow Rothman's penetrating language. Social justice

"influences how businesses structure themselves. It is altering how employers and employees relate to one another. It has utterly transformed academia. [And] it is remaking our politics with alarming swiftness."

In support of these contentions, Rothman assembles a parade of illustrations that are ... horrifying and darkly comic. Among them are the sagas of James Damore, the Google employee who was fired after composing an internal memo suggesting that the industry's "gender gap" might be explained by the differing interests of men and women; Erika and Nicholas Christakis, professors at Yale who were driven from their positions after objecting to the university's politically correct guidelines for students' Halloween costumes; and Maggie Stiefvater, whose young-adult novel *All the Crooked Saints* was condemned as racist while the manuscript was still in progress. Cited, too, are such absurdities as a Reuters report praising a Brooklyn mother's affirmation of her three-year-old's transgender identity and the New York City Commission on Human Rights' warning that employers can be fined for failing to use their employees' preferred pronouns. Columbia University's decision to reserve certain campus areas for the exclusive use of LGBT and minority students is examined in these pages, as are the University of Missouri's 2015 racial kerfuffles and the false rape allegations against the Duke lacrosse team and the University of Virginia's Phi Kappa Psi fraternity. I could go on. Rothman does.

The great accomplishment of *Unjust* is that it succeeds in synthesizing these anecdotes (and many others) into a coherent narrative. Though seemingly disparate, such illustrations in sum reveal the extent to which a movement that might have set its sights on the amelioration of legitimate societal ills has instead been transformed into a vehicle for the Left's worst ideas: "an affinity for racial hierarchies and race-based preferences, antipathy to due process and the presumption of innocence, [and the] reduction of individuals to nondescript representatives of their taxonomic class." Whatever it could have been, Rothman asserts, social justice is now "a creed born of grievances"—a crusade "fueled by anxiety, a preoccupation with oneself, and the need for a constant stream of new enemies."

In Rothman's telling, the assumptions that guide contemporary social-justice activism are dangerous in part because they cross partisan lines. While a less sophisticated conservative polemic might have trained its fire on the Left alone, Rothman is careful to demonstrate that a similar intellectual cancer has taken root on the alt-right, whose white-nationalist program can best be understood as an attempt to achieve social justice for a shrinking Caucasian majority. Thus, Rothman writes, just as "the social justice left is generally hostile toward any distribution of social goods that does not disadvantage that majority," so "the alt-right is wholly suspicious of any distribution" that fails to privilege America's white citizens. The consequence of these resentments is, inevitably, a cycle of mutual loathing in which the participants are increasingly indistinguishable. In one of *Unjust's* most cogent passages, Rothman peruses a number of Antifa websites and tracts only to find that the bile contained therein bears a striking resemblance to corresponding ravings on the other extreme of the political spectrum. "Replace the objects of [Antifa's] hatred (homophobes, frat boys, bank tellers, etc.) with the objects of white nationalist hatred (miscegenation, minorities, 'social justice warriors,' etc.), and these ugly sentiments are almost ideologically interchangeable."

Among the additional drawbacks of the grievance-mongering practiced at both political poles is its tendency to inculcate a view of the world (if they gain, we lose) that is both morally and economically illiterate. For the Left, specifically, a further flaw is the rank ahistoricism of the idea that America is uniquely deserving of progressive rage—a notion that *Unjust* skillfully dismembers. [Such an idea is the antithesis of American exceptionalism.] Few would deny—and Rothman readily concedes—that the United States has at times failed to meet the obligations set forth in its founding documents. But all must acknowledge that this nation has taken incredible strides in the direction of equality and racial reconciliation. Rothman argues that such strides are "unrivaled by any other culturally heterogeneous nation in any similar span of human history." A failure to recognize that work is a sign not only of ingratitude but of intellectual laziness.

Indeed, intellectual laziness is perhaps the most compelling explanation that Rothman offers for the enduring popularity of social-justice activism on the left. Any idiot (my term) can follow Alexandria Ocasio-Cortez on Twitter or unearth a micro-aggression or two. Few Americans—few humans—have the time and inclination to participate in meaningful policy debates or to practice sustaining an argument. "It takes work to know what you're talking about," Rothman points out. Social-justice activism is attractive precisely because it provides "a convenient method by which the ill-equipped can engage in politics and be taken seriously."

It's difficult to imagine a more thorough diagnosis than Rothman's of the condition that now afflicts us. Whether a cure can be had is, of course, a different matter, and on that subject *Unjust* is surprisingly hopeful. In part, Rothman's optimism is due to the fact that social justice is in many cases meted out in a closed loop. "More often than not," he reminds us, "the people who face retribution" for social-justice-related offenses "are social justice enthusiasts themselves." Conservatives can avoid a great deal of punishment merely by with-holding the "complicity" that is required of victims in the form of false apologies and groveling. And in the longer term? The solution, Rothman suggests, lies with "Democratic lawmakers of stature," who "must commu-nicate in clear terms why the social justice left's brand of politics is not only a dead-end but also a threat to the egalitarian system they profess to love."

Will such a champion arise in the frenzied election season to come? I have my doubts.[95]

This fair rendition of Rothman's key points and recommen-dations is germane and helpful, and yet the context for the Trojan Horse seduction is much broader, deeper, and certainly more chal-lenging. Rothman often targets the classroom, understandably so, but while the classroom has become a bully pulpit for misconstrued social justice, it has, more importantly, become a bully pulpit for the wholesale inversion of the meaning of words, the meaning of values, and the meaning of meaning.

The Death of Truth as a Precursor to the Death of Words

Some on the left and right are now perceived to be like Luddites because they continue to cling to their God and belief and/or in some form of normative truth for all cultures and civilizations. Those retaining belief in a norm on the left often emphasize sci-ence and reason, such as progressive Alan Dershowitz, formerly of Harvard. Those on the right typically emphasize revelation and/ or reason. Both still "cling" to normative truth as a plumb line for truthful communication and dialog.

These believers in normative truth affirm that semantic integ-rity helps everyone communicate more clearly and be more truly persuasive. In other words, lovers of truth and wisdom, sometimes called philosophers or true thinkers, whether left or right in the

Western context, surely should recognize that the Balkanization of words and communication ultimately helps no one and destroys civilization. When everyone is engaging in opportunistic, shameless, and even militant spin and advocacy, we eventually reach the point where no one is believed, trusted, or persuasive.

Some two decades ago, when "postmodernism" truly became a buzz word in popular culture and the academy, Dennis McCallum penned *The Death of Truth: What's Wrong with Multiculturalism, the Rejection of Reason and the New Postmodern Diversity.* McCallum echoed or agreed with countless other authors, from Francis Schaeffer to Carl F. H. Henry to Josh McDowell, that the loss of Christian influence in Western civilization was leading to, as Henry put it, a crisis of truth and word.[96] Henry warned over three decades ago that, "We live in the twilight of a great civilization, amid the deepening decline of modern culture. Those strange beast-empires of the books of Daniel and Revelation seem already to be stalking and sprawling over the surface of the earth."[97]

McDowell often referred to the rejection of "absolute truth" or what some refer to as true truth (Francis Schaeffer), and affirmed that the loss of belief in absolute truth was eroding orthodox beliefs and biblical ethics in church and culture, and especially among churched youth—the very youth who are the future of the church and state.[98] In other words, the "death" of God at the center of civilization inevitably would undermine culturally normative truth and morality. Similarly, Douglas Groothius has warned of "truth decay" in the postmodern age, and Nancy Pearcey has advocated for "total truth" as a means to liberate Christianity from its current cultural captivity to relativism.[99]

Critics have complained that "truth" has become identified with rational, modernistic, scientific, or Enlightenment truth, and that such "truth" is bad for culture and civilization anyhow.[100] Authors such as McCallum, McDowell, Schaeffer, and Groothius are dismissed for being wedded to passé modernistic assumptions. Unfortunately, even if the critics are right, we have also seen the enormous and devastating consequences of the absence of a normative, shared, cross-cultural measuring rod for truth and morality. The rejection of Enlightenment truth need not entail the rejection of normative truth and morality or civil truth and morality. And only uninformed critics would accuse some of these authors as being naive Cartesian rationalists or modernists.

Twenty years after McCallum's work, the origin and progression of the post-Christian contagion threatening civilization is never entirely clear but it is now more clearly comprehended. It will be argued that in the Western context, the death of right belief (orthodoxy) in faith communities and churches, as early as the eighteenth century, greatly contributed to the death of God or *Deus absconditus* in culture. This straying from orthodoxy was a failure of the unification of passion and polemics[101] inside the church and passionate, tactful apologetics,[102] effective evangelism, and church planting outside of the church. The death of orthodoxy in many circles led to the death of the biblical church and synagogue. What remained is what John Wesley referred to as "the form of religion without the power," analogous to a "dead sect," untethered from core biblical convictions, disciplines, and practice.

This widespread death of orthodoxy influenced the broader cultural or civilizational death of God which contributed to the functional death of truth.[103]

Decades after the death of Truth, we are now experiencing the post-mortem consequence—the death of words.

Meaningful communication and shared definitions are being replaced by tribalistic definitions (e.g., justice or marriage) and escalating conflict. We can't even agree today on the definition of a legal or illegal immigrant, child abuse, concentration camps, Nazi, or even the fundamental nature of marriage and its role in society. Virtually every term is up for redefinition, weaponization, and politicization.

In 2018, the defenders of illegal immigration and critics of temporary family separations alleged child abuse. Defenders of the temporary child separation policy argued that extreme efforts were being made to care for children put in harm's way not by workers at the border but by their parents, the smuggling industry, and/or the liberal enablers of illegal immigration. Regardless of who got it right, it is stunning to contrast the nearly antithetical semantic universes of those debating the issue. For example, many of the outspoken and sometimes vitriolic critics of this "child abuse" of allegedly thousands of illegal child immigrants on the border are also staunch and vitriolic defenders of the abortion of millions of unborn children in the wombs of American citizens, including late term abortions and possibly even post-abortion intentional euthanasia. For some, abortion is a mere choice, a surgical procedure to remove a part of a woman's body, and the freedom to control one's body in private—and therefore not child abuse. "My body, my choice" is the mantra. For others, abortion is not a surgical procedure but the murder of a scientifically and genetically distinct person (most likely female) and not a body part, never a legitimate or moral choice, and, just like child abuse, an unacceptable choice whether the action takes place in public or private.

Post *Roe-Wade* some pro-lifers are now pushing for the legal prohibition of all abortions. They believe that legality and morality are not one and the same, and they are making a moral argument that "My body, my choice" is based on false premises. Scientifically, the unborn child is genetically distinct and not part of the mother's body, so "my body" is semantically ambiguous at best and false at worst. Morally, if those engaging in abortion acknowledge that at any point in the gestation process human life or potential human life exists, then "my choice" also becomes an ethically questionable framework for deciding on behalf of these unborn—who have no voice and who are mostly women and non-white—that they are to be terminated. Hence, even the terms "my choice" and "my body" have been defined based on the respective semantic universe. Honest dialog should explore all of these nuances related to this historic debate.

In the pro-life semantic universe, the idea that the destruction of an unborn female is a reproductive right of a woman is incomprehensible and utterly self-defeating. Similarly, concerning the separated children at the border, some feel that child abuse is an abuse of the English language, whereas others affirm that child abuse accurately conveys the reality of this dimension of border enforcement and detention. The semantic breach seems nearly infinite and irreparable on this contentious issue.

Semantic universes rule mindsets and debates while they frame the meaning and usage of key terms and phrases like choice, freedom of choice, "my body my choice," right of privacy, child abuse, fetus, unborn child, and murder. The idea that the Supreme Court, or anyone, can interpret the law or legal precedents apart from mastery of the history and nature of semantic universes and the underlying philosophical and religious assumptions is more than patently and plainly absurd. The suggestion that the Supreme Court, or anyone, can deliberate on such matters with simple legal objectivity and without a shared norm is laughable. The myth that such matters can be decided without powerful predispositions of prejudice or bias is equally suspect. Herculean efforts are required to think and act judiciously on such contested and emotional matters amidst the semantic crossfire. Normed semantic clarity is the only hope for a unified and civil quest for a more perfect union. The alternative is tribalism and the seductive tooth and fang employment of the will-to-power.

Perhaps the greatest folly is the proposal that a mythological standard of secular neutrality can fairly adjudicate such matters— that secular, post Judeo-Christian, objectivity and fairness are unbiased and even possible. The reality is that it is only within the framework of the Judeo-Christian semantic universe that anything even remotely approaching objective or normative justice or fairness is even possible or sustainable. Legal and moral decisions will always be made with someone's plumb line, standard, measure, or canon. Even political discourse is shaped by the canon of a semantic universe. Semantic universes are used or created by politicians to marginalize opponents or mainstream their own views, without any agreed upon standard to assess such statements.

Anyone who challenges the universe is alleged by opponents to be a far right or far left extremist, perhaps even a despised far right-wing extremist fundamentalist or a radical left-wing extremist socialist. Socialists and fundamentalists certainly exist, with the former seemingly on the rise in America, but the point here is who

defines terms like *extremist*? What is the measuring rod and who makes the determination? Furthermore, we must ask,
- What is the standard?
- Shall we allow politicians to create their own semantic universes that will guide the future?
- Shall we allow politicians to guide the future or are they public servants charged with enhancing the American experiment?

Apart from some agreed upon measure or canon, which used to be the Judeo-Christian influenced American experiment, shameless word spin, fake news, and verbal deception are inevitable and will only proliferate.

The real issue here is which measuring rod best approximates the correct perspective that transcends time and culture, aligns with eternity, and provides an appropriate foundation for divinely ordained human and civilizational flourishing. How can we impact a world in the present that is fallen and awaiting eventual redemption from beyond itself? The world that God loves needs just such a transcendent norm and healing touch. The standard in America and much of the West for centuries was influenced by Judeo-Christian and Enlightenment assumptions and beliefs. Such a perspective and normative perspective was quickly vanishing in mid-twentieth-century America.

In 1976, just after the American Roe vs. Wade decision, Francis Schaeffer made predictions about the future of Western civilization—and all civilizations—that captured the imagination and praxis of many American evangelicals. His formula for the future seemed spot on to some and simplistic to others. He argued that

> There is a flow to history and culture. This flow is rooted and has its wellspring in the thoughts of people. People are unique in the inner life of the mind—what they are in their thought world determines how they act. This is true of their value systems and it is true of their creativity. It is true of their corporate actions, such as

political decisions, and it is true of their personal lives. The results of their thought world flow through their fingers or from their tongues into the external world. This is true of Michelangelo's chisel, and it is true of a dictator's sword.[104]

Schaeffer framed American evangelical political engagement, including pro-life activism, by his read of history. He predicted that civilizations, from Rome to the present, follow predictable patterns and attributes of emergence and decline, as outlined by Edward Gibbon:

> First, a mounting love of show and luxury (that is affluence); second, a widening gap between the very rich and the very poor;... third, an obsession with sex; fourth, freakishness in the arts, masquerading as originality, and enthusiasms pretending to be creativity; fifth, an increased desire to live off the state. It all sounds so familiar. We have come a long road since our first chapter, and we are back in Rome.[105]

It is important to remember that these words were penned nearly a half-century ago. These cultural attributes, for Schaeffer, define the latter stages of a civilization in decline. Reflecting on his own generation, he argued, the masses increasingly abandon the pursuit of noble and enduring values or the divinely grounded vision of an ideal civilization and focus on personal peace and prosperity.

Then, he predicts, as declining civilizations seek "to fill the vacuum left by the loss of Christian principles" and the chaos of increasing moral and political anarchy, people and nations will turn to "*manipulative* authoritarian government" to restore order and provide for the needs of the masses. Drawing on the thought of Samuel Rutherford, Schaeffer predicts that nations move from law and culture rooted in what is deemed as eternally revealed and divine principles that rule as king (*Lex Rex*—the Law is King), to the government itself serving as the ultimate king (*Rex Lex*—the King is Law).[106] Government becomes a god. The future of such declining civilizations includes chaos and anarchy followed by manipulative authoritarian government.

Today, authors such as James K. A. Smith, in his *Desiring the Kingdom* series, or his fairly recent publication *You Are What You Love*, engage in a form of cultural analysis that brings into question the major emphasis upon mind or thought or worldview thinking as the Rosetta stone(s) to the flow of history and the rise and fall of nations, churches, or Christian organizations. For some, Schaeffer's intellectual or mental reading of future history is simplistic and suspect.[107]

Perhaps Schaeffer had it partially right concerning the possibility that *Lex Rex* can morph into *Rex Lex* over time, and that the intellectual assault on Judeo-Christian influence puts civilization at risk. Perhaps Smith had it partially right that you are what you love, and that what you love is often formed and framed by cultural or ecclesial liturgies rather than mere intellectual ideas. Schaeffer's emphasis on art, literature, and culture demonstrates that he did not neglect the matters of the heart. And Smith, a trained and effective philosopher, emphasizes the heart but hardly neglects matters of the mind. Modernist era Schaeffer is asking *How Should We Then [Think and Love and] Live?* Augustinian influenced and postmodern era Smith is asking "How should we then love or desire [and think and live]?

Schaeffer tries to discern what we love through what we think, and Smith seems to get at what we think through what we love. Perhaps this is a classic "chicken and egg" false dichotomy, and an either/or emphasis on mind or heart, or the exclusive methodological priority of either, runs counter to experience, common sense, the biblical and Hebraic emphasis on the unity of the person, and the best intuitions of both authors.

Perhaps the erosion of Judeo-Christian influence has as much to do with matters of the heart as with matters of the head, not to mention sociological and historical forces, and that chronicling which comes first is not always easy. Having grown up in the dazed and confused 1970s and 1980s in America, a decade plus after Woodstock, much of the drifting I observed among my formerly Christian friends had as much to do with feelings, sociology, psychology, and powerful cultural liturgies like music and entertainment, as it had to do with ideas or rational reflection. Frankly, for many it had to do with their relationships with parents.

On one level it can be argued that the ideas germinated, flowered, and led culture (and music and entertainment) and civilization away from the Judeo-Christian ethos—and the process was greatly influenced by education. On another level, the matters of the heart clearly played a critical role, as evidenced by Woodstock in 1969. As Karl Barth might suggest, perhaps the answer is both/and. Influential academics are not exempt from multiple such influences on the ideas they create that shape the future.

In one sense the educational institutions clearly and indisputably led this cultural revolution, but in another sense, what took place at the more passionate grass roots and emotional level, especially since the mid-twentieth century, was potent. This grassroots influence is especially prominent now with the global digitization of information, virtual experiences, and virtual reality. Education can and probably does hold the upper hand in guiding civilization, by virtue of training leaders, but civilizational influence seems more and more symbiotic and emanates from multiple centers or domains of influence. And today, educational institutions especially focus on matters other than the mind so their influence is multifaceted.

In the Wesleyan evangelical tradition (associated with John Wesley), reference is often made to the organic unity of right belief (orthodoxy), right passion or affections (orthopathy), and right actions (orthopraxy). Perhaps this is a helpful construct for comprehending how words, terms, ideas, cultural liturgies, doctrines, and practices develop over time. Perhaps this is also a helpful construct for grasping the means by which semantic polemics and apologetics can be effective inside and outside of the church.

Perhaps we generate and maintain what we believe, and the proper definition and usage of terms, by things such as

- *what we love and worship,*
- *how we worship,*
- *what decisions/choices we make and how we implement them,*
- *what we buy,*

- *who we love, and who we associate with,*
- *how we communicate,*
- *what we teach and preach, and*
- *how we live.*

All of these realities are simultaneously essential to maintain and advance the kingdom, even if teaching and preaching plays a primary role in articulating the course.

What also seems certain, however, is that *we are what we think and desire*, and as we think and desire our semantic universes begin to morph toward the Logos and the kingdom or away from the Logos and the kingdom. This morphing is not one word at a time, as if overnight someone individually replaces a heterosexual definition of marriage with a subjectivist view of marriage in Merriam-Webster. The morphing, for better or worse, is in the air we breathe and less than easy to track, explain, or chart. Semantic definitions surf on the winds of cultural change.

To be fair to Schaeffer, however, his classic work hardly neglects desires of the heart, as noted and as evidenced by his *significant* preoccupation with art, culture, and visuals—from the beginning to the end of the *How Shall We* text. He pays very close attention to art forms, though seeing them largely as the fruit of ideas. He was no simplistic, stuffy, dispassionate rationalist. Schaeffer does prioritize thought as the framework for the flow of culture and civilizations, and the context in which desire and matters of the heart seek fulfillment. And Schaeffer goes out of his way to suggest that the authoritarian future can take on many forms, including authoritarianism of the political right or the political left. Perhaps Schaeffer's key thesis or lament is summed up in a quotation he applies to the many political martyrs seeking authentic freedom: "Forget the past and you will lose both eyes."[108]

Schaeffer's predictions may be both over-simplistic and hauntingly relevant. History is fluid and full of surprises and exceptions. In Europe, where "post-Christendom" emerged earlier than in America, there seems to be

- a combination of apathy, malaise, and preoccupation with personal peace and prosperity;

- a weariness with ideology and nationalism along with a resurgence of reactionary nationalism and ideology;
- a strong belief that strong belief and nationalistic ideology foment war and oppression and are the ruination of civilization—rather than bad ideas, moral relativism, or flawed national experiments divorced from Judeo-Christian influence;
- a Euro-system that is largely dependent on the military defense, spending, and economic vitality of America for stability;
- a diversity of free market models between nations rather than monolithic socialism;
- a general centralization of power along with concerns about that power and the long-term fiscal solvency of entitlement nations; and
- multiple wrenching conflicts over relativism, toleration, and the welcoming of different subcultures, with some of the new subcultures seeking to hegemonically replace European culture.

Perhaps fragmentation, fluidity, the emerging, subtle or aggressive suppression of Judeo-Christian values, and *Rex Lex* are the dominant European characteristics relevant to our discussion. The European lack of or opposition to shared and normative values or strong ideology may temporarily guard against extreme authoritarian movements, but this vacuum, under the right historical conditions, especially economic collapse or war, may once again lead to the specter of authoritarianism and conflict sweeping through Europe. *Perhaps*.

In America, while there are trends suggesting that America will "go European or Canadian," the conspicuous and continued presence of a sizeable American and voluntarist evangelical religious movement along with a sizeable and morally conservative Roman Catholic and Eastern Orthodox demographic—not to mention orthodox Judaism and Islam—the vast majority of which votes politically conservative, creates different dynamics and a likely different future than Europe. The Roman Catholic influence in conservative media is significant.

In the recent American Presidential election, an overwhelming number of American evangelicals voted Republican, in spite of grave concerns about the Republican presidential candidate. The alternative—which seemed to continue the near frontal assault on traditional Judeo-Christian values and ethics, the dissolution of the original American experiment, and the rejection of authentic Judeo-Christian influence upon the American civilization—clearly seemed more perilous on multiple levels to these voters. Most of these voters were not nuanced in verbal semantics, but they simply have not accepted the sales pitch by more liberal politicians who have tried to wrap themselves in the flag of the American experiment or Christian spirituality or the Bible. For them, it may look like the flag and sound like the Bible, but it is viewed as a different political experiment and a divergent and corrosive religion.

Hence, the polarization of values and future-visions in America is much greater than in Europe, because the balance of economic, political, and cultural power between those desiring a genuine and biblical Judeo-Christian influence on America and those desiring to "go European" is more equal. In America, verbal and political civil war, already well underway, or actual civil war, is more likely due to the size and clout of all the adversaries. Some astutely have spoken of the present moment as "America's Cold Civil War."[109] Predicting the future, however, is for authentic prophets, and stoning is most undesirable (Deuteronomy 13:1–5).

Please understand that some key emphases are required at this point in the discussion. First, this work is not predicting the end of the world. Indeed, I am arguing that civilizational melioration is possible, via hard work, sacrifice, and grace.

Second, this work is not suggesting that Francis Schaeffer got it all right—that culture will soon decay and a strong man (or woman) will emerge in response to the chaos an establish global or regional totalitarianism. What Schaeffer did get right in very broad and non-chronological terms is the math of fragmentation, economic decline, and power vacuums. Disintegrating and fragmenting civilizations create power vacuums and urgent economic needs that someone eventually will try to fill to restore order. If no one has the power to take charge, then Balkanization or cultural stagnation and apathy could emerge.

In the American context fragmentation may persist for some unknown duration apart from extreme economic challenges or economic collapse. Judeo-Christian influence could well be marginalized or criminalized, and life will seem to go on as normal for many even without a shared standard for truth and morality. Biblical Jews and Christians will notice, but life will go on and the sun will continue to rise for a season.

Biblical beliefs, thoughts, and behaviors may be rejected and post-Christian mob rule may find this oppressive reality quite acceptable. "Christian" spirituality may be redefined to embrace unbiblical assumptions and escape marginalization or oppression. Beneath the surface of what will likely be described, however, as a tolerant and pluralistic post-Christian civilization is a foundation built upon shifting sands that will eventually be incapable of bearing the weight. Yet the full decline of civilization may take decades or centuries to become clearly manifest.

However, the concrete will likely set in the near future. Political, economic, or international conditions will eventually arise that will expose this soft and unstable foundation. The point here is that a truly flourishing and enduring civilization that approximates the coming kingdom of God and protects religious liberty, including Judeo-Christian religious liberty, is not possible when grounded in truth and morality relativism and escalating semantic equivocation.

Regardless of the contours of the next stage of the post-Christian or anti-Christian contagion in America or the West, verbal civil war, the death of civilization, the death of free speech, and the death of "America" are real possibilities.

The death of free speech may be initially, and ironically, primarily for faith communities who embrace the very Judeo-Christian value system that gave birth to American freedom of speech. However, *the death of freedom and freedom of speech for any Judeo-Christian faith community is ultimately the death of freedom of speech for everyone.* And, as the Pew Research data confirms, "No Matter Where You Are, Religious Freedom Is Getting Worse."[110]

The death of "America" does not necessarily mean that America will cease to exist. Such a death does mean that such a future America will bear little resemblance to the original Judeo-Christian and Enlightenment shaped American experiment, will likely move from *Lex Rex* toward *Rex Lex* or multiple and often conflicting norms and Balkanization, and will more resemble a variant of Europe than the America of the *Declaration of Independence*, the *Constitution*, or the *Federalist* papers.

A totally redefined America is arguably no longer America in any meaningful sense. The term may continue to find usage, and some in the neo-America or pseudo-America may even claim to be patriotic and wrap themselves in the flag and cross of patriotic Judeo-Christian spirituality, but the reality will no longer exist. To illustrate the point, some couples are still legally married but not really married in any relationally, emotionally, or spiritually meaningful sense of the term. The name "America" does not guarantee the reality of America, any more than the term church guarantees the reality of a biblical church.

Moving beyond Schaeffer's anarchy and authoritarianism model for the future of civilizations, and learning from Smith's emphasis on desire, while broad generalizations are over-simplistic by definition and by nature, the civilizational drift or systemic post-Christian contagion that seems to be emerging disperses something like the stages found in Tables 2.1 and 2.2 and subsequent explanations and illustrations. This work does not claim to decipher the rise and fall of nations or Western civilization, but the present verbal civil warfare is illuminated by these tentatively proposed points of historical connections and context.

The chronology of these items as listed in Table 2.1 is less clear, and some may be coterminous, but the reality of their interconnectedness does seem to be emerging before our very eyes. As will be demonstrated and illustrated social commentators like *Time* magazine are noticing. Hence, it is within this broader context that the present work on the death of words, or semantic polemics and apologetics, finds its life and cultural context. As noted, such analysis is most provisional, but also potentially rather illuminative of contemporary cultural trends. The simplest analysis is a level one analysis, and the deeper analysis is level 2. The overlapping sequencing generally moves downward in each column.

Table 2.1. Level 1 and 2 Cultural Analysis

Level 1 Analysis	Level 2 Analysis
1. Death of God	1. Death of Judeo-Christian Polemics and Apologetics
2. Death of Truth	2. Death of Biblical Orthodoxy (Right Belief, Right Affections, Right Actions)[111]
3. Death of Words	3. Death of the Biblical, Orthodox Communities of Faith
4. Death of Freedom (at least for many)	4. Death of God in Culture
5. Death of Free Speech (at least for many)	5. Death of Truth
6. Death of Civilization	6. Death of Words
7. Death of "America"	7. Death of Culture and Freedom
	8. Death of Civilization and "America"

A slightly deeper or level three analysis might suggest the following as seen in Table 2.2.

Table 2.2. Level 3 Cultural Analysis

Level 3 Analysis
Key Historical Turning Points:
1. Death of Passionate Judeo-Christian Piety (Right Heart, Right Desires, Right Cultural Liturgies, Right Heartfelt and Personal Affections or Passions, or Orthopathy)
2. Death of Effective Polemics and Historic, Biblical Orthodoxy within Faith Communities (Right Belief, Orthodoxy)—see Chapter 4
3. Death of Effective Apologetics, Evangelism, Cultural Impact, and the Energetic Planting of New, Biblical, Missional Faith Communities (Right Hand, Orthopraxy)
4. Death of the Biblically Influenced Faith Communities (and the emergence of post-biblical "churches" and "denominations")—see Chapter 4
5. Death of the Judeo-Christian God Concept and the Passion for God as the Foundation for Culture (Illustrated in Nietzsche's *Parable of the Madman*, 1882)
6. Death of Any Shared Normative Standard for Truth and Morality (whether Scripture or Reason—such as "We hold these truths to be self-evident," or the "Old Deluder Act" of 1642 and 1647.[112] This Judeo-Christian influenced Deluder Act was a future-vision affirming that the Devil could be defeated, young minds purified, and it contributed to the birth of public education.)
7. Death of Words (or meaningful, shared, and accurate communication)
8. Death of Shared Meaning and the Ascent of Tribalism, Spin, and Conflict—or Apathy
9. Death of Authentic Freedom and Free Speech (for many) and the Acceleration of Conflict

10. Death of Civilization via Decay, Stagnation, Apathy, Balkanization, Anarchy, Conflict, or Totalitarianism—the options are many

11. Death of "America"—or any meaningful resemblance to the Judeo-Christian influenced and framed American experiment

This present work makes no attempt to resolve all the contentious issues related to the definition of terms and the precise nature of civilizational drift or cultural evolution or devolution. What is clear is that in the West and a global and digitized culture ever influenced by the West, stages six through nine seem to capture the spirit of the times (or *Zeitgeist*) today. What is clear as we look to the future of faith communities, church and state, in view of the present cultural barometer, is that enhanced intentionality concerning the usage and definitions of terms, concepts, and meanings (semantics) is essential to the future of orthodox mission and ministry.

Believers incapable of seeing through the redefinition of terms are vulnerable to false belief and practices. They are, according to Ephesians 4:14, "tossed here and there by waves and carried about by every wind of doctrine, by the trickery of men, by craftiness in deceitful scheming." Judeo-Christian polemics (i.e., preserving biblical and Christian orthodoxy inside of the church) and apologetics (i.e., making the case for biblical and orthodox beliefs inside of faith communities) are increasingly allied with word usage and definitions (semantics). This alliance is especially important in an age of accelerating word spin amidst an information explosion and proliferating and privatized, personalized, and digitized sources of "truth." This verbal "Vietnam" has only deepened in our so-called relativistic postmodern or ultramodern era.

Evangelicals and orthodox believers of many faith traditions incapable of surfing the ever-shifting and Promethean word meanings of the present moment risk being unfaithful to Scripture and risk their missional effectiveness. This drift and decline includes the effectiveness of evangelism, missions, spiritual formation, holiness formation, cultural influence, biblical orthodoxy, and religious ethics.

Pastors, priests, and rabbis will be indispensable leaders of semantic apologetics and polemics in this and future generations. These pastors and leaders will protect and shape the church and impact culture. Prometheus (the shapeshifter of Greek mythology) lurks in the semantic shadows both inside and outside of faith communities; hence, this work proffers the new and carefully integrated sub-disciplines of semantic apologetics and polemics to assist with the greater apologetic and polemic mission of Judeo-Christian faith communities.

Relative to polemics, the remaining churches and denominations and religions committed to Scriptural orthodoxy will drift over time, issue-by-issue, if clarion definitions of terms and concepts are not provided by clergy leadership and reinforced relationally and ecclesially. Much rests on the shoulders of preaching, teaching, and modeling relative to polemics and apologetics.

As noted and as will be demonstrated, effective semantic apologetics and polemics are interwoven and inseparable. The correct and biblically based definitions for terms such as compassion, justice, marriage, toleration, and inclusiveness—not to mention Jesus, Trinity, and the Second Coming—are imperative for the future of faith communities and civilization, and each domain influences the other. The traffic moves in both directions between culture and faith communities. This challenge is not entirely new, as will be made evident, yet contemporary cultural and philosophical realities have raised the challenge to a new level.

The Death of Words: A Prophetic Visual

The 1966 cover of *Time* magazine trumpeted the query, "Is God Dead?" Billy Graham reportedly quipped that such a metaphysical posture was impossible because "I just spoke with Him this morning." In 2017 *Time* magazine, duplicating the simple 1966 cover style, asked "Is Truth Dead?" If God and truth are dead, then the corollary question today is whether meaningful communication is also dead. Is communication dead? Is the pursuit of truth via words dead? Is the quest for truth and semantic clarity dead? In a world without God and truth, are words little more than evolutionary belches by organisms willing the power to dominate others (Nietzsche), or dominate other tribes, survive and thrive? *Are words dead?*

From *Time*. © 1966, 2017. Time USA LLC. All rights reserved. Used under license. (Time and TIME USA LLC. are not affiliated with, and do not endorse products or services of Douglas Matthews or the publisher of this work.)

The thrust of the 2017 *Time* issue was more political and less of the profoundly philosophical, cultural, and theological reflection reflected in the title "Is God Dead?" However, Nancy Gibbs, editor of the 2017 magazine, did refer to this issue as more than a mere critique of a sitting US president and at least touching on a "meta-debate" about truth. This 2017 issue did not fully grasp the significance of the truth question for our day, focused on the alleged distortions of a current president, did not entirely grasp the relationship between the two questions, utterly failed to acknowledge such falsity in the media (including *Time*), and failed to connect God, truth, and semantics—much less the future of civilization.

Indeed, and this especially applies to evident political hypoc-risy, it is more than ironic and sardonic to be lamenting the death of truth by political opponents while self-righteously ignoring the log in one's own eyes. However, the attention given to the "death of truth," while the concept and implications are distorted, is appro-priate and receiving increasing attention in many areas of culture.

Jack Grove, in an article entitled "US Watchdogs Face 'Crisis' in Post-Truth Age," documented the post-truth analysis of Dr. Judith Eaton, president of the "Council for Higher Education Accreditation (CHEA), which recognizes 85 independent accredi-tation bodies operating in the US." Dr. Eaton referred to the current "'world of post-truth, fake news and alternative facts' [that] had also made it 'difficult' for expert [accreditation and assessment] communities to function as arbiters of quality, both in higher edu-cation and outside it."[113]

However, while this current discussion could spark a healthy cultural dialog concerning norms for truth, references to the "death of truth" are hardly new, and the issue has been previously analyzed with much more depth and acumen.[114] It is somewhat incongruent to hear progressive educational, political, and media luminaries lamenting prejudice, bias, and the death of truth! Even former President Obama weighed in by mourning the loss of "objective truth," which naturally created a firestorm of allegations of extreme hypocrisy his by critics on the right.[115] First, the critics rolled out endless examples of what they believed were made up lies and shameless spin during the Obama administration. Second, they were especially incensed that anyone on the left, known today for assuming or promoting relativism, would be decrying the loss of objective truth. Regardless of the merits of their arguments, one thing is certain. The seeming loss of a shared standard for truth and ethics—the polarizing loss of our civilizational glue—is evident to all. The reality of the death of God, truth, and words is upon us.

Nevertheless, just like Caiaphas (John 11:49–52), *Time* has unwittingly and visually prophesied and diagnosed the present moment well, even if *Time*'s content is somewhat philosophically incomplete and anemic. Perhaps, inadvertently, *Time* has chronolog-ically and properly connected two interrelated, culturally defining, and paradigmatic questions for the present age, and pointed toward a seminal question of this present work, "Are Words Dead?"

Has meaningful communication expired, since there is no standard or cultural cohesiveness within which dialog can take place? There is no suggestion that words will cease to exist. The question is whether the constructive and meaningful usage of words is in jeopardy. And is the resulting cacophony, confusion, chaos, and conflict suggestive of a civilization in peril? In the American context, if "America" is completely redefined by the emerging semantic universes, does it not follow that "America," at least the "America" of the original "American" experiment, is now facing disintegration or extinction? Perhaps future *Time* magazine covers, if the magazine is philosophically and theologically perceptive, will probe three questions. Are words, free speech, and "America" dead?

These artist sketches are used with the written permission of the artist, Marcia J. Crots, and TIME magazine. © TIME USA LLC.

The Tribalistic Abuse of Words as Sheer Power

Taking these questions together—"Are God and truth dead?"—is profoundly telling. As cultural, civilizational, philosophical, and religious commentary on the present relativizing, globalizing, and digitizing generation, these questions expose the pillars of the current semantic quagmire. These queries also reveal the fountainhead of much of the shameless and militant usage of words for tribalistic advocacy. We must ask,

- Post-God and post-truth, have words become little more than plastic and manipulating sounds disconnected from any definition of truth that rises above personal or tribal interest?
- Is justice forevermore "just us"?
- Is compassionate justice defined however any group or individual so desires?
- Is *civilization* an aspirational ideal or an oppressive Western nightmare?
- Are the legion accusations of *"ophobias"* legitimate criticisms of bigotry and prejudice or a tribal based, deceptive and imperialistic means to derail thoughtful reflection and dialog?
- Are inclusion and diversity Christian concepts grounded in biblical love, compassion, and John the Revelator's "every tribe, tongue and nation" vision (Revelation 5), or have these very terms been hijacked to undermine the influence of the in-breaking Christian *eschaton?*
- Should not the love of diversity include both racial diversity and a diversity of ideas?
- Have semantics and communication entered a self-referential and self-contained infinity of mirrors?
- Is there a plumb line for the use of contested terms and phrases, and, if so, what is the plumb line and how can it be applied amidst legion competing interests and advocacy groups?
- To what degree are faith communities *in* the world and *of* (or not of) the world relative to the definition and usage of words (semantics)?
- Are the followers of the Word leaders in shaping the words that define and norm church and culture?
- What are the consequences of Promethean word morphing for the future of faith and culture?

Yes, the attempt to nail down the precise meaning of terms and phrases, from the beginning of human history, to the Sophists, to the Kafkian and Foucauldian present, has sometimes resembled whack-a-mole or the chasing of a mirage. Nietzsche is renowned for referring to words and communication as the endless reflections of mirrors divorced from normative truth or meaning. Politicians and lawyers of all ages have oft been accused of opportunistically manipulating the definition of terms and utilizing seductive spin—even parsing what the "definition of *is* is" in order to obfuscate.

The question today is whether we have taken semantic ambiguity and manipulation to a new and dangerous level? Is unprincipled semantic manipulation becoming the norm and a symptom of the emerging cultural death of God and truth?

The Semantic Quagmire

Contemporary verbal gyrations now seemingly dance in a novel and untethered post-God and post-truth context, unanswerable to any norm or judge. The Judeo-Christian conception and experience of God, defined as transcendent, immanent, personal, and self-revealing, is vanishing on the horizon and often no longer serves as the inspirational center that binds us and guides us. Spirituality is in, but as the neoorthodox theologians suggested long ago, God-talk or theology has seemingly been redefined today as speaking endlessly about ourselves, our feelings, our needs, and our desires—via digitized and amplified loud voices.

Both relativistic spirituality and militant political and cultural advocacy today no longer seem concerned with a transcendent, cross-cultural measuring rod revealed to the apostles and prophets. The subjective world and preferences of the self or tribe serve as the only "plumb line."

Words and religious experience are not obligated to conform to anything beyond personal truth, much less divine revelation. Words just are. Words are mere tools, or weapons. They are means to achieve personal or tribal outcomes, not means to align with a truth and reality greater than themselves, or sign-posts directing us to who we should be or the nature of the ideal kingdom.

The gloves are off in public discourse. Word definitions and usages may be altered at will to *persuade or manipulate or silence* — not to dialog genuinely about or uncover what is true and ethical. We used to seek to discover Truth and knowledge. Today we create truth based on personal or tribal interests. Words are means to move others to action, or shout down and silence those with unacceptable words, perspectives, or alternative desired personal or social outcomes.

The verbal quagmire is upon us — or perhaps we are fully immersed in it. Ravi Zacharias's oft-quoted proverb may be most relevant: "if you want to know what water is, don't ask a fish."

This emerging semantic universe is not associated only with a single group; it may well be the emerging dominant culture and civilization. Everyone is accused of spin, verbal manipulation, and fake news, and no one seems to understand why we are accelerating and plummeting toward fragmentation, conflict, and a semantic and, at least potentially, a civilizational abyss.

The Twenty-First Century Mission of God and Church

This work has emphasized the importance of how a variety of faith communities can assist or work with each other in keeping faith communities faithful and positively impacting culture.

The Christian church is especially needful of attention given its prominence in public life in the American context. For the historically and biblically orthodox church,[116] including the American evangelical church, centered in the Savior and deeply rooted in a very high view of inspired, written Scripture, much is at stake.

Evangelicals should be servants of the Word (both written and the personal, living Logos) and masters of words. The biblical church is animated by the good news of salvation by grace and the restoration of the image of God. The very mission of the church (and the mission of God or *Missio Dei*) totters on the edge, including the preservation of biblical Christian orthodoxy within the church. Such preservation requires impassioned, tactful, semantic polemics.

The state is in danger if the church disintegrates. The immense resources from American philanthropy or charity, given to religious causes and to the world, including Christian missions, would likely be impacted by a defection to a post-Christian or pseudo-Christian future. Other religious traditions, such as Judaism, should be equally concerned about this cultural and religious drift.

Christian influence on civilization and the constructive engagement of contemporary challenges to the faith outside of the church (i.e., apologetics) are in peril.[117] Evangelism, church-planting and disciple-making hinge on effective semantics. The evangelical church faces a historic crisis and opportunity at a time when many, even American evangelicals, herald the loss of the evangelical culture wars.[118] Fortunately, current realities, while novel in some respects, are not unprecedented, and lessons from the past (the early church, or nineteenth-century theology) should prove instructive.

Hence, increased semantic intentionality relative to apologetics and polemics is most timely and urgent. *We are in a semantic crisis.* It is arguable that never before in the history of the church have semantic polemics and apologetics been so vital. I hope this present work serves as a primer for such a mammoth and challenging task and attempts to provide Christian academics, leaders, pastors, priests, and informed laity with preliminary tools as we navigate the accelerating semantic headwinds.

It would seem that every term is being modified today because their definitions ultimately emerge from an underlying convergence of passion and thought, and passion and thought today are fermenting. A 2018 Supreme Court decision, "MASTERPIECE CAKESHOP, LTD., ET AL. v. COLORADO CIVIL RIGHTS COMMISSION ET AL.," is instructive.[119]

The Masterpiece Baker and The Colorado Butcher

The Supreme Court's narrow decision supporting the evangelical baker's refusal to bake a wedding cake for a gay wedding illustrates how shifting semantic universes redefine assumptions, terms, word usage, ethics, law, and culture. All is connected. The baker won the case because the Colorado Civil Rights Commission butchered the free speech rights and free exercise of religion of the baker. Justice Kennedy, speaking for the court, concluded, "When the Colorado Civil Rights Commission considered this case, it did not do so with the religious neutrality that the Constitution requires."[120]

I will again largely defer to legal experts on legal matters, as with the legal nuances of the Supreme Court's redefinition of marriage. However, my theological and philosophical training suggests that the philosophical, theological, and semantic confusion of the court is striking, if not stunning.

First, the false myth of religious neutrality is as naïve in the twenty-first century as it was in the eighteenth century at the birth of the republic. Today, the hidden prejudice in most legal decisions is typically post Judeo-Christian, and the bias is secular or pluralistic. For nearly two centuries in America, Judeo-Christian assumptions undergirded the judiciary and the whole of culture. We must understand that pluralism today tends to mean the acceptance of anything but the Judeo-Christian perspective. As noted in the front matter and Preface, Os Guinness referred to this as an "ABC" cultural moment.

In the eighteenth century of Jonathan Edwards intellectual honesty and awareness, and philosophical acumen, were much greater, and "neutrality" was in reference to not favoring or establishing any Jewish or Christian denomination or sect. This did not mean that atheism or polytheism were built into the warp and woof of the law and culture of the American experiment, or that such perspectives were to guide or undergird the republic or frame the definition of marriage. This role for polytheism and atheism stood in very stark contrast to the normative role of Judeo-Christian beliefs, practices, and culture relative to the experiment.

It is one thing to allow atheists and polytheists to have free speech *because* of Judeo-Christian charity and tolerance. It is quite another thing to allow atheism or polytheism to guide the state, law, and culture, to define marriage or "religious neutrality," and to replace the Judeo-Christian civilizational assumptions and pillars of the American experiment. It is one thing to allow Satan worship because of Judeo-Christian charity and tolerance. It is quite another thing to equate Satan and Christ in the name of religious neutrality or the nonestablishment of religion or let Satanism, whether metaphorical or supernatural Satanism, shape the contours of our civilization. Polytheists, atheists, and Satanists should literally "thank God," meaning the monotheistic Judeo-Christian God, for the freedom of the American experiment.

Chapter 3 will advance this argument, but the assumptions, and often the principles and practices, of law, ethics, culture, and republican political democracy in the eighteenth century were clearly Judeo-Christian influenced. This conclusion is not even a close call. This conclusion is inescapable for anyone familiar with the key documents and literature of that era, which will be referenced in Chapter 3. Was Enlightenment thought influential during the birth of the America? Of course. Yet Judeo-Christian assumptions undergirded far more of the American experiment than the Enlightenment, especially the radical Enlightenment, both in the era of the Pilgrims and Puritans, and after the first Great Awakening that laid the foundation for the American Revolution. Only the uninformed or those trying to redefine "America" and mutate—not just enhance—the American experiment would suggest otherwise, or repeat the verifiably false claim that "almost all the founders were Deists or atheists."[121]

Neutrality never was and never can be absolute or totally neutral. Postmodernists, of all people, should know this well. Neutrality is something we approximate and neutrality is defined by its semantic universe. In the case of the original American experiment the concepts of toleration and neutrality were defined by the Enlightenment *and* Judeo-Christian hybrid context. This myth of secular neutrality is extremely naïve in view of: human nature, psychology and sociology; postmodern insights on bias, prejudice, and word usage; mountains of historical evidence; and even semantics or the way we use and define terms like "neutrality" or "marriage."

Today, neutrality often means "ABC" and a rejection of Judeo-Christian influence on civilization, whereas in the eighteenth century it was assumed that nearly omnipresent Judeo-Christian values, or, as they put it, "religion and morality," served as a core requisite that made democracy *possible*—along with the possibility of some measure of tolerance and neutrality toward religious sects and denominations! "Marriage" was monogamous, heterosexual, and the heterosexual family unit or ideal was viewed as a key and indispensable pillar of a tolerant, Judeo-Christian influenced civilization. Today, marriage and gender are increasingly becoming a matter of subjective, personal preference. Marriage—as with morality in general—is defined by the user and by the moment. Our civilization is rushing toward moral and legal solipsism—the belief that the self is the ultimate reality and standard. This vapid trajectory will ultimately destroy law and civilization. Hence, in the Western democracies we are traversing from *Lex Rex* (eternal Law is King) to *Self as Law* ("me" or "self" is Law), which may ultimately return us to *Rex Lex*.

I'm not a Latin specialist, but a colleague versed in Latin suggested *Lex Ego Sum*. Hence, "Self or me is the Law," or "I myself am law" would capture this concept. Self could also be expanded to "my tribe" is the law. Civilizational solipsism is an extreme philosophical concept and will likely never exist,[122] but the concept catches the irrational spirit of where we are headed, and points out why experiments in anarchy are never sustainable or realistic. And, if Schaeffer is right, they eventually invite authoritarian versions of *Rex Lex* (the king or government is the Law) in order to fill the vacuum.

Hence, while the Supreme Court got it right that the baker's free exercise of religion was being compromised by the prejudice and animus of the Colorado Civil Rights Commission butcher, they are more than naïve to think that such matters can be resolved by an appeal to a so-called objective and secular standard of neutrality that somehow exists in an unbiased and unprejudiced void. Is the Supreme Court aware that rationalistic modernism is on life-support for some very good reasons?

Marriage is a term that exists within one semantic universe or another that is absolutely brimming with theological, philosophical, ethical, historical, legal, and cultural assumptions and precedents. The suggestion that marriage, this fundamental building block of civilization, can be defined by "just any" semantic universe or reduced to issues of personal preference, mere legal precedents, or equal rights only draws attention to intellectually dishonest semantic smuggling, historical myopia, and theological and philosophical bankruptcy. Yet for many the personal preference approach to defining marriage is because they have been verbally seduced by these new semantic sirens.

So, yes, the butcher was biased, and the baker should bake his heterosexual wedding cakes, but the referee for such matters should properly frame the definition of marriage within the context of the semantic universe of the original American experiment. Is the Supreme Court aware that some of the ethical extremes of the Enlightenment were reversed by the First Great Awakening in America on the eve of American independence and the construction of key founding documents? America is not a secular republican democracy, and only historical revisionism would define "America" in such terms.

The baker seemingly got it right—on every level—concerning the historical, legal, and ethical definition of marriage, and should not suffer coercion concerning his free exercise of religion, or, more critically, censure for his "American" understanding and definition of marriage. Gay marriage was largely unthinkable only a decade ago, even by progressives, because our civilization was still normed, to some degree, by the semantic universe of the *Judeo-Christian* American experiment in republican democracy. There must be an ethical, legal, and cultural standard in such matters and proper definitions. The standard should be the semantic universe of the authentic American experiment, not the unstable and foundationless semantic universe of the emerging post or anti Judeo-Christian culture. It is not too late to restore Judeo-Christian influence. Faith communities have faced much more challenging contexts out of which faith inspired cultural influence emerged than the current American context where many opportunities for speech and influence still exist.

The issue of slavery is often presented as a wedge strategy to suggest that the founding vision was flawed and needs to be replaced. Slavery will be addressed in this chapter, but first let's clarify the nature of semantic universes.

The Semantic Universes

Especially critical relative to the apologetic and polemic task of this work is the recognition of these organically or systemically connected verbal or semantic universes and the connected space that these contested terms occupy. Conflicts over words are symptomatic and illustrative of a much deeper conflict between semantic universes. Semantic universes issue forth from deeper belief systems, worldviews, passions, and cultural liturgies. Semantic universes *see* and *feel* things differently, including the definition of controversial words and concepts such as marriage, inclusivism, "America," or toleration.

Even in a progressively syncretistic and post-truth culture, where values and beliefs are chosen buffet style to advance personal or tribal interests, word definitions naturally cluster together. Such is the nature of language, communication, and humanity. The Bible, though written over centuries, is a relatively tight semantic universe, which is why evangelicals insist on interpreting Scripture by Scripture. The Bible was "a" or "the" dominant influence in the birth of the American experiment, influencing cultural understandings of key terms such as marriage or toleration. *Pilgrim's Progress* also was most influential as America was emerging. The McGuffey Readers series laced with Scripture and biblical morality trained generations of children from the 1830s to the 1960s. *Uncle Tom's Cabin* framed the struggle for liberation that issued forth into an American war. All of these books were dripping and oozing with biblical influence. Most radiated biblical eschatology. For centuries the American semantic universe was relatively coherent and unified.

This work directly addresses the varied uses of key terms relative to the Judeo-Christian and evangelical Christian apologetic and civilizational task. The many and conflicting definitions today are either symptoms of a diseased semantic universe or the fruit of a biblically influenced semantic universe (or some combination thereof).

John Wesley used to discuss his definition of and cure for sin in terms of "fruit" and "root," and affirmed that ignoring the root was fatal for individuals and churches seeking authentic and sustainable

Christlikeness or holiness. Similarly, the following discussion must be framed within the context of the fruit and root of a cosmic semantic shift and conflict—foundational semantic universes or verbal worlds in conflict (the roots) that will write the pages of future history (the fruit). Focusing on these semantic universes reveals or smokes out the underlying passions, convictions, beliefs, practices, cultural liturgies, and worldviews that have shaped the past, and will shape the present and the future.

Wittgenstein and many postmodernists wrongly detached words and communication from a Logocentric, Word-centered, or Christ-centered Trinitarian universe where words truly have correspondent meaning relative to reality and the divine perspective on reality, yet they were correct in noting that words and terms exist in an almost symbiotic (even systemic or organic) relation to each other. The semantic universe of the early American experiment, reflected in terms such as freedom, liberation, morality, Christian nation, marriage, and family, has largely been supplanted by a post-Christian or even anti-Christian semantic universe that redefines virtually each and every term. This introductory and simple Table 2.3 is illustrative (also see Chapter 9 and Appendix A) of semantic changes in the American context, and underscores the organic nature of the American experiment's semantic universe.

Table 2.3. Introductory Semantic Comparisons

Term	Typical Meaning Consistent with the Original American Experiment	Emerging Meanings Today
Marriage	Heterosexual, monogamous	Subjective, non-binary, possibly and temporarily monogamous
Tolerance	A hybrid Judeo-Christian and enlightenment conception	Relativistic, post Judeo-Christian, guided by the myth of neutrality
Truth	Eternally grounded, revealed in reason and Scripture and guided by reason and experiment	Absolute truth claims are dangerous, hence viewed as pragmatic, subjective, cultural
Inclusion or Inclusive	Judeo-Christian in nature, even eschatological, and rooted in the restoration of the image of God, plus Christ's death for all, in many Christian traditions	Relativistic, post-Christian and often excludes traditional Judeo-Christian beliefs and practices
Patriotism or Patriotic	Non-idolatrous support of the original American freedom experiment *under* God	Supportive of a New America and new "just" vision for America, fearful that patriotism is idolatrous nationalism, and many now affirm open borders

Term	Typical Meaning Consistent with the Original American Experiment	Emerging Meanings Today
Compassionate social justice	Defined by biblical and enlightenment values, personal opportunity and responsibility, and limited government	Typically guided by centralized governmental solutions, distributions, and entitlements
Freedom and freedom of speech	Framed and defined within Judeo-Christian values and responsible freedom	Framed by post Judeo-Christian values, relativism and pluralism, sometimes restrictive of Judeo-Christian speech

Before concluding this chapter, the slavery argument against the American experiment and semantic universe must be addressed. The critic will, of course, predictably bring up the issue and worn-out argument of slavery in order to invalidate the above comparisons. In other words, colonial slavery demonstrates that the founders and the American experiment were not truly for equality. The American experiment included slavery in its definition of freedom, it is suggested, and therefore it is justifiable to redefine the key terms of the American experiment.

First, the critics are confusing the practices of fallen individuals with the eternal principles guiding the experiment.

Second, even if their argument is sound, there is a vast difference and consequence between re-defining or enhancing and clarifying one phrase (e.g., all men are created equal means all human beings), and redefining *all* terms, which is where things are headed. It is arguable that at some point the redefinition of terms reaches a critical mass and the original American experiment is dead. For example, the Republican party could embrace some of the principles of the Democratic platform, but at some point acceptance of most of the Democratic platform would mean that the Republican party would have abandoned its own vision and, in effect, it would no longer exist other than in name only.

Third, and more fundamentally, however, the real question, which was debated by the founding fathers themselves, was whether slavery was consistent with the vision of the American experiment? For pragmatic reasons (e.g., keeping the colonies together on the eve of war), and misguided personal reasons, slavery was allowed to continue. For theological and philosophical reasons, the case can certainly be made that slavery was abolished in principle or seed form in the Declaration of Independence and the Constitution of the United States. George Washington noted that one of his "first wishes" was "to see some plan by which slavery in this country may be abolished by law." (See Federer, *America's*) Should all of the slave-holding founders have freed their slaves? Certainly, if managed well, but it is odd that today's cultural relativists are often the loudest critics of the cultural realities and political challenges of eighteenth century America. On a related note, since American sexism is also used to invalidate the founders and the experiment, it should be noted that revival influenced evangelicals led abolitionist and feminist movements in nineteenth century America based on Scripture and the founding documents. They called America back to its core principles, as did Harriet Beecher Stowe in *Uncle Tom's Cabin*. Indeed, Christian revivalism was central to virtually every social reform movement in nineteenth century America.[123]

The Fallacy of Equivocation and the Future of Civilization

A key point in this work is that the same terms can have very different meanings and applications, or entirely different meanings, *and their definitions and usages are all connected or co-dependent.* Hence, the American experiment is misinterpreted apart from the semantic universe of that experiment. Today verbal redefinitions are being used to reshape faith communities, church and state. All terms are at risk. Such redefinitions result in a near communication breakdown (and uncivil verbal warfare) between the two or more worlds or universes in conflict. Effective apologetics and polemics can bridge the worlds and assist with preserving and advancing orthodoxy and orthopraxy in faith communities, civilizational influence, civil behavior, and via apologetic and evangelistic persuasion and impact. Effective apologetics and polemics likewise sustains, advances, and applies orthopathy to the ecclesial and cultural semantic task. But this task will fail unless proper attention is given to the pervasive verbal equivocation today in church and state.

I taught logical fallacies for over a decade, and in logic the informal fallacy of equivocation is when the same words are used ambiguously, or with different definitions, whether intentionally or not. This fallacy seductively persuades someone to accept an illogical conclusion. One meaning of a term is used or assumed in one part of the argument, then a shift takes place and a slightly different or very different meaning of the term is used or smuggled in to another part of the argument.

Here is one classic example: "Logic helps you argue better, but do we really need to encourage people to argue?" One meaning of the reference to argue or argument means argumentative, whereas the intended meaning here of argue or argument is simply referencing how to present fair or logically sound arguments. Or, to connect the widespread verbal equivocation shell game today to our discussion, here is another example: "How dare you question my patriotism for America! I am fighting for an America that is just, free, and inclusive, takes care of everyone, and therefore which has eradicated all Judeo-Christian influence." The verbal equivocation on patriotism and "America" is used to persuade the reader that one can be patriotic and love America even if the founding American vision is completely eradicated. This would be like someone saying he or she is a true Roman Catholic even though they reject virtually everything Roman Catholicism affirms, because they have a new and better vison for Roman Catholicism. In reality, Roman Catholicism has been redefined out of existence.

The fallacy of equivocation is on steroids today, as verbal gyrations are constantly being used to redefine reality. If American history were a Star Wars drama, the fallacy of equivocation would clearly be one of the main and most effective weapons of the dark side. Or in the terms of C S. Lewis and his *Screwtape Letters*, seductive semantic equivocation is the enemy's best friend.

Perhaps it is preferable and more intellectually honest for those proposing a new vision of the future simply and openly to use new or different terms. In the American context, referencing neo-America or post-American America would at least reflect integrity by the advocates of an utter revision of the experiment. Chapter 4 will document how, in the Christian church, such wholesale redefinitions of key terms and Christian beliefs mainstreamed in countless denominations in the modern era. Chapters 5–9 will demonstrate how the fallacy of equivocation has engulfed and enticed Western civilization while also proffering solutions.

It should be emphasized that some verbal equivocators have been seduced by the prevailing and intoxicating semantic universe. This especially seems to be the case within religious communities.

The proliferation of such verbal seduction generates seductive semantic universes, even within faith communities, that are somewhat analogous to what Scripture refers to as having a veil over one's heart, ears, mind, and eyes. Jesus, grounded in the Old Testament, refers to his very religious generation as incapable of truly hearing and seeing. He even asks his own disciples, "Do you have eyes but fail to see, and ears but fail to hear? And don't you remember?" (Mark 8:18). Yet for those followers who were beginning to see through the fog, he affirms, "But blessed are your eyes because they see, and your ears because they hear" (Matthew 13:16).

For example, Jesus affirmed that both his followers and the religious leaders of his day had redefined the concept of "Messiah" such that they could not recognize the true Messiah who was standing before them. "O foolish men and slow of heart to believe in all that the prophets have spoken!" (Luke 24:25). The combination of spiritual blindness, hard heartedness, and a false definition of the Messiah—and many related terms (e.g., Abraham's "children," John 8:39–47)—veiled the true Messiah to an entire faith community that was eagerly expecting the Messiah.

Similarly, Paul underscored such seduction within his faith community of birth concerning the true definition of the Messiah: "But to this day whenever Moses is read, a veil lies over their heart; but whenever a person turns to the Lord, the veil is taken away. Now the Lord is the Spirit, and where the Spirit of the Lord is, there is liberty. But we all, with unveiled face, beholding as in a mirror the glory of the Lord, are being transformed into the same image from glory to glory, just as from the Lord, the Spirit" (2 Corinthians 3:15–18).

I hope this work serves as essential reading for all Christian leaders, educators, religious leaders, and pastors. Laity should request that every teachable pastor or rabbi committed to Judeo-Christian values and Scripture work proper word definitions into preaching, teaching, and writing. Informed and culturally engaged evangelical and historically orthodox laity should also benefit from grasping the core concepts of this work.

Professors teaching theology or Christian apologetics courses may be assisted by this supplemental text. Pastors and priests should be able to protect the flock (polemics) better, more effectively engage the culture (apologetics), and enhance evangelism and church planting (apologetic evangelism) with assistance from this primer. Informed Christian laity should find this material helpful relative to constructive cultural, political, and civilizational engagement. Laity are being targeted by sophisticated semantic seduction and need to be prepared.

This work is self-consciously written in and for an American context but is aware of issues such as Ameri-centrism and ethno-centrism. This book, as noted, focuses on the American context, but also makes global applications relative to semantic apologetics and polemics. Such global issues are not neglected but are also not the focus of this work. If the argument of this text is affirmed by some of our global brothers and sisters, the task remains for others to improve, translate, and apply this material to multitudinous and interdependent global contexts.

A mammoth but manageable educational task lies before the American evangelical church and American religious communities of faith relative to semantic polemics and apologetics. The

Judeo-Christian faithful are confused and drifting—lured by the semantic sirens of an alternate universe.[124] Yet the opportunity for kingdom advance in such a context is truly unparalleled.

Ask Yourself or Your Group

- *How do you agree or disagree with the author's view of how the Time magazine images tell the story of our present and future (Death of God, Truth, Words, Free Speech, America)?*
- *What was the point of discussing Ninotchka relative to the purpose and argument of the book and chapter? How might "Social Justice" be a Trojan Horse today? What has been your experience with "Social Justice"?*
- *What does it mean to say that words are not true but only means of power?*
- *Why does the author believe that the Supreme Court was very confused when debating the Masterpiece Baker case? What is a semantic universe or family and how does it relate to Supreme Court deliberations and decisions?*
- *What is the significance of the Oxford Dictionaries naming "post-truth" as the 2016 international word of the year? Did the Washington Post get it right by commenting on this word of the year by saying, "It's official: Truth is dead. Facts are passé." Is Oxford's Casper Grathwohl correct in suggesting that "post-truth" could become "one of the defining words of our time"? Did Oxford get it right when defining our age and "post-truth" as a context in which "people respond more to feelings and beliefs than to facts"?*

Chapter 3

SEMANTIC APOLOGETICS OR CIVILIZATIONAL SURRENDER?

But sanctify Christ as Lord in your hearts, always being
ready to make a defense [apologian] to everyone who asks
you to give an account for the hope that is in you, yet with
gentleness and reverence.
— 1 Peter 3:15

Culture Wars

Some believe that the culture war has been lost in the West or in America.[125] Regardless of the diagnosis, given the warp speed of the digital globalization and the flow of information, the rapidity of political shifts, and the continuing and profound American international influence, evangelical and Judeo-Christian semantic apologetics may have a critical role to play in the future of both Western and non-Western civilization(s). Indeed, the abandonment of the civilizational quest in view of Western or American decay ignores the possible role and globally significant impact of the remaining biblical faith communities in America. The relationship between faith communities across the globe should be characterized by reciprocal influence and partnering together for kingdom influence in an ultramodern syncretistic age.

Focusing entirely on the American context also ignores current missiological trends suggesting that vibrant evangelical and orthodox Judeo-Christian expansion is largely not in the West. Most expansion is in what missiologists often refer to as the "majority world." Hence, the focus of the American church should be faithfulness and optimizing future missional impact in our syncretistic context rather than the current state of civilizational decline.

This non-Western expansion especially suggests that *this is not the time to obsess or lament over whether orthodox Judeo-Christian communities have lost or are losing the culture war* in America or the West. The global semantic task is missional and lessons from the syncretistic context of early Christianity may serve as the key to effectiveness in the present.

Early Church Apologetics and Polemics

Two classic examples of Christian semantic and apologetic engagement in the syncretistic historical context of the early church concern the common allegations that Christians were *atheists* and practiced *cannibalism*, even incestuous cannibalism. Justin Martyr observes, "Thus we are called atheists."[126] Tertullian, Justin Martyr, Origen, Athenagoras, Octavius, and Theophilus all reference this semantic and cannibalistic distortion of the Eucharist and Love Feasts, and many have recounted the Christian apologetic interactions with and responses to the critics.[127] These early church verbal conflicts, however, were not limited to unpacking the allegations of cannibalism and incest (see Table 3.1). To this list could be added many other allegations, some of which especially hinged on semantic distortions (e.g., atheism, lack of patriotic nationalism, the killing of children in the Eucharist, antisocial behavior, and orgies).

In Augustine's day, of course, a central apologetic and semantic challenge was to respond to the allegation that Christianity had destroyed or led to the punishment or decline of the great Roman civilization. Sound familiar today? Hence, we now have an apologetic for the ages in the form of Augustine's *The City of God*.

Philosophy has often been described as the handmaiden of theology. Regardless of the accuracy of this characterization, this present work especially will emphasize the importance, relevance, and utility of employing philosophy alongside Logocentric, biblical, historical, and systematic Christian theology in the task of re-sanctifying words, concepts, and meaningful communication. Philosophers can be of great assistance, and robust and intricate philosophical semiotics is welcomed, but legitimate semantics and communication must primarily be rooted in a theology birthed by divine revelation.[128] The early church and Augustine sometimes drifted too far into Hellenistic influence in the name of apologetics, thus creating issues for polemics. At their best, early Christian apologists and polemicists were driven by faithfulness to divine revelation in response to apologetic and polemic challenges. They defended the church, and the constructive role of Christian influence on civilization. The challenges in the early church were many, some of which are listed in Table 3.1.

Table 3.1. Early Church and Augustinian Semantic Apologetics and Polemics

Disputed Terms, Concepts, and Sematic Clusters	Allegation and Semantic Distortion	Apologetic [and Polemic] Corrective
1. Cannibalism, infanticide	Christians initiate their services by consuming the flesh and blood of children.	Christians only consume wine and bread, and Christians not only oppose infanticide but also abortion, in contrast to pagans, in view of the *imago Dei* and sacredness of human life.

Disputed Terms, Concepts, and Sematic Clusters	Allegation and Semantic Distortion	Apologetic [and Polemic] Corrective
2. Incest and orgies	Christians meet in secret to engage in kissing, orgies, and incestuous love feasts.	Christians do not always meet in secret, have no official buildings largely due to persecution, love one another spiritually and sacrificially (not physically) as brother and sister by the command of Christ, and greet one another with a holy non-sensual kiss.
3. Atheism	Christians are atheists who deny the gods.	Christians deny false gods (polytheism) but serve the living God (monotheism) who made all things. Jews are usually allowed to worship one God and we serve the same God, so why not grant Christian believers the same freedom?
4. Unpatriotic	Christians refuse to pledge allegiance to the divine Emperor and state and thus undermine society.	Christians affirm that Christ is Lord above all humans and false gods, including deified and immoral rulers, and pledge themselves to love and sacrificial service of all (hence no killing of any kind), which enhances and preserves the state.

5. Uneducated, poor, antisocial, self-righteous	Christians consist of uneducated and gullible women, slaves, and working classes abandoned by their false god to poverty and cultural marginalization, which these strange believers seem to relish.	Christians include scholars, former pagans, and apologists, the wealthy, and even some on Caesar's staff. Most Christians are poor by the world's standards, which keeps some from rushing to be Christians for the wrong reasons, but Christians are also eternally rich. Christians do not oppose the ethical gain of wealth, but Christians are passionate for Christ and not temporary wealth. At the heart of the gospel is the forgiveness of sinners.
6. Decline of the Empire	Christian immorality, atheism, and weakness are responsible for the increasing decline of the empire.	The decline and weakness of the empire is due to increasing pagan immorality and barbarism (rooted in false gods) that is the antithesis of Christianity.
7. Punishment of the Roman Civilization by the gods	The gods are angry at the perverted Christian atheists in the midst of a great empire.	Christians are not atheists and Christians are blamed for everything that goes wrong. Any punishment from above is for rampant and accelerating pagan immorality that stands in stark contrast to the gospel.

Semantics, Apologetics, Polemics, and Civilization

As discussed in the early chapters in this work, a key and largely successful tactical maneuver in this historic conflict is the redefinition, modification, or creation of key terms and phrases that untether conversation and values from foundational biblical moorings and theological assumptions — not to mention any meaningful *after modernity* definition of reason or truth. As noted, the very term "civilization," once an aspirational *telos* or goal and ethical norm, is, via this "word theft" (see Chapter 4) viewed in many quarters as representative of an oppressive Western evil from which some form of liberation is a moral imperative.[129] Verbal equivocation attempts to redefine civilization and rules the day, but it is not a new tactic.

Lewis's contention that the "normal state of humanity is barbarism, just as the normal surface of our planet is salt water," now faces a militant semantic counteroffensive affirming that *civilization*, especially Western civilization, is the true barbarism corrupting the normal state of humanity — corrupting what Hobbes, Locke, Rousseau, and others referred to as the "state of nature." The state of nature is what humanity or human nature allegedly would be like apart from Western civilization. For many, but not Hobbes, Western civilization and even civilization itself, rather than fallen human nature or corrupt values, is the problem and certainly not the solution.

Ultramodern[130] Coates writes, "Vulgar nationalists often point to Europe [European "civilization"] as evidence of something that all humans … strive for — certain civilized ground. And yet the greatest proponents of such certainty, of Utopia, of [European, Anglo or American] exceptionalism, of solutionism, of Stalinism, of Bibles, of Qurans, of great civilization, and complete theories, are so often themselves engineers on the road to barbarism."[131] Hence, for postmodern and dystopian Coates and others, "civilization" is equated with barbarous oppression; Coates expresses exasperation not aspiration relative to the quest for civilization.

What Coates and others fail to see is that the prophetic and sometimes appropriate critique of uncivilized behavior by nations actually presupposes an aspirational civilizational ideal. Unless Coates is a consistent anarchist, the problem is not the quest for civilization. The problem is that most quests are misguided, based on false beliefs and assumptions, hypocritical, utopian, and often barbaric. What Coates should be arguing for is that civilizations should be more civilized and not built on utopian, corrupted Judeo-Christian or post Judeo-Christian sand. Abandoning the aspiration only exacerbates the problem of wayward kingdoms.

Today we have come full circle, from allegations against the early church that Christians are anti-nationalists undermining civilization to contemporary allegations that Western evangelical and conservative Roman Catholic Christian ideology[132] regularly and inevitably commits the sin of nationalism, even vulgar nationalism;[133] therefore, orthodox Christians are dangerous! As with "cannibalism," the unpacking of varied meanings of key terms (e.g., civilization, nationalism, and patriotism) is absolutely essential to orthodox semantic and cultural apologetics.[134]

Post-Christendom and the Benedict Option

Indeed, the faddish term "post-Christendom," which certainly has application to many segments of European culture and civilization, when applied to a very different American experiment and context (with a history of religious voluntarism, ongoing and significant evangelical and Roman Catholic influence), rightly points out some aspects of cultural trending in the United States. Indeed, Roman Catholics often seem to be leading the way in law, media, and scholarship relative to defending Judeo-Christian influence on civilization.

However, post-Christendom, when applied without precision in the American context, quickly short-circuits Judeo-Christian attempts to understand, influence, and meliorate culture and civilization. In other words, by using post-Christendom to describe the American situation today, some are suggesting, perhaps prematurely and recklessly, that significant evangelical, orthodox, biblical influence is now a faint echo, so we should accept this and try something else like the neo-monastic Benedict option.

If America has *arrived* at a post-Christendom state, just like Europe, then perhaps, it is argued, the church should abandon any intentional (even a shrewd and tactful) strategy to be salt and light in culture, politics, law, media, or education and simply adopt the increasingly popular Hauerwasian cultural engagement model to just "be the church," simply and radically.[135]

Hauerwas recoils at Niebuhrian attempts to transform culture. While this sentiment is understandable, it is more than tragic that some are essentially calling for the strategic withdrawal from direct and passionate engagement with culture and politics.[136] This option suggests that the monastic response to Rome's fall may be a helpful model today in view of the decline of culture and civilization.

Similar to Hauerwas, this Benedict option affirms that the church's best shot at impacting culture long-term is to focus on being faithful and modeling Christian love and character even as or if the civilizational pillars crumble. The movement here seems to be moving away from emphasizing direct cultural engagement and conflict to modeling a monastic city or community set on a hill that might lure future generations. Much could be debated concerning this nuanced yet questionable and possibly reductonistic and neo-monastic approach to interfacing with culture. The half-truths are that we should model our faith winsomely and attractively to the world in contrast to the provoking actions of some evangelicals. This Benedict option does not call for total disengagement, but the net effect of such a focus will likely be the same.

Regardless of the Benedict Option's merits, a premature evangelical and orthodox response in America based on a cultural hermeneutic more applicable to Canada or Europe could prove disastrous or become a self-fulfilling prophecy. Loving and tactful cultural and political engagement is imperative. Abandoning the civilizational task because of the inappropriate actions of some communities of faith seems a bit premature. Also, some critics perceive tactful and loving involvement as hateful or culturally imperialistic.

The answer is to be loving, engaged, and prophetic. God has granted American Judeo-Christian believers significant access to cultural influence, power, tremendous resources, and political expression. Many believers are sacrificing much to preserve a more perfect union while parasites are pontificating on strategic cultural withdrawal due to cultural setbacks and criticizing the culturally and politically engaged. To cast aside these divine gifts of the right to vote, use the media and countless means of influence, litigate, and engage is irresponsible. We don't live in ancient Rome and the faithful in that oppressive era still made a difference. Strategic withdrawal will only accelerate mod-rot and post-mod-rot. Cultural drift is not entirely due to tactless Judeo-Christian believers, any more than was the persecution of the early church.

For some, pessimistic eschatology might also be employed to justify a fatalistic and escapist posture. Perhaps, these pessimists might argue, even in a republican democracy where Christians can still hold office and influence education, law, entertainment, and politics, Christians should simply accept a new identity more analogous to Christians living in the catacombs in ancient Rome. Hence, everything is at stake regarding how we use and apply terms such as "post-Christendom." Many may have given up on evangelical and orthodox civilizational and global influence prematurely — perhaps well in advance of the game plan of Divine Providence (see Chapter 10 for a further defense and elaboration of this point).

Decaying Evangelicalism? The Sad Case of Fuller Seminary versus Robert Jeffress

Some American evangelical responses to cultural conflict and presidential politics well illustrate semantic confusion and necessitate an extended conversation. Mark Labberton is president of historic Fuller Seminary which served for decades as the flagship evangelical seminary. It was founded to move beyond American fundamentalism, energize the evangelical movement, and counter liberal theological drift in mainline denominations and seminaries. Labberton has been an outspoken critic of the evangelical response to and embrace of the Trump administration. Robert Jeffress is a Southern Baptist pastor in Dallas with a broad television and radio audience, close connections with the Trump administration, and he has given support to Trump's policies.

Labberton's critique of the broad American evangelical support of Trump, in a document ("Political Dealing: The Crisis....") with the Fuller Seminary official seal, includes representative arguments that will be listed, and which touch very directly on our discussion of how we use and define key terms and words such as compassion, justice, immigration, racism, and the American experiment. Labberton's arguments are absolutely essential to understanding semantic apologetics and polemics and contemporary arguments, including the evangelical semantics influencing major elections, thus the Labberton-Jeffress debate will require lengthy documentation and evaluation.

Labberton unabashedly claims to properly define the true Christian gospel or evangel (good news) for the present generation:

- Evangelicalism's support of Trump amounts to a crisis
- God is bigger than any contemporary crisis
- Evangelicalism has a great heritage but an uncertain future
- The "gospel of Jesus Christ has been betrayed and shamed by an evangelicalism that has violated its own moral and spiritual integrity."
- "Now on public display is an indisputable collusion between prominent evangelicalism and many forms of insidious, racist, misogynistic, materialistic, and political power."
- The term evangelical, in the American context, has devolved into meaning nothing more than "white, theologically and politically conservative."
- "Today's egregious collusion between evangelicals and worldly power is problematic enough; more painful and revealing is that such collusion has been our historic habit. Today's collusion bear's astonishing—and tragic—continuity with the past." (Note the apparent, intentional, and repeated usage of the term "collusion" in Labberton's lament.)
- Evangelicalism has demonstrated a "destructive complicity with dominant cultural and racial power" reflective of "devastating social self-interest that defends the dominant culture over against the gospel's command to love the 'other'

as ourselves." This complicity includes "complicity in the suffering and death of others." This unholy alliance is reflected by the fact that "When you Google 'evangelical,' you get Trump."

- At the heart of much of this crisis is the abuse of power. "Whether we think about US militarism, or mass incarceration, or the #MeToo movement (or mistreatment of women in general), or the police shootings of unarmed, young, black men, or the actions of ICE toward child and adult immigrants, or gun use and control, or tax policy — *all* this is about power [emphasis added, and this focus on power was written prior to congressional hearings on Ukraine]." Labberton applies this scathing critique as follows: "The apparent evangelical alignment with the use of power that seeks dominance, control, supremacy, and victory over compassion and justice associates Jesus with strategies of Caesar, not with the good news of the gospel." Note: retaining the term "apparent" in this statement seems incoherent, and making no reference to legal versus illegal immigration amounts to semantic confusion.

- This abuse of power includes narrative distortions. "Stories of devastation are often absent from a happier white evangelical narrative of promised-land life, or buried in a sanitized story that claims that past injustice is not relevant for people of color today — despite the fact that nearly all color of people experience racism and its implications every day around the nation." Indeed, "racism permeates American life, and its tinderbox was lit on fire by the rhetoric of our national life in recent years — whether in references to Ferguson, or Charlottesville, or [profanity] ... countries deemed without value." Note: no qualifying statements are included concerning what actually took place in Ferguson, an omission which surely illustrates both semantic seduction and what columnist Eric Zorn contends is "practically the recipe for perpetual injustice."[137]

- Labberton affirms that "White history narrates the story of America's heroes, and white evangelical history views those 'good guys' as the providence of a good and faithful God. When some white evangelicals triumphantly proclaim that we now have 'the best president the religious right has ever had,' the crisis underscores to millions of people of color is not an indictment of our President as much as it is an indictment of white evangelicalism and a racist gospel."

- Labberton also accuses majority American evangelicalism of nationalism: "For white evangelicalism to embrace a platform and advocacy that promotes, prioritizes, and defends America above all and overall is to embrace an idolatry that has only ever proven disastrous." Labberton carefully qualifies this statement by affirming appropriate respect for "nationhood, including borders and immigration" and the "rule of law," yet he concludes that "identification with the use of demeaning rhetoric toward other nations, not least nations of color that are facing the challenges of poverty and war, is not only confusing but violating to the dignity, value, and truth of the gospel. It is, as well, violating to the people we otherwise claim to see, serve, join, and love — nations to which, ironically, American evangelicals annually send millions of dollars for missions and evangelism" (especially see Chapter 9 on the proper use of the term nationalism).

- Evangelicals simply are ignoring "God's heart for the poor and the vulnerable," both at home and abroad. Prominent white evangelicals "speak about what is fair and beneficial for society, but then pass laws and tax changes that create more national indebtedness and elevate the top 1% even higher — while cutting services and provisions for children, the disabled, and the poor that are castigated as disgusting 'entitlements' — one has to ask how this is reconciled with being followers of Jesus." Hence, "it is very hard to recognize the influence of the gospel narrative on compassion, let alone justice" among white, pro-Trump evangelicals.

No statement could be found in the above document concerning how all political parties have, at times, contributed to exploding the national debt. These illustrative statements from Labberton's recent essay on the crisis in evangelicalism,[138] viewed as profound by some and as a reckless rant by others (see immediately following in this chapter), are consistent with his prior statements summarized below. Yet Labberton's "Introduction" in the work he edited, *Still Evangelical?* is much more nuanced.[139]

- "Evangelicalism in America has cracked, split on the shoals of the 2016 presidential election and its aftermath, leaving many wondering whether they want to be in or out of the evangelical tribe." The reason for this crisis is because American evangelicalism likely provided "determinative support for the election of Donald Trump."
- This "election made apparent that culture rivals the gospel in defining evangelical political vision; our sociological frame speaks louder than our theology." This is not a new reality, but it is "now more blatant and more critical. For a movement that has been about the primacy of Christian faith, this is a crisis."
- The "word *evangelical* has morphed in common usage from being a reference to a set of primary theological com-mitments into something akin to a passionately defended, theo-political brand." *Evangelical*, in the minds of many, has become sociopolitical, often bears more affinities to fundamentalism, and is now aligned with President Trump. Nearly 80% of American evangelicals voted for Trump. Here Labberton properly engages in semantic polemics, regardless of the soundness of his argumentation.
- This voting pattern has less to do with biblical or theolog-ical convictions because "our sociology presets our convic-tions before the teaching of the Bible has been considered and integrated into our lives. And this can be as true of the right as it is of the left. This doesn't minimize the poten-tial for biblical faith to inform our social location, partic-ularly about important matters such as these. It is striking, however, that our context is the most pervasive influ-ence that shapes us, even if we profess Jesus as Lord. The

red-and-blue-state [voting] pattern reflects the profound sway of social location." Labberton also notes that red-and-blue-state context, or coastal location (east or west), seems to be guiding evangelical responses to LBGTQ issues.

- Relative to racism, the "denial of personal racism by many in the evangelical right is often paired with blindness toward systemic racism."

- So while all evangelicals are subject to context, and no one can claim a biblical "purity of vision," what "mystifies and infuriates the evangelical left is that the voice of the evangelical right seems to be controlled by white supremacy, moral and political inconsistency, and a fearful nationalism or isolationism that bears little evidence of the fruit of God's spirit. Again, social frame matters in how we see and what we see."

- The "binary nature" of the culture wars has made it difficult for the evangelical left to speak out without being accused of heterodoxy.

- "The 2016 election extended this situation further while opting for pragmatic power (by which Trump is compared to Cyrus, the pagan King used by God for holy ends) rather than coherent piety (as seen by the endorsement of Trump despite his lack of what would usually be considered 'Christian' character qualities)." And again, Labberton affirms, with such repetition and intensity that he is rather consistent with the postmodern spirit of the times, that each "believer occupies and is occupied by a social context—that is, an educational, economic, racial, and religious ethos that permeates and shapes each of us. We are never context-free." Hence, when we went to the polls in 2016 we "may not have asked how we'd been shaped by our context and culture or asked whether we were using Jesus as leverage based on our social location." Labberton waffles on whether context is a strong influence or actually and systemically determinative of political orientation, though he ends with a hopeful note in his essay—see the last bullet.

- Yet location will also shape the future of evangelicalism, or lead to departures from evangelicalism. "As the racial diversity and generational differences among evangelical churches on the left continue to grow [especially in blue states], it will become more and more unpalatable to choose association with evangelicals on the right. It will feel like a choice between bigotry and justice, in which case faith and social location will compel the evangelical left toward justice."

- In contrast to the accommodation of the evangelical right, the biblical "trajectory of salvation leads to a new sociology—a new social location and communion that is made possible only because of Jesus, who brings divided enemies into one new social reality." This new sociology is the kind of kingdom future that can avoid the errors of 2016 and embrace an increasingly just and diverse future. 2016 was a "problem of our own doing," which also means it can be corrected. Evangelicalism does not need better branding; it needs genuine kingdom revival and the authentic "sociology of the kingdom of God."

Robert Jeffress, as a representative of the allegedly nationalist Southern Baptist "right" referenced above, that is allegedly distorting the gospel, takes great exception to much of the above. His views will be explored in short order. It should be noted that the Wheaton meeting that led to Labberton's document ("Political Dealing ...") is dismissed by Jeffress as not representative of American evangelicalism and unlikely to have much impact on the evangelical movement overall. Jeffress acknowledges that "Evangelicals knew they were not electing a choir boy" when they voted in great numbers for Trump. Jeffress argues that Reagan and Trump were flawed, and admits that perhaps Trump is even more flawed than Reagan, but that on the balance their policies were more consistent with evangelical values than the alternatives, and on the balance they were less antagonistic to the evangelical Christian faith than the alternatives. Hence, Jeffress, with qualifications, would accept and continue to defend the Cyrus analogy.

However, the heart of where Jeffress would depart from Labberton, and the why, seems to be encapsulated in his ideas and statements below that emphasize two core values: 1) abortion as a unique issue and cultural barometer; and 2) the increasing marginalization of conservative evangelical Christianity in America that has been stalled or reversed by President Trump.[140] Jeffress believes that American evangelicalism has and is under assault and that President Trump has been an evangelical ally.

As a political science minor, I would argue that neither the approach of Labberton nor Jeffress should surprise us, since a key principle of political philosophy is that individuals, groups, and nation states tend to act based on perceived self-interest. Labberton sees Trump as a threat, perhaps the greatest in recent history. Jeffress believes that Trump has brought a reprieve to the assault on what he views as biblical, evangelical Christianity, and at least one crystal clear moral issue where there should be no debate among American evangelicals. These seem to be the core points of the argument by Jeffress:

- "This [abortion] is an issue of life and death. This is so black and white, so much about good versus evil. I don't get it," He continues: "It really goes to the core of who we are as a country and what kind of a country we have in the future, and if we can't get this issue of life right, I just don't know where we're going to go down the road." (Jeffress does not address whether any of Labberton's concerns are issues of life and death or morally black and white.)
- "What you're seeing that Andrew Cuomo and others have proposed [relative to late or post-birth abortions/infanticide], it's not only sinful and wrong, it is barbaric…. It is the sign of what Romans 1 in the New Testament calls a depraved mind that would allow that to happen."
- Those opposing Trump and supporting pro-abortion candidates are complicit with a regime of death—not unlike Hitler's Germany.
- "We cannot afford to be like German Christians who, in the rise of the evil reign of Adolf Hitler, just remained neutered. They remained silent. And you saw what happened there….

I think there's a similar wave of godlessness that is rising in our country right now, and we must push back against that tide."

- "We're not having our heads chopped off like Christians in the Middle East by ISIS, but you've heard me say before, I think when you look at what happened in Germany, look, the Nazis didn't take the Jews to the crematorium immediately.... They wouldn't have been allowed to do that by the German citizens. What the Nazis did was a program of making the Jews the object of ridicule and contempt in the eyes of the German people, and only once they had marginalized them, were they able to take away their rights." (Jeffress seems sincerely concerned about abortion and infanticide, and the decline of civilization, but especially concerned about the gathering storm that seems headed directly toward the future of American evangelicalism.)

It is tempting to comment on every point above of both of these two evangelicals and the camps they represent, but what is striking concerning the emphases of Jeffress and Labberton is the depth of the divide between these approaches, sociological contexts, and semantic universes. It is reminiscent of when Erasmus commented, after Luther's publication of *The Babylonian Captivity of the Church*, that "the breach is irreparable" between Luther and the church authorities. I am tempted to suggest that after the comments of Jeffress above, and especially Labberton's publication of "Political Dealings..." replete with multiple unqualified condemnations *and* the official Fuller Seminary seal, that the breach is irreparable. These two representatives of evangelical streams are speaking different languages with different assumptions, definitions, and core values. Though both claim to be American evangelicals, they are arguably inhabiting different semantic universes. Hopefully some progress has been made in the dialog since penning these words.

It is unfortunate that, as far as I know, Jeffress has not at least fairly articulated and responded to the concerns of the evangelical left—which certainly can be affirmed and/or refuted but true dialog includes fairness of presentation and some measure of empathy for what is worthy of discussion from an opponent. Jeffress has not, as far as I know, really grappled with the kind of systemic evil and sociology that concerns Labberton—at least his locatable public statements do not seem fully to grasp Labberton's approach. Hopefully he has addressed this elsewhere but I simply could not locate such material to date. It is hard to determine whether Jeffress is clueless or dismissive of evangelical concerns concerning systemic evil.

It is also unfortunate that the more measured attempt to address the evangelical divide by Labberton in *Still Evangelical?* morphs into a seeming self-righteous vitriolic rant in "Political Dealings...." In *Still Evangelical?* Labberton probably overstates the role of context in theology, to the point of making context almost entirely determinative of belief and action, but he at least acknowledges that both left and right are subject to contextual biases and prejudices.

However, in *Still Evangelical?* what frustrates him and "mystifies and infuriates the evangelical left is that the voice of the evangelical right seems to be controlled by white supremacy, moral and political inconsistency, and a fearful nationalism or isolationism that bears little evidence of the fruit of God's spirit." That is a rather damning indictment of Jeffress and others that comes to full fruition in the "Political Dealings..." diatribe.

It is unfortunate that Labberton is inattentive to questionable alignments with power on the evangelical left, with politicians, presidents, organizations, and movements. I could find no concerns expressed in either document, or in other documents that I could locate, concerning evangelical leaders who had cozied up to other Presidents and presidential candidates, such as Tony Campolo. I did write to Dr. Labberton requesting such sources, but did not hear back prior to publication.

Most unfortunate and unprofessional is the fact that Labberton allowed the Fuller Seminary seal to be placed on his "Political Dealings..." fireball. Apparently, in view of the seal usage, Fuller has zero interest in preparing Christians with a "red state" mindset for Christian leadership and ministry—unless they repent of their ethnocentric, imperialistic chauvinism!

The most troubling feature of Labberton's argument, in addition to using such universal and caustic terms of condemnation and his question-begging on the nature and definition of social justice, is his seeming lack of self-awareness concerning his own "social location" and context, which suggests possible elitism in relation to other red state evangelicals. Would he be making similar statements today if American evangelicalism likely provided "determinative support for the election of" Secretary of State Clinton or Senator Bernie Sanders of Vermont to the presidency? He understands the threat from evangelical alignment with "Cyrus," but does he fully grasp the threat from the other available political alternatives? Labberton seems to be engaging in elitist virtue signaling.

A few clarifications related to the thesis of this book are needed. We need to listen closely to Labberton (and Jeffress for that matter), and attempt to separate the gold from the dross. Labberton is correct that we need to keep kingdom sociology and the kingdom vision of the future before us. The coming New Creation is "a renewal in which there is no distinction between Greek and Jew, circumcised and uncircumcised, barbarian, Scythian, slave and freeman [NIV, "free"], but Christ is all, and in all" (Colossians 3:11). Labberton is correct that questions of complicity and collusion with dominant cultural powers need to be asked, and that sin and evil are often systemic. However, he seems oblivious to the possible collusion and complicity of the evangelical left with, or influence by, the legion centers of power that are more politically liberal (e.g., media, education, entertainment, popular culture, blue-state political power). Indeed, according to Google, Hollywood is only thirty minutes from Fuller Theological Seminary's historic location! Yet the geographical proximity may only be a metaphor for ideological proximity and, as he put it, the blinders of context and location that guide his own theology.

More concerning, Labberton only references troubling stories of devastation, especially on minorities, the poor, or illegal immigrants, that are the result of the alleged actions of one political party—this is a significant omission. Similarly, he only mentions the negative impact on diversity employment and wage ratio differentials of the poor due to the alleged actions of one political party—and fails to mention the possible employment and compensation wins of the accused political party or the possible devastating failures of the policies of his preferred political party on the disadvantaged. If Labberton is correct that evangelicals like Jeffress have baptized the platforms of their preferred political party, then it must also be asked whether evangelical leaders like Labberton have done the same. Location, location, location?

The social justice of seemingly all entitlements is assumed in Labberton's argument, but the possible social injustice of some entitlements is never referenced. For example, the adverse impact of entitlements on diversity groups or the problem of intergenerational dependency does not seem to be a significant storm on Labberton's progressive horizon. Perhaps space limitations were prohibitive, but only mentioning the positives of entitlements is as biased and prejudiced as only mentioning the negatives of entitlements and having no concern whatsoever for reasonable safety nets and true opportunities for struggling subcultures.

Labberton nods his head to the impact of social location on the left and right, but for him it is really the right that has been hijacked by injustice and idolatry due to their social location. As noted, he just does not seem cognizant of the possible impact of his social location on his entire argument—and social location or context is the backbone of his argument and references to location and context are many.

Finally, Labberton predictably engages in the utopian fallacy. Everyone seems to agree that the faults of the current President are many—but the real issue between Jeffress and Labberton is what are the alternatives? In a utopian world Trump would run against a fantastic, competent, pro-evangelical candidate who can get things done, and the choice would be easy. In the 2016 election multiple pollsters noted that one of the reasons why polling was so difficult was because some who apparently voted for Trump would not admit such on a survey—either before or after visiting the polling booth.

Anecdotally, in my evangelical circles I encountered many evangelicals who held their nose and voted for Trump, and then were hesitant to admit such. They voted for Trump simply because they believed that the alternative was even more dangerous to the republic, to the faith, to minorities, to women, and to the poor. Each President touches literally thousands of issues, so many evangelicals are engaging in a kind of political triage or lesser evil calculation. Just because some evangelical luminaries seem to be fully and enthusiastically in bed with any politician does not mean, apart from very strong evidence to the contrary, that many or all evangelicals don't have reservations about all current presidential candidates.

A correlate illegitimate child of this utopian fallacy is the assumption that a powerful and centralized government is necessarily the cause, means, or distributor of social justice. Government certainly can assist, and as noted previously should serve as a just referee when possible, but the original vision of our more perfect union was the *provision* for the common defense and the *promotion*, not provision, of the general welfare. This qualification and limitation is rooted in Judeo-Christian assumptions about human nature and governmental leaders. A nation cannot avoid centralized responsibility for defending the nation, and even that centralization of power needs checks and balances, and hence the American experiment even put the military under elected civilian control.

Providing for the general welfare rather than promoting the general welfare has three theological or logical flaws. First, in order to provide for the general welfare, the government would need to centralize and consolidate more and more economic control, political and economic power, and amass vast wealth under its control.

The original American experiment was trying to avoid such centralization because of the European experience where centralized power led to centralized oppression, tyranny, poverty, famine, economic stagnation, imperialism, and economic immobility. The support for unchecked and overly centralized power misunderstands human nature.

Second, centralized power assumes that the federal government knows best on how to obtain, provide for, and distribute economic progress and justice. This theological assumption is also questionable relative to human nature.

Third, the American experiment sought to place the government under divinely revealed principles and Law (*Lex Rex*, eternal law is king and not the reverse; see Chapter 2 and subsequent chapters). Hence, the American experiment incentivized non-governmental organizations and business entrepreneurs to assist, imperfectly, with relief, justice, and the promotion of the general welfare. In a nutshell, because Labberton has already committed the utopian fallacy his discussion, while properly raising questions of justice about governmental actions, Labberton noticeably references the government as the center of the universe relative to justice and the general welfare. Perhaps there is no greater social injustice and oppression than a government that begins to function as a god.

More helpfully, Labberton and others of a similar mind might want to read two key articles to better or truly understand the sociological context of what they described as the current evangelical crisis. The first is by Michael Massing, who contends that sociology does indeed help in "Making Sense of Evangelical's Support for Trump."[141] Massing does not appear to be in full alignment with conservative evangelicalism, but observes that the sociology of unabated liberal elitism will guarantee a Trump reelection. The second article is by Daniel Strand, where he argues that Labberton, Michael Gerson, and the "Religious Left Misdiagnoses [the] Crisis of Evangelicalism." Strand contends that Labberton is elitist and he:

- Completely misunderstands the evangelical movement and the motives of most evangelicals (this is not all about power and racism)
- Completely misunderstands a robust, biblical and theological ethic of power and overly relies on one approach as represented by Yoder and Hauerwas (Hauerwas, by the way, despises H. Richard Niebuhr's transformer of culture approach)
- Engages in numerous straw man/woman/person fallacies
- Makes numerous assertions without evidence

Strand affirms that Labberton is "guided almost completely by the pieties of contemporary progressives. Christians have developed different political programs based on theology and the reading of scripture, but the work must be done rather than assumed." Strand concludes:

> For someone who claims not to advocate for the political left, Labberton picks a very telling list of crisis points: power, race, economics, and nationalism. Noticeably absent from his list are issues that most concern evangelicals and the reasons why some, not all, ostensibly voted for Trump: religious liberty and related issues, family and marriage, supreme court and other judicial appointments, abortion, etc. Turns out the crisis points are not crisis points at all but political differences dressed up in the garb of hyperbole. Politicization of Christianity is a temptation and a threat to evangelicalism, but instead of offering a better way, we're presented a political platform with a shallow theological justification.[142]

The outcome of the conflict between perspectives such as Jeffress and Labberton has huge implications for this work, for semantics (e.g., defining "justice" or "racism"), and for the future of faith communities and culture — but the conflict is also a bit sad. The tension between these two evangelical camps reflects the current state of at least two important subcultures of American evangelicalism. Perhaps a greater threat to American evangelicalism than either of these sociopolitical views is the evident opprobrium, and the lack of meaningful definitions and dialog and semantic clarity, that exists between these two camps, which raises serious questions about the fragmentation of American evangelicalism.

Ed Stetzer (*Christians in the Age of Outrage*, 2018), Glenn Stanton (*The Myth of the Dying Church*, 2019), plus David Kinnaman and Mark Matlock (*Faith for Exiles*, 2019), are doing very creative and constructive work and research that bears on the future of American and global evangelicalism.[143] Stetzer is doing a tremendous job quantifying the demographics and sociology that underlies the cultural polarization fostering contemporary and accelerating tribalism. These works may reveal options for a better evangelical future.

However, one key point must be made about such research. Regardless of whether numeric evangelicalism (however defined) is in decline or not in any particular country or region, *much* attention must be given to definitions, semantics, and semantic universes in order effectively to understand and nuance what is taking place relative to core beliefs in faith communities and culture. This intensive need for discernment especially applies to the semantics of surveys, and survey respondents, as such surveys often assume a kind of naïve commonsense realism or modernistic, scientific certainty relative to how terms and definitions are presented and then interpreted by survey respondents.

Kinnaman has done some helpful work in ferreting out categories such as "Resilient Disciples" as opposed to "Habitual Churchgoers" among eighteen to twenty-nine year olds,[144] yet the need for significant additional semantic theological mining remains. The gravest danger relative to Stanton's work (*The Myth of the Dying Church*) is that it may fail to clearly communicate the semantic, polemic, apologetic, legal, cultural, and civilizational crises facing both church and state in this critical hour of human history. Of equal importance is the fact that our ultramodern age is syncretistic (see the entire work, but especially Chapter 6). That means that survey respondents may affirm biblical beliefs in one context but then embrace approaches to social justice or inclusion that completely undermine biblical orthodoxy!

The true state of faith communities cannot be fully discerned apart from intensive semantic and theological analysis. This true state touches on more issues than whether the commitment to some versions of social justice often entails presuppositions largely or entirely alien to Judeo-Christian and biblical orthodoxy. It is also the case, by way of personal illustration, that, sometime late in the twentieth century I began encountering more and more Bible-believing collegians and seemingly orthodox collegians who did not bat an eye at syncretistically affirming biblical marriage, the inspiration of Scripture, cohabitation, and same-sex marriage. While some may appear religiously orthodox on surveys, their syncretistic, unbalanced, and unbiblical views on inclusion, love, and social justice may actually be in conflict with or undermine that very orthodoxy. The data I have seen and my personal interactions with evangelical students truly imply that things are a bit messier inside the evangelical church than some have suggested or what may be reflected in surveys and demographic analyses.

And even if there is a faithful remnant among all evangelical generations, and even if the dying church is largely a "chicken-little" myth, the semantic, cultural, philosophical and theological realities in both church and culture suggest that evangelicalism is facing unprecedented internal and external crises.

This work affirms that the way out of the current verbal civil war and quagmire is neither by embracing the semantics and "pieties of contemporary progressive evangelicals," nor naively associating with an ill-defined nationalism or the politicians or political programs on *either* side of the political aisle. The way forward is a Logocentric, coherent, and semantically enhanced vision of a more perfect union that far transcends the current volatile moments in presidential politics.

An Eschatology of a More Perfect Union

Relative to *civilization*, biblical theology certainly affirms human depravity and the danger of all foolish efforts, apart from repentance, grace, and radical, supernatural, Exodus-style Divine intervention, to create a perfected new humanity or a utopian new society. This biblical rejection of naive utopianism, however, certainly does not entail abandoning the quest for "a more perfect [and hence more civilized] union." This quest is evident from the command in Genesis to steward God's creation and culture, to the frequent New Testament prayers and commands that view leaders as servants ordained by God to establish an admittedly less than perfect civilized culture (see Rom. 13 and 1 Timothy 2 referenced in Chapter 1), or the call for believers to be salt and light. The quest for a more perfect order in this present age is a nonnegotiable biblical mandate. This mandate is also a manifestation of biblical neighbor-love and of being a Good Samaritan, which sums up the horizontal dimension flowing forth like living water from the vertical dimension of the Ten Commandments.

The choice is not between utopian perfection or dystopian disillusionment and fragmentation but some measure of pre-Parousia approximation of God's new creation. Hence, the term and *telos* "civilization," though certainly hard to define, retains semantic utility[145] and remains a worthy quest. The term actually implies that there is a human and historical struggle to civilize.

If the reader objects that this book is simply another antiquated defense of Western civilization, then the reader has missed the point entirely. The apologetic and polemic quest pursued here is primarily for the sake of preserving biblical faith communities. The secondary purpose of semantic apologetics and polemics is to advance biblically influenced culture and civilization(s) across the globe, and to assist with the unrelenting biblical quest toward an approximation of the aspirational ideal (civilization).

Thus the ideal of civilization in the present age is a fluid approximation, when possible, of the New Creation. It is a separate debate as to whether any "more perfect unions" exist on the face of the globe, and, if so, which best approximate this aspirational ideal. It is a separate debate as to which type of civilization should serve as the fallible and aspirational *promised land*, and to what degree the West is flawed. The point argued here is that we should not shun the ideal of civilization or uncritically reject any contemporary form of civilization, including Western, prior to careful, biblical, theological reflection and analysis.

The scope and magnitude of potential pre-Parousia influence is also a separate inquiry. Please see my academic work, *A Theology of Cross and Kingdom*, for an attempt to answer that question. Some have advocated for very optimistic postmillennialism, and others have advocated for less hopeful perspectives. It is important to note that Christian influence need not be equated with *Christianizing* or *theocratizing*. A worthy outcome may be as simple as restoring some measure of integrity, collegiality, and truthfulness to public and political discourse. Do note the semantic and conceptual connection between civilization and civil discourse, and how the accelerating lack of civil discourse today may be the tremors preceding the civilizational earthquake.

The alternative to the endless, grace-assisted quest for at least an approximative or reasonably healthy civilization (i.e., approximating the ideal in a fluid and sometimes decentralized fashion) confirms the value of the quest. The alternative to the quest includes the following: the lack of *civilis,* impolite and rude behavior and uncivil political debate; brutality; rape and pillaging; barbarism; endless bloodletting; no peaceful means for resolving disputes; the lack of religious and political freedom; unbridled and unchecked greed and corruption; the lack of human flourishing on any level; fragmented families and lives; rampant violence and drug usage; shortened life expectancies; and, widespread poverty and disease. Sound familiar? This list is not just ancient history. However, any quest not rooted in Judeo-Christian moorings is headed toward shipwreck, just as the stormy uncivilized and barbarous journeys previously referenced.

The so-called virtue of rejecting the quest for an aspirational civilization and a more perfect union, and the semantic maneuver of redefining civilization as a vice, are, frankly, rather demonic.

The survival of the Republic, *any* relatively free and just Republic — not to mention the vibrancy and even orthodoxy of biblical, evangelical, Jewish, or Roman Catholic churches, schools, and associated organizations — may well depend, in part, on the outcome of these semantic conflicts and language theft games. And these word wars outside the church and synagogue inevitably have influence inside faith communities, including via the pulpits across the globe. The outcome hinges on the ability of orthodox and biblical faith communities to engage in persuasive semantic apologetics and polemics relative to biblical assumptions and terminology that interface with culture and civilization.

This global conflict may have far-reaching implications that, in many respects, exceed the consequences of an actual, global physical military conflict or the verbal conflict may spark or frame such actual military conflict. In many respects, while the Allies and the

Greatest Generation certainly won World War II on one level, on another level the Allies lost or are losing the fierce and subsequent global truth and values conflict. This semantic World War 3 is well underway, has been for decades, and is only intensifying. The war is especially proliferating in the West.

A Tolerant, Judeo-Christian-Influenced Nation

One conspicuous example of the utilization of semantic ambiguity in order to remove, dampen, or negate Judeo-Christian influence on American culture is telling. Opponents of such Christian influence utilize the debate concerning and referencing to America as a "Christian nation" to suggest, via straw man fallacies that

1. evangelicals and conservative Roman Catholics seek to **establish a theocracy**,
2. the orthodox naively believe that the United States was **founded as a theocracy** (and perhaps even by fundamentalist founding fathers), and/or
3. the orthodox believe that **most Americans today** are still conservative or fundamentalist evangelicals.

Even former President Barack Obama, in an address to the *Call to Renewal* conference sponsored by the liberal evangelical *Sojourner's* magazine,[146] engaged in some measure of semantic distortion. He argued the following concerning the definition of America: *"Whatever we once were, we are no longer just a Christian nation; we are also a Jewish nation, a Muslim nation, a Buddhist nation, a Hindu nation, and a nation of nonbelievers."* Obama's historically false, culturally relativizing, inchoate, and historically misleading statement employs many semantic equivocations and distortions that are most illustrative of cultural appeasement and legion post Judeo-Christian cultural winds.

It would be substantially more advantageous to the discussion and any such call to *renewal*, not to mention a more historically and philosophically accurate approach and much less undermining of positive Judeo-Christian influence, if the history and religious nature of America would not be characterized like President Obama but more in line with the following and *hypothetical* call to renewal.

Perhaps President Obama could have better illuminated this critical discussion by modifying the key points of his argument to be more aligned with something like the following:

- *America's birth was primarily undergirded by profound Judeo-Christian and Enlightenment influenced presuppositions and passions that permeated the founding documents, law, and culture. Key religious presuppositions especially framed the American experiment from Jamestown to Philadelphia and beyond, yet we should not ignore the fact that some of the more constructive ideals of the Enlightenment were also influential and contributory to refining the vision.*

- *America was never intended to be or established as a secular state, or a Deistic nation, or a Christian theocracy. The grand experiment was a welcoming, tolerant Judeo-Christian democratic Republic. The Founding Fathers were unflinching in their contention that such newfound and unbridled freedom would not be sustainable apart from Judeo-Christian values and Christian virtue—defined as the principal supports of democracy in America. This historic call to renewal today, not unlike the covenant offer of Josiah, is to point out what the founding fathers would likely advise. With repentance we must confess that we have drifted from, and need to return to, the Judeo-Christian piety, values and conceptual assumptions that birthed and framed this great experiment in democracy. We are not a Christian theocracy or a secular state, and certainly not a Muslim, Buddhist or Hindu nation. We are a tolerant Judeo-Christian influenced democratic Republic, not only tolerant but most welcoming of all faiths, yet we are in urgent need of a spiritual renewal of our liberating Judeo-Christian moral, spiritual, and intellectual heritage that launched and which will sustain and nourish this miraculous experiment.*

Or, even more to the point, perhaps President Obama would have served the nation well by simply quoting Abraham Lincoln relative to the import of Judeo-Christian assumptions and the need for a biblically framed repentance and renewal, when President Lincoln declared (1861) the fourth Thursday in September as a *National Day of Prayer*:

> It is fit and becoming in all people, at all times, to acknowledge and revere the Supreme Government of God; to bow in humble submissions to his chastisement; to confess and deplore their sins and transgressions in the full conviction that the fear of the Lord is the beginning of wisdom; and to pray, with all fervency and contrition, for the pardon of their past offenses, and for a blessing upon their present and prospective action.

> And whereas when our own beloved country, once, by the blessings of God, united, prosperous and happy, is now afflicted with faction and civil war, it is peculiarly fit for us to recognize the hand of God in this terrible visitation, and in sorrowful remembrance of our own faults and crimes as a nation and as individuals, to humble ourselves before Him and to pray for his mercy … that the inestimable boon of civil and religious liberty, earned under His guidance and blessing by the labors and sufferings of our fathers, may be restored.[147]

Only the philosophically and theologically naïve would not recognize that Lincoln's declaration immediately above is not built upon the religious assumptions of just any religion or worldview, but it specifically rests on the assumptions of the personal conception of God found in the Judeo-Christian tradition.

Perhaps an even more telling and appropriate model for a Call to Renewal today that accurately reflects the nature of the American experiment is Lincoln's *Proclamation 97—Appointing a Day of National Humiliation, Fasting and Prayer*.[148] This quote is lengthy yet critical for this discussion. This extensive evidence documents and clarifies the semantic universe of Lincoln, and therefore directly bears on the present argument concerning *Christian*

nation semantics. The Judeo-Christian assumptions are conspicuous from a President reared in the very shadow of the founders
of the American experiment. The following text clearly does not
assume that the cultural norm or presuppositions for the American
experiment are found in atheism, Deism, Buddhism, Hinduism,
pantheism, or polytheism.

By the President of the United States of America [March 30, 1863]

A Proclamation

Whereas the Senate of the United States, devoutly recognizing the supreme authority and just government of Almighty God in all the affairs of men and of nations, has by a resolution requested the President to designate and set apart a day for national prayer and humiliation; and

Whereas it is the duty of nations as well as of men to own their dependence upon the overruling power of God, to confess their sins and transgressions in humble sorrow, yet with assured hope that genuine repentance will lead to mercy and pardon, and to recognize the sublime truth, announced in the Holy Scriptures and proven by all history, that those nations only are blessed whose God is the Lord;

And, insomuch as we know that by His divine law nations, like individuals, are subjected to punishments and chastisements in this world, may we not justly fear that the awful calamity of civil war which now desolates the land may be but a punishment inflicted upon us for our presumptuous sins, to the needful end of our national reformation as a whole people? We have been the recipients of the choicest bounties of Heaven; we have been preserved these many years in peace and prosperity; we have grown in numbers, wealth, and power as no other nation has ever grown. But we have forgotten God. We have forgotten the gracious hand which preserved us in peace and multiplied and enriched and strengthened us, and we have vainly imagined, in the deceitfulness of our hearts, that all these blessings were produced by some superior wisdom and virtue of our own. Intoxicated with unbroken success, we have become too self-sufficient to feel the necessity of redeeming and preserving grace, too proud to pray to the God that made us.

It behooves us, then, to humble ourselves before the offended Power, to confess our national sins, and to pray for clemency and forgiveness.

Now, therefore, in compliance with the request, and fully concurring in the views of the Senate, I do by this my proclamation designate and set apart Thursday, the 30th day of April, 1863, as a day of national humiliation, fasting, and prayer. And I do hereby request all the people to abstain on that day from their ordinary secular pursuits, and to unite at their several places of public worship and their respective homes in keeping the day holy to the Lord and devoted to the humble discharge of the religious duties proper to that solemn occasion.

All this being done in sincerity and truth, let us then rest humbly in the hope authorized by the divine teachings that the united cry of the nation will be heard on high and answered with blessings no less than the pardon of our national sins and the restoration of our now divided and suffering country to its former happy condition of unity and peace. In witness whereof I have hereunto set my hand and caused the seal of the United States to be affixed.

Done at the city of Washington, this 30th day of March, A.D. 1863, and of the Independence of the United States the eighty-seventh.
ABRAHAM LINCOLN.
By the President:
WILLIAM H. SEWARD, Secretary of State.

Lincoln's overt Judeo-Christian framework, assumptions, values, and semantic universe are irrefutably and conspicuously demonstrated via the following phrases and terms in this declaration. As the tragic haze of the battlefield enshrouded the nation, Lincoln's gaze was fixed on the in breaking rays of hope from the personal and Judeo-Christian God who birthed, nurtured, sustained, led, and judged the nation, and who could also forgive and miraculously restore the nation, vision, and reality of a more perfect union. These are not polite references to a generic civil religion or a generic god, or political pandering. Lincoln is making *explicit* Judeo-Christian theological affirmations and applications

accompanied by the Senate's approval of the declaration and the
seal of the President of the United States of America:

- The "supreme authority and just government of
  Almighty God"
- A "day for national prayer and humiliation"
- A call for all "to own their dependence upon the overruling
  power of God"
- A plea to "confess their sins and transgressions in
  humble sorrow"
- Assured "hope that genuine repentance will lead to mercy
  and pardon"
- Truth "announced in the Holy Scriptures and proven by
  all history, that those nations only are blessed whose God
  is the Lord"
- A lament, and application to America, "that by His divine
  law nations, like individuals, are subjected to punishments
  and chastisements in this world"
- Repentance for "our presumptuous sins, to the needful end
  of our national reformation as a whole people"
- Gratitude and repentant humility, since "We have been the
  recipients of the choicest bounties of Heaven; we have been
  preserved these many years in peace and prosperity; we
  have grown in numbers, wealth, and power as no other
  nation has ever grown. But we have forgotten God."
- A biblical challenge to complacency for a people that has
  "vainly imagined, in the deceitfulness of our hearts, that all
  these blessings were produced by some superior wisdom
  and virtue of our own. Intoxicated with unbroken success,
  we have become too self-sufficient to feel the necessity of
  redeeming and preserving grace, too proud to pray to the
  God that made us."
- The call to repent before a personal, single (monotheistic), and gracious God, and "humble ourselves before
  the offended Power, to confess our national sins, and to
  pray for clemency and forgiveness." (This is the personal
  Judeo-Christian God, not the disengaged god of deism or
  the impersonal divinity of pantheism.)

- The utilization of biblical and Judeo-Christian language and concepts to establish "a day of national humiliation, fasting, and prayer. And I do hereby request all the people to abstain on that day from their ordinary secular pursuits, and to unite at their several places of public worship and their respective homes in keeping the day holy to the Lord and devoted to the humble discharge of the religious duties proper to that solemn occasion."
- The biblical hope, that, "authorized by the divine teachings that the united cry of the nation will be heard on high and answered with blessings no less than the pardon of our national sins and the restoration of our now divided and suffering country to its former happy condition of unity and peace."

Lincoln's semantic universe was explicitly, unapologetically, and profoundly Judeo-Christian—so much so that these words would seem scandalous to many today since we are shifting to a post Judeo-Christian or anti-Christian semantic universe. The Judeo-Christian assumptions and clear affirmations are overflowing in this declaration, and clearly inconsistent with alternative religions and philosophies. As an avid tennis player, writing this as the Australian Open is well underway, this seems to be an appropriate point to suggest *game, set, and match*! Revisionist scholars can speculate, deconstruct, reconstruct, and psychologize endlessly concerning what the founding fathers or Abraham Lincoln "actually" believed. However, for those desiring to preserve scholarly integrity the evidence of Judeo-Christian influence on these architects of the American experiment is absolutely irrefutable. The semantic universe of the American experiment, and the defeat of slavery, was undeniably and primarily Judeo-Christian influenced in dialog with the Enlightenment. See other chapters, especially chapter 9, concerning George Washington's views that birthed and paralleled those of Abraham Lincoln.

If Abraham Lincoln, born in 1809 in my current state of Kentucky, less than a generation after the revolution and the *Constitution,* so profoundly failed to comprehend the religious nature of the American experiment, or the foundational and presuppositional role of Judeo-Christian thought for that great experiment, or the true nature of social justice, toleration, inclusion, or the establishment of religion clause, then perhaps we are all in dire straits relative to resolving such matters. I stand with Lincoln as opposed to contemporary historical revisionists. And Lincoln got it right on the public, cultural, and civilizational relevance of Judeo-Christian values to slavery and racism.

The quotes from Lincoln reinforce a critical emphasis in this work. Lincoln occupied an entirely different semantic universe than contemporary post-Christian advocates and militants. Virtually all key terms used by Lincoln's generation versus our generation (e.g., freedom, free speech, Christian, Christian influence, prayer, sin, forgiveness) have *interrelated or systemic and contextual* definitions issuing forth from largely or entirely irreconcilable semantic universes. Lincoln's semantic family was Judeo-Christian, not atheistic or Hindu or postmodern. Effective apologetics, polemics, and civilizational influence must embark on the twenty-first-century journey with this reality clearly in focus. The semantic universe and experiment in human flourishing of 1776 is parsecs away from the contemporary post-Christian semantic universe and so-called "American" experiment.

America was unquestionably founded and continued to progress as a Judeo-Christian influenced nation, undergirded by Judeo-Christian and biblical (i.e., epistemological, metaphysical and axiological) assumptions while also framed within the context of the Enlightenment. The Enlightenment is an intellectual movement often only defined in a one-sided and oppositional manner to Christianity due to the extreme critiques of traditional Christianity by certain Deists (e.g., Voltaire or Paine). The Enlightenment was sufficiently broad and diverse in scope such that it paradoxically both challenged and parasitized Judeo-Christian assumptions concerning knowledge, morality, reality, God, and ethics.

Hence, the founders, key players, and influential philosophers birthing the American experiment included orthodox mainline Christians, evangelical Christians, rational supernaturalists (see Chapter 5 concerning Locke), as well as radical and Christian Deists. "Of note is the fact that virtually all of the 55 writers and signers of the United States Constitution of 1787 were members of Christian denominations: 29 were Anglicans, 16 to 18 were Calvinists, 2 were Methodists, 2 were Lutherans, 2 were Roman Catholic, 1 lapsed Quaker and sometimes Anglican, and 1 open Deist—Dr. Franklin who attended every kind of Christian worship, [and] called for public prayer [even during the Constitutional Convention]."[149]

Yet the common thread is that this experiment emerged from the whirlwind of Enlightenment and Judeo-Christian intellectual, theological, and philosophical impulses in a conceptual and verbal universe primarily framed by Judeo-Christian and biblical presuppositions. The American experiment was a tolerant, welcoming, Judeo-Christian-influenced, republican democracy. If properly defined and nuanced, America was indeed and undeniably founded and intended to be a *Judeo-Christian influenced nation*. The American experiment of 1776 irrefutably was neither a theocracy nor a secular democracy, but a Judeo-Christian influenced republican democracy. The incorrect or false options concerning the "America is a Christian nation" debate include affirmations that America is:

1. A Christian nation in the sense that most or all today are active, engaged, historically orthodox and **Bible-believing Christians**—the Barna data suggests otherwise;[150]
2. A Christian nation in the sense that most or all are today at least **nominal Christians**—even if true, and see the Gallup data,[151] that would not guarantee authentic Judeo-Christian or biblical influence on culture;
3. A Christian nation in the sense that all or virtually all of the **founding fathers were fundamentalist, Bible-believing, evangelical Christians**—they *were* primarily historically orthodox Christians, but they were neither all evangelical fundamentalists nor anti-Christian Deists (see Chapter 9);
4. A Christian **theocracy**—while this option may have been considered early on by some of the first colonialists the American Experiment and founding documents clearly had moved beyond and rejected this theocratic option;

5. A **secular, democratic state**—this option is refuted by countless founding documents and early American practices (see previous material in this chapter and see Chapter 9).

The historical and demographic data is compelling. The American experiment was an experiment in a tolerant, Judeo-Christian-influenced republican—not direct—democracy. This democracy was to be forever guided by *Lex Rex* not *Rex Lex*. And the attempts discussed previously to redefine the experiment, either by the contemporary political left or right, jeopardize this grand and historic experiment. Perhaps one of the most confused, ludicrous and self-serving conversations today is the debate concerning whether America is or was a Christian nation.

This issue is not that complicated if folks simply read the core and founding documents of the American experiment and preserve and promote honest semantics. America was founded as a Judeo-Christian influenced republican democracy. Most Americans are nominal Christians today, yet America has a significant group of very committed and engaged Jews and Christians—in contrast to most of Europe. The Enlightenment influenced the American experiment, but Judeo-Christian values also influenced the Enlightenment and directly influenced the experiment, the culture, and the underlying assumptions of the experiment. The founders were mostly orthodox Christian believers. Judeo-Christian values made religious freedom, freedom of speech, toleration, and democracy possible. Some of the key founders and authors of core documents were influenced more by one or the other two key streams, and all were influenced by both the Enlightenment and Judeo-Christian streams.

Freedom and toleration will eventually become Balkanized, collapse, or self-devour apart from Judeo-Christian values—over the course of years, decades, or many centuries. Religion and morality were viewed as the indispensable or principle supports of democracy in America. Judeo-Christian values sparked and framed every major social reform movement in early America and countless other movements throughout the nation's history, including abolitionism, feminism, and prison reform (see the Preface, and Chapters 2 and 7). Lincoln and Harriet Beecher Stowe (*Uncle Tom's Cabin*) called the nation to repentance and the renewal of core Judeo-Christian values and threatened the judgment of a personal, supernatural monotheistic God. Such an authentic renewal is the only key to the sustenance and future of the grand experiment.

Just as with the phrase and debate concerning *Christian nation*, other related and impactful terms and phrases will be referenced in the following chapters and in the comparative mini-Lexicon in appendix A.[152] Such terms increasingly have been distorted and coopted to redefine and shape doctrine (beliefs), history, reality, values, ethics, education, preaching, entertainment, and law. This semantic seduction has also been appropriated to shift the cultural imagination and sentiments away from Judeo-Christian norms and influence. This semantic theft has thus far been rather successful, but much history may yet be written by the American experiment and the global Judeo-Christian movement.

Ask Yourself or Your Group

- *Why do some despise the very term "civilization" today?*
- *Name some of the terms that the early Church and Augustine had to rescue from improper definitions? What difference did the definitions make for apologetics? What difference did the definitions make for the church?*
- *Does the author agree or disagree with the "Benedict Option," and how does the author's view on the "Benedict Option" relate to the purpose of the book?*
- *Whose semantic universe is more accurate concerning biblical justice? Labberton or Jeffress?*
- *What does the author mean by "the eschatology of a more perfect union"? Does the author support theocracy or a secular state? Is America a Christian nation?*
- *Rod Dreher's "Benedict Option" and Timothy Keller and Jake Meador's creative arguments in the book entitled In Search of the Common Good: Christian Fidelity in a Fractured World are seeking alternative approaches concerning how faith communities should interact with culture and politics in our polarized era. Does the author of Seduced? believe that we need a new or alternative*

*approach, or instead do we need a renewal and refine-
ment of the original "City Set on a Hill" and "more perfect union" American vision? Does <u>Seduced?</u> believe
that faith communities should be only mildly engaged
with culture? Should churches and synagogues define
themselves as culturally marginal religious or neo-monastic sects, or instead should we be part of the very warp
and woof of culture and civilization—and located at the
very nexus of the intellectual and spiritual marketplace
shaping our normative ideas, passions, and future vision?
Please also see the quotations by Charles Matthewes in
the back-matter at the very end of this book.*

Chapter 4

Semantic Integrity or Semantic Ecclesial Theft?

> *For I am jealous for you with a godly jealousy; for I betrothed you to one husband, so that to Christ I might present you as a pure virgin. But I am afraid that, as the serpent deceived Eve by his craftiness, your minds will be led astray from the simplicity and purity of devotion to Christ. For if one comes and preaches <u>another Jesus</u> whom we have not preached, or you receive a <u>different spirit</u> [pneuma] which you have not received, or a <u>different gospel</u> which you have not accepted, you bear this beautifully.… For such men are <u>false apostles, deceitful workers</u>, disguising themselves as apostles of Christ. No wonder, for even Satan disguises himself as an <u>angel</u> of light. Therefore it is not surprising if his servants also <u>disguise themselves as servants of righteousness</u>, whose end will be according to their deeds.*
> —2 Corinthians 11: 2–4, 13–15 (underscoring added)

> *I tell you this so that no one may deceive you by fine-*
> *sounding arguments.*
> —Colossians 2:4

Semantic gymnastics have played a significant role in drawing Judeo-Christian faith communities away from their orthodox, historical, Scriptural, and theological underpinnings. Classical liberal "Christian" theologians and those in academia who determined that orthodox Christianity had been supposedly discredited by the modern mind realized that an overt approach to laity—telling them upfront that their orthodox faith and major beliefs were primitive, irrational, and misguided—would backfire and result in liberalism being driven from the church.

The late Walter Martin often lamented and challenged the "theobabble" that had invaded the contemporary nineteenth- and twentieth-century church.[153] Key Christian and biblical terms and phrases (e.g., the Deity of Christ, Trinity, and Second Coming) had been, rather than abandoned, subtly redefined by liberal or liberated preachers and theologians—liberated from biblical orthodox beliefs. This subtle redefinition process, Martin observed, was also being applied to ethical terms and concepts such as homosexual behavior. For example, Martin rejected the liberal argument that the sin of Sodom should be redefined primarily as non-sexual Middle Eastern inhospitality.

The orthodox terms were retained in the church and synagogue in order progressively to *win over* (or seduce) the faithful into incrementally embracing a progressive post-orthodox and unbiblical theology. This *theobabble* also allowed scholars and pastors who had unquestionably departed from the historic Christian or Jewish faiths (or denominationally required beliefs) to remain in leadership positions and ultimately subvert biblical beliefs and practices in mainline and nominally Judeo-Christian denominations, seminaries, and colleges. As noted, one of my friends completed his PhD at a Jewish university where he studied under an atheistic existentialist Rabbi! Such semantic redefinitions and departures from Scriptural intent continue to this day. All of this was done with the alleged good intention, of course, of saving Christianity from irrational irrelevancy and moving the uninformed laity in a more progressive and modernist direction. This word theft was largely successful in many religious organizations. Such word theft, however, has a long history dating back to biblical times.

Pauline Semantic Polemics and Apologetics

The Apostle Paul was not a trained philosopher (philosophy was not yet a specialized discipline) in philosophical linguistics, semantics, or semiotics, yet in the passage that opened this chapter from 2 Corinthians 11, he clearly understood what was at stake relative to the word theft of terms such as "Jesus," "Gospel," "Spirit" and "Apostle"—not to mention "angel."

Indeed, Paul clearly connects this word "theft" to the "Has God said?" original demonic temptation (11:3), which wrestled and severed the meaning of terms and concepts from the semantic intention of the Logos, the Agent of creation, who created all things. The Logos created communication, culture, and humans as *imago Dei* and capable of interacting reliably and verbally with God (and vice versa), others, and created reality. Is it surprising that Paul affirms that such word theft touches on the very nature of the gospel? Paul concludes that a redefined gospel "is really not another [gospel]; only there are some who are disturbing you and want to distort the gospel of Christ" (Gal. 1:7). Similarly, Paul references other terms, such as circumcision, and notes that there is both a "true" and "false" definition and usage of terms like circumcision (see Philippians chapter 3), which implies there are true and false definitions of terms like "God's people," "children of God," "Jew," and "Christian." Paul was not a linguistic relativist. A semantic measuring rod exists and should norm all definitions and communication.

Table 4.1. Pauline Semantic Polemics and Apologetics (Mini-Lexicon[154] Based on 2 Corinthians 11–13, Galatians 1–5)

Biblical Terms and Phrases	Revelatory Biblical Usage	Semantic Distortion
1. Jesus (2 Cor. 11:4)	Trinitarian	Non-Trinitarian (and/or legalistic and/or an antinomian doctrine of Jesus) [Note that John and 1 John also use semantic apologetics to counter false and non-physical redefinitions of "Christ"]
2. Spirit (2 Cor. 11:4)	Holy Spirit	Another spirit or an evil spirit
3. Gospel (2 Cor. 11:4, 7–9; 12:13–16, 1:6–12)	Trinitarian gospel of grace, humbly preached without charge	Antinomian or legalistic distortions and redefinitions,[155] non-Trinitarian, preached for a charge or price, burdensome, amounting to thievery
4. Apostle (2 Cor. 11:5, 13:10; Gal. 1:11–24 and also 2 Pet. 3:15–16)	Commissioned by the Triune God	Disguised selves as "apostles," deceitful workers, self-anointed and self-appointed apostles
5. Servants of righteousness, workers (2 Cor. 11:14–15)	True servants of Christ, authentic righteousness with/from God, humble, suffering with Christ	Satan's servants, disguised as messengers of righteousness and as light; deceitful, abusive, and self-exalting

6. Wisdom and knowledge (2 Cor. 11:15–21, 23–29; 12:16)	Authentic, revelatory and reasonable (consistent and non-abusive), yet often perceived as foolish and deceitful	Foolish, enslaving, absurd, deceitful and contradictory yet disguised/perceived as wisdom
7. Circumcision (Gal. 3, Gal. 5:1–14; also Deut. 30:6, Col. 2:11, Rom. 2:28, Phil. 3:3)	Authentic spiritual circumcision and election	Physical circumcision as sufficient for salvation, false claim to be elect without genuine spiritual circumcision

These semantic contrasts are only illustrative, and to this list could also be added endless comparisons from the synoptics where Jesus, the Logos, returns language and meaning to its true Center relative to terms such as marriage, divorce, children of God, children of Abraham, sinners, and the righteous. Word definitions and usages matter and are connected to the revelation of the Word of God, and the preservation of the gospel depends on orthodox and Logocentric semantics and polemics. Biblical faith communities have sometimes failed to meet the semantic and polemic challenges that have come their way, like in the eighteenth and nineteenth centuries.

Classical Liberal Theology, Semantics, and Apologetics

Friedrich Schleiermacher's classic work, *Reden*, written in 1799, is considered by many to be the *watershed* moment relative to the birth of classical liberal theology *in the church*, and the liberal attempt to separate the gold from the dross (or the kernel from the husk) of historic, orthodox Christian beliefs. Schleiermacher was trying to appeal to the eighteenth-century, "with it," vogue, modernist "cultured despisers" of Christianity by liberating these critics from traditional beliefs and asking them, relative to outmoded orthodox Christian semantics and dogmatics, why they had not "penetrated deeper to find the kernel of this shell."[156]

We face a similar challenge today in creatively responding to what is often referred to as ultramodernism or postmodernism without accommodating or being seduced as was classical liberal theology by modernism, Romanticism, Kant, and Hegel. Relative to word wars, classical liberal theology typically decided to keep, hijack, and co-opt (rather than jettison) the orthodox terms, *and confessions and doctrinal statements*, that had been carefully tested and refined over centuries. Liberals quickly and substantively redefined the terms in ways that were acceptable to them and that accommodated to the modernist and post-orthodox mind-set.

Some classical liberals emphasized ethics, and others emphasized religious experience, as they renovated the Christian faith. Does this sound familiar today? Some believe that as long as they have a passionate experience of Jesus, and/or advocate for social justice, it does not matter what they believe or why they believe it. Besides, theology is confusing and Paul the apostle, the early church fathers (East and West), Hildegard, Augustine, Julian of Norwich, Luther, Calvin, Arminius, Wesley, Edwards, Barth, and Mother Teresa obsessed over non-essentials—or so it is argued.

Most orthodox terms (e.g., the Deity of Christ) were still kept in the progressive, mainline churches and seminaries, though redefined. Some either jettisoned the crude *virgin birth* as superstition and a late addition to the early first century church or biblical narrative, or they demoted and retained its alleged kernel (i.e., Jesus and Mary were unique humans), while shelling the husk (i.e., an actual, divine, miraculous, virginal pregnancy). The underlying biblical affirmations were largely or entirely lost and unrecognizable other than by the few who grasped the mammoth implications of this classical liberal semantic theft.[157]

This theological word "theft" moved in many directions. The "Deity of Christ" became, for some, a statement about how a merely human Jesus had an extremely high or potent level of religious feeling, God-consciousness, or awareness.[158] Therefore, Jesus served as a sort of pipeline to divinity or a higher religious consciousness, and therefore Jesus could still serve or be referred to as Lord and Savior. Liberals would say "of course I believe Jesus is lord and divine; I'm a Christian ordained pastor!" And many believed. And many were seduced.

The resurrection of Christ could still be proclaimed, but it was now merely a veiled reference to Christ living on in the faith, hearts, ethics, or preaching of the disciples and all Christians. Or perhaps belief in the resurrection meant faith in his personal and global impact for the good. For others, at best, "on the third day" was a spiritual (not bodily) resurrection, which, of course, subverts the whole of Christian theology (see 1 Corinthians 15) and pulls progressive theology out of orbit from its Jewish or Hebraic roots. Yet Christ's *resurrection* could still be preached with existential zeal, as with Rudolf Bultmann, who enthusiastically proclaimed an existential resurrection. Bultmann defined the resurrection of Christ as the experience of finding faith amidst existential darkness, even while he was entirely demythologizing the historical, space–time resurrection and, to some extent, the very historicity of what he described as a very historically shadowy Jesus.[159]

The return of Christ could still be shouted from the rooftops, not as a future, decisive, actual, historical, supernatural, space–time intervention but as a symbol of how progressive liberal ideology would ultimately triumph and create a better world and perhaps usher in a "Christian Century."[160] Some of these liberal theologians doubtless had the good intent of making Christianity relevant in an age that increasingly viewed historic Christianity as a dinosaur (as with Voltaire) or an albatross (as with Feuerbach and Nietzsche).

However, the reality or truth was that, as Karl Barth, J. Gresham Machen (in 1923), and others clearly demonstrated, classical liberal theology, while retaining many Christian terms, was in many respects a new, post-Christian modernist religion smuggled into the church and culture beneath the thin surface of vestigial Christian beliefs and terminology. This is what Walter Martin meant by theobabble. In the case of Schleiermacher, he attempted to retain the piety of Christianity, connecting it to the spirit or feeling of Romanticism while exploring radical doctrinal modifications acceptable to the modernist cultured despisers of orthodoxy. Sound familiar? If you insert "postmodern" for modern then you also are tracking with the argument of this work and the spirit of our present age, even within religious communities. Table 4.2 should clarify and illustrate the classical liberal accommodation to the age of modernism.

Table 4.2. Comparative Theological Lexicon[161] (Terms Typically Retained but Redefined by Liberal Theology)

Terms	Biblical, Historic Orthodoxy	Classical Liberal Theology
1. Theological kernel and gold	Biblical, historic, Trinitarian, supernaturally revealed beliefs	Rationally or empirically discerned essence, acceptable to the modern mind
2. Theological husk and dross	Nonessential[162] theological variations	Supernaturalism, irrationalism, scriptural mythology and errors, immoral biblical ethics
3. Deity of Christ	Trinitarian Christology	Unique human, ethical genius, high level of God-consciousness
4. Virgin birth	Trinitarian Christology	Late addition to New Testament, false myth, irrational, yet (for some) still useful to illustrate the uniqueness of Jesus
5. Christ as Savior	Trinitarian Christology and soteriology	Merely human but unique God-consciousness and pipeline to divinity, and/or moral influence
6. Resurrection of Christ	Trinitarian, bodily	Lives on in preaching of disciples, spiritual influence, or a merely spiritual resurrection

7. Return of Christ	Trinitarian, space–time future event	For those still affirming Christ's return, good wins out over evil, liberal values triumph in civilization, or they opt for a realized/experienced eschatology

This slithering semantic tactic was enormously successful in the global Church, synagogue, and the academy (and beyond), as virtually all of the more established and mainstream Christian denominations chased the progressive and often unbiblical modernist elixir that originally promised a coming *Christian Century*. Classical liberalism clearly wedded this Christian advance to progressive thought and liberal ideology and semantics.

This semantic theft within the church of Jesus Christ lacked ethical and semantic integrity. Those like the radical Deists who abandoned biblical, historic, Christian orthodoxy due to the influence of modernism can be criticized for faulty reasoning or assumptions, but relative to semantics at least most evidenced some integrity. Those who engaged in semantic theft and remained in the church sparked a historic theological earthquake that redefined the faith and influenced the culture. Hence, it could be argued that this semantic earthquake in the church was a precursor and key contributor to current cultural decay and the global semantic war for the future of civilization. Has the church, or civilization, learned from these word wars?

A full analysis of all relevant contemporary terms and semantic smuggling far exceeds the limitations of a single book, although an illustrative lexicon in appendix A should assist. Yet these verbal Trojan horses certainly define and illustrate the current struggle for the church and civilization and reveal the pungent aroma of the current relativistic *Zeitgeist* (spirit of the times).

Ask Yourself or Your Group

- *Discuss the true and false meanings of the terms Paul had to properly define for polemic and apologetic reasons?*
- *What can we learn today from how Classical Liberal theology re-defined key terms? Does it really matter how we define these terms? Does polemics matter today? What key terms are being redefined today <u>inside</u> of the church or your church?*
- *Someone has said, "As goes the church, so goes the nation." Do you agree, disagree, and how does semantic analysis relate to this question? Is this statement true: "Redefine words and you will redefine or recreate the family, church, and nation"?*
- *What might happen in the American context if mainline church attendees and pastors increasingly embraced or returned to biblical semantics, beliefs and values and worked hand in hand with tactful, biblically and spiritually energized traditional American evangelical, Roman Catholic, Mormon, and Jewish faith communities? What if these groups collaborated to shape the future of semantics, culture, and civilization, and worked together to reach the increasing numbers of "religiously unaffiliated"? Consider this question in view of the fact that the Pew Research Center reported (2016), concerning America's 300 plus million population, that "the U.S. as 100 people" translates to "Two Jews, One Muslim, and 71 Christians"? Please see the Pew Research Center data: https://www.pewresearch.org/fact-tank/2016/11/14/if-the-u-s-had-100-people-charting-americans-religious-affiliations/ft_16-10-13_100religious_affiliation420px/.*[163]
- *Additional and recent Pew Research data concluded that "In [the] U.S., Decline of Christianity Continues at Rapid Pace," the "religious nones" or religiously unaffiliated are growing rapidly, and there is a huge generation gap in religious belief and practice in the American context. Are*

religious Americans and their children being seduced? How and why? Are these trends tremendous opportunities for kingdom advance, and, if so, exactly how? How might diverse and biblically faithful Judeo-Christian faith communities work together and, by God's grace, restore normative truth and write the future pages of history for church and state? Please see this additional Pew Research Center data: https://www.pewforum.org/2019/10/17/in-u-s-decline-of-christianity-continues-at-rapid-pace/.[164]

Chapter 5

TRUTH or "TRUTH"?

God usually exerts ... [His] power in connection with certain prior conditions of the human mind, and it should be
ours to create, so far as we can, with the help of God, those
favorable conditions for the reception of the gospel. False
ideas [conveyed by semantic tapestries] are the greatest
obstacles to the reception of the gospel. We may preach
with all the fervor of a reformer and yet succeed only in
winning a straggler here and there, if we permit the whole
collective thought [or semantic universe] of the nation [or
the church] or of the world to be controlled by ideas [and
words] which, by the resistless force of logic [or semantic
seduction], prevent Christianity from being regarded
as anything more than a harmless [or privatized, ghet-
toized] delusion.
—J. Gresham Machen, 1912[165]

*For the weapons of our warfare are not of the flesh, but
divinely powerful for the destruction of fortresses. We are
destroying speculations and every lofty thing raised up
against the knowledge of God, and we are taking every
thought [and word] captive to the obedience of Christ.*
—2 Corinthians 10:5

The creative, incarnate Triune Logos birthed the church to evangelize and disciple the nations, present a people "holy and blameless and beyond reproach" (Colossians 1:22), serve as salt and light, and herald and approximate the New Creation through the Triune ministry of the already/not-yet kingdom. Yet when the response of faith communities to semantic or word theft is simply to *"bear this beautifully,"*[166] including accepting theobabble (see Chapter 4) or polybabble (defined in Chapter 6), then all is at risk well beyond the walls of the church. The only enduring semantic glue holding together church and state is vanishing.

TRUTH, Truth, truth, and "Just My Personal Story"

Engaging the countless theories and nuances of truth[167] after modernity far exceeds the purpose and thesis of this book. However, to oversimplify for the purpose of the present argument, Scripture and centuries of sound biblical theology affirm that truth is trifold in nature. God alone possesses something like TRUTH, defined in the strongest or even absolute sense (and therefore capitalized) relative to God's knowledge of self and reality.[168] Because of God's amazing, gracious revelation and self-disclosure, even fallen and fallible humans, created in the image of God, have the *created* and grace-assisted potential increasingly to know some measure of reliable Truth concerning God, salvation, the physical world, the future, and how we should live in the present age. The contemporary obsession with reducing truth to the mere personal, the culturally bound, the tribal, or the subjective[169] stands in stark contrast to the understanding of Truth prevalent during the history of the church or the founding of numerous Judeo-Christian influenced countries and civilizations.

The distortion and relativizing of truth is pervasive,
even or especially in the American evangelical church.

Today, core beliefs and ethical standards are prefaced by the following:

- "This is only my perspective."
- "This is just my personal preference."
- "This is just my personal opinion."
- "I have the right to think and believe what I want."
- "My personal beliefs are nobody's business."

Now, to be fair, such phrases are usually appropriate when discussing things such as one's preferences concerning a flavor of ice cream, a favorite vacation spot, or what time an adult turns in for the evening. Such qualifications certainly can assist with collegial and open discussion on some matters. However, these terms and phrases are now applied to core truths and ethical norms. I would assert:

1. On issues that really matter, it is most redundant to say, "This is just my personal opinion." Of course it is your opinion, since you are saying it.

2. Is it really just a personal opinion or perspective that child sacrifice is immoral? Is it merely an opinion that children should not be tortured? Is it *just my perspective* that we should avoid nuclear war? Is it mere personal preference to be faithful in marriage or to treat others as we would like to be treated ourselves?

Hence, even terms like perspective, preference, and personal opinion have been defined out of meaningful existence. The language we use reflects a crisis of truth and word.[170] Such qualifiers amount to epistemological surrender—the broad acceptance of the view that no one has the right to make *any* normative truth claims. Such surrender would avow, "We can really know nothing except what I personally know and experience." Objective knowledge or absolute truth outside of "me" simply doesn't exist.

The erosion of truth is especially evident, in and outside of the church, with the current obsession with the terms "story" or "my story." "Story" certainly has a proper and legitimate usage with some stories falling into the genre of imaginative fiction and other stories closely corresponding to historical reality. The stories of World War II or Gandhi's social movement transpired in space and time, and the key is to get the details and facts correct.

The problem today is that "story" is now utilized to reduce all truth claims to a matter of personal or tribal preferences. Many would argue something like this:

"Trusting Christ for salvation is my personal story, but your personal story may be trusting in yourself or Allah. *My story* is true for me and your story is true for you. I cannot prove that my story is truer than yours; indeed, your story may be just as meaningful and *true* as mine. Any story can be a means to happiness and God, and we should not judge the stories of others."

"The Bible is a story, but there are many holy books, philosophies, and stories. It is fine to believe the Bible as long as this personal story is not imposed on others and as long as the bad and hateful parts (e.g., non-inclusive morality) are kept in the privatized and cultural closet. There is no *Story* that everyone should believe; there are only stories. There is no *Perspective* that is *True*; there are only perspectives and personal opinions that are *true* — with a small t."

This understanding and definition of truth, morality, story, and opinion, of course, amounts to personal, cultural, and civilizational insanity and sociopathology.[171] Is it only a perspective or opinion that civilizations and religions practicing human and infant sacrifice, human trafficking, ethnic genocide, temple prostitution, female circumcision, or brutal slavery are immoral? Was the Third Reich [i.e., kingdom] or the Manifest Destiny justification for the Trail of Tears just a preferential story, no worse or no better than any others?

The failure to assess and discriminate among stories, opinions, perspectives, and words is itself a devastating and dangerous attempt to smuggle in an alternate *Story*, perspective, and opinion. In America, this drift from the belief in and pursuit of Truth is most consequential.

Veritas

Relative to the American context, Edwin Gaustad has irrefutably documented how the many Colonial "Nurseries of Piety"[172] drifted from historic Christian Orthodox semantics, including drifting from the very notion of Truth.

When Harvard University was founded in 1636, it served as the first of many colonial "Nurseries of Piety."[173] All colonial nurseries of piety have largely abandoned their children and journeyed, to one degree or another, from their founding Judeo-Christian visions and missions. This shift did not happen overnight. Key terms like "truth," basic Christian doctrinal terms, or "Christian college" were redefined in order to accommodate to prevailing cultural and intellectual winds. These schools did not wake up one day and become post-Christian. The drift from orthodoxy was incremental and began with semantic drift. Evangelical, Jewish, and Roman Catholic drift today is fueled by semantic drift.

Harvard's College of Arms was a shield emblazoned with the word *Veritas* (i.e., Truth).[174] In 1636, Truth (see Chapter 9 concerning TRUTH, Truth, and truth) was especially connected to the belief in and pursuit of normative, personally and socially liberating biblical Truth — a reliable redemption seeking and civilization building Truth.

This quest no doubt was already interacting with the Truth quest of the Renaissance and emerging modernism, yet the belief in the attainability of a normative and shared understanding for Truth was primarily connected to scriptural revelation — this conception flourished in the colonial era. Harvard trained ministers. Today, however, via word theft, the claim to Truth is now often viewed only as an oppressive Western concept used to empower some and disempower others. This normative Truth should be replaced with the understanding that all truth (small *t*) is merely one or some/all of the following: personal (i.e., truth for me); lived and felt truth more so than known truth; passionate and bodily truth rather than prescriptive or cognitive truth; personally or culturally created rather than discovered truth; volitional (i.e., willed) truth; and, culturally bound or tribal truth, ultimately relative to the individual, group, or observer(s) and hence a mere matter of mere perspective.[175]

In contrast to relativized conceptions of truth, the University Laws of Harvard from 1642–1650 clearly affirmed Truth or *veritas* with an implied and divinely revealed capital *T*, and the Laws clearly rooted the concept in Scripture: "Every one shall consider the mayne End of his life and studyes to *know God and Jesus Christ which is Eternall life.*"[176] Harvard and the colonial nurseries of piety embraced Logocentric truth.

Logocentrism and *Lex Rex*

Truth and language were, much to the later dismay of Nietzsche and his minions, inseparably and organically tethered to the Logos and, hence, Logocentric—*primarily* in the theological sense.[177] They were also clearly tethered to the firm conviction of the advancing kingdom of God—hence, words were Logocentric and kingdom-centric. The semantic universe was thus Logocentric and kingdom-centric.

When *words* become separated from the Word and the kingdom, which usually takes place over time, meaningful communication collapses and all that remains is a tooth and fang will to power that *uses* words. The Word and words are inseparable. The collapse of the Judeo-Christian influence on the colonial nurseries of piety happened for many reasons, one of which was the failure of semantic polemics and apologetics to respond to verbal equivocation of the *avant-garde* arguments against core beliefs and values. This failure should be instructive today for evangelicals, evangelical educational institutions, and all proponents of Judeo-Christian influence on culture.

Today, some version or interpretation of Nietzsche's, "There is no truth,"[178] resonates in many sectors of academia, the philosophy and practice of law, and increasingly in popular culture. One might ask if this "there is no truth" statement is, in any sense, True, but this sentiment that all beliefs and ethical convictions are "perspectival"[179] is truly in the cultural air we breathe—even in some religious communities and Christian demographics.[180]

Relative to Lewis's suggested eternal vigilance regarding the future of civilization, the loss of some firm concept and definition of Truth or normative Truth is the loss of a central pillar of civilization, not to mention the cultural glue for civilized discourse and civilization. In the American context, "we hold these truths to be self-evident," the Laws of Nature and Nature's God quickly now dissolve, *along with* "certain unalienable rights,"[181] into the ocean of perspectival truth and ethics.

The knowability of some measure of Truth was an essential assumption of the *Declaration of Independence*, and the *Declaration*, with much taken verbatim from Locke, was an essential assumption of not only the American *Constitution* (and many other constitutions), but of the American experiment in forming a civilization hoped to be a "more perfect union." Relative to Truth and civilization, all is at stake. If rights are not grounded in divinely sanctioned, revealed, and knowable truth, and are merely perspectival, then they hardly qualify as self-evident or unalienable—much less real or sustainable. Rights then devolve into transient, tribal, or mob-rule preferences.

To be perfectly clear to the critics, this work is not trying to preserve the Enlightenment or modernist conception or norm of "truth." That concept was imperfect. Fallen humanity is still referred to in Scripture as being created in and having the status of the image of God (Genesis 9:6). Yet humanity is fallen and flawed at the very core (Jer. 17:9). Hence, neither a naïve optimism about fallen humanity's ability to reason properly, nor an unwarranted pessimism concerning the potential of human reason created in the image of God, is warranted. The desperately wicked human heart and the fallen mind are also objects of grace and redemption in this present age. Biblical reason is not identical to Enlightenment or modernist or postmodern reason and, by grace, prophetically critiques both modernism and postmodernism.

Interestingly, the American experiment emerged at the confluence of the Enlightenment's unbridled optimism, the Puritans unbridled realism of human nature, the Puritan vision of a City Set on a Hill and creation mandate, and the Wesleyan realism of human nature and optimism of radical grace that fueled social reform. This synthesis birthed a dynamic norm for truth, law, and ethics, and led to political realities such as the Trinitarian balance of power between branches of government, the shared awareness that religion and morality are necessary supports of freedom, and the confident quest by grace for a more perfect union. The normative truth of the American experiment was far more profound, dynamic, theological, complex, and far richer and more fecund than a simplistic conception of modernist truth. Normative truth in the American experiment was an amazing synthesis and consensus involving deep passion and centuries of careful thought and reflection, and it accommodated some healthy differences of perspective and nuance. The founders were less than perfect but it is past time that we quit looking down our elitist noses at these historic figures. The tragedy today is that many, in rejecting the modernist norm for truth and ethics, are now drifting wayward on the troubled waters of truth and ethical relativism.

One example of this truth consensus is the very structure of the American government just referenced. The very *balance of power* ideal guiding the *Declaration* and the *Constitution* was rooted in the following: a verbal and conceptual Judeo-Christian tapestry responding to the abuse of "Divine right" power in Europe; a heightened awareness of human depravity (and therefore the need to limit power); and a monotheistic, Trinitarian, theological and anthropological optimistic solution that divided government into three coequal branches pursuing a more perfect union. Power was to be subject to revealed and eternal *Lex* not sinful *Rex*, and it must be distributed and balanced.

This monotheistic experiment was not subject to a human king (the failed European experience) but subject to principled law rooted in Truth guaranteed and given by God. As many have pointed out as early as Rutherford, this Trinitarian verbal and conceptual framework affirmed that God's Law (truth and eternal principles) served as King, rather than affirming that the king or the king's truth was the law. As noted previously in Chapter 2, and this is worth endlessly repeating as our civilization drifts, the experiment was *Lex Rex*, not *Rex Lex*.[182] Apart from some normative concept of knowable Truth, this experiment inevitably fragments and fails over time. For those who reject modernist reason, the appeal at this point would be for them at least to provide a workable, shared, and normative alternative.

I have mentioned the need for us to be Logocentric. Let's turn to a further discussion of that as we proceed.

Ask Yourself or Your Group

- *Do you agree or disagree with the distinction between TRUTH, Truth, and truth? Have you ever heard or used the phrase, "well, that is just my personal opinion?" Is that phrase ever proper? Improper? Redundant? Is there a danger to having everyone emphasize their "story" today? Is there value in emphasizing personal stories?*
- *How does Truth relate to Lex Rex and Rex Lex? How do Lex Rex and Rex Lex relate to the American experiment in representative democracy? Which politicians today affirm Lex Rex and which affirm Rex Lex?*

Chapter 6

LOGOCENTRIC AND KINGDOM-CENTRIC CIVILIZATION OR HYPER-POLYTHEISTIC TRIBALISM?

The gospel is never preached in a vacuum. It is always heard against the backdrop of the culture's collective mindset and mood. Well, the cultural mindset and mood is steeped in postmodern thought that relativizes truth, knowledge, and value. As a result, people today are morally confused and biblically illiterate. Confusion, darkness, and disintegration reign.
—Paul Gould (2017)

As such, what many call postmodernity or postmodernism I will discuss as being a stance or epistemology (theory of or approach to knowledge) *within*, and only intelligible *within*, modernity.
—Rustin E. Brian (2013, emphasis added)

Professing to be wise, they became fools.
—Romans 1:22

Polybabble

When classical liberal theology creatively and/or seductively replaced biblical and orthodox theology, the echo of Judeo-Christian monotheism (i.e., belief in one personal God) still remained as a central assumption of Judeo-Christian communities and many nation states. Yet with the death of Truth today, even that remaining truth echo is now merely one personal, nonnormative preference among many. Hence, the ecclesial challenge of theobabble has now become an assault on church and Judeo-Christian influenced civilization that may perhaps be best characterized as polybabble (see Chapter 5). Polybabble is ultimately the de-tethering of language and meaning from the Trinitarian Logos. This de-tethering ultimately empties all communication of transcultural meaning, norms and authority.

Reducing Truth to "truth is merely truth for me" is, on a fundamental level, ultimately a form of polytheism (many gods or ultimate concerns). Polybabble is arguably more of a threat to civilization than polytheism (or even terrorism), since with polybabble not only does every culture have its own god or gods, *but every culture, subculture, tribe, or individual is a functional god.*

For postmodern, ultramodern, and individualistic relativism, our project is to become or function as god, defining ourselves, truth, morality and the future. Hence, we have moved from civilizations premised on many gods, usually with a supreme demigod leader, which provided some coherence and order by at least functioning as a pseudo-monotheistic surrogate, to experimenting today with civilization based on countless and competing functional gods.

Atheism does not eradicate functional religion from culture. It simply spawns legion alternate gods, and atheism is arguably a loose-knit religion with core ideological commitments, apart from authoritarian and centralized atheistic communism. Sartre reflected the heart of the new religious or non-religious hyper-polytheism today very well: Humanity's "project is to become [as] God" (i.e., function as God relative to meaning, truth and morality).[183] Yes, Sartre criticizes the desire to be God in one sense, when we try to eradicate the contradiction of our finite existence. Yet, in another sense, Sartre clearly affirms that the role that God used to occupy is now ours, which creates much *angst*. Sartre represents existentialism, which is an early and individualistic form of what is now referred to as postmodernity. Hence, with both atheistic existentialism and the New Age movement, the individual functions as god. The result is we now swim in religious and non-religious polytheism and pluralism.

Tribalism and Balkanization

It is hard to resist the conclusion that this loss of a shared norm for language and meaning—a common semantic universe—likely, eventually, and inevitably leads toward one or more of the following: cultural fragmentation, extreme polarization, militant advocacy for one's tribe, and eventually the disintegration and Balkanization, if not the dissolution, of both orthodox Judeo-Christian communities and aspirational civilization.

The United Methodist Church in America currently faces the very real possibility of a split or Balkanization as the Christian orthodox consensus continues to diminish, and the historically orthodox Wesleyan semantic universe within the United Methodist Church is in question. The church may split before this book is widely read. Methodists operating within the context of a *post-* (e.g., postmodern, post-Christian, post-orthodox, post-Wesleyan) semantic universe, inevitably *see* LGBTQ+ ordination and marriage differently than those viewing such issues from something akin to John Wesley's eighteenth-century orthodox vantage point. While it may take centuries or decades for countries and denominations and churches and synagogues to fragment or fracture, the outcome of such cosmic semantic shifts will always be the same.[184]

Based on historical experience (e.g., Russia in the 1920s or Europe of the 1930s), the result of such accelerating chaos, at the level of civilization, is typically armed conflict, and/or civil war, and/or the emergence of the extreme centralization of power to restore order. Sound eerily familiar? Europe is arguably and currently in a holding pattern after two world wars, weary of conflict and ideology, except for the ideology of post-Christian relativism, and somewhat dependent on American economic vitality and military prowess and deterrence. In strong free market economies, the first step towards the abyss will likely be or already is economic civil war, where economic power is utilized to define and enforce the semantic universe. More importantly for our discussion, this semantic polybabble is not likely to be sustainable over time. Someone or something will eventually emerge to restore order.

Ultramodern Syncretism — Beyond Postmodernity

This I am god and truth and ethics are truth and ethics for me sentiment lies at the heart of what many have referred to as the current age of postmodernism or ultramodernism. "Post," of course, means after modernism, and modernism refers to the Western, modernistic age characterized by the following: Western, (often) arrogant *reason*; the *rejection of past superstitions* (e.g., traditional superstitions such as Christianity and Judaism); *scientific reasoning* as the path to rational truth; belief in rational, scientific *progress*; *toleration* (only of reasonable beliefs and progressive thought, of course); and, tremendous zeal and optimism concerning the future and even the need for and possibility of, to some degree, *starting history over again* (e.g., the French Revolution or many forms of Communism).

In contrast, the *Encyclopedia Britannica* properly and succinctly emphasizes these postmodern themes: "a late 20th-century movement characterized by broad skepticism, subjectivism, or relativism; a general suspicion of reason; and an acute sensitivity to the role of ideology in asserting and maintaining political and economic power."[185] The *Stanford Encyclopedia of Philosophy* emphasizes the *telos* and origin of the movement: "to destabilize other concepts [and words] such as presence, identity, historical progress, epistemic certainty, and the univocity of meaning. The term 'postmodernism' first entered the philosophical lexicon in 1979, with the publication of *The Postmodern Condition* by Jean-François Lyotard."[186]

Lyotard, of course, provided the oft-quoted and classic bumper sticker definition of the movement: "Simplifying to the extreme, I define postmodern as incredulity towards metanarratives," and he defined metanarrative as "a global or totalizing cultural narrative schema which orders and explains knowledge [and words] and experience."[187] Christianity, communism, Islam, and even postmodernism itself would be classic examples of grand, overarching, totalizing, all-encompassing narratives or Stories, with a capital *S*, that seek to use semantics to interpret and explain (or dismiss) the major questions of existence. These normative and typically prescriptive big stories influence or even direct the future of human existence and civilization.

Since this is not a purist academic or philosophical work, perhaps it will be helpful to summarize briefly the **ten commandments of postmodernism**.[188] Non-specialists should be able to better grasp the essentials of the sometimes esoteric, difficult to understand (abstruse), and confusing postmodern perspective via these concise commandments. This list is based primarily on a carefully written scholarly work as opposed to popular literature, blogs, and diatribes. Nothing is simple or brief relative to explaining postmodernity; and it is more a posture than a creed. This list is presented mildly tongue-in-cheek, but should assist the non-specialist with comprehending and learning about this important movement.

1. Thou shalt use rational arguments to *reject human confidence in reason.*
2. Thou shalt confess the perspective that *all perspectives are "radically situated,"* biased, prejudiced, and perspectival. (Morality is largely or entirely a matter of perspective, although some perspectives must be rejected as immoral.)
3. Thou shalt confess with words and language that *language is "inherently unstable,"* a "mobile army of metaphors," and it does not objectively explain reality.
4. Thou shalt acknowledge the truth that *all truth is constructed or created* and "not discovered" or revealed.
5. Thou shalt recognize that *the human self is not stable, enduring, or clearly definable*, and that we can only subjectively define ourselves.

6. Thou shalt confess and make the historical and philosophical observation that *all "writing of history" is "essentially ideological."*

7. Thou shalt *reject "European and American exceptionalism"* and Judeo-Christian cultural exceptionalism and affirm and advocate for postmodern cultural exceptionalism.

8. Thou shalt confess the truth that *truth is* largely or entirely non-objective, non-normative, personally or tribally subjective, and *especially or primarily therapeutic.* (Truth, with a small "t," is grounded more in what works, what feels good, what is true to oneself, and what aligns with personal or tribal perceived needs, desires, and tribal definitions of and advocacy for social justice.)

9. Thou shalt confess the non-oppressive and grand truth that *all grand explanations of reality (metanarratives) are "inherently oppressive."*

10. Thou shalt use reason and argument to *reject the omnicompetence or super-competency of reason.*

Additional clarity, elaboration, explanation and commentary on these ten commandments is essential at this point for specialists and non-specialists. The italicized material is the extended version of the commandments, followed by my brief commentary on the commandment.

1. *Thou shalt use rational arguments to facilitate cultural progress—or at least avoid ideological and nationalistic oppression—by rejecting the Enlightenment and modernistic confidence in human reason and civilizational progress.* In other words, the myth that reason and science could save the world has been exposed as false and dangerous. Postmodernists continue to employ reason and science and enjoy many of the benefits of reason and science. Postmodernists are arguably exhausted moderns, running on the fumes of a failed non-theistic modernist project. Hence, ultramodern syncretism may more accurately describe the postmodern posture. First, it is more of a posture than rigid

monolithic beliefs. Second, postmodernists can't escape western reason and science and parasite off of both. Third, the rejection of absolute standards for truth and morality, at least common at the popular cultural level, has been replaced with a syncretistic mixing of countless values, practices, religions, ethics, and philosophies. Fourth, and most important for defining the movement, this ultramodernism is the ultimate syncretism, mixing together not only varied and inconsistent beliefs and practices, but also incoherently hybridizing the assumptions of modernism and postmodernism. Hence, ultramodern syncretism truly is the ultimate syncretism, as it inconsistently absorbs major elements of both modernism and postmodernism. The term postmodernism really does not capture this key point and mega-syncretistic reality as does ultramodernism. In any event, a more biblical approach is to acknowledge the limitations of human reason, especially fallen human reason (referred by theologians as the noetic impact of the fall), and the desperate need for divine revelation and grace.

2. *Thou shalt believe and confess that human reason and all perspectives are "heavily situated," biased, and prejudiced by one's historical and social context and that no one is a "neutral observer."*

   Statements are redundantly prefaced with "this is just my personal opinion." Everything or most everything is true for me but not true for you, including morality. Beliefs are entirely or almost entirely determined by context and/or personal preference. A more biblical position would affirm that context is very influential and must be addressed, but that context is not determinative. We are not automatons and many have prophetically challenged their cultural context, even to the point of martyrdom.

3. *Thou shalt use language and words to reject "the idea that language simply and transparently captures the world around us."*

   This commandment has been indirectly addressed throughout this work and has extreme relevance to semantic polemics and apologetics. A more biblical trajectory would affirm that fallen human reason and language is limited in its ability to capture and correspond to reality. Yet divine revelation, the divine origin of communication, and the image of God in humanity all ensure significant correspondence between reality and reason via language properly utilized. This is another reason why semantics is critical to effective Christian mission and cultural engagement.

4. *Thou shalt affirm the truth that truth is created and constructed rather than discovered as something "that is (in some sense) already out there."*
See commandment number two above, but the majority Judeo-Christian perspective has been that in spite of the limits of human knowing, and the constructive role of the human mind in perception, normative truth or True truth is more discovered and revealed than created. Individual and tribal truth creation is ultimately devastating to culture and civilization and inevitably inflames the polarization that exists already within any pluralistic culture.

5. *Thou shalt reject the idea that the human self, human nature, and human gender are set, fixed, and "stable and continuous over time."*
While individuals certainly can grow and develop over time, this commandment is much more radical than that. While Scripture acknowledges that individuals choose and are responsible for what they become, Scripture also affirms the image of God, fallen human nature, and the Christlike ideal for true humanity. Scripture frames the nature of humanity and gender. Ultramodern syncretism claims that such matters are not fixed or determined, yet their political advocacy often suggests they really believe otherwise and exposes yet another contradiction. In Scripture, Christ is the second Adam and humanity's true future.

6. *Thou shalt utilize the methods and results of historical, philosophical, and social science research to affirm the truth that we should be suspicious that historians, philosophers,*

and social scientists can "provide any hope of arriving at objective truth."

Here we have another false dichotomy. Either we are almost completely biased and prejudiced (postmodernism), or we can use reason and science to arrive at objective truth (modernism). In reality, the quest for truth is arduous, requires awareness of our contextual and sinful tendencies, is communal involving checks and balances from others, and requires receptivity to grace and divine revelation. We should be both suspicious and hopeful concerning the noble quest.

7. *Thou shalt demonstrate the moral superiority, truthfulness and objectivity of the postmodern perspective by rejecting "the traditional idea that Europe and North America are somehow . . . superior to countries" in the majority (non-Western) world.*

No culture or civilization should be assumed to be inferior or exceptional prior to honest, careful, grace-based analysis. Yet we must avoid the dangerous relativism of affirming that all cultures and civilizations are created equal and make difficult, discerning, grace-assisted, and multi-complex comparisons and assessments. While postmodernism claims to reject exceptionalism, the movement often functions as another form of exceptionalism. No culture or civilization is currently the fullness of the kingdom of God, yet all cultures and civilizations must be critiqued, compared, and contrasted by the coming kingdom of God if we have any hope for genuine and sustainable progress.

8. *Thou shalt affirm the objective truth that we can no longer affirm objective truth and therefore we must "increasingly see truth as more therapeutic in nature" rather than "static and objective."*

Postmodern truth, with a small "t," is grounded more in what works, what feels good, what is true to oneself, and what aligns with personal or tribal perceived needs and desires. Biblical truth has therapeutic value but is ultimately grounded in the amazing and divine self-disclosure that is personally true and objectively true. Indeed, personal truth divorced from objective truth is merely a truth illusion and opiate.

9. *Thou shalt proclaim the big truth that all big truths, stories, mega-narratives, and meta-narratives are "inherently oppressive" and "generally beyond the human ability to grasp them."*

   We should be cautious about "big truths," as many or most have wrought demonic devastation across the globe. However, the myth that as long as we don't believe anything too strongly, or as normative, we will avoid war, conflict, and oppression is turning out to be very short lived in human history and out of touch with the reality of human nature and the facts of history. Additionally, the rejection of meta-narratives has morphed, at least at the popular or cultural level, into yet another increasingly oppressive meta-narrative. Let's find the normative big story, live accordingly, and approximate God's ultimate and glorious future already.

10. *Thou shalt utilize careful reasoning, language, and rational argument to reject what Alister McGrath refers to as the arrogant, modernistic "omnicompetence [total or absolute competence] of reason."*

    Again, postmodernity rests on endless false dichotomies and blatant contradictions, and we have addressed this commandment previously and throughout this text. The choice is not between the worship of reason (or omnicompetent reason) and irrationality. By grace, revelation, and humble reason we can fulfill the image of God by understanding and serving as good stewards of God's very good creation.

By the way, if a critic wants to argue that these are not really commandments, they are often intentionally or unintentionally contradictory and incoherent, and they are not obligatory relative to what any postmodernist actually believes or practices, then such points will be readily conceded! The case for postmodernism is as flawed or more flawed than the case for modernism. Both need to be filtered by sound reason and divine revelation.

After constructing (or deconstructing) these ten commandments it seemed prudent to search book distributors and the internet to see if any books or articles surfaced on the ten commandments of postmodernism. I was surprised at the lack of such material, and only located one lightly sarcastic parody. I did, however, locate a lecture outline by Dr. Jim Dennison (PhD, Southwestern Baptist Theological Seminary), which could help clarify the argument of this book by responding to Dennison's top ten list.[189] I will only make brief comments on those items needful of nuancing or quick commentary.

1. *Separate Spiritual and Secular*
   This separation is more of a modern than postmodern emphasis. The recent postmodern emphasis is more open to pervasive spirituality in culture as long as it is privatized spirituality, "ABC" (see the front matter and Preface), and in alignment with postmodern political advocacy. For postmodernists, separation of church and state has become a smokescreen for ABC, not for anything but spirituality. Privatized ultramodern syncretistic spirituality and politically liberationist spirituality are acceptable.

2. *Locate Truth within the Individual*
   Locate the truth within the individual or tribe, and as always, "ABC." Many in the postmodern tribe are more than willing, however, to silence inconvenient truth emanating from non-members.

3. *Accommodate Truth to Culture*

4. *Reject Ecclesiastical Authority*
   The only nuance is especially to reject such authority unless we are referring to churches who have swallowed the postmodern bait hook, line, and sinker, and who advocate for postmodern social justice.

5. *Reject Absolute Truth*
   Except for the truth that there is no absolute truth.

6. *Deconstruct Language*

Except for the philosophy, perspective, and language used to deconstruct language.

7. *Resist Power Structures (By building your own power structure)*

8. *Affirm a Chaotic Worldview*
   As noted throughout this work, the postmodern worldview is more of a posture than a worldview, it is more ultra-modern than truly postmodern (which will be discussed momentarily), and it is more chaotically syncretistic than merely chaotic.

9. *Replace Truth with Tolerance*
   However, tolerance is selective and postmodernists actually assume a very normative view of truth and correct language.

10. *Brand Religion as Dangerous*
    Except for religion or spirituality that aligns or is not a threat to postmodernism, and except for the postmodern religion because postmodernism (or ultramodern syncretism) often functions like a very aggressive and proselytizing religion.

As noted, every culture, civilization, sub-culture, and movement has the equivalent of a ten commandments. The key is to locate and live by those which truly come from beyond human speculation.

Tom Oden sometimes preferred the terms "ultramodernism" or "mod-rot" as a superior way to characterize the current and later stages of the failed project of modernism (since 1989 and the fall of the Berlin Wall), which was now running on fumes.[190] In other words, modernism (reason and science) failed miserably at creating an ideal or utopian civilization, as well as failing to create a semantic framework and value system that could provide the social glue for a better civilization. Modernistic reason and science destroyed the reason and science that was supposed to deliver progress and the modernistic utopia.

Mod-rot means we are now running, stalling, and floundering on modernistic fumes amidst widespread fragmentation and cultural decay. Hence, we now live in the age of ultramodernism rather than the age of postmodernism. We are living in the "ultra" or last, final, exhausted, contradictory phase of modernity. Whatever this current age or phase is, the impact on semantics is incalculable. We may be in the latter stages of modernism, but we are well advanced in the era of semantic reengineering and have been for decades if not centuries.

For those with a philosophical background, it is important to note in agreement with one aspect of structuralism that the organic nature of semantics is assumed in this work. However, in contrast to structuralism this work affirms that the organic nature of Logocentric language defeats relativistic or subjectivist formulations of structuralism. It is also important to note that this work acknowledges the utility of the post-critical deconstruction of language and systems, while also affirming that Logocentric and revelation-based language and semantics can and do escape the onus of relativistic deconstruction. Indeed, deconstructionism is at its best when deconstructing deconstructionism, because it then begins to overcome its endless logical contradictions and point toward the need for a shared semantic norm. Deconstructionism is actually an excellent argument for the Judeo-Christian Logos.

Another way of communicating this academic debate would emphasize the true nature of language. "Some views of language may see linguistic meaning as involving both referential issues (what objects key terms refer to) and relational ones (how each word relates to the other words present) . . . [The more radical view is that] the full meaning is decided entirely by relational issues, not referential ones."[191] The radical view of language, rejected in this book, is not simply affirming that words find their meaning within systems or families of organically related terms, which is the view of *Seduced*. The radical view is saying that the entire system, semantic universe, or family of words does not correspond with, connect to, or objectively define reality, and that if the system or structure changes then the meaning of the individual term also changes. Terms never truly correspond to reality, according to this extreme view.

Hence, radical linguistic postmodernism is premised upon yet another logical fallacy. Either words do not correspond to reality and they are simply subjective pieces of a subjective language game, *or* words and terms perfectly and objectively correspond to and define reality and they exist as independent, objective, and static facts about reality. For those trained in philosophy, this false dichotomy would be similar to saying that the only options concerning knowing reality (epistemology) are either naïve commonsense realism *or* phenomenalism—or even solipsism. Philosophers are aware that there are other options for how and what we know about reality, such as critical realism, direct realism, and indirect realism.

From a biblical perspective, because of divine revelation, coherent, meaningful, and reliable semantics is possible. Also for those with philosophical competencies, it is important to note that there are many postmodern varieties and postures. That level of analysis exceeds the purpose of this present book. The concern in this book is primarily with relativistic and sometimes nihilistic versions of postmodernity that have captured and corrupted the popular, cultural, and academic imagination and passions. Ultramodern syncretism is more helpful at diagnosing the present semantic and cultural crisis.

Hence, ultramodern syncretism is much preferred as a late twentieth- and twenty-first-century cultural descriptor and framework for semantic apologetics. *Post* tells us little, and *ultra* only lets us know we are in the final or extreme culturally and philosophically *reductio ad absurdum* stages of mod-rot. "Post-pregnant" has little value in capturing the radical new reality and experience of a woman in contrast to the term "mother"! Ultramodern syncretism better captures the contemporary chaotic Zeitgeist. Ultramodern syncretism includes the following: truth for me or my tribe; reckless and often incoherent mixing of beliefs, values, and practices; and the ultimate syncretism of mixing a suspicion or disdain for modernism with a parasitical dependence on the assumptions, toys, and benefits of modernism—just as modernism unravels.

Ironically, parasitical ultramodern syncretists lament and denounce the evils of reason and science and the slippery nature of language while flying on jets and using electronic tablets and words via the World Wide Web. They denounce in (far more than *truth is just for me*) creatively chosen narratives the great evils of Western and Christian civilization. Really?

The expected result is a rather self-righteous polybabble that, via wholesale word theft, seeks to replace the Truth and civilization aspirations birthed by biblical and Enlightenment assumptions with all that is left: polytheistic, tribalistic, individualistic, and militant advocacy for a plethora of causes or tribes united primarily by disdain for Western and biblical values—ABC. A simple comparison of how different news networks handle the same news items is revealing: (1) contradictory news reports cannot both be right if logic exists and if logic applies to reality, and (2) words de-tethered from the plumb line of the Logos eventually degenerate into mere *"news"* advocacy parading as news, shameless spin, will-to-power, polybabble, and semantic theft.

Perhaps the most profound political word theft today in America is how the nonestablishment-of-religion concept has morphed into the militant and oppressive justification of the establishment of a functional, post (or anti) Judeo-Christian state religion. This ultramodern and syncretistic state religion ironically often functions like the very fundamentalist religions it despises.

This Nietzschean inversion of words and ethics has been underway for over a century, but took on a very public and activist political posture in 1971 in America when Saul Alinsky essentially dedicated his political activity and infamous *Rules for Radicals* to "the very first radical ... known to man who rebelled against the establishment and did it so effectively that he at least won his own kingdom—Lucifer."[192] Heroizing Satan is perhaps the ultimate word theft, polybabble, and inversion of words, values, and ethics. Alinsky was indeed kingdomcentric, he just voted for the wrong kingdom.

The point here, though worthy of note, is not the reference to the dark side, but Alinsky's (and countless others) brash and intentional Nietzschean inversion of values and terms and semantic theft seeking to usurp Judeo-Christian influence in and on civilization. Alinsky did this with eyes wide open. Nearly fifty years later the establishment-of-religion clause continues to be militantly used by some to establish an oppressive, post-Christian state religion—all in the name of toleration, inclusion, social justice, freedom, and, most ironically, religious neutrality. And this pluralistic, syncretistic, post Judeo-Christian civil religion is often very uncivil in the media, entertainment, law, politics, the ivory tower, and even in some largely post Judeo-Christian churches and synagogues. Even many in the more progressive religious groups have taken a large bite out of Alinsky's apple, if not swallowing the seductive fruit entirely.

Given space limitations, in the chapters that follow a limited number of additional illustrations of the contemporary polybabble fostered by this uncivil civil religion will have to suffice. It is important to remember that the focus of this book is not to resolve all of these endless semantic disputes but instead to argue for decreased semantic ambiguity and enhanced Judeo-Christian influence via intentional, aggressive, systematic, systemic, and thoughtful semantic polemics and apologetics. The reality is that, consistent with the thesis of this book, when semantic universes shift, the definitions of all words shift, and when one word is redefined (e.g., marriage), all words are impacted. Semantic revolutions change the church, the synagogue, and change world. The hope for the future is that the semantic universe of the biblical and orthodox Judeo-Christian tradition will lead the way. Is biblical, Logocentric truth and justice possible? That becomes our next discussion.

Ask Yourself or Your Group

- *What is theobabble? (See prior chapters) What is polybabble? Give examples of both. What is the difference? Why does the author believe theobabble and polybabble are dangerous to church and state? Have you ever heard polybabble? Have you ever engaged in theobabble or polybabble, perhaps without knowing it? Have you ever heard a preacher use either "babble"?*
- *How is polybabble related to tribalism, Balkanization, and the disintegration of civilization? Have you experienced tribalism? Why do some feel strongly that tribalism is perfectly and semantically justified?*

- *Why does the author prefer "ultramodern syncretism" over postmodernism when describing our age? What is the ultimate syncretism? How do semantic apologetics and polemics relate to ultramodern syncretism?*
- *What is the relationship between "political correctness" and verbal seduction? Is there any value in political correctness? What is the danger? What has been the impact on education and the church?*
- *Has the Logos or Christ as the center of language and communication increasingly been replaced with the principle or spirit of anti-Christ as the core? To what degree, as Nietzsche put it, has the trans-valuation or inversion of values and words taken place in the American context? In your view, who or what is primarily at the center of our cultural semantics and civilization today?*
- *What is the significance of Saul Alinsky for this discussion? Have you heard of him previously? Why is his name referenced frequently in political discourse and debate? Why does the author of this book mention him?*

Chapter 7

BIBLICAL COMPASSION AND JUSTICE OR "JUST US"?

But let justice roll down like waters
And righteousness like an ever-flowing stream.
—Amos 5:24

The trouble with socialism is that you eventually "run out of other people's money."
—Prime Minister Margaret Thatcher (and others)

I do get a sense sometimes now among certain young people—and this is accelerated by social media—there is this sense sometimes of the way of me making change is to be as judgmental as possible about other people, and that's enough. Like, if I tweet or hashtag about how you didn't do something right or use the wrong verb, then I can feel pretty good about myself, "cause man did you see how woke I was? I called you out."
That's not activism. That's not bringing about change. If all you're doing is casting stones, you're probably not going to get that far. That's easy to do.

This idea of purity, and [that] you're never compromised
and you're always politically woke and all that stuff — you
should get over that quickly.
—Former President Barak Obama (2019)

Barack Obama seems more concerned with cancel culture
than reversing America's right-wing slide.
Jacob Bacharach (November 4, 2019)

Socialism guarantees failure and suffering—so why do so
many Americans support it?
—Victor Davis Hanson

Columbia professor who fled communism resigns, says
university is becoming communist.
—Jeremiah Poff, *The College Fix*

Designer Justice

One of the most controversial and illustrative areas of semantic distortion today regards compassion and social justice. Social justice is often referenced in this work because it has become for many, with support inside and outside of faith communities, the functional state-sponsored and aggressively enforced civil or uncivil religion. The reader may want to review the illustrative Labberton and Jeffresss conflict discussed in Chapter 3 to grasp fully the intensity of the conflict and its enormous implications for semantics, faith-communities, and civilization. The social justice wars, proffering answers to the question of "what is a just civilization," certainly lie at or near the heart of the definition of an evangelically or orthodoxy influenced aspirational civilization, and the answers are legion and contradictory. For example, definitions of "justice" according to the American Center for Law and Justice (ACLJ) or *Sojourners* magazine simply do not dwell in the same semantic universe (see Chapter 2). Indeed, the ACLJ and *Sojourners* do not dwell in the same universe, period.

These additional examples of equivocation regarding social justice should suffice. First, New Wave Feminists, Feminists for Life, the Liberty Counsel, and numerous Roman Catholic women's groups affirm that the core values of social justice and feminism require a pro-life position (even referring to "reproductive justice" for the unborn—with the abortion "choice" being the ultimate semantic theft). Countless other social justice groups (e.g., NARAL, NOW, Catholics for Choice, Women's March) view pro-abortion advocacy as central to feminism, social justice, and a better civilization.

Second, groups such as Proclaiming Justice to the Nations, Christians United for Israel, and the International Christian Assembly Jerusalem affirm that justice requires strong (sometimes nuanced) support for the Jews and Israel, whereas *Sojourners* ("building a movement to transform the world") and Evangelicals for Social action view such support as one-sided, unbalanced, Zionist, and leading to an unjust and racist world.

The reality is that most everyone claims to be questing for a better civilization via social justice these days, even though many of these groups mix like oil and water. Has social justice become question-begging, and is it being used to silence dissent and avoid true dialog? Has social justice semantics lost its utility? Should we not press these justice advocates for an *apologia* for or clarification of their question-begging calls to join them in social justice, especially *biblical* or Judeo-*Christian* justice efforts?

It is also critical to remember that countless post-Christian and anti-Christian atheistic and humanist organizations engage in social justice advocacy[193] (e.g., Orbit, the American Humanist Association, the Foundation Beyond Belief, Silence, People of Color Beyond Faith, the Appignani Foundation). And many, not unlike Marxism, view the false illusion (or opiate) of biblical Christianity or religion as a central pillar of social injustice and oppression. Indeed, at the core of Marxism was an atheistic argument for a social justice that could transcend religion and class warfare.

Socialistic Nazism was much more than nationalism or fascism. It was an occult influenced and angry anti-Semitic struggle (*Mein Kampf*) to reestablish order, justice, German pride, and prosperity and move beyond authentic biblical roots. Radical liberation theology is a social justice ideology and views the orthodox semantics and hermeneutical approach to Scripture and theology as an ethnocentric abuse of power. In our own day, many radical groups across the globe regularly defend savage terrorism as just and apply the term "terrorism" to the critics of terrorism. In a world of polybabble, with no plumb line, justice has become designer justice and terrorism has become designer terrorism. In other words, designer justice, like designer clothes, is justice as imagined or created by the individual designer. When American was founded, justice was grounded in, designed, and revealed to humanity by one divine Designer or Creator. Today, the individual or tribe is the designer of justice. Even terrorism is in the eye of the beholder.

Question-Begging Justice

It is certainly a legitimate debate as to which political theory, form of government, or means to and definition of justice or social justice maximizes biblical compassion, biblical justice, and the quest for an aspirational civilization. Unfortunately, the identification of compassion and social justice with a specific conclusion concerning the *only* alleged means to achieve that justice is becoming pervasive and sometimes rather militant.[194]

It is critical at this juncture to empathize with those who have been the victims of demonic injustice and oppression, from the slave trading ships of Wesley's day to twentieth-century lynchings to twenty-first-century racial and religious genocide. It is absolutely critical for orthodox Christians, Jews, Roman Catholics, and evangelicals, especially conservative evangelicals, to empathize and understand that many of the oft distorted terms and semantic clusters connected to social justice today (e.g., inclusion, toleration, *ophobias*, globalism, colonialism, multiculturalism, ethnocentrism, inclusion) do not exist in a vacuum. People have been enslaved, oppressed, physically and emotionally maimed, and unfairly excluded, and some evangelicals and religious leaders have been on the wrong side of Scripture and history. I remember being literally stunned in the 1990s when encountering a KKK rally in the center of southern city. I could not resist telling one of the proselytizers, hopefully with love in my heart, "shame on you."

Unfortunately, many of these terms have now moved far beyond legitimate prophetic critique or cries for authentic compassion and justice and they have morphed into post- or anti-Christian political ideology and movements. This is a classic example of what is meant in this work by semantic theft. For example, inclusion is certainly a virtue if properly defined and connected to biblical agape, but if inclusion means accepting unbiblical behaviors then inclusion has become toxic to civilization. Should we be inclusive of the KKK or spouse-beaters? Compassion and justice, certainly biblical concepts, have likewise been coopted by post- and anti-Christian ideologies.

The assumption that a specific political agenda is compassionate (even biblical) social justice, prior to or apart from careful biblical reflection and ongoing dialog is question-begging. Dialog is often manipulatively silenced in advance since elitist, social justice Gnostics already have secretly divined the best or only means to the messy quest for social justice. Progressive social justice today, often prejudiced against Judeo-Christian values and the American experiment, is littered with questionable assumptions. The alleged or proffered means (a specific and fallible political ideology) often masquerades as the thing in itself (social justice). Multiple evangelical social justice movements today may illustrate a strong measure of social justice hubris, elitism, Gnosticism, and semantic confusion, as will be discussed in more detail in this chapter.

My PhD minor at Baylor was in political science—mainly political philosophy. I was honored to study with and learn from great scholars holding to a variety of perspectives. What is clear from such an education, however, is that the assumption that there is only one approach to defining and implementing compassionate (or biblical or social) justice is more than intellectually flawed and ignores numerous Western and global perspectives.

Even if it is argued that compassionate social justice has to be contextualized within the framework of Western political realities, that hardly justifies ignoring views of justice affirmed by Plato, Aristotle, Augustine, Aquinas, Hobbes, Hume, Kant, Mill, Rawls,

Nozik, Novak, Hayek, Okin, Nussbaum, and many others. It is less than helpful simply to beg the question concerning which single view of compassionate justice is superior. Yet *social justice* often is presented as "if you disagree, you are unjust and unbiblical." Social justice is also presented as easily defined.

Compassion and justice are now typically confused, conflated, or identified with advocacy for Leviathan-like (massively centralized and bureaucratic), secular, and/or religiously pluralistic, socialistic governmental solutions to real crises of poverty and human brokenness. These solutions often may be less than biblical or compassionate and should be carefully evaluated. Many of these *compassionate* solutions may actually foster intergenerational governmental dependency,[195] spawning more crime and poverty, and destroying families and community. The family is the stable foundation of healthy communities and nations. These pseudo-solutions typically increase governmental power and indebtedness to dangerous levels along with spawning economic stagnation or decline.

If this assessment has any validity, then such solutions hardly sound biblical, compassionate, or just and they certainly compromise the second great commandment. In addition, centralized power, even in the name of justice, without appropriate checks and balances and submission to higher principles like the Constitution (*Lex Rex*) or shared power with other branches of government, ignores history, radically fallen human nature, and the seduction of power.

The Trojan horse of justice (or social justice), with biblical window dressing on the eyes of the horse, is often confused with the political-economic theory of some variant of socialism or contemporary (not classical) liberal political theory. *Social justice is not necessarily socialism*,[196] and that verbal distinction and the careful, patient renewed debate about the means to compassionate justice are critical for the future of civilization.

This rejection of the conflation of social justice and socialism is not found only among religious conservatives. Unitarian and "theological radical" A. Powell Davies contended that socialism emerged from irreligion, birthed many more evils than capitalism, and obstructed moral, ethical, and economic development.[197] Social justice seemingly has been hacked, coopted, or hijacked today to the point where one wonders if the term any longer assists with its own worthy goal. Socialism also may have backfired relative to its much-touted compassionate goal.[198]

Shrewd Biblical Justice

Biblical justice and compassion must be shrewd. Simple illustrations should suffice. Parents could decide to give away everything they own in the name of biblical compassion and justice, but if they fail to take account of the impact on other family members and children, not to mention the longitudinal economics of the surrounding community or state, then their compassionate justice would properly be viewed as foolish injustice. Parents also must care for their posterity, not just their children, if love has any bearing on justice.

Paul the Apostle, who sacrificed everything for others and engaged in many compassionate activities nevertheless prescribed the following rules: "But if anyone does not provide for his own, and especially for those of his household, he has denied the faith and is worse than an unbeliever" (1 Timothy 5:8). "For even when we were with you, we used to give you this order: if anyone is not willing to work, then he ['the one,' NIV] is not to eat, either" (2 Thessalonians 3:10). Parents are even obligated to save up for their children (2 Corinthians 12:14). Hence, these parents may give away much, but if not done in a shrewd manner the compassionate justice claim is falsified and unbiblical. Indeed, such justice is, in reality, injustice and such compassion (or love) is actually devastating folly.

Similarly, a country could, in the name of compassionate justice, lavish all its resources in a short period of time to assist the poor and the oppressed. However, the failure to account for the impact on future economic sustainability, medical care, social security and the elderly, poverty assistance, or even the impact on international conflicts, other countries, and national defense, removes the veil of biblical compassionate justice and exposes foolish pseudo-compassion and rank injustice. Countless millions of lives would be impacted by such folly. Perhaps this is like the classic lesson from the *Miracle Worker*, where the teacher finally erupts during a teachable moment with the parents and tells the parents, to paraphrase, "Your love [i.e., the enabling of dependence and self-destructive behavior] is killing her." Thank God for this semantic clarification, Helen Keller's shrewd and persevering teacher, and Helen Keller's cultural influence that emerged from the true love and true compassion of the teacher.

Massive governmental handouts will always be appreciated by someone (even if creating dependency) and may truly help some individuals or communities—but only for the short run if not sustainable. Handouts also fuel political prostitution. Conservatives waste their time trying to prove that handouts are not desired by or helpful to some individuals. The real issues are whether the handouts are truly helpful and sustainable, wise short and long term, and if helping some with handouts or the cumulative impact of such handouts potentially destroys us all.

In the run up to presidential elections in the American context the political pandering of some politicians has perhaps reached unprecedented levels. Some of our politicians have turned into political prostitutes by promising virtually everything free (or nearly so) to everyone in order to get votes. The fiscal implementation of all of these handouts is not sustainable and could break the economy and ultimately end up hurting the diverse poor more than any segment of our society. Additionally, while some critics would love to see American military power decrease, for some majority world countries or even less powerful western democracies, a weakened American deterrence could prove calamitous.

By the way, another semantic seduction related to compassion and socialism is the argument that "everyone believes in socialism—some believe in socialism to help the poor and some believe in corporate socialism." We can and should debate to what extent corporations should receive tax incentives or be able to utilize tax loopholes, and whether such incentives truly help the average worker trying to provide for their family. However, that argument is a misuse of the term socialism for political purposes.

Socialism means that the government owns and/or controls the means of economic production, distribution, and exchange. Tax incentives and tax breaks for corporations and individuals can exist apart from a socialistic economy, so tax breaks and loopholes to corporations should be defined as just that—tax breaks and loopholes. Confusing and conflating socialism as an economic system and theory and corporate handouts and tax loopholes, even if the handouts and loopholes are unjustifiable, amounts to semantic opportunism. Critics should challenge the tax loopholes and corporate assistance if they are truly unjust, but conflating such with socialism is less than helpful to the debate.

In addition, some define socialism as if the community, or the people, or the workers own and/or control the economy, but history has demonstrated over and over again that community control is a euphemism for government control, which is then actually controlled by the elite and prosperous few, which is always the inherent danger of socialism.

Some have legitimate concerns about global capitalism, and global corporations should be monitored and appropriately regulated (refereed, not state owned or controlled). Any corporation, government, or individual with unchecked power, given fallen human nature, is a potential threat to a flourishing and just civilization. And corporations can accumulate enough wealth to sometimes negatively influence nation states or laborers or foreign policy or war. Even Republican President Eisenhower warned of the military-industrial complex.

However, when governments control both the military and the economy, you move from the perils of global capitalism to something even worse—global socialism backed by officially authorized and directly connected to military power—not just military power influenced by corporations. In rushing away from the dangers of global capitalism some are jumping out of the frying pan and into the fire of global socialism. Should we not have learned something from the dangers of military backed global socialism in recent centuries? Social justice prophets should give prophetic attention to militarily backed dictators and global corporations *and* militarily backed global socialism.

Common sense dictates against some of the arguments for government enforced compassion and social justice. Someone could argue that hacking *your* bank account and redistributing *your* life savings and social security benefits to the poor is biblical compassion and justice. After all, you are more wealthy and healthy than most people who have ever lived, even if you think you are middle class. However, without knowing all the facts of an individual case, such redistribution is more likely to be better designated as *theft* rather than compassion or justice, and such theft typically does not provide a longitudinal solution to the poverty or oppression of anyone, and such theft undermines ethical integrity and economic stability.

Poverty is never really assisted with charity alone. Poverty is only assisted when the creativity of economic power and freedom is unleashed. Yes, unjust corporations must be refereed, held accountable, and replaced with better corporations. But to we really need more historical lessons in the dangers of the governmental control of politics, economics, and religion? Really?

Especially in the West, specifically the United States, this semantic pivot from theft to compassion is striking. In America, the founding documents ("by the people and for the people") are explicit concerning the American social contract. The money collected by the government is not ultimately the government's money but stewarded money from and "of the people" to be managed for the people and not by the will of a supreme executive branch, judiciary, or congress (any option of which would be *Rex Lex*). Even the usage of stewarded money for the people must *only* be utilized consistent with God's revealed eternal justice (*Lex Rex*).

Hence, the government coffers administered by public servants (not lords or *Reges*) hold the people's money, which is ultimately God's money (from nature's or creation's God), since it is subject to the norms of eternal justice. Hence, a tax cut should not be defined as a decrease in the rate of increase of taxation but as an actual reduction of taxes, and every cent spent must be just and justifiable to the true lords (the people through their representatives) and the true Lord who is the source of eternal law and justice. Economics must be Logocentric and kingdomcentric.

To illustrate, a people attuned to the true nature of the American experiment should sometimes be shouting from the rooftops to the governmental lords, "Not your money!" Or "You have enough already!" Instead, even religious conservatives today are often thrilled with a miniscule tax refund *from the government*, rather than being appalled that, relative to fiscal resources, *Rex* is increasingly *Lex* as states and the nation waste endless resources and spend us all toward a fiscal crisis. The problem goes far beyond one political party.

There is nothing particularly compassionate or just about spending a state, city, or civilization into oblivion. Evangelical and orthodox Christians should be shouting "not your money" to governmental bureaucrats while also shouting "Not my money" to themselves, as ultimately all resources are granted by nature's God.

These illustrations are not theoretical extremes. In the European and American context, countries and American states are often spending themselves into just such a fiscal oblivion (with massive unsustainable debt) in the name of economic justice and compassion, and jeopardizing everyone's future. Predictably, such states and countries then demand that others bail them out.

Safety nets seem compatible with compassionate biblical justice, but not Leviathan-like social entitlements that foster dependence. As noted previously in this chapter, Paul worked day and night and risked life and limb to share the gospel and care for the needy. He certainly illustrated compassion. Yet even Paul minced no words when declaring: "For even when we were with you, we used to give you this order: if anyone is not willing to work, then he is not to eat, either" (2 Thessalonians 3:10).

Is it just or compassionate, in the name of helicopter or bulldozer parent compassion or justice, to become enslaved by a national debt that will jeopardize social security for seniors? The pursuit of justice and compassion require complex or shrewd long-term calculations and much planning and dialog. Spending like a generous, benevolent, drunken sailor hardly reflects biblical justice. The simple co-opting of the term "social justice" as equivalent to "socialism" or "capitalism," without intense reflection on numerous political and economic models and the significant marshalling of evidence, is unworthy of those claiming to pursue the lofty goal of justice and the lofty quest for an aspirational civilization.

There are also issues of ethics and compassion when governments forcibly compel citizens to surrender personal earnings and resources, often under penalty of law, in order to redistribute these resources to those who can but do not contribute to society. Limits on the amount and nature of such taxation or redistribution must be carefully assessed. Governmental or hand-out dependency must be avoided at all costs. Indeed, governmental handouts and regulations can de-incentive faith-based charitable organizations that not only bring the resources of faith and faith communities to assist with social problems, but faith-based philanthropy also mediates accountability and an informed understanding of local contexts. De-motivating faith-based social justice entrepreneurship by exclusively relying on centralized and inefficient governmental programs is disastrous for those in need.

When faith communities punt to the federal government as a means for actualizing compassion, not only does this punting create or feed Leviathan, it also robs the responsibility of the common citizen to be responsible for one's neighbor, social justice, and compassion. Leviathan will devour much before it ever helps the needy, and the help is often not the best means of assistance. Leviathan like social justice has a chilling impact on the common citizen and culture-wide as people of faith abdicate their God-given responsibilities to the mythology and idolatry that Leviathan is always wiser and far more effective concerning how to meet individualized needs at the local level. Of all people, postmodernists should understand why effective compassion must be contextual.

True compassionate justice especially requires that non-governmental and local organizations, where personal knowledge and accountability is possible, *must* be a key piece of the strategic and tactical safety net and opportunity game plan for the needy in a healthy civilization. If any group should understand this truth concerning delivering true compassion it should be the Judeo-Christian faith community, for both theological and historical reason. Faith communities have often led the way and deeply experienced the need for direct, personal, intensive compassion and accountability.

Faith communities should lead the way for theological reasons—the divine calling to kingdom advance and neighbor love.

The utopian fallacy would suggest that only the government can consistently provide such services nationwide, but the reality is that in a fallen world government is often a very inefficient means of compassion, as has been demonstrated by the Great Society or more recently by the VA (US Department of Veterans Affairs), though some improvements have been made recently with the VA. Marvin Olaskey's classic work, *The Tragedy of American Compassion*, well documents the value of compassionate initiatives being local, faith-based, spiritually transformative, having personal knowledge of the recipients of assistance, and including appropriate accountability and systemic (e.g., families, communities) engagement.[199]

The relevance of these illustrations to Judeo-Christian cultural apologetics and polemics should be more than self-evident. If the church or civilization comes to define key terms related to compassion and justice inconsistent with key biblical assumptions about the nature of justice or the possibilities of human nature, then not only has Christian polemic (internal) and apologetic (external) influence waned, but the very nature of the church, synagogue, and civilization will have been radically altered. Aspirational civilization "is a rarity, attained with difficulty and easily lost."[200]

Certainly, our civilization faces many terrorist threats, but semantic terrorism is rarely publicized by the media. What do I mean? Read on.

Ask Yourself or Your Group

- *Have you ever observed "just us"? What is "designer justice"?*
- *Have you ever encountered "question-begging" social justice?*
- *How would you define shrewd, biblical justice and differentiate it from the many alternative definitions today?*
- *Are you or is your church involved with any form of authentic social justice?*

Chapter 8

DIALOGICAL SEMANTICS OR SEMANTIC TERRORISM?

But speaking the truth in love . . . .
—Ephesians 4:15

The Semantic Jungle

The volume of the current verbal cacophony is especially elevated today in view of undiscerning, manipulated, and lazy semantics. All semantic projects, including this present work, are most fallible. Reining in words is more challenging than herding cats. The thesis of this work is that the future of the church and civilization depends on passionate semantic intentionality and the acceptance of a shared norm for evaluating semantic universes. Judeo-Christian semantic apologetics and polemics can lead the way with diminishing polybabble and advocating for Logocentric and kingdomcentric communication.

No doubt, undisciplined semantics issues forth, in part, from a sound bite and twitter culture where the clarification and nuancing of terms is all but impossible. Many celebrities and politicians are exacerbating the problem. Some of this issues forth from an ultramodern syncretistic culture where Truth is in question and all that remains is hyper-polytheistic tribal advocacy and passionate self-expression.

Regardless, the gloves have now come off and the claws and daggers are now out of the closet in much public and political discourse, at least in the West. This is not entirely new, but it does seem accelerated and systemic. Semantic tactics have often become weapons used to bully an unsuspecting public into submission toward a specific, unfounded, unbiblical mind-set without rational or open discourse. Hence, public discourse is a critical area of attention for semantic apologetics.

Ultramodern syncretistic public discourse inevitably, over the long haul, may trend toward militant verbal advocacy and even physical violence. As noted, today there is increasingly no shared standard (scientific reason and/or Judeo-Christian revelation) to which all parties can ultimately appeal to adjudicate truth and advocacy claims. The loss of such a norm also has led to the loss of shame. Hence, words are simply tools of power and the advancement of an agenda. There is no longer a requirement for public or political discourse to be coherent, or rational, or collegial, or evidence based, or subject to any standard or norm because all facts are *"interprefacts"* embedded in a story of a person or group or nation seeking control. Of course if all facts are interprefacts then the fact that all facts are interprefacts is also an interprefact and the interprefacts theory of facts may be dismissed as merely perspectival.

The only reasons for relativistic public discourse to appeal to reason or some objective standard include the following: 1) the *imago Dei* cannot be suppressed, or 2) some are still running on the fumes of modernistic reason or a faint Judeo-Christian memory, or 3) the appeal to reason and evidence at least gives the appearance of being reasonable in order to persuade or control.

Reason and truth are simply embodied evolutionary skills that either do or do not persuade or control and advance the will to power of individuals or groups. Welcome to the semantic jungle! If "God is dead" is at the core of the semantic universe, then Nietzsche is correct concerning much relative to the nature of language and the will to power. All that remains is semantic terrorism. If you disagree with me, I will verbally blow you up by calling you a "___ist."

Modernism had its flaws, especially salient arrogance relative to human reason and prescribed and mandated social and civilizational utopian programs, but at least there was a final appeal to the bar of reason or science to adjudicate competing perspectives. Postmodernism (used broadly for the more skeptical variations) increasingly exhibits the same intellectual arrogance concerning denying certain knowledge while militantly knowing *the good* for civilization, and for you, all the while rudderless and cloaked by the semantic ambiguity surrounding terms such as inclusiveness, justice, toleration, love, and hate.

It is ironic that postmodernity, supposedly frustrated with the arrogance and dangerous ideological fanaticism of modernism, often reflects that very same arrogance. Amidst this ultramodern syncretism there really is no standard by which to evaluate arrogance, or any claims to knowledge or morality, other than the question-begging, self-referential norm of self or tribe. This can only be described as a trajectory of cultural sociopathology (no conscience) and incredible cognitive dissonance. Indeed, to affirm eschatological dystopia,[201] based on postmodern assumptions, while also aggressively seeking to mandate acceptable behavior and ethical norms with utopian zeal, is utterly contradictory and irreconcilable. In other words, if there is no standard of truth or an ideal future we are all pursuing, then why are so many postmodernists mandating how we speak and live? Such behavior betrays the fact that they are created in God's image and they are also pursuing something akin to the kingdom of God.

Relativistic Advocacy or Shrewd Advocacy

When relativistic advocacy is all that is left, perhaps the obvious question in a truth-for-me culture is, "Why should I, or anyone, care about your advocacy, unless you have power over me?" A few illustrative examples of such foundationless advocacy will have to suffice.[202]

To be perfectly clear, biblical justice and compassion should motivate American evangelicals and orthodox Judeo-Christian faith communities to have great concern for, and give passionate attention to, issues such as global refugee crises, legal and illegal immigration, racism, discrimination, sexism, inclusion, diversity, and colonialism. The problem is that these terms often have, via semantic smuggling, prejudiced and biased honest inquiry and careful analysis.[203] As a result, there is often only one single narrative permitted by the elite regarding compassion and social justice, and any honest inquiry or careful analysis is quickly dismissed with strong accusations often leveled at those advocating different views.

For example, the church's and society's response and public policy concerning legal and illegal immigration is a needed and fair debate. This debate bears on the character of the church, the nation, and civilization. Yet it is ethically troubling and a semantic red flag to conflate illegal and legal immigration *prior* to open inquiry and debate — not to mention it is rather question-begging.

A biblically oriented, compassionate, justice-seeking individual might be very supportive of aggressive, greatly accelerated, expansive, well-managed legal immigration while also having concerns about illegal immigration. They might call for doubling the number of legal immigrants by 2025, though some nations already attempt to absorb some one million per year, so realism must balance optimism in countries who already have much skin in the game. A common sense business model suggests that there must be some caps on even accelerated legal immigration. Proponents of illegal immigration and open borders seem incapable of expressing any appreciation for nations that have received millions of legal immigrants, or for individuals who spent years if not decades on the difficult journey culminating in legal immigration status.

Such an individual who supports legal immigration but not open borders might passionately advocate for well-vetted refugee assistance and generous overseas refugee assistance, while also viewing reckless illegal immigration and reckless refugee assistance as lacking wisdom, compassion, or justice. The semantic ploy that conflates everything related to immigration and the refugee crisis has been so effective that the word "illegal" relative to immigration is vanishing and an unsuspecting public has been convinced that to use the term "illegal" is promoting hatred, prejudice, and injustice toward those who are not citizens of the United States. Simply put, deviating from the party line means one is anti-immigrant and racist.

Hence the only allowable term in this debate is now "undocumented." This semantic ploy lacks ethical integrity. See the Preface, but the term undocumented is not only misused and question begging, as it assumes conceptually that everyone essentially is already a citizen and simply needs documentation, but it is also philosophically and semantically confused. First, as noted in the Preface, the term implies illegal status even though it is being used to obscure illegal status. Second, imagine if we start using the term undocumented to justify other illegal behavior. One could claim to be an undocumented police officer, or IRS agent, or parent, or member of a family, or a CNN or White House staff member. How "___ ist" for CNN to deny a minority access to their still mostly white anchor dominated studios in Atlanta just because someone doesn't have documentation! It is amazing how many who live behind high security and armed borders oppose borders that protect others. Perhaps bank robbers are simply undocumented police officers or undocumented bank employees who genuinely need assistance? Either someone is or is not justifiably categorized according to the rules that make civilization possible.

Unfortunately, however, in our post-Truth culture, justice has become for many, on all sides of the political spectrum, a tribalistic and hyper-polytheistic *just us*. Polybabble rules. Language is not used to dialog, communicate, or discover Truth but simply for tribal advocacy.

Dan-el Padilla Peralta seemingly provides a classic illustration of using a false dichotomy to not only defend but glorify justice as postmodern tribalistic "just us." Peralta teaches, ironically, at the formerly traditional Christian and early American nursery of piety still known today as Princeton University. Mary F. Williams appropriately or inappropriately raised concerns about the subjective and tribalistic paper Peralta presented at a conference affirming that "journal publication in classics is a 'whites-only neighborhood.'" Peralta, in a subsequent conversation, said that what he heard Williams saying was that the only reason he had gotten his job at Princeton was because he was black. Regardless of what Williams said—she claimed she was misunderstood in a noisy room—or the soundness of Peralta's thesis concerning the classics—his response to Williams's concern was telling and reflected classic ultramodern syncretism.

> What I found myself returning to in the hours and days after the incident was the strong belief that has informed so much of my own work and teaching: My merit and my blackness are fused to each other. It is impossible to think of my scholarship, my achievements, without thinking about my blackness.

> Undeniably there have been people, and there will continue to be people, who think the ideal should be this depersonalized objective scholarship. But I don't believe in the possibility of this type of scholarship, or in its desirability. That's not to say one has to center the voice of the ego on every single page in every single sentence. But that voice is there, whether we like it or not. The histories behind the voice are there, whether we like it or not. So why not make the effort to attend to that voice as diligently as possible.[204]

Peralta is guided or misguided by the logical fallacy of the false dichotomy. Either we have absolute, modernist, rationalistic and totally objective knowledge and scholarship or we reject "the possibility of this type of scholarship, or … its desirability." Either we are omniscient gods, or we can make no meaningful and largely objective distinctions. Either we hire professors and choose classic books to sustain a "whites-only neighborhood," or we accept the postmodern premise of the relativism, unattainability, and subjectivity of truth and ethics (and justice). We can make no distinction between merit and the possible positive contribution of minority ethical experience to the candidate pool or the pool of books that contribute to a robust classical education. Either we reject the ideal, which is the key problem in Peralta's argument, or we simply accept our "situatedness" and get on with our militant advocacy. Peralta's "justice," even in view of some of his qualifications, leans in pretty far toward the subjective, tribalistic, and therefore nearly if not entirely reduces to "just us."

Much of the point and value of divine revelation is to create the possibility of rising above being totally dependent on or embedded in our social, economic, political, or historical context. Divine revelation ultimately undermines human sacrifice, child sacrifice, the gladiatorial games, infanticide, and dehumanizing polygamy—which were all normative and situated cultural contexts. Situatedness has become a postmodern epistemological shibboleth and idol.

The relevance and utility of revelation influenced semantics is well demonstrated by the non-situated *Barmen Declaration* of 1934, barely one year after Hitler came to power, which intuitively and prophetically accused Nazism of idolatry. Barth and Bonhoeffer continued to raise the prophetic flag throughout Hitler's short lived *Reich* or kingdom, and Bonhoeffer paid the ultimate price for *The Cost of Discipleship*.

Having served on many search processes that include minority search team members, I am grateful to have been associated over the years with faculty and staff (including minority) members who passionately advocate for minority hires while all of us, with feet of clay, and by God's grace, at least attempt to discern appropriate qualifications and merit and diversity contributions to our community. In one such hiring process, I was chastised by minority search team members for not moving more quickly to hire the non-diversity candidate! Peralta's ivory tower view of justice as just us, that well reflects how the educational system indoctrinates future cultural leaders like Peralta, may help to explain, frame, or contextualize Ocasio-Cortez's statement quoted in the introduction. As the reader may recall, Ocasio-Cortez argued that inaccurate facts and semantics are not that critical when one knows, seemingly *a priori*, that one is morally right. Ocasio-Cortez was educated at progressive Boston University.

This "just us" approach to the illegal immigration debate may have grave consequences for civilization. The reality is that if (legal and illegal) immigration is not well managed, with shrewd compassion, then the very fiscal and cultural strengths in some nation states that motivate millions to relocate legally to "more perfect unions" across the globe, at risk of life and limb, will be irreparably harmed. Naïve or utopian biblical compassion and social justice self-destruct over time. Such naiveté jeopardizes those nations, the broader civilization, and the flourishing of untold masses. Such naiveté may set in motion forces that could spawn even greater injustice than the current and well-advertised ills endlessly rehearsed by militant illegal immigration advocates.

Yes, the plight of those beyond the borders seeking assistance and safe harbor from a state, like the Jewish refugees during World War II, deserve urgent, accelerated, and compassionate consideration. Indeed, the argument that all legal immigrants (rather than a specified percentage) should have demonstrative and significant economic value and merit lacks compassion and is inconsistent with Judeo-Christian values.

Far more important than merit or economic merit, though a good business model suggests that some should be quick economic contributors, is whether legal immigrants are acculturated into the core values, culture, and foundational principles and documents of authentically flourishing civilizations. In the American context, do legal immigrants fully understand, passionately embrace, and totally commit to the American experiment and vision? Does the legal immigration process properly educate and prepare those going through the process? Yes, legal immigrants bring value to the American experience, but that does not mean appropriate acculturation is unnecessary. And yes, the fiscal ability of a specified percentage of illegal immigrants to sustain themselves after immigration is a very reasonable business model consideration for accelerated legal immigration—as is the overall business model of the host nation. We need to move beyond what some have referred to as "sloppy *agape*" (servant love) and embrace an authentic *agape* and shrewd compassion that maximizes human flourishing for all. And how tragic or bittersweet if our legal immigration process actually exceeds our public school systems in acculturating future citizens.

However, it is important to reemphasize to American evangelicals that only allowing the legal immigration of the economically advantaged falls far short of the ethos of a Judeo-Christian influenced civilization—not to mention the rich history and story of constructive and contributory legal immigration in multiple countries. The success stories of some famished, oppressed, and diverse legal immigrants are inspiring and instructive. Some responses to needs such as the plight of refugees seem rather heartless, as when Jews were turned away from many countries during the Nazi terror, while other responses to such human crises seem rather naïve and identify compassion with recklessness and pseudo-justice.

The shrewd and compassionate solution is likely multi-complex. Indiscriminately allowing illegal and legal immigrants to migrate to the United States in massive numbers is less than shrewd or compassionate. Setting up insurmountable barriers and delays to legal immigration is immoral. The failure to devise a coherent plan for accelerated legal immigration, either due to the desire for cheap labor or the attempt to protect and sustain illegal immigration in order to expand a voting base or play to a political base, is *shamefully opportunistic*. The failure of immigration policy seems to involve more than one political party, yet no attempt is being made to suggest moral equivalency.

The task of just, legal, and accelerated immigration is massive, but surely we can do better. Yet we should also herald the accomplishment of welcoming millions of legal immigrants in rather substantial numbers each year to multiple nations. Smart and legal immigration is an arduous and time-consuming task.

In like manner (see the illustrative Lexicon in appendix A), related semantic clusters such as multiculturalism, diversity, inclusion, feminism, sexism, globalism, and colonialism, all of which have potential theological and philosophical utility, sometimes are defined (or redefined) and employed such that genuine dialog and critical reflection are never really allowed. Sometimes dialog is intentionally silenced. Diversity and inclusion now demand the mainstreaming and sanction of unbiblical morality or even penalize minority Judeo-Christian perspectives.

Yes, many of these "social justice" terms attempt to counter abuses, but as with political revolutions (e.g., Russia, Cuba, Southeast Asia), identifying injustice is much easier than

241

proffering more just alternatives Or, as former President Obama put it recently, it is easy to self-identify as woke. It is much more difficult actually to live as one who is authentically and shrewdly woke.

Terms and phrases such as white privilege, male privilege, micro-aggression, Christian privilege, and Euro-American privilege easily, recklessly, and frequently flow off of the lips of the progressively liberal and alleged champions of multiculturalism, diversity, anti-colonialism, compassion, and social justice.[205] Some of these concerns are legitimate, some are not, and some need to be better defined and nuanced.

Let me assure the reader that the goal of this work truly is finding the biblical zone for justice. I have advocated for and written concerning racial reconciliation when speaking at the prestigious Wheaton Theology conference or writing in the pages of the *Alliance Academic Review*. The context of this present work is Judeo-Christian, evangelical and orthodox apologetics and polemics, meaning a defense of Judeo-Christian orthodoxy and especially evangelical, biblical, orthodoxy, yet throughout this work the various forms of social injustice, *when properly defined*, have been freely acknowledged and condemned.

Nevertheless, the classic speck-and-log fallacy and moral failure referenced by Jesus in Matthew 7:1–5 are most evident in such discussions of privilege, often by the privileged and so-called progressives. Where is the reference in such discussions of privilege to the politically liberal privilege that dominates art, music, entertainment, countless major corporations, media, law, and certain regions of the country—not to mention public and higher education? These are arguably the primary centers of power in the West.

Such militant advocacy seems tone deaf to theological anthropology (we are all fallen) when theological anthropology needs to be applied to such liberationist and revolutionary movements themselves. Why do so many justice advocates seem incapable of acknowledging the log in their own eyes while becoming experts on the specks in the eyes of others—especially American evangelicals and orthodox or conservative Roman Catholics and Jews?

It is past time to begin to openly speak of liberal privilege and liberal-centrism as frequently as other kinds of privilege and "centrism" in response to the endless allegations of privilege. Ethnicity is not the only privilege evident in civilizations. Failure to counter this ideological and cultural privilege simply enables, at times, anti-Judeo-Christian privilege and weakens the orthodox Judeo-Christian mission and influence.

Illustrations of Semantic Terrorism

These culture forming terms, such as privilege and woke, at times, have become mere tools of advocacy and indoctrination rather than means for genuine reflection, analysis, and enhanced communication. This approaches being a kind of verbal terrorism—"Agree with me or the nuclear option of name calling will utilized to silence you." Proper semantic analysis of just one of these terms, such as globalism, likely exceeds the limits of a single book given the endless definitions.[206] However, the following is a brief sampling of the possible verbal distortions of common terms that are often enforced with threats, power, privilege, and name calling, and which jeopardize the potent influence of the Judeo-Christian movement on the future of civilization:

- Terms such as *sexism and feminism* have become uprooted from very healthy and fertile nineteenth-century Judeo-Christian soil[207] and cast into the relativistic, self-referential reflections of our ultramodern syncretistic infinity mirror. For example, in view of the nineteenth-century context of evangelical feminism, if any advocacy group today should be pro-life and anti-pornography it is feminism, yet much of contemporary feminism is now post-Christian if not anti-Christian. Nineteenth-century feminists understood the connection between their own dehumanization, the dehumanization of the slaves, and the dehumanization of the unborn (mostly women).
- *Multiculturalism and pluralism* should be viewed primarily as a celebration of and learning from other cultures, nations, and perspectives, or a prolepsis of the day when "every tribe

and tongue and people and nation" (Revelation 5:9) will be united in love and worship before the throne of the Lamb. The already-but-not-yet rule or kingdom of God does not abolish cultural variations but instead utilizes, judges, and redeems all diverse cultures. In the light of God's kingdom true multiculturalism is instructive and eschatologically celebratory. In the present age, true multiculturalism experiences the coming kingdom of God. Unfortunately, multiculturalism and pluralism have sometimes morphed into a multicultural (concerning truth and ethics) and perspectival relativism—and/or an undiscerning anti-Western (or anti-American) prejudice and advocacy. Then anyone who expresses concerns about relativistic multiculturalism is defined as an ethnocentric racist. Only someone completely ignorant of human history, or indoctrinated in a multicultural relativist ideology, would suggest that all cultures, beliefs, and nations are at all times morally equal.

- Are all cultures and civilizations flawed? Of course, but that admission is a far cry from a radical multicultural relativistic and ethical leveling. Both stealing a cookie and committing a murder fall short of the glory of God, but the failure to discriminate between the two actions amounts to the genocide of meaningful communication and the subversion of ethics. Equating religions and nations that practice human sacrifice or female circumcision with all other religious perspectives and nations undermines the true and potentially constructive meaning of pluralism and multiculturalism. Pluralism should refer to the reality and constructive response to living, with great discernment, in a civilization characterized by multiple perspectives and values. Multiculturalism should not mean turning a blind eye to cultural differences or evil practices. The idea that one nation is perfect, and all others are worthless is imperialistic and idolatrous. The idea that one nation, often America, is evil, and all others are morally superior, is intuitively suspect and should require a significant marshalling of evidence and great discernment about the actual conditions that exist in other countries. I remember some years ago visiting a country that had been described to me in utopian terms. Within hours of visiting this country, while appreciating elements of the culture, it became clear that I had been greatly misinformed of the facts on the ground. This utopian country was a hot mess.

The other pervasive idea today that all nations are morally equal, or the correlate mantra that nations or cultures should not be compared and contrasted, is ultimately relativistic, nihilistic, or polytheistic—and idolatrous. And disastrous. And absurd. Nations and cultures can and should learn from each other but learning from each other means acknowledging the strengths and weaknesses of each, and making difficult but necessary overall assessments of cultures and civilizations that will doubtless acknowledge that some are inferior. Hitler's Third Reich, or China's and North Korea's totalitarianism, can properly be judged as inferior and evil when engaging in macro-evaluations. Additionally, a sound theology or theological anthropology, that we are all fallen, requires a frank recognition that some criticisms are actually of individual and corporate human nature more so than a country or ideology.[208] For example, a sound view of human nature recognizes that nations or groups with more power typically exert that power over nations or groups with less power. Abusive colonialism was practiced by countless nations. Even native American tribes and other native people groups around the world were sometimes rather ruthless to each other.[209] Human nature is not always pretty.

The Rousseauean myth of the Noble Savage is just that; it is a historical myth based on bad theological anthropology. There is no possibility, in a fallen world, of a noble savage who is pure because she is untainted by civilization. Hence, the determination that certain nations or their ideologies and political philosophies are evil or oppressive due to them engaging in colonialism needs to be appropriately nuanced and complex. Oppression is sometimes what fallen, powerful, groups do, even those associated with Christianity.

But the idea that non-religious or non-Christian or non-capitalistic players would not be oppressive or colonialist is truly inane and historically falsified. For example, it is fashionable to blame religion, as did John Lennon's naïve twentieth-century song "Imagine," for war and oppression, and play the song boorishly and redundantly on New Year's Eve—when in fact the carnage and suffering of irreligion in the twentieth century is incalculable.

The fact remains that in the twentieth century anti-religious, non-Christian, and post-Christian movements were responsible for a lion's share of oppression, persecution, war, torture, and genocide. They key is to assess how the ideology or belief system logically, psychologically, or sociologically engenders the oppression. In some cases, the connection is logical and direct. In other cases, the oppression is more of an abuse of the ideology or national vision than a logical outcome of the ideology or vision. Martin Luther King, Jr., and Harriet Beecher Stowe (in *Uncle Tom's Cabin*), viewed America's evils as largely a failure to live by its own God-given eternal principles of justice. Any system or ideology can be abused. Yet some are inherently abusive, oppressive, or morally relativistic.

• Historically, the *freedom of religion* has included a robust definition of the freedom of worship that propels believers toward, impacts, and engages culture and civilization. Indeed, in the American context, religion, including worship, was viewed as an absolutely essential and positive influence to bridle and season democracy and encourage virtue. Increasingly worship is being redefined as a personal and private ultramodern syncretistic experience, properly restricted (legally and in terms of post-Christian advocacy) to a privatized and ghettoized reality that is intentionally excluded from civilizational influence. Worship belongs, as is typically the case under functional and secularized state religions, only in the closet. Faith communities therefore need to lose their tax exempt role of civilizational melioration, according to many critics, and stay out of politics even as politics crushes faith communities and faith-based companies and organizations.

- *Diversity and inclusion* are viewed not primarily as an eschatological and multicultural prolepsis, or a mutually beneficial welcoming of racial and intellectual diversity, but instead these terms move far beyond the healthy encouragement and celebration of racial diversity. These terms are now often used to mandate ideological conformity and the marginalizing or excluding of biblical values (e.g., biblical sexual ethics). Diversity or inclusion now includes subjectively chosen gender identity. Evangelicals appear to be *the* one group, according to the Pew Research Center, that is increasingly excluded from protection via principles of toleration, diversity, and inclusion in contemporary American society.[210]

  Inclusiveness, diversity, tolerance, and multiculturalism are legitimate concepts within shrewd biblical parameters of Truth but divorced from Scripture they too easily devolve into socially and personally destructive attacks and truth relativisms. For example, we certainly want to reach out lovingly to alcoholics and drug abusers, but that hardly entails accepting unbiblical or personally and socially destructive behaviors. Unfortunately, the once worthy concepts of dialogical and celebratory multiculturalism and inclusivism have now, in many quarters, morphed into a relativism concerning sexual ethics. And a related term, racism, which certainly needs to be prophetically articulated at times, has now morphed into "if you disagree with me on ethics or the best course for the future of civilization," then you are a racist (and a sexist). As noted in the introduction, racism and sexism have now morphed into neo-racism and neo-sexism. The loudest anti-racists are often the most racist, and most self-righteous, social justice advocates. How far we have strayed from common sense and Scripture!

- A classic and ongoing case study in America reflecting the word theft of a legitimate term and concern—*discrimination*—involves the Little Sisters of the Poor. Leviathan-sized government used a discrimination claim to bully and discriminate against the free exercise of religion and sacrificial service to the needy. The Little Sisters of the Poor are engaging in a type of faith-based community service that has been affirmed and fiscally encouraged by nation states for centuries. Any fair observer can only conclude that the opposition to the Little Sisters was anti-Christian semantic and legal bullying. Fortunately, the Little Sisters received a temporary reprieve, though the future is still uncertain for this unnecessary church-state conflict.

- The terms *globalism and colonialism* are often not utilized to learn from the past and identify civilizational principles or even kingdom values that must supersede at times the interests of individual nations or eras. Instead, these terms have been used to dismiss everything of value in a biblically influenced (but admittedly flawed) Western or American civilization. An amazing great reversal in our American experience is the semantic journey from an American education where the strengths of the relatively esteemed colonial founding fathers were heralded—while it was noted that the founders were flawed, lived in a certain historical context, and clearly did not agree on everything (e.g. slavery)—to the contemporary ideological tyranny that equates all things *colonial* and all "founding fathers" with oppression, racism, sexism, privilege, and evil. Again, the cultural relativists today are ironically often those most critical of the founding fathers (and mothers) who were culture-bound and flawed, or situated, while also moving history toward increased freedom and liberty.

The polarized colonialism/exceptionalism and anti-colonialism debate is telling concerning the reality of speck-and-log human nature. Racism and abuse are unquestionably part of the American colonial heritage. The primary problem, however, is not white guys, white skin, gender, Anglo-Saxon Protestants, or Judeo-Christian or Enlightenment-influenced ideology and culture. The problem is human nature or the realities of theological anthropology. Systemic evil must be addressed. However, *it is past time for all to look closely in the mirror.*

Paul Hiebert's wise words concerning globalism, pluralism, and colonialism continue to be muted in many circles, including evangelical Christian circles:

> Missions has always had to deal with cultural and religious pluralism. In the past its response has often been colonial. In recent years there has been a strong reaction that has sought to eradicate the ethnocentrism and arrogance of the previous era. This reaction is an important corrective, but in itself leads us into pragmatism, relativism, and a superficial acceptance of the other. We need to go beyond anti-colonialism to find a solid base for affirming the truth of the gospel.[211]

Relative to colonialism and to the often despised belief in American exceptionalism, there are many views with three basic options or points on the continuum:
1. Either America (or any country or civilization) truly is exceptional and desirable (e.g., **American exceptionalism**);
2. Or all countries and civilizations are morally equal (**moral and cultural relativism or multicultural relativism**), and/or morality is merely a matter of cultural or personal perspective (moral **perspectivalism**)—and there is really nothing to criticize or affirm;
3. Or America (or any country or civilization) is morally inferior and some other country or civilization is morally superior (which ironically, for relativists, means that exceptionalism and universal morality of some sort are "true")—which then also logically entails belief in American mediocrity, American inferiority, or, more common today, passionate **anti-Americanism.**

We must make, and cannot avoid making, moral distinctions between nations and cultures. Winston Churchill and R. Niebuhr noted long ago, in one form or another, that the inability to discriminate ethically between cultures dominated by the demonic (e.g., Hitler's Reich) and very fallible experiments in civilization and freedom laced with or influenced by Judeo-Christian assumptions is devastating to the church, missions, and human flourishing. This lack of discrimination and discernment reflects option two above. So the only real choice for lovers of Truth is to identify aspirational countries and civilizations in a less than perfect world prior to Christ's return and seek to form and sustain more perfect civilizations. Loving our neighbor and our progeny requires such difficult discernment.

Much can be learned from a central insight of Winston Churchill and R. Niebuhr: "Democracy is the worst form of government [on the face of the earth], except for all the others." Regardless of the veracity of their conclusion concerning democracy the principle is essential to pursuing a just civilization. No governmental system is the kingdom of God, but all approximate or deviate from the values of the coming kingdom to one degree or another, and it is important, even obligatory, to discern the degree of approximation among available alternatives.

It also should be noted, in view of how history has repeated itself over and over again, that *utopian dreams, when implemented, often bear a remarkable resemblance not to heaven but to hell. Some nations and cultures approximate hell, and we need to be compassionately but brutally honest about such civilizational failures.*

Another potent term today is "post-Christendom." As previously noted, in the American context the lack of precision concerning the degree to which America is moving toward a post-Christian or post-Christendom reality, or going European, could be crippling to the Judeo-Christian quest for a better civilization.

It has been argued previously that the American experience and context was and is different from Europe's, including religious voluntarism (as noted in De Tocqueville's visit to America in the 1830s), the Reformed revivalism and social concern of the 1700s, and the largely Wesleyan-inspired revivalism and social reform of the 1800s.[212] Declaring America in an absolute and un-nuanced sense as part of post-Christendom may be premature, oblivious to a unique religious heritage or current religious (orthodox and evangelical) vibrancy and influence, and thus amounts to an insufficiently nuanced and deleterious assessment.

And while faithfulness amidst persecution is one of the glories of church history, many seem almost gleeful that we might be headed back toward the days of Christian cultural marginalization,[213] or even possibly persecution and martyrdom. This embrace of post-Christian culture and possible oppression could become a self-fulfilling prophecy and is certainly not good news or a loving gift for our progeny. As noted, surely neighbor love applies to our own progeny. We need to stand firm for Judeo-Christian influence on culture, not for ourselves or our power or to prove we are right, but because we care deeply for others. Sheepskins and human torches are not inevitable and certainly should be avoided if possible.

We can and should have an influence on our semantic universe and semantic universes around the globe. We have an incredible obligation to lead on semantic apologetics and polemics.

While it has been helpful historically to condemn what should be called "manipulative colonialism," in some quarters this critique has been replaced with an equally unproductive anti-Western climate and ethos. The well-known ills of the West are legitimately identified, yet this nearly militant version of anti-colonialism majors on the evils of the West and ignores both the evils of other cultures and the sacrificial benefits of orthodox, evangelical, and Western missions, philanthropy, medical missionary work, or even legitimate assistance from Judeo-Christian influenced nation states to those in dire need.

This reckless allegation of colonialism also commits the anthropological fallacy discussed previously, and fails to compare fallen nations to fallen nations. Evangelical colleagues now proclaim privately or even publicly that they are ashamed to be American citizens and would prefer to identify with other nations and cultures. Long live Rousseau and belief in the naïve state of nature and the noble savage? Flawed theological anthropology? We must discriminate, and we need to be just judges of cultures and civilizations.

Another controversial and related phrase deserving of some semantic archeological reflection is "America First." In the political arena, the civilizational chants of "America First," "We're number one," or "Let's make America great again" (used for two successful Presidential candidacies) could be, and likely are reflective, for some, of a rather unbiblical *just us* or nationalistic posture. All that matters are American flourishing and American or Western hegemony for this form of pseudo-patriotism. For some, America and the American church have no responsibility to or for the world beyond our borders. "Just us" might even mean, for some, that America was just fine when sexism and racism prevailed and was even overt. "Just us" may mean, for some, total indifference to the plight of the suffering and oppressed around the world. For Judeo-Christian faith communities with a global kingdom vision, such callous indifference is not a biblical option. The key is to be compassionate and shrewd on such global entanglements.

Yet there are other possible nuances of these terms and chants that have possible connections to biblical, compassionate justice and the quest for an aspirational civilization. For some, racism and sexism are acknowledged as past evils (ills that have been in the fluctuating process of being redeemed), but the seeming loss and abandonment of any moral standards causes some to yearn for an apparently abandoned and now despised or forgotten moral past and greatness, before our ethical feet became "planted firmly in mid-air."[214] That is what some mean by "great again." Not all are racist or sexist.

For some, "America First" (AF) actually reflects a politically libertarian (even liberal) concern that American foreign policy has been incautiously interventionist, such as former Presidential candidate Pat Buchanan.[215] For others, AF is a call to utilize resources in service of domestic justice and fiscal stability first, since a weak and unjust nation cannot lead, sustain, or model international assistance or justice. And for some, AF is more of a "pep rally" morale builder for sports-like enthusiasm, or even for the necessary public galvanizing for the international use of force that might indeed reflect some measure of justice (e.g., defeating Nazism). It is hard to imagine how the Allies in World War II could have succeeded apart from a rather spirited belief that the Allied kingdoms, though flawed, were vastly superior to Axis powers such as the Third Reich (or kingdom). My father was technically a World War II veteran, and that was his read and the read of his fellow soldiers on the national spirit.

While "Let's make America great again" (MAGA) can certainly be a classic example of a statement made by someone who is insensitive and who has a just-us mentality, a bit of history might be of assistance with this analysis. In the case of the 1980 Reagan candidacy, the MAGA campaign slogan was more likely intended to capture a host of concerns and sentiments and transcend the following: an era of profound national malaise; military incompetence and national insecurity; blatant international disrespect for America and "America held hostage;" moral drift and relativism; the accelerating loss of Judeo-Christian influence and cultural sanity near the time of the nation's bicentennial; crippling runaway inflation, unemployment and rampant crime; the devaluing of the founders and the core values of the American experiment; and disillusionment with political corruption (e.g., the Watergate scandal). The political and almost revivalist call to MAGA was not a crippling pessimism about the present suggesting that America in 1979 lacked any greatness; MAGA simply meant that much could be gained by returning to the core values of the American experiment and creatively applying such values in a late twentieth-century context. Reagan's MAGA and Trump's MAGA should neither be conflated nor completely polarized—they should be carefully contrasted and compared. And Reagan's MAGA was not perceived as endorsement of racism or sexism by all who voted for his landslide victories.

The flawed theological anthropology and hence self-righteousness undergirding the mind-set of so many of these contentious and reckless verbal exchanges today between the political left and right is sometimes stunning. While not at all suggesting the moral equivalency of the political ideologies of the left and right, Scripture is explicit that "there is none righteous, not even one" (Romans 3:10; Psalms 14; 53), and, "from within, out of the heart of men ["out of a person's heart," NIV], proceed the evil thoughts, fornications, thefts, murders, adulteries, deeds of coveting and wickedness, as well as deceit, sensuality, envy, slander, pride and foolishness. All these evil things proceed from within and defile the man ["person," NIV]" (Mark 7:21–23).

It is rare that participants in such passionate conversations seek understanding as opposed to tribalistic semantic, political, and legal victories. It is rare that the noetic impact of the fall on discourse, careful reflection, and the pursuit of justice is confessed by all.

I am convinced that some political parties, flawed as they are, resonate more with Judeo-Christian and biblical values than others. Yet some of the spokespersons for that more biblical political party hardly emulate biblical tone or self-awareness of their own human depravity. It is rare that semantic combatants distinguish between shared goals and less than certain proposed means. Nietzschean ethics and semantics seem to rule. Semantic terrorism seems to rule the day.

Those who have concerns about poorly vetted immigration and refugee assistance are often viewed as hate-mongers. Those who sense that biblical compassion and justice have some relevance to such discussions and an obligation beyond our borders (e.g., refugees) are often viewed as weak and anti-American. There are countless other motives attributed to ideological opponents. Perhaps the starting point for envisioning a better civilization, a Judeo-Christian-influenced civilization, is the bended-knee recognition of the log in one's own eye?

This speck-and-log truth from theological anthropology is especially applicable to a host of immensely polarizing semantic games. There are certainly those who truly hate or fear homosexuals or hate or fear those who claim or advocate for nongender binary identity, and such attitudes should be dishonored. However, the indiscriminate application of terms such as *homophobia* to anyone advocating for scriptural ethics is primarily an attack on scriptural authority, as well as a very hateful and *ad hominem* attack on specific individuals who simply have scriptural convictions. The *ophobia* accusation is quickly becoming a default mechanism against anyone with a different view on anything in this supposedly inclusive and tolerant cultural age (see Appendix A). Again, this increasingly feels like verbal terrorism. Agree or else. Any means necessary. Let's go with the verbal nuclear option immediately.

If there is one thing of which postmoderns and ultramoderns have reminded us, it is that words are contextual, part of a sometimes fleeting and fluid matrix of meaning, and hence rather slippery. Unfortunately, many postmoderns, instead of better defining, nuancing, and contextualizing word games in the pursuit of an approximation of Truth, meaning, and communication, simply lather on infinite Vaseline to the verbal interactions. They do so by rejecting the Truth quest altogether and viewing words as entirely contextual and driven by the tribalistic pursuit of power.

As Dr. Bob Patterson often said, "We have known for thousands of years that words are slippery." [216] Yet the solution is cautious, patient semantic refinement and the hermeneutical circle of dialog, not a semantic relativism that is incapable of discriminating among the ideologies and actions of George Washington, Mother Theresa, Adolph Hitter, Pol Pot, and Abu Bakr al-Baghdadi. No current political movement fully reflects the values of the coming kingdom, yet if we cannot morally discriminate, for example, between the cultures and countries that did or did not enable the female circumcision of some 200 million victims, then the ethical task now is entirely bereft of life. If we can't discriminate between nations and cultures, then there is no rationale for pursuing any ideal. The quest has effectively ended for a more perfect union.

As noted, this author and the argument of *Seduced?* is fully cognizant of the fallible limitations relative to refining word choice, word usage, hermeneutics, and contextualization—especially when simultaneously dealing with countless words! Yet this attempt at semantic apologetics and polemics may have never been as urgent in the history of the church as this present moment.

The semantic analysis of the selected terms in this work should be sufficient to at least draw attention to the importance of this area of inquiry (aggressive semantic apologetics and polemics), which is the primary purpose of this book. The subsequent chapter will amplify and expand upon this analysis and especially frame this inquiry within the context of how better understanding these many terms and the contemporary semantic conflict requires cognizance of how terms are symbiotically and organically related within a fluid tapestry and matrix of semantic clusters. These macro issues must now be examined.

Ask Yourself or Your Group

- *What does the author mean by "semantic jungles"? Have you seen such jungles in the media, law, or entertainment?*
- *What is the difference between relativistic advocacy and shrewd advocacy? How should the church be advocating for issues today?*
- *What is your favorite or most helpful illustration of semantic terrorism from the book or from your own experience?*
- *What does the author believe are the primary options concerning the debate over American exceptionalism? What have you heard people say about American exceptionalism and do you agree or disagree? Why or why not? Is Barack Obama a supporter of American exceptionalism? Is Rush Limbaugh a fan of American exceptionalism? Do you have friends or family who are anti-American? Do you have friends or family who are nationalistic idolaters? What is the proper biblical and Christian response to this debate?*
- *How does this chapter reinforce the argument, introduced in the introduction, concerning neo-racism and neo-sexism?*

Chapter 9

REFINED SEMANTIC CLUSTERS OR SHAMELESS "WILL TO POWER"?

Death and life are in the power of the tongue,
And those who love it will eat its fruit.
—Proverbs 18:21

There is one who speaks rashly like the thrusts of a sword,
But the tongue of the wise brings healing.
—Proverbs 12:18

But I tell you that every careless word that people speak,
they shall give an accounting for it in the day of judgment.
—Matthew 12:36

Language is the first casualty of wars over foreign policy.
To paraphrase Thucydides, during ideological conflict,
words have to change their ordinary meaning and to take
that which is now given them.
—Bruce Thornton (2015)

At this juncture it will be helpful and appropriate to review, advance, illustrate, and augment the argument of this work. Resolving the esoteric, highly contested and philosophical disputes concerning the nature of meaning and language raised by such scholars as Nietzsche, Frege, Lyotard, and Wittgenstein exceeds the scope of this present work.

However, a brief, technical excursus or detour of roughly two pages should help some readers prior to engaging in the true focus of this chapter. For those finding this philosophically technical discussion a bit overwhelming, please fast forward to the sub-section in this chapter on civilization. The academic sidebar that follows has been translated as much as possible to be more accessible to a general audience, and it is critical to understanding the argument of this text.

One emphasis in Wittgenstein, though needing modification, is helpful with the present argument. Wittgenstein's "language games" concept well-articulated and demonstrated the interdependent and organic nature of terms, language, and communication.[217]

Unfortunately, Wittgenstein's language game concept, like Nietzsche's approach to language, was not squarely grounded in theological and biblical assumptions concerning reality, revelation, and the *imago Dei* (humanity defined as being the image of God). Wittgenstein rejects Augustine's Neoplatonic, essentialist, and realist approach to language and affirms that words and terms and meaning do not correspond to reality. Diminishing Augustine's Neoplatonism may be justified, but much in Wittgenstein counters biblical and Judeo-Christian core semantic beliefs:

- Yes, words or terms do not exist independent of each other and form an organic tapestry and bear a family-like relational resemblance. For example, in the contemporary context, words such as inclusion, diversity, love, tolerance, compassion, and social justice, not to mention infinite *ophobia* terms, are best understood in relation to each other and the underlying ideology and activity of the primary group utilizing the semantic cluster. Many such terms today are members of post-Christian or anti-Christian semantic families.

- Yes, such semantic clusters may or may not correspond to reality and only reflect the usage (or, with Nietzsche, the ideology) of such terms by those sharing and advocating for the semantic cluster.
- Yes, such semantic clusters are likely to be fluid and the individual terms within the cluster may be less than precise and not static.
- Yes, there is an endless plurality of such semantic clusters.

However, the idea that the indeterminacy of the terms within the cluster necessitates the conclusion that all semantic clusters fail to correspond to reality is a grand and unjustified assumption:

- First, the clusters certainly reflect the activity, presuppositions, ideology and family resemblances of the words of the group using such semantic clusters.
- Second, there is no *a priori* reason to assume that such fluidity—or perhaps a better term would be adaptability—inherently and entirely severs meaning and language from reality. Indeed, such fluid clusters might assist with accurately describing, corresponding and effectively interacting with reality. This adaptability may be analogous to biological adaptability to changing environments. The tapestry of the semantic clusters may actually assist with adapting to and understanding the dynamic tapestry of reality.
- Third, from a Logocentric revelatory perspective, the semantic clusters are also organically, systemically, and symbiotically related to each other and a common and ultimate source and perspective. The tapestry of these semantic clusters is part of the larger tapestry and texture of language and meaning. While specific languages are largely human inventions over time, language and meaning, broadly speaking, are potentially revelatory mediums and allow humans created in the image of God to know and communicate effectively concerning God and reality. In Genesis, God named the elements of the creation, humans named the animals, and Adam named Eve. We should not be distracted with hermeneutical debates about Genesis. The relevant point in Genesis chapter 1 and 2 is that language

is a divinely created, Logocentric, *imago Dei* compe-
tency capable of reliably interfacing with God and reality.
Humans possess co-creative competencies through which
God and God's will can be manifest.

- Fourth, acknowledging that individual terms may not
have (or may not always have) a simplistic and atomistic
one-to-one essentialist correspondence with reality hardly
requires the conclusion that semantic clusters or language
as a whole lacks any essential connection with reality. The
linguistic whole truly may be greater than the sum of its
parts when ultimately revelatory in origin and application.

- Fifth, as noted, if semantic clusters are rooted in a theology of Logocentric creation, revelation, and the *imago
Dei*, then the revelation-dependent ability of humans created in the image of God to understand, communicate, and
interact effectively with created reality across cultures is a
justifiable and central axiom of a Judeo-Christian view of
language and meaning. Augustine may have been overly
syncretistic and indebted to Greek thought, but he certainly
had it right (and Wittgenstein had it wrong) that in some
sense and to a significant degree language and meaning
truly reflect reality.

- Sixth, linguistic nominalism properly underscored the inter-
relatedness and functional nature of terms, as well as the
slippery nature of words, yet nominalism utterly failed to
frame the entire discussion within a biblical, revelatory,
Christian, and theological context.

- Seventh, Nietzsche and others properly noted the relationship between power and semantics, and that hermeneutical
"power" tool is critical to the argument of this book. Nothing
seems more evident in the twenty-first century than that
words are manipulated, even in the church. In many circles
shameless and deceitful spin is in. However, what is being
argued in this work is that the failure of some advocacy
groups to deconstruct or at least refine and decrease the
ambiguity of the very semantic clusters claiming to counter
power (e.g., privilege, inclusion) amounts to semantic and

cultural suicide. *When advocacy groups say anything to advance the cause, they are just as guilty of the abuse of language and power as their opponents.* There can be no abuse of language or power if semantic clusters are utterly incapable of corresponding to reality. There can be no abuse of language or power if semantic clusters rest on the shifting sands of personal or cultural preferences and they are not grounded in revelatory, Logocentric reality. There can be no abuse of language or power if semantic clusters are incapable of refinement or corruption based on a transcendent plumb line and vantage point.

- Finally, those questing for a more just civilization will ground the quest in the Logocentric and revealed kingdom of God. *Meaningful and truthful language is revelation based, Logocentric, and kingdom-centric.* For example, justice is ultimately determined and measured by the Logos, and true justice conforms to the revealed and coming kingdom of God. Those seeking to participate in the epic drama of moving from the kingdoms of paradise lost to the kingdom of paradise regained will seek semantic alignment with the kingdom. They will aggressively but lovingly advocate for the proper use of terms and enhanced semantic clarity. Those pursuing and practicing effective apologetics and polemics will ground apologetics and polemics in Judeo-Christian theology.

Most informed Protestant believers are familiar with the concept of *Ecclesia Reformata Semper Reformanda*—the Protestant Reformation understanding that that the church of Jesus Christ has been graciously reformed by the Father, through the Son and the work of the Spirit, under the authority of Scripture. However, in view of theological anthropology and biblical eschatology, this reformed church, though reformed, is always in need of reformation.

While the strength of this Reformation analogy is debated, the task of decreasing semantic ambiguity, increasing semantic clarity, and increasingly conforming terms and semantic clusters to reality and divine revelation is a never-ending process of refinement. Judeo-Christian semantics, analogous to the Protestant Reformation, is reformed but ever being reformed. Roman Catholics may prefer the analogical principle of doctrinal development. Yet just as with the Reformation, measurable gains and transformative historical watersheds can obtain in church and state. Historic losses are always possible as well. What follows summarizes the application of much of this work and expands this process relative to the contemporary semantic context.

Representative terms and clusters will be reviewed, assessed, and addressed in this chapter. A supplementary Lexicon is presented in appendix A to assist with this task of recapitulation, review, and application. Hence, I will begin by returning first to the overarching term and concept of civilization introduced early in this work. For each term or cluster, an attempt will be made to present contemporary distortions followed by a trajectory for increased semantic clarity. The word theft of the terms discussed undermines biblical fidelity and the apologetic mission of Judeo-Christian faith communities, including civilizational influence. Some of these terms have already been introduced, so what follows is recapitulation, expansion, supplemental narrative, and systemic reflection.

Civilization

As noted and documented previously, the assumption that civilization is a shared goal is no longer shared. In some quarters, the goal of civilization is viewed as a smokescreen for Western or American hegemony or international dominance. Civilization is often viewed as an oppressive, imperialistic, colonial, arrogant Western concept seeking global power, control, and profit. Judeo-Christian civilization is likewise sometimes viewed as an attempt to impose a certain kind of culture on other cultures in the name of Christian evangelism or the civilizing of the heathen. The critics view Christian influence as a smokescreen for personal, corporate, and national self-interest.

The allegations are many, but a few illustrations should suffice. The power grab is baptized in holy language with holy terms. The semantic cloak invokes the following: "spreading the gospel," saving or civilizing the heathen, advancing *The Christian Century*,[218] promoting Christian democracy, compassion, and medical missions. Sometimes the cloak involves eschatological evangelism and semantics, meaning saving as many souls as quickly as possible from the sinking ship known as *The Late Great Planet Earth*. This eschatological fervor allows for accelerated imperialism, hegemony, and colonialism, it is argued. This semantic dagger ultimately results in the distortion or destruction of native cultures and contexts, or perhaps even genocide. This definition of kingdom advance does not exactly align with what many in churches have heard concerning the Christian global mission!

No attempt will be made to justify such cloak-and-dagger Roman Catholic or evangelical colonialism or abuses, but as previously noted such allegations of semantic manipulation are often presented in a very one-sided manner. So let's use semantics to deconstruct some of these one-sided narratives. For example, it is more than arguable that the increase of life expectancy and the rescuing of those in tremendous suffering as a result of medical missionary work is authentic civilizational advance. And the failure to acknowledge any benefits of global Christian evangelism and missionary work is evidence that the critics are also engaging in verbal manipulation and the self-serving pursuit of power in the name of "justice." Paul Hiebert's words, quoted previously in this work, are worthy of repetition.

> Missions has always had to deal with cultural and religious pluralism. In the past its response has often been colonial. In recent years there has been a strong reaction that has sought to eradicate the ethnocentrism and arrogance of the previous era. This reaction is an important corrective, but in itself leads us into pragmatism, relativism, and a superficial acceptance of the other. We need to go beyond anti-colonialism to find a solid base for affirming the truth of the gospel.[219]

Challenging female circumcision or elevating the status of women due to biblical influence is a civilizational gain and a foretaste of the *eschaton*. The impact of the Quakers and John Wesley on the abolition of slavery across the globe (and Wesley's revival influence on Wilberforce) should be acknowledged. Positive Christian influence in the ancient world relative to undermining infanticide, the Roman gladiatorial games, the cheapness of life, temple prostitution, and pederasty is undeniable. Abandoning the quest for an aspirational civilization because of abuses by those doing the questing is tragic. Abandoning orthodox Christian evangelism because of colonial abuses is also tragic, not to mention unbiblical. Theological anthropology confirms that the quest will always fall short of the ideal, yet the ideal has and should drive the quest. Let's be transparent, candid, and honest about the strengths and weaknesses of all programs for social betterment—such is the biblical approach.

Civilization is an aspirational ideal or an ideal to be approximated—a fallible but superior reality to the alternatives, and an endless, ongoing quest. In biblical thought, the future kingdom of God is the ideal. The cancerous utopian logical fallacy—discarding all present and partial accomplishments because they fall short of utopia while offering a utopian alternative that is less ameliorative—has been demonic in recent centuries. The utopian fallacy is the ultimate and cloaked power grab. Proponents of utopian revolutions parasitically use and enjoy the benefits of a given civilization while corrosively undermining that civilization, promising a superior utopian alternative overflowing with compassion and justice, then delivering an elitist, tyrannical, and blood-soaked hades.

Truth

As already noted, the attempt to replace the Logos with utopian and impotent usurpers has led to the current, parasitical, and unsustainable polybabble. *What is disguised as truth today is merely personal, cultural, tribal, subjective, embodied, felt, or contextual self-interest.* Truth is merely self-justificatory truth and not prophetic Truth. Truth with a small "t" is often a smokescreen for a mega-tribal story seeking power that disguises itself as Story but reduces to mere story. Many of the new stories that try to distance themselves from Christian or Logocentric roots also parasite off of the strength and gains of those very roots.

Marxism is a Christian eschatological heresy (e.g., the prophesied classless society) that can hardly justify its affirmations, its view of human nature, and its extreme moral outrage based on its own materialistic, atheistic assumptions. Many contemporary movements for social justice and compassion lack an identifiable or stable foundation apart from the Logos and often assume core Christian values while decrying the oppression of Judeo-Christian civilization. Such movements also splinter into countless alternatives apart from bowing to the plumb line of the inspired words of Scripture. Such movements also increasingly reflect the arrogance of utopianism.

This proliferation of increasingly militant movements naturally follows when truth and ethics are reduced to personal or tribal preferences. Polybabble rules. Personal, cultural, and contextual inclinations and desires should not be confused with Truth.

Truth refers to God's knowledge and perspective, of which humans have a limited or approximative but valid grasp via God's amazing revelation mediated through creation, history, miraculous revelation, conscience, and the image of God in humanity. Revealed Truth is the only legitimate basis for evaluating false and oppressive truth claims and false and oppressive civilizational movements.

As noted previously, truth is trifold in nature: TRUTH, Truth, and truth. Civilizations built on truth are built on the shifting sands of history and personal and tribal preference. Logocentric civilization that approximates the ideal is built on Truth and the already-but-not-yet assured future.

Faith

The eclipse of truth—*Is Truth Dead?* (see Chapter 2)—birthed polybabble and ultramodern syncretism. Biblical faith, therefore, has had to be adjusted and divorced from Truth in order to accommodate the postmodern spirit of the age.

Faith has now been redefined, often in mainline and evangelical churches, and synagogues, as an irrational leap to trust in something personally true and meaningful, though not True. This redefinition of faith is in response to the irresolvable questions and chaos concerning the nature of human existence and knowledge. Redefined faith is the detour around and cultural accommodation to the substantive challenges of modernism and postmodernism. Faith is not *reasonable*, not only because arrogant modernist reason is passé but also because there is simply no means by which to make the case that Judeo-Christian beliefs (or any normative meta-narrative) is True for all.

In contrast to ultramodern faith, biblical faith is primarily an interpersonal rather than an epistemological (pertaining to how we know) concept or category. The modern and postmodern epistemological redefinition of faith is truly at the core of the destruction of biblical Judeo-Christian faith communities and Judeo-Christian mission.

Biblical faith emphasizes relational trust in the Triune Christ alone for salvation and for kingdom advance and the individual and corporate kingdom journey. Biblical faith is Abraham (see Genesis 21–22; Hebrews 11), after the evidence of the amazing and miraculous acts of God (e.g., Sodom, Isaac's birth), trusting God when offering up Isaac. Biblical faith is Joseph, most aware of the mighty acts of God and the existence of God and the superiority of YWHW, trusting God in the pit and in prison.

Viewing blind or "leaping faith" as *a* or *the* only means by which to respond to the modern and postmodern intellectual challenges to and criticisms of the Judeo-Christian worldview redefines biblical faith and ultimately disengages faith communities from the critical intellectual and cultural challenges of the day. Faith and the very tenor of the Judeo-Christian faith are redefined.

Biblical faith, from Genesis to Revelation, assumes and states that the object of that faith, the Triune God, is clearly and demonstrably the one and only true God. The Bible considers it foolish to worship many gods, false gods (Romans 1–2), or to bow and worship a manufactured idol (Isaiah 44). Biblical faith is primarily relational and dispositional. Biblical faith is not a bypass around the intellectual challenges of modernism and postmodernism. Biblical faith is trust amidst the storm, or in the Garden of Gethsemane or on the cross. An extended discussion of faith is of paramount importance to this work, because faith properly conceived and experienced is central to the Judeo-Christian semantic universe, mission, tradition, and future.

Faith without Truth is dead!

Sometime in the 1980s and early 1990s, in order to counter endless distortions of biblical faith in the church (polemics) and outside of the church (apologetics), I began to emphasize in my course materials and radio broadcasts (entitled *More than Reasonable*) that *"faith without truth is dead."* To what degree this emphasis is original is unknown and of little importance.

Faith without truth is dead was hardly a defense of reason as defined by the Enlightenment or Modernism, as the radio broadcast's program title attempted to clarify. While not defining truth as modernistic truth, the critique of faith without truth did contend for some form of normative truth. *More than Reasonable* meant that the Christian faith could withstand the assaults of the modern and postmodern critics and hold its ground in the face of the strictures of rigorous logic, the challenges of science, and uncounted but pervasive relativistic assertions. Yet the Christian faith and assent to Christ was much more, much deeper, more holistic in nature relative to knowledge, and more profound than what was reasonable to the critics of the faith. Faith as More than Reasonable emphasized that faith also involved the heart, desires, affections, passions, imagination, and actions of the faithful.

More than Reasonable especially attempted to counter the tragic response within some Judeo-Christian circles to the apologetic challenges of the day. Rather than responding to the critics or proffering a better understanding or definition of reason, human assent, and belief, faith became a justification for neglect of disciplined and serious inquiry, dialog, and reasonable reflection. Faith became an excuse for abandoning serious polemics and apologetics. Faith was a means of punting to God.

One does not have to be a Cartesian modernist or foundationalist to affirm the value of at least some refined and applicable understanding of human reason. Scripture certainly affirms that worshiping the creation rather than the Creator or bowing before a piece of wood or a meteorite is folly. Scripture certainly affirms that putting one's trust in various gods other than YHWH or in cultures that deliver their children to the sacrificial fires is not acting in one's own self-interest much less being reasonable. John Wesley affirmed that to renounce religion was to renounce reason. Renouncing arrogant modernistic secularized reason is certainly in order, but the task always remains to integrate biblical faith and reason with contemporary definitions and expressions of reason. Abandoning reason while reacting to modernism puts individuals, church, synagogue, and state in great peril.

Faith without truth is dead. Truth without faith is dead. Faith and truth are closely wed.

To illustrate, in 1997, when speaking to a more general or popular audience via the *More Than Reasonable* radio broadcast, I made the following observations. The quote is lengthy but most relevant on multiple levels to the present discussion and broad or popular application of the semantic argument of this work. Annotations have been added for the purpose of clarification and contemporary contextualization.

> Faith without truth is dead. Do you believe this statement, or does it almost sound like heresy to your ears? Faith without truth is dead. Most of us would agree with the statement that faith without works is dead because we are reluctant to argue with the Bible [the book James—even though Luther did!]. We may not always and fully live out the principle of 'faith without works is dead,' but at least we agree with the concept. The Bible, however, emphasizes [normative and shared] truth from Genesis to Revelation. Yet our century, and especially our generation, no longer seems to care about truth [and

not just modernistic truth, but any normative, cross-cultural, shared conception of truth and morality].

Philosophers speak of the death of truth in our—as they call it—postmodern era. Many national surveys [e.g., Barna and Gallup] suggest that the Christian church—and I am talking about the Bible believing, born again variety—is not all that interested in truth anymore. In fact, this disbelief that there is anything called truth is directly related to why we ignore the biblical admonition "faith without works is dead...." Faith without truth leads to faith without works—and an immoral church.... In other words, many people have a Christian experience. They go to the altar. They praise and worship. They feel born again,... [yet] many Christians have not learned to think like Christians. They know how to have a religious experience, and they love to revel in talk of God's love and forgiveness, but they do not think biblically and value truth. Grace is cheap, and truth [Truth] is boring for these Christians.

Now please don't misunderstand me. Praise, worship and a warm [evangelical] heart are all very valuable and important, but [revealed and biblical] truth must lead [or ground] experience [and that which we desire and love]. We have to know what we believe, why we believe it, and how to live it, or our emotional warm fuzzies will evaporate quickly in the heat of life's troubles and temptations. Truth matters, and if we do not know how to think like Christians then we are neglecting one of the more important elements of our walk with the Lord.... Many Christians are better described as religious [or evangelical] relativists—truth and morality are relative—than as [fully] Christian because like most people in our society, they believe that truth is relative.... We are losing the battle in evangelizing [and influencing] our cultural leaders, and we are losing our own families—in part—because we have lost our commitment to truth.... Feeling-oriented relativistic morality rules.... We are much more interested in what will make us feel good than in what is true or moral.... Shouldn't the Church of Jesus Christ, more than any other people or institution on this planet, be in the truth business? Shouldn't we present Christ as *the* Truth, [and relational Rosetta Stone relative to] the meaning, purpose and destiny of human existence, rather than just another self-help quick fix to feel happy?

I do believe that Christ puts lives back together and ultimately brings [a depth of] peace, but it often takes years of hard work and it only [persists] ... within the context of Truth. John, the author of the fourth gospel, said that Jesus was the Logos, the Truth, wisdom and spoken Word of God. Jesus called himself The Truth—not just one of many paths to heaven or happiness but the only true path. The apostle Paul said don't listen to anyone, including himself, if they come preaching a different Jesus or a different message of salvation [gospel] than the true one. What we believe matters, for it guides how we live. Relativism is destroying families and [effectively] torturing children [via brokenness]. Truth, however—the Truth of Christ—sets us free. Faith without works, and faith without Truth is dead.

One who knows Jesus may or may not have powerful emotional experiences.

Josh McDowell reported that initially, after receiving Christ, he actually felt "sick to his stomach." He wondered if he had made a mistake. It took time for him to experience [the calming of his self-confessed troubled spirit and] what the Bible calls the peace that "passeth understanding." That peace is not a superficial giddiness, but a sense of God's presence and an assurance of

His working in even the most difficult situations. One who truly knows Christ will, however, encounter Truth and begin to view all of life—morality, work, marriage, children, the meaning of it all—from God's perspective. Those who claim to have felt or experienced Christ but who are unwilling to accept God's perspective on life are only fooling themselves when they call themselves [fully biblical] Christians.

Faith without works is dead and faith without Truth is dead. The truth that faith without works is dead is addressed to those who claim to be believers even though they are constantly hurting others or practicing [things such as] racism or sexism [or the oppression of the poor, as noted in Hosea and James]. The principle that faith without Truth is dead is for those who claim to have met the Lord but who reject the Truth of the Lord. Those who practice faith without Truth and faith without works become real obstacles for unbelievers who are evaluating the truthfulness of the Christian message, and they set up their own children for a devastating fall.... Faith without Truth is dead—and it is killing the church....

National surveys conducted by groups such as the Barna and Gallup organizations reveal a startling trend among evangelical Christians. Many Christians believe in Christianity in a very limited sense. They enjoy feeling born again, and they enjoy moving music and [ecstatic] worship experiences. They enjoy Christian fellowship. They also believe that while Christianity is true for them, it is not absolutely True. It is the best thing they have found so far—it is a good bet—but Jesus may not be the only way. The moral teachings of the Bible, according to these evangelical relativists, are helpful but not absolute. Adultery and premarital sex, for example, are generally not good, but each individual has to determine whether such moral teachings should guide his or her life today. In recent programs we have found that [increasingly] the younger members of our evangelical churches who claim to have been born again often live lives indistinguishable from unbelievers. The younger members of our churches who are *most* likely to say "adultery is wrong," period, are those who believe that Christian Truth is [in some sense, not necessarily a modernistic sense] absolute. They don't say, "Truth and morality are whatever I determine them to be," but instead say, "God has revealed Truth and morality—my job is to follow the Lord's instruction, regardless of the cost...." [Subsequent research suggest that this truth relativism is not limited to the younger generations.]

[If this Gallup and Barna information is correct it dispels] a dangerous myth in our evangelical churches. The myth is that if we can just get a person to the altar to get born again then everything will be ok. It would appear that if the born-again experience is really going to make a difference, then the new convert must understand that following Christ means accepting the absolute truthfulness and authority of Christ, Christian Truth, and morality as revealed in the Bible. Stated very simply, our churches need to wake up to the fact that faith without Truth leads to faith without works ... and such faith is not biblical faith [but is postmodern syncretistic faith]. The Bible argues that true believers walk the walk—true faith works, loves, and fights for [authentic] justice.

The Bible also affirms that believing in Christ is believing in the Truth and the way, not just one of many ways to heaven. Christ is not just a good bet [on heaven or happiness]. He either is or is not the only way to God. The idea that all religions lead to God—there are many paths or roads, but they all get you to the same place—is flawed, and a bit silly. Some Eastern religions are atheistic—they deny the existence of God. To say that a religion that rejects belief in God is equivalent to Christianity is laughable. Some religions teach that when you die that's it. Others teach that you come back over and over again—perhaps as a frog, a dog, a hog, or a cockroach. Or some teach that if you are really good you may cease to exist as an individual person at death, and, like a drop of ink in a vast ocean, you are absorbed back into oneness with the one. Now that is something to look forward to! [And some religions teach and practice human sacrifice or female circumcision.] We need a reality check here.

In our relativistic late twentieth-century culture [and yet today] we make ultimate faith commitments like we play [a] Super Powerball lottery—we place lots of bets and hope we win. Christ says, however, if you don't draw upon my strength and lay it all on the line for me, then you are not worthy to be called by my name and spend eternity in Paradise. Make your choice, but don't play games with the King of the cosmos. Partial belief is really no belief at all. A [constantly or chronically] skeptical [and relativistic] Christian is just a skeptic who likes to be called a Christian, or who wants some fire insurance. Now please don't misunderstand me.... It is not wrong for a believer to occasionally have honest questions if they are truly seeking the Truth—I've been there. The problem emerges, however, when we play games with the Lord and take or leave His moral teachings depending upon what is expedient or what we think will make us happy in a given situation.

This program is called *More than Reasonable* because Christianity makes [much more] sense out of existence [than the alternatives],... [including the] past, present

273

and future,… and even more so it involves [much more than reason and] a personal and intimate and transformational relationship with God—the God who called this vast universe into existence and who created each one of us. Yet the national surveys have uncovered an evangelical church that rejects absolute [or normative] Truth and morality—a church that loves religious experience but not [revealed, normative] Truth.… For some 1,700 years the [majority of the] Christian church recognized the importance of Truth and reason. The church [as a broad generalization] usually did not worship reason—such hyper-rationalism [and modernism] is dangerous as well—but Christians recognized the value of using our God-created capacity to think. [Hence, as noted, Wesley argued in the 18th century that "to renounce reason is to renounce religion," while also strongly challenging the arrogance of latitudinarian or liberal modernism while he also emphasized the need for a warmed heart and vital religious experience.]

Reason must function under the authority of the Bible and under the guidance of the Spirit, but reason, logic and thinking were viewed as God-ordained means to arrive at Truth. Today, even in the [orthodox, biblical, evangelical] church, there is a need to go back to the very basics of how reason relates to faith, for many Christians [still] think that faith is blind, irrational faith, and that reason is no longer necessary or reasonable. By the way, as a former skeptic I can testify to the fact that irrational Christians who are unable to state what they believe or why they believe it are a real turn-off to those considering Christianity. Such irrational Christians never give a good answer for the hope that is in them [in contrast to Paul in Acts or Peter]—which the Bible commands … in 1 Peter 3:15. They just say, "Take it by faith," or, "Your questions show that you have a disobedient heart."[I remember when I was a skeptic and being told that my problem was my "reason."]

I was [also] once told, as a skeptic considering Christianity, to just pray the sinner's prayer—even though I wasn't sure that Jesus [even] existed as a historical person—and that I would then *feel* the truth. I suppose that it is only by God's grace that I did not reject Christianity once and for all after that encounter with some blind-faith Christians. I am glad that I came to know some Christians who followed the Bible's commands to give an answer, and they followed the apostle Paul's example when he [repeatedly, in every city] reasoned with the skeptics [Jews first, pagans second] of the day. In the New Testament book of the Acts of the Apostles chapter 17 is a passage that takes us back to a basic truth about the relationship between faith and reason.

The basic truth is that Christianity is an apologetic faith. This doesn't mean that Christians go around apologizing ... [but instead] Christians are commanded to give an *apologia*—a reasoned defense of their faith in Christ.... [In Acts 17 it is clear that] Paul believed that faith in Christ was more than reasonable, and [though some objected and did not believe his message yet still] his apologetic evangelism brought many into the kingdom. [The sad reality is that many neglect this apologetic task, and] ... many evangelical Christians have crucified Truth and reason and view their faith primarily [or only] as a warm experience that makes them temporarily happy, or helps them to cope with the stresses of life.

Warm fuzzies have their place—they inspire and encourage—but they quickly evaporate in the heat of life's tribulations and leave the believer vulnerable to moral compromises if the emotional experiences are not guided by a firm commitment to the absolute truthfulness of the [entire] Christian message.... I believe absolutely that if the ... Christian church does not follow [Paul's example and the scriptural apologetic and polemic] example and find creative ways to persuade the skeptics of our day, then ... [many] will be right about America's future,... that we are slouching toward Gomorrah.

While this quotation is a bit dated and contextual, and needs many qualifications and modifications today, it is most relevant, broadly applicable, illustrative, predictive, and it drives home the polemic and apologetic challenge for the present century. Faith without Truth is dead, and the voluntary acceptance and consequences of a *truthless* faith by the Judeo-Christian faithful are many, including the eventual and extreme privatization and ghettoization of orthodox faith.

And the Judeo-Christian faith community without true faith is also dead, ineffective, and unresponsive to God's true calling to love and engage our world. We better get faith right.

Perhaps no faith passage of Scripture has been more abused than Hebrews 11 in order to justify blind faith—or more accurately, using philosophical terminology, to justify the existentialist (from existential philosophy, an early and typically individualistic form of postmodernism) or postmodern redefinition of biblical faith. Even a cursory reading of Hebrews 11 counters this redefinition of faith as an intellectual escape from Truth.

As noted, faith is primarily a theological and interpersonal category in Scripture, not an epistemological (how we know) category. The following are representative passages from Hebrews 11.[220] These biblical citations are lengthy, but absolutely essential to comprehending the biblical—as opposed to ultramodern and syncretistic—definition and understanding of faith. A proper understanding of faith is at the core of Judaism and Christianity, and a watershed for Judeo-Christian influence and impact for time and eternity. Faith rules.

> Now faith [from πιστεύω] is the assurance of *things* hoped for, the conviction of things not seen. [The emphasized semantic category in 11:1 is confidence and hope, not epistemology, as the rest of the passage will repeatedly illustrate.] For by it the men of old gained approval. By faith we understand [from νοῦς, which affirms the possession of knowledge, perception, understanding, pondering, and even heeding the truth] that the worlds were prepared by the word of God, so that what is seen was not made out of things which are visible [c.f. Rom. 1:18–32 and subsequent chapters in Romans where Paul describes how the lack of faith in what has been clearly revealed results in immorality, condemnation, and idolatry, in contrast to the faith that justifies both pagans and Jews].

> By faith Abel offered to God a better sacrifice than Cain [Abel and Cain both clearly affirmed God's existence, so the faith in this narrative is theological and inter-personal, not epistemological or "does God exist?" in nature or focus], through which he [Abel] obtained the testimony that he was righteous, God testifying about his gifts, and through faith, though he is dead, he still speaks. By faith Enoch [who was not wrestling with the existence of God or the problem of evil, hence the faith referenced here referred more to trust and he] was taken up so that he would not see death; and he was not found because God took him up; for he obtained the witness that before his being taken up he was pleasing to God. And without faith it is impossible to please *Him*, for he who comes to God must believe that He is and *that* He is a rewarder of those who seek Him. [The context in this verse and the entire passage is not a philosophical debate concerning God's existence but trust in YHWH

amidst a polytheistic culture and persecution. The issue in the first century for most everyone was not whether God exists but which God? Hebrews is emphasizing a better or superior way of salvation and faith, rather than how to know if God exists. God's existence is assumed.]

By faith Noah, being warned *by God* about things not yet seen, in reverence prepared an ark for the salvation of his household, by which he condemned the world, and became an heir of the righteousness which is according to faith. By faith Abraham, when he was called, obeyed by going out to a place which he was to receive for an inheritance; and he went out, not knowing where he was going. By faith he lived as an alien in the land of promise, as in a foreign *land*, dwelling in tents with Isaac and Jacob, fellow heirs of the same promise; for he was looking for the city which has foundations, whose architect and builder is God. By faith even Sarah herself received ability to conceive, even beyond the proper time of life, since she considered Him faithful who had promised. Therefore there was born even of one man, and him as good as dead at that, *as many descendants* as the stars of heaven in number, and innumerable as the sand which is by the seashore. All these died in faith, without receiving the promises, but having seen them and having welcomed them from a distance, and having confessed that they were strangers and exiles on the earth. [Note that this narrative emphasizes trust and action, motion, and a journey, rather than blind faith.]

For those who say such things make it clear that they are seeking a country of their own. And indeed if they had been thinking of that *country* from which they went out, they would have had opportunity to return. But as it is, they desire a better *country*, that is, a heavenly one. [Faith is especially connected in Scripture to obedient, loving trust on the kingdom journey.] Therefore God is not ashamed to be called their God; for He has prepared a city for them. By faith Abraham, when he was tested, offered up Isaac, and he who had received the promises was offering up his only begotten *son*; *it was he* to whom it was said, "In Isaac your descendants shall be called." He considered that God is able to raise *people* even from the dead, from which he also received him back as a type. [The author here recounts the stories of Noah, Abraham, and Sarah to illustrate the journey of faith and trust to the readers. All, especially Abraham and Sarah, after many miracles and just after the judgment of Sodom and Gomorrah, certainly and already had *innumerable and sound reasons* to believe in the Abrahamic God's existence. Abraham was not an upper-class ivory tower philosopher reflecting on God's existence. Abraham was traversing through the real world crucible of trust in the face of God's undeniable presence and existence.] By faith Isaac blessed Jacob and Esau, even regarding things to come. By faith Jacob, as he was dying, blessed each of the sons of Joseph, and worshiped, *leaning* on the top of his staff. By faith Joseph, when he was dying, made mention of the exodus of the sons of Israel, and gave orders concerning his bones.

By faith Moses, when he was born, was hidden for three months by his parents, because they saw he was a beautiful child; and they were not afraid of the king's edict. By faith Moses, when he had grown up, refused to be called the son of Pharaoh's daughter, choosing rather to endure ill-treatment with the people of God than to enjoy the passing pleasures of sin, considering the reproach of Christ greater riches than the treasures of Egypt; for he was looking to the reward. By faith he left Egypt, not fearing the wrath of the king; for he endured, as seeing Him who is unseen. [The biblical author here recounts the origins of the Exodus narrative, and again defines faith as primarily theological and as active interpersonal trust, especially illustrated by the reference to the faith of Moses after the plagues. After the miraculous plagues on Egypt and the death of the first born YWHH's superiority and existence was hardly a point to be debated or a rational issue for Moses.]

By faith he kept the Passover and the sprinkling of the blood, so that he who destroyed the firstborn would not touch them. By faith they passed through the Red Sea as though *they were passing* through dry land; and the Egyptians, when they attempted it, were drowned. By faith the walls of Jericho fell down after they had been encircled for seven days. [By the time Israel reached the walls of Jericho, one could make the case that the denial of YHWH's superiority and existence would require incredibly irrational and blind faith, so clearly biblical faith is theological and interpersonal in nature, and not an epistemological blind leap.]

If any doubt still remains that biblical faith, or the faith referenced in Hebrews 11, is fundamentally and primarily theological, active, and interpersonal in nature, rather than an epistemological detour around tough modern and postmodern questions, this summation by the author of Hebrews 11 is quite conclusive:

And what more shall I say? For time will fail me if I tell of Gideon, Barak, Samson, Jephthah, of David and Samuel and the prophets, who by faith conquered kingdoms, performed *acts of* righteousness, obtained promises, shut the mouths of lions, quenched the power of fire, escaped the edge of the sword, from weakness were made strong, became mighty in war, put foreign armies to flight. Women received *back* their dead by resurrection; and others were tortured, not accepting their release, so that they might obtain a better resurrection;

and others experienced mockings and scourgings, yes, also chains and imprisonment. They were stoned, they were sawn in two, they were tempted, they were put to death with the sword; they went about in sheepskins, in goatskins, being destitute, afflicted, ill-treated (*men of whom the world was not worthy* ["the world was not worthy of them," NIV]), wandering in deserts and mountains and caves and holes in the ground. And all these, having gained approval through their faith, did not receive what was promised, because God had provided something better for us, so that apart from us they would not be made perfect. (Hebrews 11:32–40)

Faith is primarily radical (it goes to the root of who we are), allegiant (to *Christos Kurios* as King of the kingdom),[221] personal, relational, active (see Hebrews 11 above), and eschatological trust (an assured future vision and epic kingdom journey of trust). Grace-based transforming faith involves integrity and our faith or lack thereof is a statement about who we really are at the core of our being—hence, the heroes of the faith above are, by grace, "worthy." Grace-based faith trusts in and commits to Christ as forgiving Savior, Lord, and becomes baptized in or immersed in the Trinitarian work of the Spirit to replace the dead or unresponsive heart of stone with a responsive new covenant heart of flesh. This new heart becomes capable of overflowing love for God and others in God's kingdom and good creation (Ezekiel 36:26). The unwillingness to respond to love, grace, and to be transformed is un-faith or anti-faith and makes a huge statement about who we are at the core. In contrast, biblical, radical, transforming trust includes allegiance and intellectual assent, yet faith is much broader, richer, and deeper than either since biblical, saving faith is rooted in the Triune new covenant and kingdom.

Such faith is not foolish but firmly grounded in the clearly revealed Creator (Romans 1–2) and the many revealed and mighty acts of God in history. Scripture views the rejection of such faith as unworthy and foolish. Faith clearly has a moral dimension and touches on the very essence of our character, as those with or without true faith are viewed throughout Scripture in moral or ethical terms (e.g., Joseph, Moses, David, Saul).

In reality, it is not biblical faith communities but contemporary alternatives that revel in blind faith.

- It takes blind faith to believe that our deepest, profound, eternal, emotional, and spiritual needs can be truly fulfilled through romance or illicit sex with a finite human being. Human love and romance are wonderful gifts but ephemeral if not rooted in something beyond ourselves.
- It takes blind faith to try and find personal fulfillment and the meaning of life at the bottom of a fifth of whisky, at the end of a syringe, or by self-medicating with pills or opioids.
- It takes blind faith to believe that we can destroy the biblical definition of the family without deleterious and pathological long-term personal and civilizational consequences.
- It takes blind faith to affirm that the symphonic universe, life, and the infinitely complex, interrelated, artistic creation are self-generated and not created.
- It takes blind faith to know or affirm that nothing can be known or affirmed.
- It takes blind faith to use words to affirm that words are meaningless.
- It takes blind faith to believe in blind faith.

The contemporary narrow, privatized, existential distortion and definition of biblical faith is directly related to and feeds into the attempt to eradicate Judeo-Christian influence from the marketplace of culture and ideas. This semantic distortion is also an urgent matter for semantic polemics and apologetics as the church accommodates to culture on the meaning of its core experience and cognition of faith.

Blind faith undermines apologetics. Blind faith undermines fidelity to core Judeo-Christian beliefs and ethics, because when reason and faith are divorced, and faith is viewed as a blind leap, then right doctrine is inevitably devalued if not deemed irrelevant. Experience and personal preference or feelings reign supreme. Polemics dies. Apologetics dies. Orthodoxy dies. Such muted, weakened, and unbiblical faith is easily hidden or forced into the civilizational closet or reeducation camp.

Establishment of Religion and Freedom of Speech

Today, it is often alleged that any, or virtually any, especially Judeo-Christian, religious beliefs and values allowed in the public sphere of civilization amount to the establishment of religion. Biblical faith belongs in the closet or the graveyard. Freedom of religion (defined as mere religious *truth*) is best exercised in ghettoized churches and in the privatized metaphorical closet.

A functional post- or anti-Christian syncretistic state religion has been largely established by those falsely claiming to keep church and state separate. Freedom of speech (originally primarily political speech) has evolved greatly over the last few centuries and especially in recent decades such that virtually anything is considered by some to be freedom of speech (e.g., abusive pornography), including art, music, and freedom of expression that would truly stun the original framers of the very concepts of the free exercise of religion and freedom of speech. The point here is not that the founders had a narrow view of the freedom of speech. The point is that they would view some definitions of "speech" as an improper and seductive definition of speech. So on the one hand, they would oppose restrictions on the free exercise of speech and religion. On the other hand they would attempt to refine our conceptualization and articulation of what was intended by speech.

Hence, Washington, Madison, Samuel Adams (the Father of the American Revolution), John Adams, and Jefferson, yes even Jefferson, are likely turning in their graves concerning the semantic theft and abuse of the concept of the freedom of speech. And, it might be noted, all of these founders would be in violation of contemporary pseudo-definitions and secularized definitions of the separation of church and state in view of their alleged ethnocentric and Judeo-Christian bias.[222] The debate concerning the founders exceeds the scope of this present work, but a few illustrative quotes from America's first President should be of assistance:[223]

The propitious smiles of Heaven can never be expected on a
nation that disregards the eternal rules of order and right which
Heaven itself has ordained.
—George Washington, First Inaugural Address, 1789

I am still in the land of the livg [sic] by the miraculous care of
Providence, that protected me beyond all human expectation; I
had 4 Bullets through my Coat, and two Horses shot under me
yet escaped unhurt.
—George Washington, July 18, 1755

Went to church and fasted all day.
—George Washington, June 1, 1774—
[Washington's response to the recommended
fast by the Virginia legislators]

[T]he Brigadiers and Commandants of Brigades [are] desired to
give notice in their orders and to afford every aid and assistance
in their power for the promotion of that public Homage and ado-
ration which are due to the supreme being, who has through his
infinite goodness brought our public Calamities and dangers (in
all humane probability) very near to a happy conclusion.
—Washington's General Orders, February 15, 1783

It would be peculiarly improper to omit in the first official Act,
my fervent supplications to that Almighty Being who rules over
the Universe, who presides in the Councils of Nations, and
whose providential aids can supply every human defect, that this
benediction may consecrate to the liberties and happiness of the
People of the United States.
—First Inaugural Address, 1789

Of all the dispositions and habits which lead to political prosperity, **Religion and morality are indispensable supports**. In
vain would that man claim the tribute of **Patriotism**, who should
labour to subvert these great Pillars of human happiness, these
firmest props of the duties of Men and citizens.… The mere

Politician, equally with the pious man ought to respect and
cherish them.
— Farewell Address, 1796

Samuel Adams (known as the founder of the American
Revolution) concurred:

> A general dissolution of principles and matters will
> more surely overthrow the liberties of America than the
> whole force of the common enemy. While the people
> are virtuous they cannot be subdued; but when they lose
> their virtue they will be ready to surrender their liberties
> to the first external or internal invader.... If [true] virtue
> and knowledge are diffused among the people, they will
> never be enslaved. This will be their great security.

> Neither the wisest constitution nor the wisest laws will
> secure the liberty and happiness of a people whose
> manners [morals] are universally corrupt.

> He therefore is the **truest friend to the liberty of his
> country** who tries most to promote its virtue, and who,
> so far as his power and influence extend, will not suffer
> a man to be chosen into any office of power and trust
> who is not a wise and virtuous man.... The sum of all
> is, if we would most truly enjoy this gift of Heaven, let
> us become a Virtuous people.

> Let divines and philosophers, statesmen and patriots,
> unite their endeavors to renovate the age, by impressing
> the minds of men with the importance of educating their
> little boys and girls, of inculcating in the minds of youth
> the fear and love of the Deity [a personal and mono-
> theistic Deity] and universal philanthropy, and, in sub-
> ordination to these great principles, the love of their
> country; of instructing them in the art of self-govern-
> ment without which they never can act a wise part in

the government of societies, great and small; in short, in leading them in the study and practice of the exalted virtues of the Christian system.[224] [This last paragraph was written on October 4, 1790 to Vice President John Adams, who replied, "I agree," on October 18, 1790. This correspondence is years after the Constitutional Convention, which counters the ludicrous suggestion that the entire young nation moved from a theologically undergirded foundation for the American experiment in the Declaration to a secular foundation in the Constitution.]

I would like to suggest, as politely as possible, that no one has the right to speak on America's religious heritage or church–state relations, and the many nuances and expressions of this heritage from actions and legislation to architecture and prose, or claim the banner of patriotism, prior to first spending much time with primary sources such as *The Federalist* (Hamilton, Madison, Jay).[225] For those pressed for time, an alternative is to review every page carefully in works such as William J. Federer's encyclopedia of documented and direct quotations in his *America's God and Country*,[226] or the series of scholarly articles in *The Founders on God and Government*.[227] Both works irrefutably establish that the semantic universe of the true American experiment was decidedly and conspicuously Judeo-Christian influenced.

Some will criticize Federer as beholden to political ideology, an argument which is known in philosophy and logic as the genetic fallacy, or the logical fallacy of origins. An idea cannot be discounted simply because of the source or genetic origin of the idea. Or as some have put it, even a broken clock is right twice a day. Federer's work on *America's God and Country*, no relation to Roger Federer of which I am aware, is essentially an unbelievably detailed and rigorously documented anthology. Let the careful reader review such evidence for the pervasive Judeo-Christian influence on every dimension of the American historical experience and reconsider the public school and media indoctrination that many have experienced regarding the American experiment.

Former socialist Michael Novak aptly summarizes such compelling evidence *in Founders*, and comments on "how little one can learn on these subjects from recent scholars.... In particular, scholars since about 1950 have thoroughly misconstrued the high achievement of the founding generation with respect to religious liberty." In addition, "recent scholars have also failed to grasp the comparative advantage of Judaism and Christianity among world religions, that is, their rare and sophisticated understanding of liberty of conscience."[228] Consistent with the argument of this work, Novak notes,

> Even American deism seems to owe more to Jewish and Christian conceptions of God than to ancient pagan religious philosophies. The most common form of deism in the founding generation appears to have been the worship not of the god of Plato, Aristotle, Cicero, or even Descartes, but the Jewish-Christian God (Creator and Providence), abstracted from the historical particulars of Judaism and Christianity.

> As a consequent, historians since 1950 do not place the American founding in a true international [or global] perspective [even while ironically criticizing others via historical revisionism for being ethnocentric]. They seem uncommonly cut off from its historical roots in centuries of philosophical reflection on God, creation, and the proper relation of rational creatures to their creator.[229]

For the original American experiment,

> Duties to one's Creator were held to be inseparable from the self and not transferable to anyone else; they were "unalienable." This particular vision of man's interior life is not part of the universal inheritance of humankind; its specific narratives, horizons, and concepts [and semantic universe, to use the language of this

work] were worked out in Jewish and Christian history over many centuries. While there are many divergences between Protestant and Catholic versions of this vision of the interior life of Christians, the Americans of the founding period drew to a remarkable extent from traditions of reason they held in common with Catholics and to a commonsense reading of the political history of the Bible. One rarely finds among them the disdain for "reason" common among some of the reformers in Europe, on the one hand, or the total disdain for the Bible found among many of the "enlightened" in Europe, on the other.[230]

Even Benjamin Franklin, often falsely cited as the exemplar of anti-Christian Deism, affirmed, with other colonial leaders, the pragmatic value for the American experiment of Judeo-Christian religion and the world-changing "principles of primitive Christianity." He viewed traditional Judeo-Christian religion as the pervasive and foundational or principal support and sustainer of democracy in America that would restrain the tiger of vice that could devour the virtue requisite for responsible and unbridled human freedom and flourishing. Franklin even affirmed the following:

Hence, bad examples to youth are rare in America [rarer than in Europe], which must be a comfortable consideration to parents. To this may be truly added, that serious religion, under its various denominations, is not only tolerated, but respected and practiced.

Atheism is unknown there; Infidelity rare and secret; so that persons may live to a great age in that country without having their piety shocked by meeting with either an Atheist or an Infidel.

And the Divine Being seems to have manifested an approbation [approval or praise] of the mutual forbearance and kindness with which the different sects treat each other; by the remarkable prosperity with which he has been pleased to favor the whole country.[231]

Franklin even affirmed that "A Bible and a newspaper in every house, a good school in every district—all studied and appreciated as they merit—are the principle support of virtue, morality, and civil liberty."[232]

By way of comparison, Novak affirms that the "concept of God in Muslim thought and in the Christian (and also Jewish) thought is in such matters profoundly different...." In contrast to the all-consuming or even fatalistic will of God, the founders had a very different vision "of the way in which God's freedom and human freedom interrelate." Humans were viewed as "free, independent, self-reliant, cooperative with one another in civil society, and responsible for their own destiny. This is, as the world goes, a unique God [concept and semantic universe], and these men and women are, in their way of relating to him, a unique people."[233]

Indeed, the "impress of the God of Abraham, Isaac, and Jacob on these views is unmistakably deep, even when the idiom in which his character and actions in history are discussed is practical, related to actual events in then contemporary history, and rather more commonsensical than strictly speaking theological or academic."[234] Biblical semantics was nearly omnipresent and influenced everything. So even those imbibing deeply of the Enlightenment or Deism (Jefferson, Franklin, and "maybe" Madison) were consciously or unconsciously operating in a Judeo-Christian semantic universe and Judeo-Christian worldview. Even "Jefferson's argument for a natural right is in this case not merely a philosophical argument, but, rather, a philosophical argument that in one of its premises borrows a Christian conception of God."[235] It is no surprise, then, that "Nearly all other signers of the Declaration of Independence and the Constitution were publicly rather more devout and more orthodox than" Jefferson, Franklin, and Madison. And most importantly, post Judeo-Christian scholarship has obscured the "forgotten founders" who tilled the soil and laid the cornerstones of the American experiment, such as "John Witherspoon, George Mason, Charles and

Daniel Carroll, and James Wilson"—not to mention John Adams, "the father of the nation's independence."[236]

In the early nineteenth century, not long after the birth of the nation, as "Alexis de Tocqueville pointed out in *Democracy in America*, America was most distinguished from continental Europe by the fact that here religion and liberty were seen to be interdependent. Each had been present at the founding. Each had heightened the prestige of the other. Each continued to nourish the other."[237]

This consensus allowed for a precise formula for religious liberty, which contrasts greatly with the flawed contemporary and relativistic model of our own day:

> First,... they allow for the religious liberty even of those who do not share the religious views of Jews or Christians and even of those who declare themselves to be agnostic or atheist.... Second,... they protect religious liberty on the premises that are not relativist, nihilist, or cynical. In other words, a commitment to religious liberty, or liberty of conscience does not entail a commitment to the moral equivalence of any and all points of view. On that premise of moral equivalence, there would be no intellectual defense against the will to power. For if it were true that reason has no capacity for deciding that one point of view is better than another, then the power of decision would have to be vested outside of reason, in raw power or something like it. On that foundation, neither liberty nor civilization could ever be secure. The possibility of liberty requires the possibility of truth.[238]

As argued throughout this work, the American experiment was a tolerant and welcoming Judeo-Christian republican form of democracy, and not a secular democracy. Only the historically myopic or intellectually dishonest would suggest otherwise. Novak also anticipates the postmodern or ultramodern challenge to his claim concerning Truth and contends that "the commitment of a civilization to the idea of truth does not require the belief that any one person actually possesses the [or all] truth. All that it requires is respect for rules of evidence on the part of all. If all of us are subject to the rules of evidence, we are each servants of such truth as humans may come to. The truth is not our servant; we are its servants."[239] Or to borrow and modify language from earlier in this work, the guiding assumption was not *Rex Lex*—the King or government is Law and Truth—but *Veritas Lex*, or truth is King and therefore *Lex Rex*. Harvard was founded upon just such a *Veritas* assumption. Novak concludes his summary with a contemporary assessment:

> The long cherished project of the Enlightenment to discover a universal ethic based upon reason alone has ended in failure or more precisely, in relativism, subjectivism, "nihilism with a happy face," and other such forms of take your pick. Post-Enlightenment ethics has been reduced, in effect, to an individual *boo!* Or *burrah!* As we have seen, a commitment to some principle less than finding the truth provides no reasonable basis for either civilization or liberty.... Neither Europe, nor the rest of the world has in the past paid much attention to the world-altering originality of the American experiment in liberty.[240]

And so, we have come full circle from a semantic universe rooted in Judeo-Christian conceptions that guarantee, foster, and nourish, liberty, to relativistic conceptions of liberty rooted in the shifting sands of ultramodern syncretism and the shameless, misguided, and sometimes deceitful semantics of the will to power. And the latter option will prove terminal.

Patriotism was once inherently anti-nationalistic if nationalism ever became idolatrous given the desire to escape the prior experience of European totalitarianism. Patriotism was supportive of the national experiment, but not nationalism if defined as putting any nation above God's truth and law. There should be an important semantic distinction made between nationalism and "nation-olatry," or between *Lex Rex* nationalism and vulgar or naïve *Rex*

Lex nationalism. That very distinction, that the nation was to be founded upon divine law and most honored *if* subject to divine law (*Lex Rex*), was the whole point of the American experiment. Today patriotism is viewed by some as vulgar nationalism—especially by those who are clueless concerning the actual contours of the original experiment. And for others likely on the far political right, equally clueless of the original experiment, some expressions of patriotism may well be nationalistic and idolatrous.

To be clear, a proper use of patriotism does not mean worshipping the nation or suggest the idolatry of any nation. Judeo-Christian faith communities put the kingdom of God above all kingdoms and judge all kingdoms by the kingdom of heaven. No current nation is the kingdom of God, but some are better and worse when judged by reason and Scripture. As argued previously, not making moral distinctions between nations and cultures is as ethically irresponsible as naively baptizing any current nation as the fullness of God's kingdom.

When one is properly patriotic one is showing appropriate but not unqualified respect for governmental authorities (Romans 12), while not sanctioning all government actions (e.g., genocide—for we must obey god rather than human beings, Acts 5:29). In the American context, patriotism should not become completely aligned with any particular administration or political party, in view of theological anthropology—the fallen nature of humanity and leaders. Yet some leaders, ideologies, political parties and programs are more informed by biblical influence than others, and careful discernment is required. Legitimate patriotism in the American context is primarily focused on the value of the American experiment, rather than any particular historical moment or regime.

Respect for nation or flag in the American context should be appropriate appreciation for the less than perfect gains and trajectory of the American experiment—if one is convinced by evidence that such gains are real. The argument for viewing the American experiment as a gain includes many layers and factors. Christianity and Judaism were, in principle, allowed to flourish. Judeo-Christian influence guided the nation, but skeptics were to have legal protections under the law. Religious involvement was voluntary. Law, rooted in divine principles and ethics, was to be king, or *Lex Rex*. Both free press and political speech were protected. Disputes were to be settled peaceably whenever possible based on divine principles of justice and equality that were self-evident to all. Virtue, religion, political and economic freedom working together were viewed as a means to alleviate suffering and unleash human creativity and flourishing.

Critics will try to discount these principles by the practices of fallen humanity, but this would be a striking and opportunistic fallacy. Such critics typically propose some alternative experiment modeled on countless failed experiments in history, especially those that concentrate immense power in a supposedly benevolent state that will guarantee justice and equality of outcomes. Unfortunately, such utopian visions misunderstand human nature and fail to provide the kind of checks and balances on power that characterized the original American experiment in tripartite or Trinitarian democratic capitalism.

The argument that patriotism toward the original American experiment is nationalistic in the negative sense, or even idolatrous, is inane. The original experiment was founded upon the very principle that no nation is above the divinely grounded law, and any nation that subverts that order may be legitimately resisted (see the *Declaration*).

Disrespect for nation or the American flag is misguided at this juncture in history because it means disrespect for the very principle of subjugating the nation to law and ethics. The flag should be used as a prophetic critique of injustice rather than opposed as a symbol of injustice. The kneeling NFL or World Cup players simply illustrate the rampant poverty of their education and the extreme naiveté of their perspective. There may come a time when the flag is completely disassociated from the experiment and the nation is totalitarian, but that time is not here yet and democratic processes for peaceful change still exist. And burning the flag in protest unfortunately can imply that one is burning the American experiment, which is the very mechanism and framework by which many injustices have and can be remedied.

Many are misinformed or have historical amnesia and fail to grasp that the total lack of patriotism for a fallible but reasonable civilizational experiment can ultimately undermine the very possibility of justice or equality. Protest injustice by using the American flag, not by protesting against the flag, if the original experiment was a reasonable attempt at a more perfect union in a fallen world. Use the flag, at least in the American context—just as Martin Luther King, Jr. or Harriet Beecher Stowe used the founding American documents and Scripture—to call a nation to live up to its own inspirational vision. That approach is far more persuasive, effective, unifying, and historically and philosophically sound. Or provide a defensible superior civilizational eschatology prior to torching the American experiment.

In such a fallen world, no country should be compared to perfection and then rejected in favor of inferior utopian or hypothetical alternatives. Every nation falls short of perfection. Instead, all nations and cultures should be compared to each other, realistic alternatives, God's future kingdom, and the sobering realities of a fallen world under redemption yet awaiting full redemption. Unfortunately, many compare nations to perfection, then promise deliverance and paradise, only to deliver a civilization that is as bad or worse than the one replaced, along with much bloodletting and social purgatory—or something worse.

Today, many who have moved far beyond the influence of the Judeo-Christian context and presuppositions of the American experiment in Trinitarian democratic capitalism still claim to be patriotic,[241] and metaphorically wrap themselves in the flag and identify with the cross. Those of a variety of political perspectives (e.g., left or right,[242] in the American context) or political parties certainly are capable of drifting away from the patriotism of the actual American experiment in a variety of ways. However, certainly President Washington's standard for patriotism properly defined is nonnegotiable:

> Of all the dispositions and habits which lead to political prosperity, Religion and morality are indispensable supports. In vain would that man claim the tribute of

> Patriotism, who should labour to subvert these great
> Pillars of human happiness, these firmest props of the
> duties of Men and citizens.... The mere Politician,
> equally with the pious man ought to respect and
> cherish them.[243]

The semantic universe of authentic American patriotism is essential to the proper definition of patriotism. And it should be noted that this early American patriotism included a rejection of idolatrous nationalism, deified conceptions of the role of government or the divine right of presidents or kings, and rejected a secular state liberated from Judeo-Christian influence.

In this increasingly post-Christian Western context, often the only check on morally and culturally relativistic extremism today is the appeal to the principle of local community values, an appeal that ultimately reduces to yet another form of tribalism. In the American context, Logocentric influence on a national scale is waning and we are chasing the European model—a model that Nietzsche aptly referred to as retaining church buildings only as the sepulchers of God. Yet the freedom of Judeo-Christian speech, rooted in a key and Logocentric basis of freedom of speech in the West, is often viewed as the kind of speech that undermines the contemporary redefinition of free speech. Again, the parasites have attached to the vital organs of our corporate body's quest for a stable, flourishing, Judeo-Christian influenced aspirational civilization.

Theocracy and the establishment of a single denominational or sectarian tyranny (e.g., Cromwell, or Iran) certainly amount to the establishment of religion. The American experiment was not a secular nation, or a CHRISTIAN nation (a theocracy or the belief that all were Christians), or a "christian" nation (i.e., widespread but merely privatized faith). The experiment was a tolerant or welcoming Judeo-Christian, democratic republic. Yes, the Enlightenment and Deism were influential during this period, but, as demonstrated previously, Deism and the Enlightenment were also emerging while lathered with Judeo-Christian ontological, epistemological, and axiological assumptions and influence. Even as Deists challenged core Christian assumptions, the scent of

Judeo-Christian assumptions was pungent in the assumptions, articulations, and actions of those operating within the Deistic universe.

This point concerning Deism is critical to the future of the American state or similar experiments in republican democracy. Relative to understanding the philosophical and theological assumptions guiding the American experiment, not to mention the influential *Zeitgeist* of the founding fathers (and mothers, e.g., Abigail Adams who greatly influenced John Adams), Deism and the Enlightenment should be viewed as very progressive variations on basic Judeo-Christian assumptions concerning reality, law, culture, and civilization. These progressive thinkers did not fully escape orbit from Christianity, as later atheists would lament.

Yes, some Deists (e.g., Voltaire or Paine) were very critical of traditional Christianity. Some leaving Mormonism today have been most critical of their prior faith while still retaining many core assumptions about reality from their Mormon past. There is arguably much more in common between Deism and Christianity than between Deism and atheism (or atheistic Marxism) or Deism and the New Age movement.

John Locke, who was practically plagiarized by the *Declaration of Independence*, is appropriately classified as an Enlightenment influenced "rational supernaturalist,"[244] who discarded some elements of traditional belief and yet continued to affirm the reality of revelation, miracles, and resurrection as truths above, but not contrary to, reason. Locke is representative of the fluid and interdependent ideas and terms enveloping the genesis of the American experiment, as his rational supernaturalism stands at the juncture of Christianity and Deism. His influence on the experiment was unrivaled, and he well represents the many theological and philosophical options of that era. Locke's perspective is instructive, and stands in stark contrast to the false and extreme polarizations of Deism and Christianity today seeking to marginalize the narrative of Judeo-Christian influence on the experiment.

Relative to civilizational presuppositions, such as law, morality, human nature, democracy, the needed balance of power, education, or eschatology, it is clearly the case that Christianity, Deism, the Enlightenment, and Rational Supernaturalism all worked in concert together as midwives of the American experiment. These were sometimes contentious midwives, yet ultimately successful contributors to the delivery of a more perfect union.

As demonstrated previously, there is a significant difference between affirming that the grand experiment was Judeo-Christian influenced versus a theocracy or a secular state. It is a false dichotomy to suggest that either the experiment was a theocratic fundamentalist (or conservative evangelical) project through and through or it was entirely a secular or Deistic vision. The best answer and remedies to these fallacies is simply to read the words of the founding fathers and mothers of the experiment. Diverse intellectual views within a Judeo-Christian and Enlightenment framework characterized the seventeenth and eighteenth-century milieu, which is why shameless advocates of a narrow view certainly can find quotations that seemingly back their reductionistic attempts to redefine American history.

For the sake of argument, even if Deism was a major force or player in the American experiment, that hardly discounts the enormity of Judeo-Christian influence or the presence of influential orthodox, biblical Christian founders such as Patrick Henry and Samuel Adams. Removing the Judeo-Christian assumptions and influence from American civilization and culture is akin to removing the hard drive from a computer, roots from a tree, or business ethics from a business curriculum. Free speech and the free exercise of religion are Promethean or shape-shifting concepts apart from the welcoming Judeo-Christian conceptual and cultural roots. The non-establishment clause has been used to establish a functional state religion. Sematic theft is alive and well and thriving.

Educational Neutrality

Similarly, with the increasing eclipse of Truth and the eradication of the once pervasive biblical influence on education, public education adopted the shallow myth of educational neutrality. This especially gained momentum in America in the 1950s and 1960s. Secularized students were to be provided a *neutral* education that no longer acknowledged the Judeo-Christian roots of the entire educational endeavor and the quest for truth dating back to the colonial nurseries of piety. The utopian dream was that publicly funded schools could simultaneously marginalize or eradicate Judeo-Christian educational influence (the very historical and conceptual pillars of education) while providing totally objective and neutral education. The modernistic naiveté of this neutral proposal concerning human nature, psychology, philosophy, the nature of communication, semantics, and semiotics, not to mention the nature of educational instruction, is stunning. Only blind faith in a secular utopian dream, or post-Christian ABC prejudice, can explain such naiveté.

The pursuit of balance and enhanced objectivity is noble, but the idea that neutral teachers in public institutions across fifty states, K–12 and higher education, would not intentionally and unintentionally influence students in one direction or another relative to politics and worldview options is farcical. The shifting *Zeitgeist* will always provide the conceptual glue for so-called neutral public education and function as a covert or overt religious framework for the quest. The semantic universe inevitably rules education. Even *facilitating* instructors can create a classroom culture that implies that all perspectives are equally valid or that traditional religious beliefs are threats to everyone's future and freedom.

As we have seen, the conceptual glue for the American nation and for education for centuries was a welcoming Judeo-Christian framework honed within the historical context and influence of the Enlightenment. Indeed, basic Judeo-Christian and Enlightenment assumptions defined and made possible the pursuit of free intellectual inquiry, which was analogous to and interdependent with the American flavor of political and religious freedom.

Without the cultural glue, especially in recent decades, most anything can be advocated for in public education except biblically influenced values and ideas. This is truly a *Great Reversal*. Relative to the American context, the very biblically influenced foundation for America's educational quest for Truth is now the one perspective that is the most consistently marginalized and viewed as a violation of educational neutrality.

I have personally experienced so-called educational neutrality in classes taken at public schools and at a state college. Atheistic and existentialist (and what can only be described as pornographic) literature, including existentially framed introductions to primal therapy, were presented in a positive fashion. Scientific evidence that *proved* that Genesis was wrong was presented without dialog as part of a lecture. No reflection on proper biblical hermeneutics or the nature and limits of science were deemed as relevant during this anti-Genesis diatribe. One state university class lacked such educational value and objectivity that I finally dropped the class. As a very young student, it seemed odd to pay for what clearly was not education.

Teachers and professors and coaches in many grades and settings were not hesitant to interject their different perspectives or lifestyles *contra* Scripture. One teacher was well known for his interest in illegal marijuana. To be fair, as a skeptic in high school, two teachers were rather open about their Christian faith, but that was prior to the common gag orders in so many publics today. My personal experience has been verified in numerous research studies and personal stories, from surveys of the beliefs and values of college professors to the actual documentation of such widespread propagandizing. Even more politically liberal studies and reporting have confirmed a nearly 12 to 1 hegemony of liberal to conservative professors, and the imbalance is apparently only increasing.[245]

There is much debate concerning whether public education is playing a role in driving young evangelicals out of the evangelical church, never to return or not to return for a significant time period.[246] This is important, but relative to this work the key issue is the degree to which biblically orthodox beliefs and semantics are being eroded by the publics and how effective orthodox polemics and apologetics are at countering such influence.

In contrast to the strictly enforced myth of educational neutrality in the American context, educational neutrality should mean that public education does not serve as a propaganda arm of any particular church or denomination *or worldview or philosophy*. This would especially apply to philosophies and worldviews that are propagandized and function like a religion and attempt to eradicate Christian influence in a nation and educational process shaped by and presupposing Judeo-Christian influence. The state should not establish a sectarian religion or a secular or post-Christian syncretistic religion, which is the current trajectory.

The tolerant or welcoming Judeo-Christian democratic experiment makes possible such grounded but free inquiry because of values such as humility, empathy, and love, even the very passion for Truth. This experiment planted education into Judeo-Christian soil and assumptions about knowledge, reality, human nature, Truth, and a vision of the future—to name a few. Or, stated another way, free inquiry emerged from Judeo-Christian and Enlightenment soil.

Even the linear concept of history surrounding the American experiment and the "more perfect union" as opposed to a quest for perfect union are Judeo-Christian-influenced assumptions. It has already been noted that the Enlightenment contributed to this experiment. Yet by way of reminder, the focus of this work is orthodox and Judeo-Christian polemics and apologetics, not Enlightenment apologetics, and Judeo-Christian assumptions about reality remained in many of the assumptions of Enlightenment thought even while the Enlightenment departed from other Judeo-Christian convictions.

Educational neutrality as secular education cannot sustain education or civilization. Secularized, syncretized education functions as a state religion and is often militantly post-Christian, and hence the myth of educational neutrality today often means that "educational neutrality" actually is the establishment of a functional post- and sometime anti-Christian religion.

As opposed to the myth of neutrality, the way forward is to acknowledge and be grateful for the intellectual roots of the American experiment and American education. Rather than seeking utopian educational neutrality, which is clearly unraveling, or theocratic instruction, what is needful is balanced dialog and an intellectually representative educational diversity that honors the experiment.

This next point is controversial, but it is important to be crystal clear concerning the American context. Judeo-Christian values had a foundational and integrating status in the American experiment, including public education. Judeo-Christian values served as the presupposed norm for the experiment and for liberating educa-tion—this was neither theocratic nor secular in nature. The solution is not to replace this norm with a secular, syncretistic, or polythe-istic alternative. The solution is to enhance the Judeo-Christian norm and heritage with grace, dialog, free but respectful inquiry, humility, and a genuine intellectual diversity that honors the founding assumptions of the experiment. Yes, this is a most dif-ficult project and balance but far less difficult than sustaining the failed myth of educational neutrality or a civilization enhancing education rooted in self-referential polytheism, militant tribalism, and polybabble.

On a related note, one could argue that the American experi-ment was birthed by numerous Judeo-Christian assumptions and hybridized with Enlightenment assumptions without fully cor-rupting the former. Yet a workable foundation remained for the political and educational experiments. All religions and philoso-phies were, in principle, welcomed to the shores of America, but the epistemological, ontological, and axiological foundations of the experiment were grounded in numerous biblical suppositions, often unconsciously.

The American experiment was intended to be a welcoming, non-sectarian, tolerant, Judeo-Christian influenced democratic republic. America was never intended to be a secular, theocratic, post-Christian, or syncretistic experiment.

Hence, it is most ironic that some seek to gut the core of the experiment while claiming to be patriotic proponents of the experi-ment and freedom. Neither freedom nor ameliorative education can survive or persist in a theological and philosophical vacuum. There is nothing patriotic about shattering the foundation of freedom, and the global implications of a redefined experiment just for the evangelical church, evangelical missions, and evangelical public engagement, and massive evangelical philanthropy should not be dismissed. The negative implications beyond the evangelical world are equally stark. Over time a post-Christian civilization characterized by polybabble will not flourish, and over time evangelicalism and orthodox belief, as in Europe, will be sent scurrying to the secret closet or will be criminalized. This process is already well under way.

A key means by which the journey to the closet is encouraged is via the claim that biblical faith violates its own faith commitments to be loving, tolerant, nonjudgmental (Matthew 7), and non-legalistic (note the theme of Galatians). In other words, Jesus and Scripture call Christians to be loving and nonjudgmental, and culturally and politically engaged Christians, especially evangelicals and Roman Catholics, are hateful and judgmental. The alleged virtue of this proposed ostrich posture is often lauded in both evangelical and mainline churches.

Judgmentalism, Legalism, and Forgiveness

A primary contemporary pseudo-virtue is the claim that no one has the right to judge anyone else. This belief holds that Jesus is the model for humility (e.g., identifying with sinners), and Jesus even said, "Do not judge"—which is interpreted as do not judge anyone, or anything, ever! This relativistic conclusion is allegedly based on the words of Jesus in Matthew 7:1-5. This relativistic Jesus fits well, it is argued, with truth being perspectival; no one has the right to judge anyone else, and truth is a matter of personal perspective and preference. Of course, this fluid and foundationless approach to ethics is not practicable if someone experiences a great personal injustice or, ironically, if someone encounters a believer in Truth, in which case it is quite acceptable to judge and militantly condemn that individual.

The reality is that the biblical admonition not to judge, perhaps the most abused verse in the Bible in our post-truth era, taken in context, is unquestionably and primarily a rejection of hypocritical judgmentalism but not the rejection of making essential biblical judgments concerning Truth and Morality (i.e., how shall we be saved, and how shall we live). Indeed, judging judgementalism is a judgment. Jesus and the apostles exercised many strong judgments (e.g., "You brood of vipers"; "you hypocrites"; "If anyone preaches a different gospel ... let them be under God's curse").[247] The immediate context of Matthew 7, "Do not judge," includes the following: "For in the way you judge [judgments are necessary, biblical and inevitable], you will be judged; and by your standard of measure, it will be measured to you." Jesus goes on to ask why some focus on the speck in the eye of another individual while ignoring the log (or telephone pole or plank in our day) in their own eye. "Do not judge" means "do not judge hypocritically," and when judgments are made they are to be done "in a spirit of gentleness. Keep watch on yourself, lest you too be tempted" (see Matthew 7 and Galatians 6).

Pseudo-tolerance and compassion include an unbiblical definition of forgiveness, often most evident in evangelical churches and organizations. I have repeatedly observed evangelical believers, students, laity, and leaders equate forgiveness with virtual anti-nomianism. Antinomianism (anti-*nomos* or anti-law) refers to the rejection and polarizing of law in favor of so-called grace. Grace has also been redefined and distorted. Legalists exist in the church, including the evangelical and Roman Catholic church, but so do antinomians, and both are threats to biblical theology and ethics.

Yes, Christians are saved by grace alone but also created in Christ Jesus for good works (Ephesians 2), and true faith works and produces fruit (James; John 15). Likewise, forgiveness by God or others does not entail the eradication of consequences in this life (e.g., David and Bathsheba, Moses, the Apostles, Pauline church discipline) or the age to come (e.g., rewards). God and others can and should forgive a sincerely repentant adulterer or murderer, but that hardly suggests the individual should experience no consequences in this life or the next. Salvation is by grace alone, so the sincerely repentant and trusting individual will not forfeit salvation for forgiven sins, but there is more to the age to come than merely escaping eternal judgment.

Legalism increasingly refers, even in some evangelical churches,[248] to requiring *any* fixed moral boundaries. Rather than legalism, antinomians affirm, "Ethics is like art" (Sartre), and that any moral standards not self-created or self-chosen rob the individual of creativity and freedom (and for the religious such fixed standards allegedly contradict love and grace). Today, fixed moral standards are often viewed as legalistic, oppressive, psychologically destructive, and personally stifling. Self-actualization is lost in such smothering environments, it is argued. Normative ethics is rejected in favor of creative, individualistic, or tribalistic ethics. In the evangelical church, this relativism sometimes takes the form of "love Jesus and follow the Spirit" (or some spirit), or "my interpretation" of that passage (e.g., premarital sexual ethics) is different, or "I love Jesus and I live under grace not law."

The church, including the evangelical church, which is increasingly syncretistic, retains evangelical spirituality (e.g., born again piety, the warmed heart, the Christ alone experience, prayers for miracles) mixed with relativistic morality and ethical antinomianism. Are we witnessing the emergence and proliferation of evangelical Christian hearts and pagan minds? The heart says, "I love Jesus," and the head says, "Ethics is like art," and there is often little recognition that such a state of affairs is a volatile and unstable formula relative to maintaining biblical piety and orthodoxy.

In terms of proper definitions, relative to biblical theology, legalism primarily refers to seeking salvation by works, not to the essential *fulfillment* of the Law—including every jot and tittle—via transformed hearts created in Christ Jesus for good works (Ephesians 2:10). As many have said, head and heart must go hand in hand for biblical Christians. Reducing morality to personal preference is ethical heresy. Reducing Truth and Ethics to truth and ethics is often justified in the name of false tolerance and false love.

Tolerance and Love

In the age of rationalistic modernism, "tolerance" meant toleration of beliefs that were deemed rational as well as (sometimes militant) intolerance toward socially destructive superstitions and allegedly oppressive religion (e.g., traditional Christianity—witness the French Revolution). Today, tolerance, including love and compassion, means toleration of beliefs and practices that fall under the rubric of liberal political ideology and, increasingly, includes the militant intolerance of Judeo-Christian values, beliefs, and practices, especially the affirmation of Truth and Ethics. Such militancy, even *shouting down* and suppressing dialog, is often articulated via accusations of *isms* and *ophobias* (e.g., racism, sexism, and homophobia) and ironically justified by appealing to love, compassion, and social justice.

Perhaps the real sentiment is, "You evangelicals or Roman Catholics are haters and we hate you." It is amazing that we have reached the point in Judeo-Christian-birthed Western culture where individuals hatefully yelling and screaming at the top of their lungs that Christians who believe in heterosexual marriage are haters are even taken seriously. And of course those who disagree with their hateful allegations prove that they are haters.

Racism, once a useful prophetic critique, rather than referencing any sinful and inappropriate attitudes or actions toward different races, now often means "you disagree with me and you are a hater and a bigot." Or it is argued that racism is a sin that can only be committed by one race or the more powerful race. Redefined racism has become incredibly racist. These semantic shifts attempt to claim the moral high ground in opposition to allegedly hateful Judeo-Christian and traditional biblical morality. Even privatized or ghettoized biblical morality is increasingly unacceptable to the true believers of militant, post-Christian tolerance and love.

True tolerance is more than indifference. It values and respects real differences in the pursuit of Truth and authentic civilization, and fosters genuine dialogical inquiry, the truth quest and the educational task. Tolerance is not to be confused with relativism, and pseudo-tolerance is often not so tolerant today. Contemporary tolerance is actually pseudo-tolerance and such tolerance ultimately collapses apart from Judeo-Christian assumptions. If there is no Truth, then why bother with tolerance, and what is tolerance? True tolerance and authentic love for others hardly means enabling self-destructive, other-destructive, and civilization-destructive values and behaviors—not to mention spiritually and eternally corrosive values and lifestyles. Such love is pseudo-love and arguably a form of negligence and complicity. Militant accusations of *isms* and *ophobias*, if not grounded in reality (genuine cases of irrational fear and hate), amount to nothing more than crass, hateful, intolerant propaganda.

Sexual Ethics

The area of sexual ethics is most illustrative of the semantic distortion of love and tolerance. Our culture has often attempted to replace the infinite God-shaped vacuum in culture and restless human hearts with romantic love and sexual or other extreme experiences, and this has clearly failed.

The new truth-for-me-oriented semantic universe for sexual ethics naturally births the following terms: homophobia, sexual preference, sexual orientation, and nonbinary gender identity, etc. All of these terms are paradoxically affirming the sometimes militantly enforced truth that sexual ethics is a matter of truth, not Truth, and (incongruously) that the only truth is that sexual ethics is mere preference as with art, and part of free self-creation. Any suggestions otherwise amount to the hateful and repressive suppression of sexual freedom. Freedom, once defined more as political, religious, and economic freedom within a Judeo-Christian context, now refers to virtually unbridled freedom to do and be anything one wants, *as long as no one gets hurt*. Of course avoiding hurt is not so easy to discern or obtain.

When post-Christian relativists attempt to define what *no one gets hurt* means, relativistic chaos and polybabble are smoked out, seen for what they are, and such impracticable relativism is forced to emerge from hiding. I have observed the utopian *no one is getting hurt* ideology justifying mind-expanding drug usage, adultery, and teen pregnancies—just to name a few illustrations. I lost two friends to drug usage, so the argument, that I once embraced, became less and less persuasive as reality kept intruding on this fanciful, idealistic, and extremely naïve and individualistic ideology. People do get hurt, terribly so, by choices that are heralded as "nobody gets hurt." We are all short-sighted and, in the West, especially prone to the individualistic fallacy concerning the impact of our choices and actions.

The scarlet letter of adultery is now only reserved for those whose personal truth commitment was to monogamous marital fidelity and thus a violation of one's own self-selected ethical position (faithfulness in marriage). Otherwise, adultery is simply an *affair* or an *open marriage*. Fornication typically has no scarlet letter attached and is simply referred to as cohabitation, hooking up, a test ride, or *friends with benefits*. In contrast, sexual ethics and terms supportive of a free and flourishing civilization are properly rooted within the framework of Trinitarian and biblical Truth and a covenantal theology of relationships, family, community, and the body.

It is critical to affirm that homosexual or gay bashing is immoral, as are the legion behaviors and semantic distortions of biblical morality.

Quite some time ago in the West, a critical context and framework for biblical sexual morality, the definition of "family," was severed from Judeo-Christian assumptions that had been affirmed, tested, and refined by multiple millennia of civilizational questing dialog. It is also critical to distinguish between the primary or aspirational meaning of family, the proper secondary uses of the term "family," and usages of "family" that run counter to core biblical and Christian convictions. The aspirational family is clearly built upon monogamy and heterosexuality. When such a marriage and family function properly, all things being equal compared with other alleged forms of family, the greatest lessons in modeling and restoring the image of God are possible. God made them "male and female" (Genesis 1:27; Jesus in Mark 10:6) to reflect his image, and the whole story of the Bible is about paradise lost becoming paradise regained. Today many wrongly define additional and almost endless gender categories as created categories rather than as consequences of a fallen world.

The restoration of the image of God in humanity is a paramount theological and eschatological theme. Monogamy, covenantal fidelity, male and female are all divinely sanctioned and created realities. This created norm is the best building block and context for a healthy civilization, a missional church, and godly children prepared for time and eternity. That norm is the ideal.

Yet realities such as death, divorce, and a not yet redeemed creation must not be ignored. A single mother or father raising a child is certainly and properly referred to as leading a family, but it is lovingly and properly classified as a single-parent family. This family should celebrate being a kingdom family. These heroic single parents also need to find dynamic and influential equivalents for the absence of an opposite gender spouse. Single parent families and dual parent families are properly referred to as families, yet this should not mean abandoning the biblical and aspirational ideal and framing all such discussions of family within biblical parameters.

Polygamous and homosexual unions certainly can evidence more care, compassion, and peace than abusive and violent and/or drug-addicted heterosexual marriages. The solution, however, is not to divorce the primary and aspirational sense of the term "family" from biblical revelation. Just because some polygamous arrangements may be less physically abusive than some heterosexual marriages hardly justifies a return to treating women as chattel.

Likewise, gay bashing may very well emerge from homophobia, but homosexual advocacy may also emerge from heterophobia or bibliophobia—fear of biblical morality. The contemporary consequence for civilization of the emerging semantic universe is the ever-growing disdain or even verbal violence toward biblical morality, especially sexual ethics, as well as the verbal eclipse of the cultural, psychological, spiritual, and social benefits of monogamous heterosexual marriage and families. This should not be surprising. When sexual experience attempts to fill the infinite void left by Trinitarian presence, any attempt to restrain sexual ethics is viewed as akin to a mortal sin and an abridgement of freedom, compassion, and social justice.

Compassion and Social Justice

Compassion and social justice have already been directly addressed, but in order to review, clarify, and amplify the subject a few additional comments are in order. A great intellectual personage recently passed from the global stage. Michael Novak, a former socialist passionately committed to social justice his entire life, reflected on social justice, and attempted to live social justice, over the course of a lifetime. As an introduction to this section, his thoughts on social justice semantics—"not what you think it is"—are instructive:

> For its proponents, "social justice" is usually unde-fined. Originally a Catholic term, first used about 1840 for a new kind of virtue (or habit) necessary for post-agrarian societies, the term has been bent by secular "progressive" thinkers to mean uniform state distribu-tion of society's advantages and disadvantages. **Social justice is really the capacity to organize with others to accomplish ends that benefit the whole commu-nity.** If people are to live free of state control, they must possess this new virtue of cooperation and association. This is one of the great skills of Americans and, ulti-mately, the best defense against [oppressive] statism.[249]

Novak notes, "The problem with 'social justice' begins with the very meaning of the term." Novak draws on the work of Hayek to point out "that whole books and treatises have been written about social justice without ever offering a definition of it. It is allowed to float in the air as if everyone will recognize an instance of it when it appears. This vagueness seems indispensable." Why? Because "social justice" is used as "an instrument of ideological intimidation, for the purpose of gaining the power of legal coercion."[250]

Whether Novak landed on the right definition of social jus-tice (primarily the habits and virtues of individuals who organize with others) can be debated. The point of his quoted material is intentionally to run counter to what can only be described as an increasingly pervasive *social justice* advocacy and spirituality. This spirituality distorts the social justice to mean, as Novak put it above, the "uniform state distribution of society's advantages and disadvantages." This spirituality has been evident in many mainline denominations (e.g., my denomination of birth, United

Methodism) for quite some time, and now this spirituality is quite evident in American evangelicalism and Roman Catholicism. To be spiritual, biblical, compassionate, and just, it is assumed one must support massive, "uniform state distribution of society's advantages [including wealth] and disadvantages."

The Sojourners' movement and magazine may be the best evangelical representative of this approach.[251] *Sojourners* makes clear that to love mercy and do justice is to align with their understanding of political and social justice advocacy. This debate will not be settled here, though questions have already been raised about the dangers and effectiveness of relying on massive governmental dependence for justice.

The main point for now is simply to reaffirm that the means of social justice must not be confused with the goal of social justice such that the very term "social justice" is defined so that anyone who disagrees with the proposed means clearly does not love justice, mercy, and compassion and has utterly missed the boat on authentic biblical spirituality. The Sojourners' movement may also be the most egregious evangelical offender relative to that semantic distortion.

Sojourners reflects an increasingly influential evangelical piety and spirituality. If sixty years ago one had to be politically conservative to be an American evangelical leader, today the situation is shifting and more nuanced. American evangelicals continue to support more conservative political candidates,[252] yet the Sojourners' movement has conflated evangelical piety and a specific approach to social and political issues that seems increasingly influential with evangelicals with more education and in positions of leadership. In other words, sixty years ago, evangelicals were broadly politically conservative, and it was hard for many to conceive that a true evangelical could have liberal (contemporary liberal or leftist, rather than classical liberal) political sentiments. Today, most evangelicals are still politically conservative, yet the political views of younger evangelicals and evangelical leaders are less predictable.

For many, to be Christlike, holy, loving, and compassionate requires a different sociopolitical orientation than the 1950s—to be spiritual is to be politically liberal. True spirituality is viewed as politically liberal. Jerry Falwell, Moral Majority, Focus on the Family (from the 1980s), and even Franklin Graham represent ill-advised, dated, and privileged spirituality. Hence, compassion and social justice are often confused with a single political party platform or agenda, and social justice and compassion are often confused with a proposed compassionate means to social justice, typically some variant of democratic socialism or European socialism.

The naïve embrace or affirmation of democratic or European socialism is not without peril. It is arguable that, to some extent, democratic socialism is an oxymoron—a contradiction of terms. Surely someone else has made this argument, but when any economic socialist government attempts to increasingly control the means and distribution of goods, even with good or naively good intentions, the government increasingly gains more power over the people.

Even if the people vote for more power to be vested in the governmental bureaucracy (democratic socialism) the result is that the people turn over massive power to the government which not only robs the people of political and economic power but it also diminishes economic freedom. While the hope may be to limit the power of corporations the result, predictably, is the limitation of economic freedom or capitalism.

While the government can and should serve as an accountable referee—accountable to the people and their representatives— in a free economy, once the government takes on the role of the benevolent and socially just director of the economy it is just a matter of time until the government functions more and more like a dictator. Economic freedom is squelched and economic power is usurped. And once economic power and the "just" distribution of goods and wealth is controlled by the government, the people and economic entrepreneurs also lose political power. In other words, you can't have it both ways—hence democratic socialism has an internal and irresolvable conflict. It self-destructs. It is arguably an oxymoron.

Democratic socialism is also based on a faulty theological anthropology—in other words, the centralization and control of economic power by the fallen human beings who run government is a theological recipe for disaster. Just governments must be subject to higher principles (e.g., truths, Constitutions, divinely sanctioned rights) and accountable to the people and their elected representatives in order to maintain a balance of power that must submit to these higher principles. Governments that serve as just, principled, and accountable referees advance human flourishing. Governments that delude themselves into thinking they are the means of universal justice are susceptible to the demonic.

In any event, the common ground in this heated discussion is to view compassion as caring for one's neighbor as one would care for loved ones, or self, and justice should be defined in very biblical terms based on Old and New Testament passages and themes plus other noble texts. The Judeo-Christian tradition emphasizes servant love and "do unto others" (Matthew 7:12), and the Confucian and other commonsense traditions emphasize "don't do unto others what you don't want done to you." Social justice advocates should be careful to distinguish between the biblical vision, their passion for the vision, and the proposed action plan, political theory, or program.

The debate about the role and approach utilized by government either to provide, assist with, support, or facilitate compassionate justice should not be decided prior to robust analysis and discussion of the options, consequences, and evidence from historical realities. In today's context it is important to at least affirm the possibility that massive godlike, centralized governmental compassion and justice could lack compassion and foster injustice or even tyranny over time. Similarly, the idea that the invisible hand of a free economy will always promote justice has been discredited as intellectually bankrupt for decades.

It bears repeating that social justice is not necessarily socialism, communism, or capitalism. All models, including those vesting extreme power in corporations or punting to an invisible economic hand must be evaluated with Scripture and robust discernment—yet attempts at ethical discrimination between systems *must* be made. Sometimes attempts to criticize the reigning orthodoxy in the academy, which is typically some variant of a socialistic solution, have unfortunately yielded accusations of Nazism, terrorism, and extremism.

Terrorism and Extremism

The alleged extreme lack of justice has been used to justify global terrorism or to apply the term "terrorist" to the West rather than to those the West often defines as terrorists. In other words, England and France or the United States are the true terrorists and extremists opposing justice, and the alleged terrorists and extremists are the heroic defenders of the victims of the West. This sentiment may have been illustrated in November of 2019 when Oberlin college students made headlines across the nation by erecting memorials to fallen Jihad Palestinian terrorists and condemning "Zionist," "colonial" terrorists.

This semantic debate concerning terrorism may well be one of the starkest examples of extreme semantic polarities. Similarly, and interestingly, opponents of massive, centralized governmental power are increasingly being referred to as extremists, Nazis, and even terrorists, just as the proponents of massive governmental distributed justice are accused of being Nazis. It seems that everyone is a Nazi these days.

Relative to American evangelicals, who still tend to vote against contemporary and politically liberal centralized governmental policies and candidates,[253] they are increasingly encountering an anti-Western culture, even in America. The terms "terrorism" and "Nazi" are more frequently and recklessly applied to any group, organization, or political party using *any* kind of power, including the utilization of power in Western or Jewish democratic states, that counters contemporary liberal or leftist political ideology.

In other words, those who are skeptical of massive government are accused of being extremists when trying to reign in governmental power, or when trying to preserve some measure of Judeo-Christian influence on the state. Thus, the real extremists are those who disagree with the ideology of the post-Christian, syncretistic state religion. Nazis are, ironically, according to this perspective, those who want to use the political process to reduce the governmental power that establishes so-called social justice (e.g., new definitions of marriage, or pro-environmental enforcement). This is a tricky issue. Apart from evangelical libertarians, evangelicals typically want to selectively reduce government but maintain the moral framework of the American experiment. Evangelicals are thus perceived as hypocritical because critics don't grasp the conversation immediately above concerning the true nature of the American experiment (e.g., not a secular state or a theocracy).

In recent years, numerous critics of immigration border enforcement policy and centers and family separations were widely reported on multiple networks as comparing these holding centers at the border to World War II detention centers or concentration camps, and comparing the enforcers to Nazis. The family separation policy can and should be debated, but the rush to unprincipled semantic warfare is telling and illustrates and reinforces the thesis of this present work. Semantic universes rule, and they are becoming opportunistic tools for political advocacy. All words are viewed as the will-to-power for individuals or groups, and therefore can be manipulated at will without shame, because there is no transcendent or revealed standards for words or truth. Everyone ultimately loses in such a sematic culture.

It should also be noted that relative to global terrorism, some now affirm that the intentional targeting of civilians (or using human, hospital, or religious gathering shields) is no longer a distinguishing characteristic of terrorism, for in oppressive Western capitalistic regimes, all citizens are arguably extremists and terrorists, and some nations (e.g., America) are terrorist nations. Every American enables American oppression and terrorism, it is argued. As noted, we now have extreme semantic polarities regarding terms such as terrorism.

A more helpful approach to the semantics of terrorism, based on the long tradition of Just War theory, is to accept that terrorism is a complex term but certainly has a possible application to the intentional targeting of civilians or noncombatants (e.g., the Orlando or Paris shootings). While it is not always easy to avoid noncombatant casualties in modern warfare, terms such as "civilian" and "noncombatant" must be retained if any measure of compassion and justice applies in an age of messy modern warfare and rampant terrorism.

Likewise, it would be more helpful if allegations of Nazism would have some connection to many or all of the following National Socialist party tenets: anti-Semitism, massive governmental control, socialism, post-Christian values, extreme religious nationalism, dictatorship, and/or racist genocide. Nazism should not refer simply to anyone with a different view and an undesirable use of power (e.g., a pro-life thirty-year-old mother who happens to believe that life is sacred from conception and that abortion on demand and late term abortion is sexist). Some naively believe that terrorism and extremism can be overcome by inclusive globalism and multiculturalism, when in fact the lack of a semantic plumb line in most forms of globalism and multiculturalism only encourages the conflict

Inclusive Globalism and Multiculturalism

As previously noted, globalism has many meanings, but one questionable meaning, related to transcending national interest in favor of global interests, is the idea of moving beyond Western Christian influence, renouncing all association with the colonial age or even Western culture, and rejecting virtually any recognition of progress made in Western and American culture. This globalism or inclusivism has many dimensions and applications.

Sexism and feminism, it is argued, in order to escape the clutches of Christian misogyny and Western oppression, must be now defined in a secular, relativistic, often subjective, and ultra-modern syncretistic fashion. Multiculturalism often means global multicultural relativism, and diversity or inclusion often means not only the embracing of different races (which is good) but also the leveling of all ideas (relativism) and behaviors with the possible inconsistent exception of liberal ideology (affirmed) and Christianity (rejected). Multiculturalism may well be the dominant and umbrella term used to advance inclusive globalism. Racism, sexism, and discrimination now refer to any opposition to opposing views. Discrimination claims are used to discriminate against religious freedom, as seen in the Little Sisters of the Poor case study discussed previously. Post-Christian liberal ideology is elevated, and Western Judeo-Christian assumptions are typically viewed as inferior and oppressive. It is within this context that "profiling" is often defined as any recognition of ideological, religious, ethical, or cultural differences that might bear on sheer statistical probability relative to terrorism, law enforcement discernment and effectiveness, and the triage of limited anti-terrorism resources.

From a biblical perspective, the *telos* or goal of Revelation 5, where *every* tribe and tongue and nation worship together at the throne because of a cross carried for all humanity, certainly means that Christians must have a global kingdom perspective (not to mention the injunction, "Go ye into all the world").[254] And, as discussed previously, Christ's kingdom is above and stands in judgment of all human kingdoms.

Yet careful discernment is needed. Comparing present governments to perfection is prophetic, but governments must be compared to each other and historical precedents as well in order to avoid the utopian fallacy discussed in prior chapters.

If utopia is the standard, then the dissolution of every government could be justified. If utopia serves as a prophetic critique within the context of realism about possibilities of justice in the current age, then clearly the dissolution of a state could also be a great evil. Biblical anthropology also reaffirms that the fallen nature of revolutionaries and the fallibility of revolutionary ideologies could turn (and have turned many) utopian dreams into hell on earth. Hence, biblical multiculturalism (i.e., learning from the strengths and weaknesses of all cultures and civilizations and celebrating the genuine contributions of multiple cultures) is to be preferred over a very dangerous multicultural relativism or an ambiguously defined multiculturalism. Discussing multiculturalism without a biblical plumb line is like chasing a black cat at midnight while wearing sunglasses—to use an oft-quoted illustration.

Multiculturalism should be viewed as the proleptic and dialogical celebration and appreciation of multiple cultures and ethnicities within the context of the essential and most urgent assessment of the strengths and weaknesses of all cultures and nation states.

Are Nazi or Rwandian or Ugandan or Soviet or KKK cultures and subcultures really just a matter of perspective? Are all nations morally equal? Will any civilization do? An affirmative answer to those questions is silly, dangerous, and fatal—just as is the uncritical acceptance of the glories of any culture, including Western culture and civilization. The current supposedly relativistic proponents of multiculturalism often communicate, with nonrelativistic certainty, a total disdain for Western civilization, all the while parasitizing the plethora of benefits from the centuries of advancements that Western culture brought to the world.

Not only is there a parasitical relationship with Western culture, but post-Christian critics also fail to realize that many of their ethical and philosophical assumptions about justice and related values are the vestigial remains or leftovers of Christian assumption about knowledge, reality, and values. They unknowingly parasite off and advocate for Judeo-Christian values (e.g., justice, love) that are unsustainable by their post-Christian philosophical assumptions. The American Humanist Association would be an example of such parasitizing. In any event, the disdain for the West is frequently well-articulated (e.g., racism, the treatment of Native Americans), and replete with semantic distortions (e.g., unintentional colonial genocide due to disease is equated with the intentional anti-Semitic genocide of Hitler or the political and/or atheistic genocide of Hitler and Stalin).

Such conversations should seek semantic refinement and should also explore possible Western contributions to the following:
- the quest for civilization, such as philanthropy, and medical missions over the centuries
- social reforms sparked by Christian values (see the research by Smith and Dayton mentioned previously)
- the defeat of Nazism
- the self-correcting nature of democracies who abolished slavery
- the advocacy of religious freedom
- the increased possibility of upward economic and political mobility

- the constructive rebuilding of Europe after World War II including the sacrificial and massively expensive rebuilding rather than raping and pillaging of conquered nations
- the global benefits of space exploration
- the halting of the spread of genocidal or totalitarian atheistic ideologies
- the liberation of the concentration camps and the protection of the persecuted Jews
- the contributions to medical health and life expectancy

The list of Western evils is real, well rehearsed, and easy to come by. What is being argued for here is full disclosure and dialog.

Similarly, the age of colonialism certainly had abuses, but the failure to acknowledge the selfless labors of some for the world, or the real benefits taken to the world (e.g., health and life expectancy, enhanced means of combatting poverty and famine), reflects the narrow anti-colonialism and arrogant multiculturalism previously referenced. Bruce Thornton, in a lengthy but relevant quotation, may not prove all of his points, but this article underscores the need for a transparent and non-question-begging dialog on colonialism.

> Language is the first casualty of wars over foreign policy. To paraphrase Thucydides, during ideological conflict, words have to change their ordinary meaning and to take that which is now given them.

> One word that has been central to our foreign policy for over a century is "colonialism." Rather than describing a historical phenomenon—with all the complexity, mixture of good and evil, and conflicting motives found on every page of history—"colonialism" is now an ideological artifact that functions as a crude epithet. As a result, our foreign policy decisions are deformed by self-loathing and guilt eagerly exploited by our adversaries.

> The great scholar of Soviet terror, Robert Conquest, noted this linguistic corruption decades ago. Historical

terms like "imperialism" and "colonialism," Conquest wrote, now refer to "a malign force with no program but the subjugation and exploitation of innocent people." As such, these terms are verbal "mind-blockers and thought-extinguishers," which serve "mainly to confuse, and of course to replace, the complex and needed process of understanding with the simple and unneeded process of inflammation." Particularly in the Middle East, "colonialism" has been used to obscure the factual history that accounts for that region's chronic dysfunctions, and has legitimized policies doomed to fail because they are founded on distortions of that history. [255]

Thornton makes some questionable historical points and moral assessments in this article, but underscores the complexity and perils of using "colonialism" like "social justice" to end dialog. "This leftist interpretation of words like colonialism and imperialism transforms them into ideologically loaded terms that ultimately distort the tragic truths of history." He concludes that "Perhaps we should start crafting our foreign policy on the foundations of historical truth and precise language." [256]

The reality is that nations or groups that have power often abuse that power because of human nature, not necessarily because of the associated ideology. If a non-Judeo-Christian religion had birthed advanced scientific and technological nations, be assured that the projection of power would have followed. Indeed, countries controlled by post-Christian, atheistic, or polytheistic ideologies have been historically genocidal. The *progressive* French Revolution was soaked in blood. Judeo-Christian assumptions often tempered the abuse of Western power in the colonial age (e.g., the abolition of slavery) and the twentieth century (e.g., the defeat of Hitler). Feminism, which is now subsumed under globalism in many quarters, should return to its nineteenth-century Judeo-Christian birthing soil, centralize a normative plumb line for truth and ethics, and be pro-life.

The age of colonialism certainly was flawed and evidenced elitism and oppression, but some truly Herculean and Christian missional, medical, economic, and political work overseas by Westerners have brought tangible and life-saving or life-extending benefits to millions. Hence, the discussion concerning colonialism and the use of the term needs to be nuanced. Both the Trail of Tears and the trail of medical missionaries are relevant to the conversation and proper definitions and semantics

To sum up, relative to the semantic cluster of globalism and multiculturalism, it is being argued that globalism, multiculturalism, diversity, and inclusion should celebrate many (not all) cultural differences while using reason and Scripture (i.e., Truth) to make important distinctions and decisions relative to civilization building, civilization enhancement, and the discerning assessment of political and cultural options. If commitment to inclusion is defined, as per the Mormon church, as a commitment to move beyond a racist past, that is worthy of commendation and celebration. However, defining inclusion as embracing unbiblical, personally and socially destructive lifestyles amounts to seductive semantic theft. Similarly, racist profiling compromises the Scriptural vision. Racist profiling should be replaced with sheer, *blind*, unbiased statistical probability analysis of threats that does not turn a blind eye to real-world realities. Let computer statistics do the probability calculations and ensure that the programmers are represented by diverse perspectives? I shall defer to the experts, but neither naiveté nor racist vulnerabilities advance civilization, reduce crime, or combat authentic terrorism.

A global and multicultural Christian certainly should be one who is, above all, committed to kingdom global impact, the Great Commission, and the *missio Dei* and not be captive to any particular culture, including colonialist culture or the post Judeo-Christian culture of multicultural relativism. That very commitment requires shrewd analysis of civilizational options and both the negative and the positive impact that Western civilization has had or can have on world history.

The God and Bible of historic, Judeo-Christian orthodoxy is most inclusive and global — properly defined. The Abrahamic promise is to bless all nations. Every sinner, tongue, tribe people, and nation are again and again welcomed, by grace, into this line of promise. Murderers and prostitutes are most welcome, and the invitation to join the eschatological banquet is universal. Christ died for all and heaven is for all who sincerely repent and believe. This *global inclusiveness* for everyone (Revelation 5), however, is predicated on the assumption of universal brokenness and a cosmic redemption.

Authentic biblical and global inclusiveness is most inclusive and most candid about the real human condition. Yet the God and Bible of Judeo-Christian orthodoxy is not inclusive of rebellion, deception, intellectual dishonesty and moral relativism. Therefore, if love, toleration, globalism, and inclusiveness mean acceptance of a terminally diseased creation with no real solution that gets at the very core or root of hate, war, self-destruction, and other-destruction, then such inclusion utterly fails and betrays itself.

To be clear, biblical inclusiveness (and eschatological, multicultural globalism) is the only true inclusiveness that leads to the new creation. Post-Christian or anti-Christian and anti-biblical *inclusiveness* offers no real solution to the tragedy of human and civilizational suffering and brokenness. Such pseudo-inclusiveness is actually exclusive of the only path from paradise lost to paradise regained, and perpetually propagates civilizational decay, suffering, and undermines human flourishing. Genuine globalism includes the *via* to the new creation. This discussion of globalism, inclusiveness, and multiculturalism naturally raises, once again, the question of the place of nationalism and patriotism in the life of Judeo-Christian faith communities and orthodox and evangelical Christians.

Nationalism and Patriotism

Nationalism (along with "religion too," e.g., from John Lennon's *Imagine)* is typically viewed as *a* or *the* key source and cause of wars and conflicts, poverty, and oppression. In Europe, after two world wars, strong belief in any ideology (except for politically liberal ideology or anti-ideology) is viewed as another key factor contributing to aggression and conflict. This anti-ideological sentiment is somewhat understandable in Europe, but it is also hopelessly utopian and ignores the cultural and civilizational implications of the ideology of anti-ideology.

Let's recapitulate and clarify the prior discussion concerning nationalism and patriotism. "Nation-olatry" is evil. Yet anti-ideology, or the anti-metaphysical posture, creates a religious vacuum that will be eventually filled by individuals and nations or tyrants. Europe has tried this experiment only to find that many are glad to fill the void.

Ideology is inevitable, so the question for civilizations is not *if ideology* but *which ideology*, and I have already outlined the broad contours of the ideology of the American experiment. The American experiment should at least be included in the marketplace of ideas when cultural and global leaders earnestly and prayerfully reflect on all of the options.

The Judeo-Christian influence on the original intent of the American experiment is no mystery, as reflected in this quote from George Washington referenced earlier in this chapter:

> Of all the dispositions and habits which lead to political prosperity, **Religion and morality are indispensable supports.** In vain would that man claim the tribute of **Patriotism,** who should labour to subvert these great Pillars of human happiness, these firmest props of the duties of Men and citizens.... The mere Politician, equally with the pious man ought to respect and cherish them. [Farewell Address, 1796, emphasis added]

America First (AF) is often viewed as nationalistic, racist, and dangerous. Critics argue that this rallying point should be replaced with compassion first, social justice first, or a new borderless global order first. Such critics often view patriotism as vulgar nationalism. Indeed, if *America First* or any *nation first* creed is an idolatrous nationalism that undermines the reality and values of "Thy kingdom come," then such sentiment is vulgar and idolatrous. If the kingdom of God is ever subjugated to personal or national interests, such interests are, by definition, in conflict with the kingdom of God. If borders and walls are reflective of nationalistic idolatry and narcissism, then God's rule is under assault.

However, the growing hostility toward a Judeo-Christian influenced civilization, even with a less than perfect but significant positive global influence, is also a threat to the future. The opposition to the kind of national defense (including borders and walls) requisite for protecting and preserving such influence, liberty, and human freedom, are very susceptible to a misguided elitism. This elitist, often naïve and self-righteous narcissism, replete with a heavy dose of idealistic and self-righteous anti-nationalism, often replace true kingdom values with post-Christian conceptualizations of "justice," "love," "compassion," and "inclusiveness." This elitism proffers a way forward that achieves none of these lofty goals. When Judeo-Christian influence is overrun by post-Judeo-Christian civilization, culture, and values, then anything remotely resembling biblical love, compassion, and inclusiveness begins to evaporate. The semantic universe of freedom, liberty, and the divine blessings and human flourishing advocated for by the likes of Abraham Lincoln also is at risk. And these new and fluid definitions are less than stable guides for any civilization.

Biblical revelation certainly condemns the idolatry of nations and leaders. Nevertheless, in a fallen world, the quest for and discernment concerning a better civilization or more perfect union need not be abandoned simply because the ideal will never be realized in this current age. Utopianism and pessimistic fatalism stand in stark contrast to core and foundational biblical theology. And there is an immense difference between blind patriotism and nationalism and discerning patriotism and nationalism.

Why is it acceptable to love one's family, community, or even one's school (in a non-idolatrous fashion), but not discerningly to love or at least appreciate one's country? The realities of wartime, like World War II, are illustrative. Idolatrous nationalism, apathy, moral relativism, and indifference all proved to be demonic and only enabled the advance of evil kingdoms.

Nations had to courageously mobilize and firmly believe that their less than perfect nations were worthy of the ultimate sacrifice and that other nations had so traversed the law of God that they were a threat to everyone's future. These were not easy political or moral wartime calculations, but evil is enabled by relativistic evaluations of the morality of nations. We may not get it right, but we have a commonsensical and biblical obligation to at least try.

At some point we have to strike up the band and unite the national community, with passion, behind our best moral calculation of just international policy. Yes, sometimes we only have enough information for lesser evil calculations, but in World War II we had *Mein Kampf* (1925), the *Kristallnacht* (1938), and increasing numbers of reports of likely genocide in the years subsequent to the invasion of Poland (1939). That nuanced approach requires a nuanced but heartfelt nationalism and patriotism. Wrong ideology, not strong ideology, is the enemy of the future. We can't send melancholy twenty year olds into battle to engage malevolent darkness and risk life and limb. The demonization of such proper and discerning patriotic support is less than human or realistic and fundamentally misunderstands the communal dimension of human nature and existence.

During World War II theological luminaries like Reinhold Niebuhr, Karl Barth, C. C. Morrison, and Dietrich Bonhoeffer, many of whom were former pacifists exhausted by World War I carnage, enthusiastically led the world and inspired the opposition to totalitarianism after making such seemingly impossible and difficult calculations. And, as Niebuhr often put it, love taking the form of justice in the real and fallen world is not typically advanced either by reckless hawks or naïve doves.

Such patriotism born of the American experiment also and especially includes prophetic critique, but appreciation for civilizational gains, a healthy sense of national community, and the desire for and pursuit of aspirational civilization are potentially virtuous. Most importantly, the quest for aspirational civilization should avoid both utopianism and fatalism and should properly guide and define Christian allegiance to nations and states. So, where do we go from here?

Ask Yourself or Your Group

- *What are semantic clusters or families and why does the author believe that understanding the nature of these semantic families is absolutely critical to understanding and engaging with culture today? How might the current political and cultural vitriol today result, in part, from the failure to grasp the clustered, connected, or familial nature of terms and definitions? How might the inability to talk to each other also result from semantic confusion?*

- *Select at least three terms or phrases (civilization, establishment of religion, educational neutrality, tolerance, love, compassion, terrorism, extremism, globalism, multiculturalism, nationalism, or patriotism) and discuss different definitions of these terms and what is at stake in how we define these terms?*

- *Why is the author so passionate about "Faith without Truth is dead"? Agree? Disagree? How does the author believe that faith has been distorted in the church, and how has that impacted the effectiveness of the church and the intellectual and spiritual preparation of countless Christians? What is the proper relationship between truth and faith? What is blind faith? What does it mean to say that biblical faith is not primarily epistemological but interpersonal? Are there any Bible stories that back up the idea that faith is more about trusting God than debating whether God exists? How might a right definition of faith impact one's walk with the Lord?*

- *Discuss how terms are used today related to sexual ethics (gender, marriage, morality, etc.).*

- *How have terms and phrases like "do not judge," legalism, and forgiveness been distorted today? What are the true biblical definitions of such terms and phrases? What difference does it make in the church or in our walk with the Lord?*

Chapter 10

LOGOCENTRIC MELIORATION OR CIVILIZATIONAL CACOPHONY, CONFLICT, AND FRAGMENTATION

*See, I have set before you today life and prosperity, and
death and adversity.*
—Deuteronomy 30:15

*I call heaven and earth to witness against you today, that
I have set before you life and death, the blessing and the
curse. So choose life in order that you may live, you and
your descendants.*
—Deuteronomy 30:19

These semantic clusters and this semantic game, dance, or verbal cold war have real-world implications for the church, the academy, and beyond. Western, and to some degree global, culture is running on the fumes of the failed modernist project amidst the rising and putrid aroma of the failing ultramodern project. Hence, we see mod-rot and pomo-rot seemingly flourishing and being celebrated as civilization careens downward. The stunning arrogance and relativism of both "mo" and "pomo" are fatal to civilization and can only lead to civilizational decay and fragmentation over time.

The arrogance of modernism arguably birthed the Nietzschean predicted and bloodiest century thus far in human history and contributed to untold genocides. The absolutistic relativism of postmodernism is sowing the seeds for Balkanization, militant and shameless political and cultural wars, civil wars, and eventually the fraying of any meaningful semblance of a civilized society. It is difficult to assess at this juncture the possible relationship between pomo-rot and global conflicts, but instability is usually not helpful.

We are truly feasting on the leftovers of a once great but imperfect Logos influenced civilization. The fuse is lit and time is finite for a recovery. Both the modernists (e.g., Marxism's heretical and perverted version of Christian eschatology) and the postmodernists (e.g., relativistic postmodernism's absolutistic emphasis on pseudo-love, pseudo-justice, and pseudo-toleration) are doubly parasitical on Logocentric civilization.

First, the modernists and postmodernists parasite off the benefits of Judeo-Christian influenced democratic civilization while also trying to eradicate that very Judeo-Christian influence.

Second, the lofty values of both movements simply are groundless and thus firmly planted in midair. These two movements are simply not sustainable apart from Logocentrism and kingdomcentrism. Semantics not grounded in divine revelation ultimately unravels. Civilization not influenced by Logocentrism and kingdomcentrism eventually staggers.

The illustrative and comparative lexicon in Appendix A seeks to summarize, illustrate, and extend the discussion, as well as encourage dialog concerning the assumptions and usage of related terms. Appendix A also should reinforce and assist with communicating how semantic choices impact the real world, which will be summarized and emphasized in the next section of this chapter. The Judeo-Christian faithful including American evangelicals often fail to grasp the real-world significance of ideas and words. Roman Catholics and Orthodox traditions, more connected to history, seem to be more aware of such consequences. Words express ideas and concepts, and words and ideas, as many have noted and as I have emphasized in this work, are most powerful relative to culture and civilization.

The Power of Words and Ideas

A superior and more biblical response than accommodation to these seismic semantic shifts in an age that often disdains ideas, ethical norms, ideology, or *Veritas* is to reanimate and reify our commitment to the power of words and ideas relative to Judeo-Christian higher education and the potential cultural impact of faith communities.[257] This does not require a return to modernistic or rationalistic definitions of reason; it only requires a passion for serving the Logos, Scripture, and the pursuit of a better world. The idea that ideas no longer matter is simply the latest flavor of false ideas, and this contradictory culture needs a loving but firm and broad orthodox response from educators, pastors, and laity.

Archbishop Temple warned that philosophers (or thinkers) rule the world—500 years after they are dead—and often via their words. The evidence for the power of words and ideas is compelling. Napoleon confessed that in the long run the sword is always beaten by the mind. Emerson cautioned that we should beware when God lets loose a thinker on this planet, for all things are at risk. Moore, Bruder,[258] J. Gresham Machen, and many others all have, in one form or another, warned that ideas move armies, raise empires, and tear down civilizations.

If we really care about people,[259] then we will really care about words and ideas, including the false concept that ideas don't matter, and that truth is nothing more than a personal or tribal perspective. Ideas have put food on the table or sent people to reeducation camps in Siberia or death camps at Auschwitz. Adolf Eichmann may have organized the trains leading to the death camps, but in a very real sense Nietzsche was driving the genocidal trains. Ideas and words spark blood-soaked revolutions and indiscriminate terrorism. Ideas contribute to values that build or disintegrate families and enable constructive or self-destructive lifestyles. Terrorism and nuclear conflicts are truly threats to civilization, but even more may be at stake due to the word theft and false ideas that are corrupting and stealing our individual, ecclesial, and cultural souls.

Recall Machen's amazingly prophetic warning cited at the beginning of Chapter 5 from over a century ago: "We may preach with all the fervor of a reformer and yet succeed only in winning a straggler here and there, if we permit the whole collective thought of the nation or of the world to be controlled by ideas [and words] which ... prevent Christianity from being regarded as anything more than a harmless delusion." Or, one might add today, having Christianity regarded as nothing more than just another perspective (a truth, a story) — and frequently viewed as the major socially and politically dangerous triumphal perspective — undercuts evangelism, the mission of God, and certainly Judeo-Christian civilizational influence.

Tactful and loving cultural and intellectual engagement and the enhancement of clear dialog, issuing forth from overflowing love of God and others and rising to the surface in the stellar moments of Church history, are fundamentally and essentially biblical, Judeo-Christian, and imperative for those who care about the future of civilization.

The Way Back and Forward

Because words and ideas are most powerful and can correspond to some degree to reality and even create new realities, one key dimension of the way back and forward is to invoke language games that play fair and have a biblical connection (the way back) that imparts a foundation, norm, meaning, and purpose to the cultural dialog (the way forward). Our words will always be somewhat slippery in this present age and have limitations, but the ceaseless attempt to enhance clarity and quest for Truth is essential. The assumption that some measure of Truth is knowable and can be communicated will guide the endless refinements of our semantic tapestries.

To sum, in our contemporary context, the way back is semantic refinement that should be rooted in the Logos, the already coming kingdom, Scripture, an appropriate use of tradition, reason and experience, the best insights of the Enlightenment, communal and collaborative theological and philosophical reflection, and much love and prayer. This foundation will allow for the potential melioration and enhancement of our semantic and civilizational future, which is the way forward. Civilization is easily lost, especially if some measure of Judeo-Christian influence and semantic clarity is utterly abandoned, which is the current trajectory in the West.

It was noted above many times that this book was written in and for the American context, yet with global implications—especially in a globally digitized culture. As Walter Kaiser and others used to say, "I'm not a prophet, or a son of a prophet, and I work for a non-profit organization!" Predicting the future is a fool's errand, apart from divine revelation. However, given the intensity and persistence of the semantic revolution that has been underway for generations in the key centers of cultural and political power, especially educational institutions that train our cultural and political leaders, time is of the essence.

Institutions of higher education are especially complicit in redefining terms such that the Judeo-Christian influence that birthed and provided the fertile soil and stable but adaptive pillars for a relatively successful experiment in a more perfect union is forever marginalized, eradicated, or even criminalized. It is hard to resist the conclusion that unless the educational system is renewed in this generation, if not within a decade after 2020, then it is simply a matter of time before the full implications of the verbal revolution will have redefined the American experiment out of existence. Something called "America' will likely still exist, but such an "America" can only be described as a seductive sham and a very faint echo of the original American experiment.

The complex semantic tapestries reflected here and in appendix A are ultimately propellants embedded within powerful vision statements concerning the desired future of civilization. Hence, while civilization certainly refers to what exists in the present, it also refers to a vision of what should be in the future—an ideal that we attempt to approximate. Hence, *civilization* also serves as a secular or religious eschatology (all cultural eschatologies function to some degree as religions) that is inseparably connected to a

331

multilayered semantic tapestry. The Judeo-Christian semantic universe is the stable and generative context of the true future.

Conclusions and Recommendations

First, *much is at stake* and much can be learned from history regarding semantic power, semantic clarity, semantics and ecclesial orthodoxy, and the quest for Judeo-Christian influenced civilization. This ongoing quest for the refinement of words and meaning is especially urgent amidst a postmodern, sound bite, Twitter, and tabloid news culture that is often antithetical to careful and nuanced communication. Given the countless Judeo-Christian losses in culture, even the minimal restoration of some measure of firmly grounded semantic integrity to public discourse would be a major gain for civilization. Judeo-Christian believers need to ramp up semantic polemics and apologetics if they desire to see their religious movements exist, persist, and flourish beyond the present generation. As already noted many times, the loss of the biblically influenced semantic universe will inevitably lead to interim fragmentation, and/or accelerating conflict, and/or economic war, and/or tyranny or actual international or civil war (to establish or reestablish a guiding semantic universe as the requisite glue of civilization). We have a tremendous obligation to persuade others concerning proper semantics, apologetics, and polemics.

Second, *tactful, aggressive intentionality relative to semantic clarity* is essential for the future of effective orthodox Judeo-Christian polemics and apologetics and the future of global, orthodox, Judeo-Christian, evangelical, and biblically influenced faith communities. Indeed, as we have seen from the Barna research, semantic drift from biblical orthodoxy and orthopraxy is very much inside, not merely outside, the evangelical church (e.g., Christian cohabitation has become a euphemism for fornication, and marriage and family semantics are quickly morphing for younger evangelicals). Even if the culture war is being lost, or if Lewis's civilizational quest is rejected, enhanced semantic apologetics and polemics are critical to the survival of the biblically influenced faith communities, synagogues, and churches. Many

Protestants, Protestant evangelicals, Roman Catholics, Orthodox believers, and other major religious faiths should find common ground relative to this intentional semantic task.

Hence, **third**, *aggressive, reverent, and gentle semantic orthodox polemic and apologetic training* is essential for Judeo-Christian pastors, priests, educators, leaders, and laity. The heuristic tables in this work and appendices may provide some assistance as tools.

Fourth, relative to the American and global context, the future of Judeo-Christian-influenced civilization depends, in part, on the critical semantic distinctions I've presented concerning these civilizational options. Here are at least three critical options: (1) a theocracy; (2) a secular and/or spiritually syncretistic state; and (3) a *welcoming Judeo-Christian democratic republic*. The latter, based on the evidence to date, likely provides the most defensible cultural glue and stable pillars for a truly aspirational civilization, and authentic human and religious flourishing.

Fifth, and more fundamentally, apart from meaning, value, and *semantics ultimately influenced by the Logos and the Judeo-Christian kingdom vision*, there is no stable civilizational foundation or social, political, ethical, and semantic plumb line. Polybabble, polylogos, and selflogos ultimately degenerate into tribalistic advocacy and tooth-and-fang will-to-power conflicts. Sound eerily familiar? The recent proposal of confident pluralism[260]—the idea that we might survive the current cultural chaos and coexist amidst irreconcilable differences via constitutional commitments and virtue—is commendable but built on epistemological and ontological quicksand. Confident pluralism is an unsustainable house of cards apart from the influence of the civilizational pillars of the kingdom and city that endures forever. It could serve as a stalling mechanism to avoid the nightmarish Balkanization of the West or America, but a much better solution is the refinement, upgrading, contextualization of and re-advocacy for grand experiments in welcoming Judeo-Christian-influenced civilizations.

A Call to Action! If the message of this work resonates, the straightforward call to action should include items such as the following:

333

1. Request your teachable pastors, priests, rabbis, members of pastoral or clergy staff, and political or cultural leaders to work semantic polemic and apologetic material into their ongoing public statements, preaching and instruction. Encourage religious leaders to work through the proper definitions of terms patiently, key word by key word, with those they are leading. Some terms will be more relevant than others given the particular context. If this work has value it will be need to be translated and contextualized for cultures and subcultures across the globe. Yet it should be remembered that digitized culture is becoming similar in some respects across the globe. Proper word definitions can easily be grafted into sermons and instruction over time. For example, there are countless biblical passages that address issues of justice that could be connected to contemporary social justice debates and news coverage.

2. Utilize social media to spread the word about words, or write loving, tactful, and informed letters to newspaper or magazine editors that utilize principles in this or similar works. Expect criticism but lovingly persist. Speak the truth in love (Ephesians 4:15).

3. Call in to talk shows and give loving, tactful, and informed perspectives.

4. Pray for a Logocentric and kingdomcentric resurrection of meaning, values, and words. Work with political and community leaders to fund and restore the authentic education of our future leaders, and politely defund toxic education.

As noted in Chapter 1, the semantics advocated for in this work is ultimately Logocentric, Word-centered, kingdom-centric, theological, and eschatological. The Judeo-Christian kingdom-centric semantic universe provides a solid foundation for flourishing civilization. For biblical Christians, the ongoing quest for an ideal of civilization is the quest for an appropriate (pre-*Parousia*) approximation of the New Creation kingdom that has already established a decisive beachhead amidst all civilizations via the enveloping Christ event. For proponents of Judeo-Christian values who may not fully embrace this Christian, orthodox, evangelical, and eschatological vision, the similar goal and values of approximating a civilizational ideal remain. Multiple faith traditions and denominations can and should labor together for the future, and for the sake of future generations.

Hence, *viva la* civilization is a fitting aspiration, and Lewis essentially had it right regarding the need to preserve and pursue civilization. The contours of this civilizational future-vision are ever being clarified and refined via intentional semantic dialog in the light of God's amazing and personal revelation. However, as noted in the introductory material, the future of the civilization is contingent upon the future of religious communities and families, so semantic apologetics and polemics must first commence in our own back yards. The last hope for a more perfect union is a robust renewal of our faith communities.

Religious believers and organizations that are serious about mission, polemics, and apologetics must increasingly be passionate, intentional, proficient, and agile at surfing the tumultuous waves of our contemporary, ultramodern, syncretistic Promethean ocean of words. Present trends cannot continue without mammoth consequences for civilization, human flourishing, communities, families, churches, and future generations. Yet a key assumption of Judeo-Christian influenced faith, certainly evident during the tumultuous days of the birth of the American experiment, is the many surprises of grace and Providence in history. Semantic apologetics and polemics may well be one of the important avenues of such grace, reform, renewal, and progress.

The abbreviated, preliminary, illustrative and comparative Lexicon in Appendix A is offered as a trajectory for future dialog and a reference tool or didactic aid to preaching and teaching. Those who sense that the attempt to enhance such semantic clarifications is urgent and relevant to the endless quest for a more perfect civilization may find this information useful. Appendix B also includes illustrative responses to possible or likely objections.

The goals of this work are modest. The hope is to spark increased awareness of the importance of this issue, to contribute to enhanced semantic clarity, and to assist with effective polemics and apologetics. To slightly modify the words of Andrew Jackson and abolitionist Wendell Phillips, the price of liberty is eternal semantic vigilance. Perhaps Carl F. H. Henry's quote from early in this book said it best when he observed that we are facing a "crisis of truth and word."[261] Should not the people of the Word lead the way on the redemptive and impactful usage of words?

Ask Yourself or Your Group

- *What is the author's argument for the power of words and ideas?*
- *So how has this book impacted your life, the life of your family, or the life of your church?*
- *How might polemics and apologetics benefit from the content and arguments in this book?*
- *In terms of churches, synagogues, and other faith communities, where do we go from here?*
- *How can you personally use this book to advance the kingdom?*

Appendix A

Mini-Lexicons of Contemporary Terms and Semantic Clusters[262]

Dictionaries and encyclopedias of philosophy (e.g., Oxford, Stanford) simply do not list most of the terms discussed in this work. When such terms are referenced (e.g., "justice" is an entry but not "social justice"), multiple theories and definitions are referenced, which far exceed the limitations of a lexicon or the purpose of this present work.

More helpful as part of the preliminary research for this project was the utilization of the *Oxford Learner's Dictionary*,[263] the *Oxford Dictionary*[264] (with historical and common usage definitions), and *Merriam-Webster* as reference points for reflection and analysis and as preparation for construction of Table 5. The online versions of these reference works were selected for a variety of reasons, including the fact that hard copy reference works are increasingly falling into disuse.[265] Users today refer to the online definitions.

Table 5 is annotated via additional explanations below the table in order to clarify and justify the analysis that led to many of the conclusions in the text and in Table 6. Table 6 then contrasts contemporary semantic distortions and alternatives relevant to Judeo-Christian apologetics and polemics with possible semantic clarifications. Column two of Table 5, which is from the *Oxford Learner's Dictionaries,* illustrates definitions targeted at younger ages. Column three of Table 5 is from *Merriam-Webster*, and column four is from the standard *Oxford Dictionary*. Table 6 then presents how these terms are being used today, especially contra Judeo-Christian civilizational influence and contra Logocentrism and kingdomcentrism. The contemporary distortions, as noted, are then contrasted in Table 6 with a suggested and more Logocentric usage. Such Logocentric usage, it has been argued, should assist religious communities with biblical fidelity, enhance Judeo-Christian influence, and assist with the melioration of culture and civilization.

Table 5. Illustrative and Comparative Dictionary Definitions[266]

Term or Semantic Cluster	*Oxford Learner's* definition	*Merriam-Webster's* Definition	*Oxford Dictionary* Definition
Civilization	A state of human society that is very developed and organized	A relatively high level of cultural and technological development. The culture characteristic of a particular time or place. The process of becoming civilized. Refinement of thought, manners, or taste	The state or condition of being civilized; human cultural, social, and intellectual development when considered to be advanced and progressive in nature. The culture, society, and way of life of a particular country, region, epoch, or group.
Compassion [First Semantic Cluster, SC #1]	A strong feeling of sympathy for people who are suffering and a desire to help them	Sympathetic consciousness of others' distress together with a desire to alleviate it	Suffering together with another, participation in suffering; fellow-feeling, sympathy. The feeling or emotion, when a person is moved by the suffering or distress of another, and by the desire to relieve it; pity that inclines one to spare or to succour.

Social Justice, Justice [SC #1]	NA[267] "Justice": the fair treatment of people	A state or doctrine of egalitarianism	To have compassion: to have pity, take pity. Justice at the level of a society or state as regards the possession of wealth, commodities, opportunities, and privileges [Reference is made to multiple theories]
Establishment of Religion [SC #2]	NA. "Establishment Clause": the article in the First Amendment to the American Constitution which created the separation of Church and State in the US by forbidding the government to establish a state religion. The US Supreme Court used it in 1962 for a decision that stopped prayers in schools, and this upset many US Christians. However, 'In God We Trust' is still the National Motto and is on US coins.	NA. "Establishment Clause": a clause in the U.S. Constitution forbidding Congress from establishing a state religion "Freedom of Exercise": the clause in the First Amendment to the U.S. Constitution prohibiting Congress from making any law prohibiting the free exercise of religion "Freedom of Religion": the right especially as guaranteed under the free exercise clause of the First Amendment to the U.S. Constitution to practice one's religion or exercise one's beliefs without intervention by the government and to be free of the exercise of authority by a church through the government	NA "Freedom of Religion": freedom to practise the religion of one's choice, esp. when regarded as a right
Educational Neutrality [SC #2]	NA	NA	NA

Table 5., continued

Term or Semantic Cluster	*Oxford Learner's* definition	*Merriam-Webster's* Definition	*Oxford Dictionary* Definition
Freedom of Speech [SC #2]	The right to express any opinions in public. This right became part of American law under the First Amendment. If the opinions expressed are false or damage a person's reputation, however, that person can take legal action under US law. In Britain, people are free to express most opinions, but it is against the law to express some ideas, e.g., ideas that aim to cause racial hatred.	The legal right to express one's opinions freely	Freedom to express one's opinions without censorship, legal penalty, or any other restraint, esp. when regarded as a right.
Faith	Faith (in somebody/ something) Trust in somebody's ability or knowledge; trust that somebody/ something will do what has been promised	Allegiance to duty or a person Belief and trust in and loyalty to God Firm belief in something for which there is no proof	To have faith, believe. To give credence to, believe in, trust. To place or rest one's faith on a person. Belief, trust, confidence. Belief in and acceptance of the doctrines of a religion, typically involving belief in a god or gods and in the authenticity of divine revelation. Also (Theol.): the capacity to spiritually apprehend divine truths, or realities beyond the limits of perception or of logical proof, viewed either as a faculty of the human soul, or as the result of divine illumination. Chiefly with in (formerly also … of). Firm trust or belief in or reliance upon something (e.g., the truth of a statement or doctrine; the ability, goodness, etc., of a person, the efficacy or worth of a thing); confidence; credence. Belief based on evidence, testimony, or authority.

Globalism [SC #3]	NA. "Globalize": if something, for example a business company, globalizes or is globalized, it operates all around the world	A national policy of treating the whole world as a proper sphere for political influence — compare "Globalization": the development of an increasingly integrated global economy marked especially by free trade, free flow of capital, and the tapping of cheaper foreign labor markets	The belief, theory, or practice of adopting or pursuing a political course, economic system, etc., based on global rather than national principles
Colonialism [SC #3]	The practice by which a powerful country controls another country or other countries	Control by one power over a dependent area or people A policy advocating or based on such control	The colonial system or principle. Now freq. used in the derogatory sense of an alleged policy of exploitation of backward or weak peoples by a large power.
Ethnocentrism [SC #3]	Behaviour or beliefs that favour one particular culture and judge other cultures against it	NA "Ethnocentric": characterized by or based on the attitude that one's own group is superior	Tending to view the world from the perspective of one's own culture, sometimes with an assumption of superiority; limited as regards knowledge and appreciation of other cultures and communities.
Sexism [SC #3]	The unfair treatment of people, especially women, because of their sex; the attitude that causes this	Prejudice or discrimination based on sex Discrimination against women Behavior, conditions, or attitudes that foster stereotypes of social roles based on sex	Originally: the state or condition of belonging to the male or female sex; categorization or reference on the basis of sex (now *rare*); (in later use) prejudice, stereotyping, or discrimination, typically against women, on the basis of sex.
Feminism [SC #3]	The belief and aim that women should have the same rights and opportunities as men; the struggle to achieve this aim	The theory of the political, economic, and social equality of the sexes Organized activity on behalf of women's rights and interests	Advocacy of equality of the sexes and the establishment of the political, social, and economic rights of the female sex; the movement associated with this
Multiculturalism [SC #3]	The practice of giving importance to all cultures in a society	NA. "Multicultural": of, relating to, reflecting, or adapted to diverse cultures	The characteristics of a multicultural society; (also) the policy or process whereby the distinctive identities of the cultural groups within such a society are maintained or supported.

Table 5., continued

Term or Semantic Cluster	*Oxford Learner's* definition	*Merriam-Webster's* Definition	*Oxford Dictionary* Definition
Racism [SC #3]	The unfair treatment of people who belong to a different race; violent behaviour towards them	A belief that race is the primary determinant of human traits and capacities and that racial differences produce an inherent superiority of a particular race	A belief that one's own racial or ethnic group is superior, or that other such groups represent a threat to one's cultural identity, racial integrity, or economic well-being
Discrimination [SC #3]	The practice of treating somebody or a particular group in society less fairly than others	The act, practice, or an instance of discriminating categorically rather than individually Prejudiced or prejudicial outlook, action, or treatment	Prejudice, discrimination, or antagonism directed against people of other racial or ethnic groups (or, more widely, of other nationalities), esp. based on such beliefs. Orig. *U.S.* Unjust or prejudicial treatment of a person or group, esp. on the grounds of race, gender, sexual orientation, etc.; freq. with *against*.
Diversity [SC #3]	The quality or fact of including a range of many people or things	The inclusion of different types of people (such as people of different races or cultures) in a group or organization	Also (with *in favour of*): favourable treatment of a person or group, in order to compensate for disadvantage or lack of privilege.
Inclusion [SC #3]	The fact of including somebody/something; the fact of being included	The act or practice of including students with disabilities in regular school classes	Orig. *U.S.* The action, practice, or policy of including any person in an activity, system, organization, or process, irrespective of race, gender, religion, age, ability, etc. (Now frequently without complement specifying who is included.)

Profiling [SC #3]	The act of collecting useful information about somebody/something so that you can give a description of them or it	The act or process of extrapolating information about a person based on known traits or tendencies	[Chiefly U.S.] The recording, itemization, or analysis of a person's known psychological, intellectual, and behavioural characteristics, esp. as documentation used (in schools, businesses, etc.) in the assessment of an individual's capabilities; (also) the compilation of databases which store such information and that can be used to identify any particular subgroup of people.
Judgmentalism [SC #4]	"Judgmental": judging people and criticizing them too quickly	"Judgmental": characterized by a tendency to judge harshly	The quality of being judgmental; overly critical or moralistic behaviour.
Legalism [SC #4]	"Legalistic": obeying the law too strictly	Strict, literal, or excessive conformity to the law or to a religious or moral code	*Theol.* Chiefly *derogatory.* Adherence among Christians to the Mosaic law or to a similar system of laws, as opposed to the gospel expounded in the New Testament; the doctrine of justification by works; teaching resembling that doctrine.
Nationalism [SC #5]	A feeling of love for and pride in your country; a feeling that your country is better than any other	Loyalty and devotion to a nation Exalting one nation above all others and placing primary emphasis on promotion of its culture and interests as opposed to those of other nations or supranational groups	Advocacy of or support for the interests of one's own nation, esp. to the exclusion or detriment of the interests of other nations. Also: advocacy of or support for national independence or self-determination. [Theology, rare] The doctrine that certain nations (as contrasted with individuals) are the object of divine election.
Patriotism [SC #5]	Love of your country and willingness to defend it	Love for or devotion to one's country	The quality of being patriotic; love of or devotion to one's country.

Table 5., continued

Term or Semantic Cluster	Oxford Learner's definition	Merriam-Webster's Definition	Oxford Dictionary Definition
Far Right [SC #5]	"The New Right": (in the US) politicians and political groups who support conservative social and political policies and religious ideas based on Christian fundamentalism	The group of people whose political views are the most conservative	The extreme right wing of a faction, group, or party
Far Left [SC #5]	"The New Left": a group of people who developed left-wing political ideas in many countries, especially the US, in the 1960s. They protested against the conditions of poor people in society, and against the Vietnam War, but they did not support the Soviet Union. The New Left included many students and writers.	The group of people whose political views are the most liberal	The extreme left wing of a faction, group, or party
Sexual Preference [SC #6]	NA	NA "Sexual Orientation": the inclination of an individual with respect to heterosexual, homosexual, and bisexual behavior	NA "Sexual Orientation": Originally: (the process of) orientation with respect to a sexual goal, potential mate, partner, etc. Later chiefly: a person's sexual identity in relation to the gender to whom he or she is usually attracted; (broadly) the fact of being heterosexual, bisexual, or homosexual.

Gender Identity [SC #6]	The way somebody considers their own gender (1) (= whether they are male or female), which may be different from the gender (1) they were given when they were born	A person's internal sense of being male, female, some combination of male and female, or neither male nor female [Facebook provides more than 50 options beyond "male" and "female" for users to describe their gender identity, from "gender questioning" and "neither" to "androgynous." —*The Chicago Tribune*	NA
Adultery [SC #6]	Sex between a married person and somebody who is not their husband or wife	Voluntary sexual intercourse between a married man and someone other than his wife or between a married woman and someone other than her husband	Voluntary sexual intercourse between a married person and another who is not his or her spouse, regarded as a violation of the marriage vows and hence as a sin or crime; the state or condition of having committed this.
Fornication [SC #6]	The act of having sex with somebody that you are not married to	Consensual ... sexual intercourse between two persons not married to each other	Voluntary sexual intercourse between a man (in restricted use, an unmarried man) and an unmarried woman. In Scripture extended to adultery.
Family [SC #6]	A group consisting of one or two parents and their children A group consisting of one or two parents, their children and close relations	A group of individuals living under one roof and usually under one head The basic unit in society traditionally consisting of two parents rearing their children; *also* : any of various social units differing from but regarded as equivalent to the traditional family	A group of people living as a household, traditionally consisting of parents and their children, and also (chiefly in early use) any servants, boarders, etc.; any household consisting of people who have long-term commitments to each other and are (usually) raising children; such a group as a fundamental social unit or institution. A group of people consisting of one set of parents and their children, whether living together or not.

Table 5., continued

Term or Semantic Cluster	*Oxford Learner's* definition	*Merriam-Webster's* Definition	*Oxford Dictionary* Definition
Terrorism [SC #7]	The use of violent action in order to achieve political aims or to force a government to act	The systematic use of terror especially as a means of coercion	The unofficial or unauthorized use of violence and intimidation in the pursuit of political aims; (originally) such practices used by a government or ruling group (freq. through paramilitary or informal armed groups) in order to maintain its control over a population [e.g., French Revolution]; (now usually) such practices used by a clandestine or expatriate organization as a means of furthering its aims.
Nazi [SC #7]	Belonging to or connected with the National Socialist party which controlled Germany from 1933 to 1945 Using power in a cruel way; having extreme and unreasonable views about race	A member of a German fascist party controlling Germany from 1933 to 1945 under Adolf Hitler One who espouses the beliefs and policies of the German Nazis One who is likened to a German Nazi: a harshly domineering, dictatorial, or intolerant person	A member of the National Socialist German Workers' Party (now *hist.*); a member of any similar organization. In extended use: a believer in or sympathizer with the aims or doctrines of Nazism or any similar doctrines. Also more generally: a person holding extreme racist (esp. anti-Semitic) or authoritarian views, or behaving in a brutal and bigoted manner. *hyperbolically.* A person who is perceived to be authoritarian, autocratic, or inflexible; one who seeks to impose his or her views upon others. Usu. *derogatory.* Intensely racist (esp. anti-Semitic), intolerant, or right-wing.
Extremists [SC #7]	A person whose opinions, especially about religion or politics, are extreme, and who may do things that are violent, illegal, etc. for what they believe Left-wing/right-wing/political/religious extremists	Advocacy of extreme measures or views	One who is disposed to go to the extreme, or who holds extreme opinions; a member of a party advocating extreme measures.

Mini-Lexicons of Contemporary Terms and Semantic Clusters

Civilians [SC #7]	A person who is not a member of the armed forces or the police	One not on active duty in the armed services or not on a police or firefighting force	A person who is not professionally employed in the armed forces; a non-military person
Non-Combatants [SC #7]	In a war, a person who is not a member of the armed forces	One that does not engage in combat Civilian	A person who is not a combatant, as a civilian during a war; *spec.* a member of the armed services whose duties do not include active fighting, as a surgeon, purser, or chaplain, etc. Not involved in fighting; of, belonging to, or characteristic of a non-combatant.
Tolerance [SC #8]	The willingness to accept or tolerate somebody/something, especially opinions or behaviour that you may not agree with, or people who are not like you	Sympathy or indulgence for beliefs or practices differing from or conflicting with one's own	The action or practice of tolerating; toleration; the disposition to be patient with or indulgent to the opinions or practices of others; freedom from bigotry or undue severity in judging the conduct of others; forbearance; catholicity of spirit.
Love [SC #8]	A strong feeling of deep affection for somebody/something, especially a member of your family or a friend	Strong affection for another arising out of kinship or personal ties Affection based on admiration, benevolence, or common interests Unselfish loyal and benevolent ... concern for the good of another	A feeling or disposition of deep affection or fondness for someone, typically arising from a recognition of attractive qualities, from natural affinity, or from sympathy and manifesting itself in concern for the other's welfare and pleasure in his or her presence. In religious use: the benevolence and affection of God towards an individual or towards creation; (also) the affectionate devotion due to God from an individual; regard and consideration of one human being towards another prompted by a sense of a common relationship to God.

347

Table 5., continued

Term or Semantic Cluster	Oxford Learner's definition	Merriam-Webster's Definition	Oxford Dictionary Definition
Homophobia [SC #8]	A strong dislike and fear of homosexual people	Irrational fear of, aversion to, or discrimination against homosexuality or homosexuals	Fear or hatred of homosexuals and homosexuality.
Truth [also see previous chapters concerning "story" and "Story," as well as "my opinion," "my personal opinion," "my perspective" or "only my perspective"]	The true facts about something, rather than the things that have been invented or guessed The quality or state of being based on fact A fact that is believed by most people to be true	The body of real things, events, and facts The state of being the case *Often capitalized*: a transcendent fundamental or spiritual reality A judgment, proposition, or idea that is true or accepted as true The property (as of a statement) of being in accord with fact or reality	Belief; (as a count noun) a statement of belief, a creed. Something that conforms with fact or reality. Understanding of nature or reality; the totality of what is known to be true; knowledge. In [a] general or abstract sense: that which is true, real, or actual; reality; *spec.* (in religious use) spiritual reality as the subject of revelation or object of faith (often not distinguishable from sense. The fact or facts; the actual state of the case; the matter, situation, or circumstance as it really is. That which is real or genuine, as distinguished from an imitation; the genuine article.

These terms are, of course, illustrative and not exhaustive and assist with laying the foundation for Table 6 and an orthodox and evangelical response to the contemporary semantic debate. Many other terms, phrases, and contemporary distortions could be added, such as "pro-choice [debated endlessly]," "freedom of the press," or "shutting down freedom of the press" (allegedly by even criticizing the press—though not legally restricting the press), "fake news," "fake facts," "reason," or an "alternative reality" of truth.[268] The distortions and hypocrisy have seemingly reached a new level, as when one politician recently complained about the death of truth and reason, alternative mental realities, and the distortion of facts in a commencement address and then quickly distorted the facts

348

and history concerning past American impeachments in the next sentence! The distortion of words is an easy form of deception and distortion of Truth and, as previously noted, goes back to the Garden of Eden and the first Adam. The Second Adam, the Word, in contrast, restored and is ever-restoring Truth and Word.

Other terms and phrases also need restoration and redemption, or at least better contextualization. The *problem of evil*, for example, contextualizes the entire semantics surrounding the discussion of suffering and evil around the alleged failure or inaction of God (or moral failure of God) when, in fact, the problem of evil may be more properly framed around the failure and evil of those opposing the God who is incarnationally actualizing Paradise regained, even through the suffering of His beloved Son. The real problem of evil or the mystery of the problem of evil is why so many reject grace and restoration and thus ultimately battle *for* evil and suffering. Similarly, concerns about "the contradictions and errors" of the Bible merit serious, considered, gentle, and respectful responses, yet the contradictions and errors of sinful human perceptions deserve equal consideration relative to the matrix and tapestry of words, meaning, and communication. The Judeo-Christian faithful and American evangelicals often *give away the store* by accepting the semantic and philosophical presuppositions of Christianity's critics.

The following are additional and illustrative observations on Table 5 that contribute to the argument of this present work:

- CIVILIZATION: The dictionary definitions of civilization do not conform to the anti-civilizational definitions of civilization as oppressive. Note that the civilization is used in both a descriptive and aspirational sense in these definitions, which comports with the argument of this present work.
- COMPASSION AND SOCIAL JUSTICE: The definitions I've already provided do not improperly conflate the definition of compassion or social justice with a proposed political agenda such that if one disagrees with the agenda (e.g., the Sojourners' movement) one is thereby lacking compassion. It is proper to argue that some means better serve compassion and justice, whether the proposals are

typically associated with conservative groups such as the ACTON Institute,[269] or more politically liberal groups such as Sojourners. Yet question-begging definitions that immediately suggest that different perspectives lack compassion or justice, even prior to genuine dialog, certainly lack the very justice (treating others fairly) they claim to champion.

- ESTABLISHMENT OF RELIGION AND FREEDOM OF SPEECH: Apart from the increasing British restrictions referenced in the previous discussions, and the increasing-practice of growing restrictions in the United States, these definitions are reasonable. The problem is that the non-establishment clause is now being used to establish a secular and/or syncretistic post-Christian religion, or at least an ideology that functions as an aggressive religion.

- FAITH: Most of the definitions of faith emphasize trust, yet the *Oxford English Dictionary* does reflect to some degree, though the definition is cautious, the improper classification of faith as epistemological in nature. The problem here is not that faith lacks any epistemological implications but that faith has been reduced to an epistemological detour.

- [LARGE SEMANTIC CLUSTER] GLOBALISM, COLONILISM, ETHNOCENTRISM, SEXISM, FEMINISM, MULTICULTURALISM, RACISM, DISCRIMINATION, DIVERSITY, AND INCLUSION: Most of these definitions have constructive utility. Biblical Christianity should place Scripture above the agenda of any nation but also above any global agendas. Colonialism's definitions speak generally of the international reality of colonialism, yet one definition (far right column) points out that the term increasingly is only used in a derogatory sense. As noted, the abuses of the colonial era are well-known and should be acknowledged, yet there is more to the story of the colonial age that increasingly is taboo for honest inquiry. Ethnocentrism's definitions should avoid question-begging by emphasizing the tendency "to view the world from the perspective of one's own culture" or ethnicity, with limited "knowledge and appreciation of other cultures and communities."[270] The other elements of the proposed definitions of ethnocentrism tend to be question-begging and/or presuppose multicultural relativism. As already argued, some cultures are inferior (e.g., Nazi culture circa 1939) and moral discriminations are inevitable and necessary. The remaining terms and definitions in this cluster have value, yet it has been argued that multiculturalism must avoid relativism while being anchored in eschatology in order to be sustained and flourish. It has also been argued that terms such as multiculturalism, discrimination, diversity, and inclusion are increasingly being redefined such that biblical morality is viewed as unjust.

- PROFILING: The two key nuances of profiling (legitimate, illegitimate) are adequately reflected in these definitions. See my recommended approach to law enforcement issues in the text.

- JUDGMENTALISM AND LEGALISM: These definitions are adequate, and the theological definition (far right column) rightly limits the meaning of the term such that it is not expanded to include any moral boundaries or the appreciation of the role of biblical Law in the life of the believer.

- NATIONALISM, PATRIOTISM, FAR LEFT AND FAR RIGHT: If both definitions of nationalism and patriotism are simultaneously utilized (general and possibly appropriate love of country, or the possible idolatry of a nation), clarity is gained. However, as noted, nationalism can also be defined improperly in a multicultural and relativistic sense, thus disallowing moral discernment, which is dangerous to civilization. The *far right* definition (i.e., far left column), including the connection to Christian fundamentalism, could be useful, but unfortunately the term "fundamentalism" is sometimes used to refer to all American evangelicals or all conservative or moderate evangelicals. *Far or extreme right* and *far or extreme left* may have become mere terms of advocacy and marginalization, seeking to disqualify some views prior to meaningful dialog.

- SEXUAL ETHICS SEMANTIC CLUSTER: While there are elements of accuracy in some of these definitions, the primary problem with most is the implied severing of sexual ethics from biblical morality. Sexual morality becomes personal or cultural preference. This subjectivity has already resulted in progressive critics rejecting binary (i.e., heterosexual and homosexual, or even the feminist category and movement) or trinary (i.e., binary plus bisexual) categories in favor of endless personal options (see column 2). The definitions of adultery and fornication are largely accurate but fail to juxtapose these definitions with euphemisms that, in the contemporary context, relativize and subjectivize these definitions. In other words, adultery is only adultery if someone agrees, going into a marriage, that consensual sex outside of marriage is wrong. An *open marriage* would view *adultery* more as *an affair*. Or, as portrayed in legion movies, adultery may actually be only an affair if the marital situation is intolerable and divorce is not the best option. Our feet are truly and firmly planted in midair. The biblical ideal of *family* should not be abandoned due to unavoidable crises or relativistic assumptions.
- [LARGE SEMANTIC CLUSTER] TERRORISM, NAZI, EXTREMISTS, CIVILIANS, AND NONCOMBATANTS: The key to semantic clarity relative to these terms and many definitions and nuances is moral discernment (as opposed to cultural relativism) and historical accuracy (e.g., the term "Nazi" should not be used in such a general fashion that it refers to anyone with whom we disagree). From a Judeo-Christian perspective, the synthesis of biblical values and classical just war theory in Christian just war theory (e.g., Aquinas, Michael Novak) is a fallible yet helpful template for defining and employing these terms.
- TOLERANCE, LOVE, AND HOMOPHOBIA: There are proper and improper definitions and applications of tolerance, love, and *ophobias*. When such terms become a means for condemning authentic biblical morality, the

civilization has lost its Logocentric glue, and the circle of crudity, immorality, and barbarity ever widens.

- TRUTH: This book contains extended discussions of truth. A simplistic but helpful popular approach is to at least recognize the tri-fold nuances of this term: TRUTH, Truth, and truth.
- Table 6 attempts to summarize the application of this analysis.

Table 6. A Narrative Explanation of Logocentric Versus Non-Logocentric Semantics

Key Controversial Words, Phrases, and Semantic Clusters	Semantic Distortions Undermining Civilization	Semantic Clarifications Enhancing Civilization
Civilization	An oppressive, imperialistic, colonial, arrogant Western concept seeking global power, control, and profit.	An approximated ideal, a fallible but superior reality to the alternatives and an endless, ongoing quest.
Compassion and social justice	Compassion and social justice are often confused with a single political party platform or agenda, and social justice and compassion are often confused with a proposed compassionate *means* to social justice, typically some variant of socialism or European socialism.	Compassion is caring for one's neighbor as one would care for loved ones or self, and justice is defined in very biblical terms based on Old and New Testament passages and themes. The debate about the role and approach utilized by government either to provide, assist with, support, or facilitate compassionate justice should not be decided prior to robust analysis and discussion of the options and historical realities. The possibility that massive, godlike, centralized governmental compassion and justice could actually lack compassion and foster injustice is at least a matter of fair debate. Social justice is not necessarily socialism, communism, or capitalism. All models must be evaluated with Scripture and robust discernment.[271]

Educational neutrality

With the increasing eclipse of Truth and the eradication of the once pervasive biblical influence on education, public education adopted the shallow myth of educational neutrality. This especially gained momentum in America in the 1950s and 1960s. Secularized students were to be provided a neutral education that no longer acknowledged the Judeo-Christian roots of the entire educational endeavor, culture, and law. In short order, and especially so in recent decades, most anything can be advocated for in public education except biblically influenced values and ideas. This is truly a Great Reversal. The very biblically influenced foundation for America's educational quest for Truth is now the one perspective that is consistently marginalized and viewed as a violation of educational neutrality.

In the American context, educational neutrality means that public education should not serve as a propaganda arm of any particular church or denomination. The state shall not establish a sectarian religion, or a secular religion (often the current state of affairs). The tolerant or welcoming Judeo-Christian democratic experiment makes possible such grounded but free inquiry, and this experiment planted education in Judeo-Christian soil and assumptions about knowledge, reality, human nature, and Truth. Educational neutrality as secular education cannot sustain education or civilization. Secularized, syncretized education functions as a state religion, often militant, and hence the deconstructed myth of educational neutrality today is that educational neutrality actually is the establishment of a functional religion.

Table 6., continued

Key Controversial Words, Phrases, and Semantic Clusters	Semantic Distortions Undermining Civilization	Semantic Clarifications Enhancing Civilization
Establishment of religion, freedom of speech	Any or virtually any, especially Christian, religious beliefs and values allowed in the public sphere of civilization amount to the establishment of religion. Freedom of religion (mere truth) is best exercised in ghettoized churches and in the privatized metaphorical *closet*. A functional post or anti-Christian syncretistic state religion has been largely established. Freedom of speech (originally primarily political speech) has evolved greatly over the last few centuries, and especially in recent decades, such that virtually anything is considered freedom of speech (e.g., abusive pornography), even art, music and freedom of expression that would truly stun the framers of the very concepts of the free exercise of religion and freedom of speech. Yet the freedom of Judeo-Christian speech is viewed as undermining this contemporary redefinition of free speech.	Theocracy and the establishment of a single denominational or sectarian tyranny (e.g., Cromwell, Iran) certainly amount to the establishment of religion. The American experiment was not a secular nation, or a CHRISTIAN nation (a theocracy or the belief that all were Christians), or a Christian nation (mere privatized faith), but rather a tolerant or welcoming Judeo-Christian, democratic republic. Removing the Judeo-Christian assumptions and influence from American civilization and culture is akin to removing the hard drive from a computer, roots from a tree, or business ethics from a business curriculum. Free speech and the free exercise of religion are Promethean concepts apart from welcoming Judeo-Christian conceptual and cultural roots. The non-establishment clause has been used to establish a functional state religion. This new and syncretistic state religion often bears much resemblance to the psychological and sociological dynamics that it claims to despise in religious fundamentalism.

Faith

Faith is an irrational leap to trust in something personally true and meaningful, though not True, in response to the irresolvable questions and chaos concerning the nature of human existence and knowledge. Faith is not *reasonable*, not only because arrogant modernist reason is passé but also because there is simply no means by which to make the case that Christianity (or any normative meta-narrative) is True for all. Hence, faith should remain in the metaphorical closet of culture and civilization.

Biblical faith is primarily an interpersonal rather than an epistemological (pertaining to how we know) concept. This epistemological redefinition of faith is truly at the core of the destruction of biblical Christianity—from within. Biblical faith, by grace alone, emphasizes relational trust in the Triune Christ alone for salvation and for the kingdom journey. Viewing faith as *a* or *the* only means by which to respond to the modern and postmodern intellectual challenges to and criticisms of Christianity redefines biblical faith and ultimately disengages Christians from the critical intellectual and cultural challenges of the day. Faith and the Christian faith are redefined. Biblical faith, from Genesis to Revelation, assumes and states that the object of that faith, the Triune God, is clearly and demonstrably the one and only true God. The Bible considers it foolish to worship many gods, false gods (Rom. 1–2), or to bow and worship a manufactured idol (Isa. 44). Biblical faith is primarily relational and dispositional. Biblical faith is not a detour around or escape from the intellectual and cultural challenges of modernism and postmodernism.

Table 6., continued

Key Controversial Words, Phrases, and Semantic Clusters	Semantic Distortions Undermining Civilization	Semantic Clarifications Enhancing Civilization
Globalism, colonialism, sexism, feminism, multiculturalism, racism, discrimination, diversity, inclusion and profiling (also ethnocentrism)	Globalism has many meanings, but one meaning, related to transcending national interest in favor of global interests, is to move beyond Western Christian influence, renounce all association with the colonial age, and reject virtually any recognition of any progress made in the colonial age. Sexism and feminism, in order to escape the clutches of Christian misogyny and Western oppression, must now be defined in a secular, relativistic, ultramodern, syncretistic vacuum. Multiculturalism often means multicultural relativism, and diversity or inclusion often means not only the embracing of different races but also the leveling of all ideas (relativism) and behaviors with the possible inconsistent exception of liberal ideology (affirmed) and Christianity (rejected). Racism, sexism, and discrimination increasingly refer to any opposition to opposing views, or are sins that can only be committed by one race or religion. Discrimination claims are even used to discriminate against religious freedom, as seen with the Little Sisters of the Poor case study. Post-Christian liberal ideology is elevated, and Western Judeo-Christian assumptions are typically viewed as inferior and oppressive. It is within this context that "profiling" is often defined as any recognition of ideological, religious, ethical, or cultural differences that might bear on sheer statistical probability relative to terrorism, law enforcement discernment and effectiveness, and the triage of limited anti-terrorism resources.	From a biblical perspective, the *telos* or goal of Revelation 5, where *every* tribe and tongue and nation worship together at the throne because of a cross carried for all humanity, certainly means that Christians must have a global perspective (not to mention the injunction, "Go ye into all the world," in Mark 16:15). The age of colonialism certainly had abuses, but the failure to acknowledge the sacrificial labors of some for the world, or the real benefits taken to the world (e.g., health and life expectancy, enhanced means of combatting poverty, political freedom and economic mobility in some areas of the world, and countering famine), reflects the narrow anti-colonialism as previously defined. The reality is that nations or groups that have power often abuse that power because of human nature, not necessarily because of the ideology. If a non-Christian religion had birthed advanced scientific and technological nations, be assured that the projection of power would have followed. Indeed, countries controlled by atheistic or polytheistic ideologies have been historically genocidal. The *progressive* French Revolution was soaked in blood. Judeo-Christian assumptions often tempered the abuse of Western power in the colonial age (e.g., the abolition of slavery) and the twentieth century (e.g., the defeat of Hitler). Feminism should return to its nineteenth-century Judeo-Christian birthing soil and be pro-life. Multiculturalism, diversity, and inclusion should celebrate and learn from many (not all) cultural differences while using Scripture (i.e., Truth) to make important distinctions and decisions relative to civilization building, civilization enhancement, and the discerning assessment of political and cultural options. Racist profiling should be replaced with sheer, *blind*, unbiased statistical probability analysis of threats that does not turn a blind eye to real world realities.

Judgmentalism, "Do not judge," and the leveling of all sins	A primary contemporary virtue is the mandated recognition that no one has the right to judge anyone else, believing Jesus even said, "Do not judge"—anyone, ever. With truth being perspectival, no one has the right to judge anyone else. Of course, this is not practicable if someone experiences a great personal injustice or, ironically, if someone encounters a believer in Truth, in which cases it is acceptable to judge and condemn that individual militantly.	The biblical admonition not to judge, perhaps the most abused verse in the Bible in our day, taken in context, is unquestionably a rejection of hypocritical judgmentalism, but not the rejection of making essential biblical judgments concerning Truth (e.g., how shall we be saved and how shall we live). Jesus and the apostles exercised many strong judgments (e.g., "You brood of vipers"; "you hypocrites"; "If anyone preaches a different gospel … let them be under God's curse"). The immediate context of Matthew 7, "Do not judge," includes the following: "For in the way you judge [judgments are necessary, biblical and inevitable], you will be judged; and by your standard of measure, it will be measured to you." Jesus goes on to ask why some focus on the speck in the eye of another individual while ignoring the log (or telephone pole or tree in our day) in their own eye. "Do not judge" means "do not judge hypocritically," and when judgments are made do so "in a spirit of gentleness. Keep watch on yourself, lest you too be tempted" (see Matt. 7 and Gal. 6).
Legalism	Legalism increasingly refers, even in some evangelical churches, to any fixed moral boundaries. Rather than legalism, it must be affirmed that "Ethics is like art" (Sartre), and that any moral standards not self-chosen rob the individual of creativity and freedom (and for the religious it would be added that such fixed standards contradict love and grace). Fixed moral standards are viewed as legalistic, oppressive, psychologically destructive, and personally stifling. *Ethics* is rejected in favor of creative, individualistic, or tribalistic ethics.	The church, including the evangelical church, increasingly syncretistic, retains evangelical spirituality (e.g., born again, warmed heart, Christ alone experience, prayers for miracles) mixed with relativistic morality and ethical antinomianism. In terms of biblical theology, legalism refers to seeking salvation by works, not to the essential *fulfillment* of the Law, including every jot and tittle via transformed hearts created in Christ Jesus for good works (Ephesians 2:10).

Table 6., continued

Key Controversial Words, Phrases, and Semantic Clusters	Semantic Distortions Undermining Civilization	Semantic Clarifications Enhancing Civilization
Nationalism and patriotism (also far right and far left)	Nationalism (along with religion, e.g., John Lennon's *Imagine)* is a key source and cause of wars and conflicts, poverty and oppression. Strong belief in any ideology (except for politically liberal ideologies or anti-ideology) is another key contributing factor. *America First* is nationalistic, racist, and dangerous and should be replaced with compassion first, social justice first, or a new borderless global order first. Patriotism is often viewed as vulgar nationalism.	Biblical revelation certainly condemns the idolatry of nations and leaders. Nevertheless, in a fallen world, the quest for and discernment concerning a better civilization or more perfect union need not be abandoned simply because the ideal will never be realized in this current age. There is a major difference between blind patriotism and nationalism and discerning patriotism and nationalism. Why is it acceptable to love one's community or even one's school (in a nonidolatrous fashion) but not discerningly love one's country? Such love also includes prophetic critique, but appreciation for civilizational gains, a healthy sense of national community, and the desire for and pursuit of aspirational civilization are potentially virtuous. This quest for aspirational civilization should avoid both utopianism and fatalism. The simplistic demonization of nationalism is a form of utopianism and fails to make critical moral discernments between nations. Indeed, anti-nationalism is often a smokescreen for a new kind of political totalitarianism.

Sexual ethics terms, family (also see sexual preference and gender identity)

Amidst a truth culture that has often attempted to replace the infinite God-shaped vacuum in culture and restless human hearts with romantic love and sexual or other extreme experiences, the new truth-for-me-oriented semantic universe for sexual ethics naturally births the following terms: homophobia, sexual preference, sexual orientation, and nonbinary gender identity, among others. All of these terms are paradoxically affirming the sometimes militantly enforced truth that sexual ethics is a matter of *truth* not *Truth* and that the only Truth is that sexual ethics is mere truth, like art. Likewise, the scarlet letter of adultery is only reserved for those whose personal truth commitment was to marital fidelity and thus a violation of one's own self-selected ethical position (faithfulness in marriage). Otherwise, adultery is simply an *affair* or an *open marriage*. Fornication typically has no scarlet letter attached and is simply referred to as cohabitation, hooking up, a test ride, or friends with benefits.

Amidst a truth culture that has often attempted to replace the infinite God-shaped vacuum in culture and restless human hearts with romantic love and sexual or other extreme experiences, the new truth-for-me-oriented semantic universe for sexual ethics naturally births the following terms: homophobia, sexual preference, sexual orientation, and nonbinary gender identity, among others. All of these terms are paradoxically affirming the sometimes militantly enforced truth that sexual ethics is a matter of *truth* not *Truth* and that the only Truth is that sexual ethics is mere truth, like art. Likewise, the scarlet letter of adultery is only reserved for those whose personal truth commitment was to marital fidelity and thus a violation of one's own self-selected ethical position (faithfulness in marriage). Otherwise, adultery is simply an *affair* or an *open marriage*. Fornication typically has no scarlet letter attached and is simply referred to as cohabitation, hooking up, a test ride, or friends with benefits.

Table 6., continued

Key Controversial Words, Phrases, and Semantic Clusters	Semantic Distortions Undermining Civilization	Semantic Clarifications Enhancing Civilization
Terrorism, Nazi, extremists, civilians	In an increasingly anti-Western and anti-colonial context, the terms "terrorism" and "Nazi" are (recklessly) applied to any government or party using any kind of power, including Western or Jewish democratic states, that counters liberal political ideology. Extremists include anyone who disagrees with the ideology of the post-Christian, syncretistic state religion. The intentional targeting of civilians (or using human, hospital, or religious gathering shields) is no longer a distinguishing characteristic of terrorism, for in oppressive Western capitalistic regimes, all citizens are arguably extremists and terrorists. Most ironically, the term "Nazi," which was a very liberal, socialist, occult, Nietzschean, post- or anti-biblical regime, is now applied to those suspicious of massive governmental solutions to issues of social justice.	Based on the long tradition of Just War theory, terrorism is a complex term but certainly has a possible application to the intentional targeting of civilians or noncombatants (e.g., the Orlando or Paris shootings). Allegations of Nazism should have some connection to many or all of the following National Socialist party tenets: anti-Semitism, massive governmental control, socialism, post-Christian values, dictatorship, and genocide. While it is not always easy to avoid noncombatant casualties in modern warfare, terms such as civilian and noncombatant must be retained if any measure of compassion and justice applies in an age of often indiscriminate modern warfare and terrorism.
Tolerance, love, *isms* and *ophobias*	In the age of modernism, "tolerance" meant toleration of beliefs that were deemed rational as well as (sometimes militant) intolerance toward socially destructive superstitions (e.g., traditional Christianity—witness the French Revolution). Today, tolerance, including love and compassion, means toleration of beliefs and practices that fall under the rubric of liberal ideology and, increasingly, includes the militant intolerance of Judeo-Christian values, beliefs, and practices, especially Truth and Ethics. Such militancy, even *shouting down* and suppressing dialog, is often articulated via accusations of *isms* and *ophobias* (e.g., racism, sexism, and homophobia).	True tolerance respects real differences in the pursuit of Truth and civilization and fosters genuine dialogical inquiry, the truth quest, and the educational task. Tolerance is not to be confused with relativism, which is not so tolerant, and tolerance ultimately collapses apart from Judeo-Christian assumptions. Tolerance and loving others hardly means enabling self-destructive, other-destructive, and civilization-destructive values and behaviors—not to mention spiritually and eternally corrosive values. Militant *isms* and *ophobias*, if not grounded in reality (i.e., genuine irrational fear and hate), amount to nothing more than crass, hateful, intolerant propaganda.

362

| Truth (and "story," "my perspective," etc.) | Merely personal, cultural, tribal, subjective, embodied, felt, or contextual. Merely truth not Truth. Truth is a smokescreen for a mega-tribal Story seeking power. Ironically, this "truth" is presented as Truth. | Personal, cultural, and contextual preferences should not be confused with Truth. TRUTH refers to God's knowledge and perspective, of which humans have an approximative but valid grasp via God's amazing revelation. This revealed Truth is the only legitimate basis for evaluating false and oppressive Truth claims. Truth is trifold in nature: TRUTH, Truth, and truth. |

Appendix B

POSSIBLE OBJECTIONS CONSIDERED

The list of potential objections to the book and tables utilized in this work is likely endless given the scope, complexity, the sheer volume of terms discussed, and controversial nature of the argument and terms. I am aware of many areas that could have been refined, but that would have required significant expansion, and this work is intentionally presented as a primer for discussion and further research.

Four non-comprehensive, illustrative, proactive responses, however, might be of assistance with reader comprehension relative to this book's methodology, argument, intent, and the nature of these potential concerns.

A Response to Four Illustrative and Interrelated Objections Concerning this Book:

- *This Work is Oversimplistic and Semantically Ambiguous*
- *This Work is Western, Americentric, Xenophobic, Imperialistic, Arrogant and Presumptive*
- *This Work is Political, Not Apologetic, and a Failed Project*
- *This Work is Biased, Prejudiced, and the Logocentric Plumb Line is Oppressive*

1. As previously noted, this project is heuristic in nature and a primer, and the scope and complexity of this argument are immense. The scope of a subsequent book should address this concern to some degree. However, as noted, "words are slippery," so the goal here is the illumination and refinement of word usage not the perfection of word usage (*teleos* not *perfectio*). At a minimum, some of the post-Christian tribalistic "will to power" underlying contemporary semantic usage should have been exposed. It is arguable that this work delivers a net gain on semantic clarity.

2. It was tempting to engage in correlating many of these terms with identical or similar biblical terms and concepts, and providing an exegesis of such key terms and passages. While this work did engage in some of that throughout the text, it became clear that such analysis would significantly expand the scope and length of this work. Hence, this work is a first step in moving toward correct definitions and appropriate and relevant translations rooted in Scripture. Much work has already been done on such biblical terms (e.g., "justice"), and perhaps it is best to have the biblical specialists and philologists lead on the biblical foundations for semantic apologetics and polemics. This work intentionally focused on the contemporary usage of terms, the interrelated and interdependent nature of terms (semantic universes), the Judeo-Christian semantics of the American experiment, and the way in which word usage and definitions are being shamelessly redefined today. Much work yet remains.

3. While it is fair to recognize that this book affirms that some of the criticisms of the Judeo-Christian influenced Western (especially American) civilization are misguided, excessive, and hypocritical, it is also true that the methodological proposal (semantic refinement) allows for a dialog that could lead to rather harsh criticisms of the West (past or present), or any civilization or culture, and the advancing of non-Western or other alternatives. For example, in principle all political and economic theories should be on the table, so

to speak, for discussion and analysis. The problem today seems to be two-fold: (1) Judeo-Christian-influenced alternatives are increasingly not given a fair hearing given the militant attempt to marginalize, entirely privatize, ghettoize, or even criminalize Judeo-Christian culture, and (2) the alternatives presented are often wedded to the utopian fallacy rather than to reality. Cautious optimism concerning alternatives and enhancements to civilization is reasonable, but comparing realistic options to unattainable perfection and then discarding the realistic options as irredeemable or evil amounts to semantic deceit. The point here is that debate and dialog should precede and interface with advocacy rather than be silenced or shouted down by advocacy. Advocacy should exist within a hermeneutical circle of dialog, not a vacuum of the militant silencing of alternative views. The critical and transparent semantic presupposition of this work would better be classified as a heuristic argument but hardly as presumptive. It has been openly stated that the attempt to engage in meaningful communication apart from Judeo-Christian assumptions is ultimately incoherent polybabble and akin to building a house on presuppositional sand. If others can provide newly fashioned and truly stable and fecund political or economic foundations, and not rule out Judeo-Christian influence *a priori*, then let the dialog proceed. The problem today is that so many militant advocates do not even understand the American experiment, much less the alternatives. As to the need for loving, respectful, and gentle polemics and apologetics, see the previously discussed 1 Peter 3:15 in the introduction and throughout the text. It is never easy to strike the perfect and biblical balance and tone when engaging with such heated and controversial issues, but the attempt certainly was made to be firm, respectful, direct, dialogical in nature, and to speak the truth in love.

4. Yes, as I noted, this work is rooted in the concerns of American evangelicalism, historic Christian orthodoxy, relatively conservative Judeo-Christian faith communities,

and intentionally written in and primarily for a Western and American context. This book is intentionally written in and primarily for an American context as we move into the next decade of history. If I tried to overstate global implications, even in an increasingly global and digitized culture, postmodern sociologists would doubtless dismiss the work as misunderstanding the global context anyhow! I do believe that this dialog certainly has global applicability — certainly in Western and Christian influenced areas of the globe and certainly in view of digitized global culture. Yet it will be left to others to determine if this work has any significant value related to other global contexts. This book is replete with criticisms of current trajectories in the West, so culture is hardly being baptized. It has been argued that the core features of the American experiment appear to be superior to many contemporary and proffered alternatives. Consistent postmodernists should celebrate the intentional contextualization of this work by, from their perspective, one who could not possibly transcend the American context even if they wanted to do so.

5. One could also object that this work is *America-centric* because it does not acknowledge that Europe has moved to a post-Christian context without economic or political tyranny or military conflict. It is hard to resist asking, "Really?" at this juncture. Stalin's anti-Christian semantic universe filled some twenty million graves. Europe's move to a post-Christian semantic universe has been accompanied by countless pathologies over the last 250 years, and even the current tolerant and inclusive European culture is being stretched to the breaking point due to the fruits of ambiguous post-Christian conceptions of compassion, inclusiveness, and toleration. Civilizations that lack a cultural glue and a shared semantic universe are ultimately in peril and will either fragment or be conquered from within or without. It is quite arguable that the current and unstable European formula for civilization is not only resting on sand but also

somewhat dependent on American defense spending and economic strength, and certainly not the reverse.

6. An apologetic task that ignores potential Christian influence on all aspects of civilization (including semantics and the integrity and tone of public discourse) and culture, not to mention influence on and essential ethical reflection concerning contemporary polarizing issues, breaks with the great tradition of a Christian apologetics (e.g., Augustine) rooted in Scripture. This work has already critiqued, multiple times, the antiquated argument that Christian influence on global culture is (or ever will be) a failed project and the oversimplistic analysis suggesting that even America has now been forever enveloped by post-Christendom. Ironically, those proclaiming that such ameliorative efforts are now a lost cause sometimes seem almost giddy concerning the prospect of a marginalized and persecuted church in the West,[272] while parasitizing on the remaining benefits and freedoms of culture and civilization often being preserved by evangelicals and Roman Catholics who are taking shrapnel while heroically serving in the cultural and civilizational trenches. The shrapnel includes friendly fire. The loving trench warfare of these Christians, done with insufficient resources, is often exhausting and sacrificial in areas such as law, politics, media, education, and entertainment. These oft-despised cultural heroes have secured freedoms not only for the American experiment, our children, grandchildren, and great grandchildren, but also for their evangelical critics. The list is endless, but includes these illustrative wins:[273]

    - The Supreme Court ruled that the Bladensburg Peace Cross in Maryland will continue to stand and commemorate the sacrifices of nearly 50 soldiers.
    - The Supreme Court ruled that it is legal to require the "humane disposal of the bodies of aborted babies" and not treat these babies as "medical trash."
    - The Supreme Court "rejected a federal lawsuit to have 'In God We Trust' removed from our national currency."

- Federal funding for research on aborted babies was successfully challenged.
- A "bonded laborer" was saved "from years of harsh imprisonment in Pakistan after being falsely accused of theft." A Christian family of five that had been enslaved and tortured by captors was freed in Pakistan.
- Pro-life medical professionals received protections from being forced to perform operations that violated their conscience.
- A school's decision to confiscate a young child's Bible was successfully challenged.

Yes, these wins only reflect a limited segment of social justice issues, and evangelical cultural hawks sometimes abandon tactful, loving cultural engagement. Nevertheless, evangelical cultural doves often deceive themselves by thinking that compassion, love, and purity require avoidance of the biblically required messy conflicts in the cultural trenches of the inevitable culture conflicts reflected in the above list. These culture wars will not cease simply because Christians surrender or retreat. Cultural surrender and appeasement are never effective. Reckless hawks often leave a bad witness, and doves often abandon the world that God loves, not to mention abandoning responsibility for the human flourishing and religious and political freedom of their own children, grandchildren, and great grandchildren. The gift of political freedom should not be squandered in the name of a false spirituality or because some believers have been less than tactful when engaging with culture.

7. In the global and American context, heroic and Herculean Judeo-Christian believers live and proclaim the gospel regardless of politically granted freedoms, while also taking abuse and frontal assaults for protecting the parasitical freedoms of those who think it is now time to abandon the civilizational quest. In the American context, the parasites who suggest giving up on culture and civilization seem either unaware of or ungrateful for the efforts of those, to cite just a few examples, who regularly stand before the Supreme

Court or hold their ground amidst the scorn of Hollywood or Washington, DC and protect the very flourishing and freedom of the parasites. These despised evangelicals and Roman Catholics have had numerous successes that benefit everyone, including the parasites. It seems that much of the religious cultural fatalism accelerated after the United States Supreme Court's Obergefell versus Hodges decision of 2015. This was certainly an important, defining, historic decision, but there are countless other changes, challenges, and conflicts (e.g., law, education, media) in America and around the globe that will greatly impact the mission of the church, future generations who are the proper objects of neighbor love, and the character of future civilization(s). The decay of American civilization is impactful on the global mission and philanthropy of American Christians and should not be understated or dismissed as trivial, yet this same mission also needs to be multifaceted and global and not entirely dependent on any single country.

8. In addition, the nuance distinguishing between whether Christians have lost or are losing the culture war could have a significant impact on evangelical semantic apologetics and cultural engagement.[274] Cultural engagement (e.g., law, education, politics), analogous to war at times (but not referring to the tone of apologetics), is a messy and complex business, and viewing the cultural war as *lost* leads some (see Chapter 3) to conclude that cultural withdrawal is the best way forward. Some believe that since evangelicals and conservative Roman Catholics are not terribly popular these days, perhaps if they focused on compassionate activity and stepped back from cultural and political engagement their influence would rebound—or at least the church would "be the church," unpolluted by politics, and the church would be faithful to God and not enamored with Caesar. No doubt some have been less than loving or tactful when culturally engaging, and compassionate, tactful engagement and service to the needy is certainly desirable and influential, as with Christian compassion in ancient Rome, but it is

questionable as to whether a change in social posturing alone will significantly soften the desire of many to eradicate evangelical, Roman Catholic, and biblical influence from culture and civilization. The fallacy here is similar to the assumption by some that if we would accommodate the concerns of terrorists that they would abandon their savage and hateful terrorism. Reckless hawks and appeasement doves jeopardize Christian influence. Appeasement never really works, it just "kicks the can down the road" and others inherit even deeper problems. The strength of the ideological and spiritual opposition to Judeo-Christian values, in spite of scriptural warnings that this is the norm apart from grace-filled culture, is often ignored. Cultural disengagement by Christians who are giving up on the task of intentional, strategic and tactical civilizational influence will likely only invite additional restrictions on faith, practice and mission.

9. American religious doves also often obscure the fact that they reside in a "we the people" political context, where they have the right and ethical obligation to engage. This is not ancient Rome where Christian influence on the state can typically only be indirect. American Christians have rights and responsibilities to engage directly with civilization and employ semantic polemics and apologetics.

10. Doubtless some critics, especially those who did not read the work carefully, will allege that this entire work amounts to politically conservative spin—especially those who believe that everything is ultimately spin. The best answer to that allegation is for the critic to reread a number of carefully nuanced statements throughout the text. The target audience of this book was clearly defined upfront as conservative to moderate faith communities who sense that their practices, beliefs, and even thoughts are increasingly being marginalized, ridiculed, harassed, and sometimes criminalized. Many traditionalists are hesitant to endorse any flawed cultural or political leaders, yet they are desperately engaging in lesser evil calculations while seeking

at least some political, legal, and cultural recourse and redress in the face of this proliferating anti-Judeo-Christian (AJC) semantic terrorism. *We are now moving from an ABC moment to an AJC moment in history.* This work intentionally utilized some political leaders as alleged and controversial examples of polarized verbal seduction (e.g., Trump and Ocasio-Cortez), especially illustrations that would be relevant to or most resonate with traditional faith communities. This work meticulously documented many of the criticisms of the current administration by Mark Labberton, as well as the criticisms typical of Labberton and "woke" evangelicals. President Trump's alleged verbal distortions are arguably the most thoroughly scrutinized and documented of any President in American history by investigators, opponents, and the media. Alleged semantic distortions by traditional faith community leaders (e.g. Franklin Graham), along with incessant allegations of being "ist" and "ophobic" likewise have been thoroughly documented and trumpeted by educational and media critics—amidst a post-truth and post-American culture where the accused are often found "guilty by allegation." Yet *Seduced?* intentionally did not focus or elaborate on all of the alleged falsifications by current or former Presidents, presidential candidates, cultural luminaries, or other elected representatives because the issues addressed in this book, while most relevant to the present moment, are also profoundly timeless. It is freely acknowledged that political and religious conservatives engage in shameless spin. Such spin should be condemned. Such spiritually camouflaged power games only feed the frenzy of postmodernists who affirm that all language is nothing but power and manipulation. However, traditional Judeo-Christian and core values and conservative Judeo-Christian faith communities are under direct assault as never before during the American experiment. Let's not lose sight of that important context for this discussion. Yes, such conservatives often betray their own ethos and should be chastened but the city is under siege just in case no one has noticed. Most power centers of culture, such as education, law, music, entertainment, popular culture, mainstream media, most older and mainstream denominations, and most political power hubs, increasingly marginalize, obscure, and sometimes oppress Judeo-Christian believers and culture. The cultural power grid certainly is more connected with the political left. Major entertainers, Hollywood, and corporations like Nike or BMW—even Disney to some extent—flaunt and milk their progressive political agendas. Nike seems absolutely clueless concerning the utopian fallacy and is shameless at identifying the Nike product with Colin Kaepernick and disassociating with Betsy Ross. Is it really necessary to mention social media and Internet behemoths such as Google? Two trillion searches per year, 3.8 million searches per minute, and 63,000 searches per second? Almost all of the twenty plus presidential candidates as of the time of this writing are radically pro-abortion, for some version of open borders, for endless government handouts to the tune of trillions, and define key points of traditional Judeo-Christian morality as unjust.

11. In addition, many of these power centers are advancing perspectives that not only eradicate the plumb line of the American experiment, but which *also corrode the very notion of normative, self-evident, shared truth and morality.*

12. Besides, endless arguments have been made elsewhere concerning the alleged errors of biblical and orthodox Judeo-Christian or evangelical-influenced semantics and civilization. The entire Judeo-Christian and evangelical semantic universe is regularly criticized,[275] and need not be rehearsed or assessed here.[276] Others have devoted much time to documenting and analyzing the alleged semantic theft and fake news or lies of more conservative political candidates.[277]

13. One must not forget, as noted immediately above, that *most* of the long-term, extremely influential, and major centers of power in Western and American culture—media,

entertainment, education, and law — are not politically conservative or biblically grounded. This is especially important relative to public education, funded by billions of dollars from tax paying Americans, which often trains the next generation of leaders in a post Judeo-Christian ethos and future-vision.

14. This work provides a miniscule measure of counterbalancing.

15. This book, as stated many times, is intentionally contextualized in an American context where the centers for power often seem determined to eradicate Judeo-Christian and biblical influence. This present heuristic is transparently attempting to counter non-evangelical and non-orthodox semantic distortions and reestablish a dialogical place in the marketplace of ideas for moderate and conservative American and Judeo-Christian semantics. This one work can't address all of the global semantic challenges in today's world. The assumption is that such a heuristic connects or reconnects the scriptural foundation to the quest for any truly aspirational civilization.

16. It has been argued that the contemporary word "theft" by the political left and right, is especially moving away from, not toward, Judeo-Christian and evangelical assumptions and Judeo-Christian influenced civilization. This is not to say, however, that so-called Christians do not engage in less than helpful semantics. For example, referring to all terrorism as *Islamic terrorism* may violate the golden rule — would evangelicals or Roman Catholics approve of "evangelical terrorism" or "Roman Catholic terrorists" being applied to all terrorist actions associated with an allegedly Christian ideology — or the mentally unstable actions of someone connected to a specific Christian faith tradition? Do evangelicals appreciate the simplistic conflation of American evangelicalism and American fundamentalism such that all are viewed as fundamentalists? *Radical* Islamic terrorism may be a more accurate appellation for current terrorism, but would evangelicals or Roman Catholics be comfortable with "radical evangelical terrorism" or "radical Roman

Catholic terrorism"? Yes, it is a legitimate inquiry as to what extent the core beliefs of any religion or ideology encourage terrorism, and it is certainly arguable that it would be entirely inconsistent with any religious movement rooted in the New Testament, the gospel (or evangel), and the Christ event to engage in savage terrorism, especially terrorism that intentionally targets noncombatants. The murder of non-combatants — or the definition of all citizens in any culture or civilization as combatants — is impossible to reconcile with biblical ethics or Judeo-Christian influenced just war theory. There is no easy semantic resolution to the challenge of defining the current wave of global terrorism on a bumper sticker. Given the undeniable frequency of terroristic acts in our day, a more robust descriptor of the savage worldwide movement responsible for the current spike in terrorism, even in a sound bite culture, might be needed if Truth and genuine civilization meliorating reflection and dialog are desired. Such radical terrorism is emerging from a rather sizable, non-progressive or medieval wing of Islam with a definable hermeneutic concerning contemporary events and the Koran. Such historical, conceptual, and sematic qualifications (e.g., Medieval Radical Islamic Terrorism?) concerning terrorism might birth a better appellation and better serve all faith traditions, Truth, and civilization. I tutored or mentored a college student from Iran once, and based on many conversations he certainly would be better characterized as a progressive, gentle, informed, compassionate, Westernized, anti-terroristic, devout Islamic Iranian. Semantic clarifications need to move in many directions, not just toward the interests of American religious groups.

17. The objection that a return to Logocentrism, or a biblical Logocentric plumb line, is biased, prejudiced, xenophobic, and oppressive is flawed. That very objection is overworked, hackneyed, threadbare, prejudiced, non-inclusive, and historically fallacious. The objection suggests that a return to biblical norms is oppressive because Scripture allegedly

endorses slavery, racism, the subjection of women, and even genocide. The critics rehearsing this objection seem to be clueless concerning key principles of biblical hermeneutics—the science and methodology of proper biblical interpretation. Properly responding to this criticism of Scripture has been the subject of many books, and could easily provide the subject matter for another chapter. Hence, the response here will only be representative:

- Understanding the nature and implication of progressive revelation is critical to properly interpreting Scripture. God's revelation to the world via Scripture took place over millennia. This revelation was inspired (2 Timothy 3:16–17), but the biblical authors were not automatons or mere stenographers. Scriptural revelation came through personalities and historical contexts. The Gospel of John was written in a very different style than the Gospel of Matthew or the Old Testament book of Numbers. Proverbs is markedly different from Jeremiah.

- God's progressive revelation through Scripture intersects history and humanity at specific points in time in the progress of revelation that encompasses the changing cultures over these millennia. In the Old Testament era women were treated as chattel, and human sacrifice, abortion, polygamy, pederasty, and slavery were common. The biblical revelation bursts into this world and begins to undermine the very assumptions that serve as oppressive pillars for ancient culture and civilizations. Child sacrifice is condemned (Deuteronomy 18:10). Male and female are both created in the image of God, and both male and female are coconspirators in the tragic and cosmic fall of humanity and the creation. Both male and female are objects of redemption. Jesus used the "male and female" from the Genesis creation narrative to criticize what was essentially a polygamous culture of divorce and remarriage that denigrated and devastated women. Many biblical heroes of the faith in the Old Testament were women, including Deborah the "judge." The Messiah was born of a "blessed" woman, Mary, and the first witnesses to the resurrection were women, in a culture that devalued the testimony of women.

- In the Old Testament God's people are reminded over and over again that they were foreigners and treated as slaves, therefore they should treat foreigners with decency and have protections for foreigners and slaves. Many centuries later, in the New Testament, Paul the apostle and leader of the Gentile church forever theologically undermined slavery in the epistle of Philemon (verses 16–17). Paul referred to a former slave as one to be viewed and treated "no longer as a slave, but more than a slave, a beloved brother, especially to me, but how much more to you, both in the flesh and in the Lord. If then you regard me a partner, accept him as *you would* me."

- The light of progressive revelation grows brighter over the millennia as the blind eyes of humanity and culture are progressively opened. Culture and civilizations do not turn on a dime. Progressive revelation speaks through historical contexts over the centuries, meeting us where we are but leading us from paradise lost to the paradise regained of the new creation, where "There is neither Jew nor Gentile, neither slave nor free, nor is there male and female, for you are all one in Christ Jesus" (Galatians 3:28, NIV). As demonstrated in the prior chapters of this work, this Logocentric vision of the future has inspired and liberated millions.

18. Some will object to the thesis of this work by arguing that American evangelicals and conservative/moderate faith communities need a new or alternative model for cultural engagement. As noted previously, that is the appeal by scholars and authors such as Timothy Keller and Jake Meador (*In Search of the Common Good*), Stanley Hauerwas (the *Resident Aliens* just "be the church" option), and Rod Dreher

(the neo-monastic or *Benedict Option*). Such creative work is truly appreciated and has valuable supplemental insights when absorbed and utilized in a very limited fashion by the larger vision of this work. Many of these authors are correct that countless models of civilizational engagement have proven inadequate or unnecessarily polarizing, such as the following: a) theocracy; b) secularism; c) relativistic syncretism; d) pietism and/or separatism; e) most formulations of the politically engaged Religious Right (e.g. Jeffress); f) reactionary and populist blue state or red state evangelicalism; g) Niebuhr's triumphalist "Christ the transformer of culture" approach; h) politically liberal or progressive evangelicalism (e.g., *Sojourners*, Labberton); or i) various and endless proposals for a civil, minimalistic, negotiated, and compromised common good that typically lack a secure and normative semantic and worldview foundation. These many models will be addressed in a forthcoming book by the author. Some of these models have been directly or indirectly addressed by Matthews, *A Theology of Cross and Kingdom*. However, as noted previously in this book, we really don't need new models like neo-monasticism or Meador's creative common good approach. This work has repeatedly argued that the way forward to civil community and true flourishing is a renewal and dynamic enhancement of the authentic "more perfect union" American experiment. The nature and contours of this experiment are reflected in the core founding documents, historical precedents, unfolding civilizational and liberating gains over time, and the writings of authors such as Michael Novak (*The Spirit of Democratic Capitalism Thirty Years Later, The Founders on God and Government*) and Os Guinness (*Last Call for Liberty*). This unique vision and experiment profoundly synthesized and appropriated some of the better instincts of the Enlightenment within a Logocentric semantic and worldview framework capable of fostering genuine, tolerant, normed, and spiritual flourishing within human and civilizational community. And

to be clear, this optimistic vision and Logocentric community proved capable of embracing and synthesizing the
very diverse perspectives of conservative Deists, more radical Deists like Thomas Paine, rational supernaturalists in
agreement with John Locke, countless traditional Judeo-
Christian faith communities and civilizational founders,
plus legion denominations, sects, and religions. This dig-
nified, realistic, compelling, and unifying vision is nurtured
via shared historical roots, is capable of defragmenting our
polarized historical moment and uniting multiple generations, and can masterfully and constructively guide and
inspire newer, floundering, and future generations. *E pluribus unum*. The suggested new models are rather shallow
compared to this profoundly rich, historically vetted, but
oft-criticized, misunderstood, and underappreciated model.
Only a semantic renaissance conjoined with a heartfelt and
Spirit-inspired renewal is capable of restoring and enhancing
this Logocentric, visionary, normed, and common quest for
a shared and more perfect union, and a city truly worthy to
be "set on a hill."

19. The final objection to this work perhaps could be described
as the "not woke" argument. Perhaps it could be stated as
follows: "You just aren't woke. You don't get it on how
the experience of diversity groups in your so-called Judeo
Christian influenced culture has been unbelievably racist
and oppressive, and how that racism and oppression continues to this very day. Wake up! We need militant and if
need be relativistic semantics to respond to militant oppression, and to respond to the violent and militant semantics that
have brutalized millions and justified that very oppression."
At the experiential and existential level, it is very difficult
to respond to this critique, so I will have to defer to others
who have experienced unrelenting oppression. However,
my consistent point throughout this work has been that
militant, tribalistic, and seductive semantics, lacking any
shared norm for truth as a foundational plumb line, serve no
one and such word weaponization or seduction destroys the

experiment in a more perfect union that has often self-corrected, liberated millions, and advanced human flourishing far better than utopian or dystopian promises of liberation and freedom. Victories achieved by shameless spin are short lived and ultimately kill the experiment. It truly is analogous to someone who quickly builds a house on sand or quicksand. The strength of the experiment is not mere racial or ethnic diversity. The experiment is not that out of the one come many. The strength of the experiment in Trinitarian republican democracy is that out of the many cultures is emerging a shared vision of one nation, celebrating and enriched by the strengths of these cultures, yet always under God and subject to *Lex Rex*. Our diverse cultures and perspectives embrace, refine, and contribute to a more perfect union of human flourishing, yet the experiment lies at the core. This experiment is the worst form of government on the face of the earth thus far, except for all the rest, as many have noted. It would seem to this author, with self-confessed feet of clay, that the militant critics of the experiment are actually the ones who are "not yet woke."

20. These points are only illustrative and not exhaustive responses to potential objections. Perhaps a rejoinder to the *too political, biased and prejudiced* concern is a fitting way to conclude this work. The false definitions of terms (e.g., social justice, compassion), especially in a tribalistic and polytheistic culture where everything is becoming Balkanized political advocacy, are a critical polemical issue for faith communities. Pseudo-definitions are redefining Christian piety, spirituality, holiness, and political and cultural engagement. Polemics and apologetics are connected at the heart and walk hand in hand to maintain and creatively advance a dynamic, biblical, culturally engaged Judeo-Christian orthodoxy. Cultural accommodation in church and synagogue demonstrate that semantic apologetics and polemics operate in similar semantic domains and the issues in and outside of faith communities are nearly one. Hence, avoiding the political in such a biased

and prejudiced age of outrage is clearly not an option. We cannot escape from semantic and political distortions even *within* our own Judeo-Christian faith communities. The present crisis of truth and word suggests that the greatest semantic, polemic, and apologetic challenges in the history of the Judeo-Christian movement may well have arrived.

RECOMMENDED READINGS

"Americans Express Increasingly Warm Feelings Toward Religious Groups." Pew Research Center, 15 February 2017. http://www.pewforum.org/2017/02/15/ americans-express-increasingly-warm-feelings-toward-religious-groups/.

Ankerberg, John. "Homosexuality and Sexual Ethics–Program 1." *The John Ankerberg Show*, 1989. https://www.jashow.org/articles/general/homosexuality-and-sexual-ethics-program-1/.

Axford, Barrie. *Theories of Globalization*. Cambridge, England: Polity Press, 2013.

Aylesworth, Gary. "Postmodernism." *Stanford Encyclopedia of Philosophy*, rev. 2015. https://plato.stanford.edu/entries/postmodernism/.

Bailey, Sarah Pulliam. "Russell Moore Wants to Keep Christianity Weird," *Christianity Today*, 8 September 2015, http://www.christianitytoday.com/ct/2015/september/russell-moore-wants-to-keep-christianity-weird.html.

Barna Group. Christians React to the Legalization of Same-Sex Marriage: 9 Key Findings," 1 July 2015. https://www.barna.org/barna-update/culture/723-christians-react-to-the-legalization-of-same-sex-marriage-9-key-findings#.VINO8XarRD8.

— — —. "5 Reasons Millennials Stay Connected to Church," 17 September 2013. https://www.barna.org/barna-update/

millennials/635-5-reasons-millennials-stay-connect-
ed-to-church#.VlNFVXarRD8.

— — —. "Scotland: Lessons for Effective Ministry in a Post-
Christian Context," 27 August 2015. https://www.barna.org/
barna-update/culture/730-scotland-lessons-for-effective-
ministry-in-a-post-christian-context#.VlNMXnarRD8.

Barry, Brian. *Why Social Justice Matters*. Cambridge, England:
Polity Press, 2005.

Beckwith, C. A. *The New Schaff-Herzog Encyclopedia of Religious
Knowledge*. Vol. 9, *Petri–Reuchlin*. Grand Rapids, MI: Baker
Book House, 1954. https://www.ccel.org/s/schaff/encyc/
encyc09 /htm/ iv.iii.x.htm.

Beckwith, Francis J., and Gregory Koukl. *Relativism: Feet Firmly
Planted in Mid-Air*. Grand Rapids, MI: Baker Books, 1998.

Berkhof, Louis. *Systematic Theology*, new comb. ed. Grand Rapids,
MI: Wm. B. Eerdmans Publishing, 1996.

Bultmann, Rudolf. *New Testament and Mythology and Other Basic
Writings*. Selected, edited, and translated by Schubert M.
Ogden. Minneapolis, MN: Fortress Press, 1984.

Carter, Joe. "Founding Believers." *First Things*, September 22,
2010. https://www.firstthings.com/web-exclusives/2010/09/
founding-believers.

Coates, Ta-Nehisi. "The Myth of Western Civilization." *The Atlantic*
(Dec 2013). https://www.theatlantic.com/international/
archive/2013/12/the-myth-of-western-civilization/282704/.

Crosley-Corcoran, Gina. "Explaining White Privilege to a
Broke White Person ..." http://occupywallstreet.net/story/
explaining-white-privilege-broke-white-person (accessed
July 6, 2018).

Cruse, Alan. *Meaning in Language: An Introduction to Semantics
and Pragmatics*, 3rd ed., Oxford Textbooks in Linguistics.
Oxford, England: Oxford University Press, 2011.

CT Editors. "Is it Time for Evangelicals to Strategically
Withdraw from the Culture: Four Evangelical Thinkers
Consider What Rod Dreher's Benedict Option Means for
the Church." *Christianity Today*, February 27, 2017. http://
www.christianitytoday.com/ct/2017/february-web-only/

benedict-option-evangelicals-strategically-with-draw-culture.html.

Dayton, Donald W. *Discovering an Evangelical Heritage*. Grand Rapids, MI: Baker Academic, 1976.

Dochuk, Darren, Thomas S. Kidd, and Kurt W. Peterson, eds. *American Evangelicalism: George Marsden and the State of American Religious History*. Notre Dame: University of Notre Dame Press, 2014.

Dreher, Rod. *The Benedict Option: A Strategy for Christians in a Post-Christian Nation*. New York: Penguin Random House, 2017.

Duigman, Brian. "Postmodernism," *Encyclopedia Britannica*, 2014. https://www.britannica.com/topic/postmodernism-philosophy.

Federer, William J. *America's God and Country: Encyclopedia of Quotations*. St. Louis, MO: Amerisearch, 2000.

Gallup. "In Depth: Topics A to Z—Religion." http://www.gallup.com/poll/1690/religion.aspx (accessed July 6, 2018).

Gaustad, Edwin S. *Faith of the Founders: Religion and the New Nation, 1776–1826*. Waco, TX: Baylor University Press, 2004.

Gaustad, Edwin, and Mark Noll. *A Documentary History of Religion in America to 1877*, 3rd ed. Grand Rapids, MI: Wm. B. Eerdmans Publishing, 2003.

Geisler, Norman. *Christian Apologetics*, 2nd ed. Grand Rapids, MI: Baker Academic, 2013.

Goldstein, Laurie. "Outraged by Glenn Beck's Salvo, Christians Fire Back." *The New York Times,* March 11, 2010. http://www.nytimes.com/2010/03/12/us/12justice.html.

Grove, Jack. "US Watchdogs Face 'Crisis' in Post-Truth Age: Increased Scrutiny of US sector and Distrust of Academics Puts Traditional Quality Assurance Models in Question." *CHEA Accreditation in the News*, from *The Times Higher Education Word University Rankings*, May 10, 2017. https://www.timeshighereducation.com/news/us-watchdogs-face-crisis-post-truth-age#survey-answer.

Hamilton, Alexander, James Madison, and John Jay. *The Federalist.* Edited by Benjamin Fletcher Wright. New York: Barnes and Noble Books, 1961.

Harvard University, Harvard at a Glance, History, the "Harvard Shield," http://www.harvard.edu/about-harvard/harvard-glance/history (accessed July 6, 2018).

Hauerwas,, Stanley and William H. Willimon. *Resident Aliens: Life in the Christian Colony: A Provocative Christian Assessment of Culture and Ministry for People Who Know That Something Is Wrong*, exp. 25th anniv. ed. Nashville: Abingdon Press, 2014.

Henry, Carl F. H. *God, Revelation and Authority.* 6 vols. Wheaton, IL: Crossway Books, 1999.

Hiebert, Paul G. "Beyond Anti-Colonialism to Globalism." *Missiology: An International Review* 19, no. 3 (1991): 263–81.

Horn, Norman. "Christians Cannot Be Nationalists." Libertarian Christian Institute, 1 September 2011. http://libertarianchristians.com/2011/09/01/christians-cannot-be-nationalists/.

Inazu, John D. *Confident Pluralism: Surviving and Thriving through Deep Difference.* Chicago: University of Chicago Press, 2016.

James, Paul. *Globalism, Nationalism, Tribalism: Bringing Theory Back In.* London: Sage Publications, 2006.

Kelley, Stewart E., with Dew, James K. *Understanding Postmodernism: A Christian Perspective.* Downers Grove, IL: IVP Academic, Intervarsity Press, 2017.

Lewis, C. S. *Mere Christianity*, rev. and amplified ed. San Francisco: HarperSanFransciso, 2001.

— — —. "Our English Syllabus." In *Rehabilitations and Other Essays*, 79–93. Oxford, England: Oxford University Press, 1939.

Lincoln, Abraham. "Proclamation 85 — Proclaiming a Day of National Humiliation, Prayer, and Fasting." August 12, 1861. Online by Gerhard Peters and John T. Woolley. *The American Presidency Project.* http://www.presidency.ucsb.edu/ws/?pid=69979.

Livingston, James C. *Modern Christian Thought: From the Enlightenment to Vatican II*. New York: MacMillan Publishing, 1971.

Lyotard, Jean-François. *The Postmodern Condition: A Report on Knowledge*. Translated by Geoff Bennington and Brian Massumi. 1997. Reprint, Minneapolis, MN: U of Minnesota Press, 1984.

Machen, J. Gresham. *What is Christianity? And Other Addresses*. Grand Rapids, MI: Eerdmans, 1951.

Martyr, Justin. "The Defence and Explanation of Christian Faith and Practice." *Apologies*. Translated by A. W. F. Blunt. Cambridge, England: Cambridge Patristic Texts, 1911. In *The Early Christian Fathers: A Selection from the Writings of the Fathers from St. Clement of Rome to St. Athanasius*, 58-65. Edited and translated by Henry Bettenson, Oxford, England: Oxford University Press, 1956.

McCallum, Dennis, ed. *The Death of Truth: What's Wrong with Multiculturalism, the Rejection of Reason and the New Postmodern Diversity?* Minneapolis, MN: Bethany House Publishers, 1996.

McCracken, Brett. *Gray Matters: Navigating the Space between Legalism and Liberty*. Grand Rapids, MI: Baker, 2013.

McGowan, Andrew. "Eating People: Accusations of Cannibalism against Christians in the Second Century." *Journal of Early Christian Studies* 2 (1994): 413–42.

Moore, Brooke Noel, and Kenneth Bruder. *Philosophy: The Power of Ideas*. New York: McGraw-Hill, 2014.

Nietzsche, Friedrich. *Book Three: Principles of a New Evaluation of The Will to Power*. Edited by Walter Kaufmann, Translated by Walter Kaufmann and R. J. Hollingdale. New York: Random House, 1967.

———. *On the Genealogy of Morals*. Translated by Francis Golffing. New York: Doubleday, 1956.

———. "On Truth and Falsity in Their Extramoral Sense (1873)." In *Philosophical Writings*. Edited by Reinhold Grimm and Caroline Molina y Vedia. New York: Continuum, 1997.

Novak, Michael. "Foreword." *The Founders on God and Government*. Edited by Daniel L. Dreisbach, Mark D. Hall, and Jeffrey H. Morrison. Lanham: Rowman and Littlefield Publishers, Inc., 2004.

— — —. "Social Justice: Not What You Think It Is." *The Heritage Foundation. Report: Poverty and Inequality*, 29 December 2009. http://www.heritage.org/poverty-and-inequality/report/social-justice-not-what-you-think-it.

— — —. *The Spirit of Democratic Capitalism*, rev. ed. Lanham, MD: Madison Books, 1990.

— — —. *Writing from Left to Right: My Journey from Liberal to Conservative*. New York: Image, 2013.

Obama, Barack. "'Call to Renewal' Keynote Address." *New York Times*, 28 June 2006. http://www.nytimes.com/2006/06/28/us/politics/2006obamaspeech.html.

— — —. "'Call to Renewal' Keynote Address." *YouTube*, 28 June 2006. https://www.youtube.com/watch?v=BFeGY5gbpCM.

Oden, Thomas C. *After Modernity ... What? Agenda for Theology*. Grand Rapids, MI: Zondervan Publishing, 1990.

Olaskey, Marvin. *The Tragedy of American Compassion*. Washington, DC: Regnery Publishing, 1992.

Orelus, Pierre Wilbert. *Social Justice for the Oppressed: Critical Educators Speak Out*. Lanham, MD: Rowman and Littlefield, 2017.

Ross, Tara, and Joseph C. Smith, Jr. *Under God: George Washington and the Question of Church and State*. Dallas: Spence Publishing, 2008.

Rothman, Noah. *Unjust: Social Justice and the Unmaking of America*. Washington, DC: Regnery Publishing, 2019.

Rutherford, Samuel. *Lex, Rex, or the Law and the Prince: A Dispute for the Just Prerogative of King and People*. Seattle, WA: CreateSpace Independent Publishing Platform, 2012.

Sartre, John Paul. *Being and Nothingness*. New York: Washington Square, 1966.

Schaeffer, Francis A. *How Should We Then Live: The Rise and Decline of Western Thought and Culture*, 50th anniv. ed. Wheaton: Crossway Books, 2005.

Schleiermacher, Friedrich. *On Religion: Speeches to Its Cultured Despisers*. Translated by John Oman. New York: Harper and Row, Publishers, 1968.

Shellnut, Kate. "Americans Warm Up to Every Religious Group Except Evangelicals." *Christianity Today*, 15 February 2017. http://www.christianitytoday.com/gleanings/2017/ february/americans-warm-feelings-religious-groups-evangeli-cals-pew.html.

Smith, Timothy. *Revivalism and Social Reform: American Protestantism on the Eve of the Civil War*. Eugene, OR: Wipf and Stock Publishers, 2004.

Swaim, Barton. "The Left Won the Culture War. Will They be Merciful?" *The Washington Post*, 27 May 2016. https://www. washingtonpost.com/opinions/the-left-won-the-culture-war-will-they-be-merciful/2016/05/27/5c5014c2-2024-11e6-8690-f14ca9de2972_story.html?utm_term=.86a113384093.

Tooley, Mark. "Falwell, Trump, Christianity and Nationalism." *The Christian Post*, 28 January 2016. http://www.christianpost.com/news/falwell-trump-christianity-nationalism-156066/.

Williams, Donald T. "Discerning the Times: Why We Lost the Culture War and How to Make a Comeback." *Journal of International Society of Christian Apologetics* 9 (2016): 4–11. http://www.isca-apologetics.org/sites/default/files/JISCA-2016-v9.pdf.

Wittgenstein, Ludwig. *Philosophical Investigations*. Translated by G. E. M. Anscombe. London: Pearson, 1973.

Endnotes

All quotations on this page were attributed to said authors according to multiple sources. Regardless, the sentiments are thought-provoking and relevant to the task of this work.

1. Bill Federer, "American Minute," November 15, 2019, accessed November 15, 2019, https://myemail.constantcontact.com/ Rev--John-Witherspoon-Signer-of-Declaration-of-Independence- -A-Republic-must-either-preserve-its-Virtue-or-lose-its-Liberty-. html?soid=1108762609255&aid=OnoOEGgEA2A.

2. A simple and introductory definition of semantics is that the discipline of semantics refers to the study and analysis of word definitions and usage. Semantics as used in this work will be progressively defined and illustrated in most chapters and the appendices.

3. The contrast between university and "multiversity" conveys the drift from the unified or same verse (universe) goal of Judeo-Christian influenced liberal arts universities reflecting upon and integrating diverse academic disciplines. Today, the unified quest has largely been abandoned, with the only unity revolving around some contemporary version of aggressive political advocacy.

4. My best read from countless web pages and articles concerning the general chronology of the many Chick-fil-A controversies—and no organization is above criticism or should naively be put on a pedestal—is that Chick-fil-A's Judeo-Christian influenced value system birthed a business that emphasized selling and serving its products with a quality control and customer service culture rooted in religious values. As this business succeeded it supported other Judeo-Christian influenced organizations, some of which required commitment to a traditional and biblical view of marriage. As criticisms of non-inclusiveness or bigotry mounted, Chick-fil-A openly confirmed and defended its support for traditional marriage, which only enraged the critics further. Attempts by Chick-fil-A to accommodate concerns have not been met with real reciprocity thus far. Colleagues who went through employee training at Chick-fil-A have confirmed that the attempt to separate selling Chick-fil-A products from its religious value system is impossible and a non-starter, unless the younger and newer leadership drifts from the heritage. This is, or at least was originally, far more than an organization that just sells chicken. Whether Chick-fil-A spokespersons could have been more diplomatic or not in public pronouncements is a separate issue that should not detract from the significance of prior attempts to suppress Chick-fil-A's freedom of religion, freedom of speech, and free enterprise—if such terms and phrases are properly defined. The critics are the true bigots and suppressers of freedom. Faith communities should recognize that the attempt to restrict Chick-fil-A, and Chick-fil-A's attempts to accommodate, are likely a foretaste of the future. Whether the future unfolds in five or fifty years, all faith communities and Judeo-Christian influenced organizations and businesses should be interested and engaged.

5. Decision Staff, "Hostility on the College Campus: A Conversation with Os Guinness," Billy Graham Evangelistic Association, May 27, 2016, accessed November 22, 2019, https://billygraham.org/decision-magazine/june-2016/hostility-on-the-college-campus-a-conversation-with-os-guiness/.

6. Let me clarify the comment above in the text about the context of this list. This list below is constructed in order to spark dialog, illustrate, communicate, and resonate with the intended, likely, and primary audience for this book—politically conservative or moderate, theologically traditional, religiously orthodox, and biblically influenced communities of faith. If more progressive, politically (and contemporary) liberal, or "blue state" audiences were the likely and intended audience of this book, this list would be modified in order to better resonate and communicate with that type of audience. However, this work directly and repeatedly addresses and navigates the very polarized perceptions concerning what qualifies as deception, dishonesty, verbal seduction, shameless spin, and fake news. The hope is that, regardless of political leanings, the primary argument is sound and fertile soil for dialog. Judeo-Christian faith communities, and their impact and influence, are in jeopardy because they are tardy relative to providing specific and detailed semantic instruction or catechesis. And regardless of political leanings, Judeo-Christian beliefs and practices are unquestionably under assault, as will be documented throughout this work.

7. See Bradley C. S. Watson, "Treason," *The Heritage Guide to The Constitution*, accessed June 24, 2019, https://www.heritage. org/constitution/#!/articles/3/essays/119/treason.

8. "Cydney Henderson, "Lady Gaga Slams Mike Pence as the 'Worst Representation of What It Means to be a Christian,'" *USA Today*, accessed November 20, 2019, https://www.usatoday. com/story/life/people/2019/01/21/lady-gaga-slams-vice-president-mike-pence-christianity/2636241002/.

9. Jackie Salo, "Why You'll No Longer Find 'Convicted Felons' in San Francisco," *New York Post*, August 22, 2019, accessed September 30, 2019, https://nypost.com/2019/08/22/ why-youll-no-longer-find-convicted-felons-in-san-francisco/.

10. Brian Riedl, "The Unaffordable Candidate: Bernie Sanders's $97 Trillion Agenda would impose Incomprehensible

Costs," accessed October 19, 2019, https://www.city-journal.org/bernie-sanders-expensive-spending-proposals.

11. Concern for this quadrillion-dollar trajectory was first heard on a late night radio talk show. The name of the host was not captured, but reference was made to Brian Riedl's research.

12. Robert Bellafiore, "Summary of the Latest Federal Income Tax Data, 2018 Update," Tax Foundation, November 13, 2018, accessed November 1, 2019.

13. Rod Dreher, "Social Justice: Our New Civil Religion," *The American Conservative*, July 10, 2019, accessed August 10, 2019, https://www.theamericanconservative.com/dreher/lgbt-pride-social-justice-our-new-civil-religion/.

14. Victor Davis Hanson, "America Does Not Have to be Perfect to be Good," Fox News, July 18, 2019, accessed July 25, 2019, https://www.foxnews.com/opinion/victor-davis-hanson-america-does-not-have-be-perfect-to-be-good-despite-what-radical-progressives-tell-us. Italicized emphasis added.

15. Greg Lukianoff and Jonathan Haidt, *The Coddling of the American Mind: How Good Intentions and Bad Ideas Are Setting Up a Generation for Failure* (New York: Penguin Press, 2018), 24.

16. "Worship at Union," September 18, 2019, accessed September 30, 2019, https://utsnyc.edu/worship-at-union/.

17. Richard Pallardy, "Christopher Hitchens," *Encyclopaedia Britannica*, accessed October 4, 2019, https://www.britannica.com/biography/Christopher-Hitchens. The quality of research varies relative to articles in Wikipedia, but also see "Criticism of Mother Teresa," accessed October 4, 2019, https://en.wikipedia.org/wiki/Criticism_of_Mother_Teresa.

18. Shawn Windsor, "Dear Lebron James: You Either Believe in Social Justice or You Don't," *Detroit Free Press*, accessed October 18, 2019, https://www.freep.com/story/sports/columnists/shawn-windsor/2019/10/16/lebron-james-china-hong-kong-protests/3991430002/.

19. Christina Maxouris, "You Can Now be Fined up to $250,000 if You Call Someone an 'Illegal Alien' in New York City," CNN, accessed November 20, 2019, https://www.cnn.com/2019/10/01/us/nyc-illegal-alien-discrimination-guidance/index.html.

20. Emphasis added to quotations by italics. Please see the standard reference works or web sites referenced, and for the IRS official definition please see: IRS, "Immigration Terms and Definitions Involving Aliens," accessed October 18, 2019, https://www.irs.gov/individuals/international-taxpayers/immigration-terms-and-definitions-involving-aliens. Also see the DHS website's "Definition of Terms," accessed October 19, 2019, https://www.dhs.gov/immigration-statistics/data-standards-and-definitions/definition-terms.

21. Shawna Mizelle, "Chicago Police Superintendent Says He's Skipping Trump Speech," CNN, October 24, 2019, accessed October 25, 2019, https://www.cnn.com/2019/10/24/politics/eddie-johnson-chicago-police-trump-speech/index.html.

22. "Obama Calls Out Call-out Culture: 'That's Not Bringing About Change,'" CBS News, October 30, 2019, accessed November 11, 2019, https://www.cbsnews.com/news/president-obama-calls-out-woke-culture-says-not-bringing-about-change-2019-10-30/.

23. *Evangelical Call for Restitution-Based Immigration Reform,* Evangelical Immigration Table, accessed November 21, 2019, http://evangelicalimmigrationtable.com/evangelical-call-for-restitution-based-immigration-reform/.

24. Ravi Zacharias, "Timeless Words," accessed January 15, 2019, https://www.rzim.org/read/just-thinking-magazine/think-again-timeless-words. Emphasis added.

25. "From John Adams to James Warren, 22 April 1776," *National Archives*, Founders Online, accessed August 27, 2019, https://founders.archives.gov/documents/Adams/06-04-02-0052.

26. The literature on and nuances of the Logos doctrine are seemingly innumerable. For the purpose of this more general work on polemics and apologetics, the many nuances of the Judeo-Christian and biblical Logos doctrine are viewed as interrelated, mutually reinforcing, and include (1) the thought, speech, and word of God; (2) the revelation and communication of God; (3) the mind, wisdom, and reason of God; (4) the spoken or written words of God; and, most importantly and centrally, (5) the Triune personal and preexistent person of Christ who incarnates, reveals, exemplifies, and unifies all of these nuances and dimensions of the biblical Logos (John 1). Those not espousing Christianity should still resonate with many of these nuances. Much of Western civilization was Logocentric and measured by the norm of the Logos for centuries. Since the core of Christ's teaching and ministry was the kingdom rule of God, semantics, culture, and civilization were thus Logocentric and kingdomcentric. The American experiment was not theocratic, but it was greatly influenced by Logocentric and kingdomcentric semantics, values, aspirations, and civilizational assumptions. The founding documents guiding this experiment, law, the Triune structure of government, freedom of speech, freedom of religion, culture, and architecture—to name a few—all were largely in orbit around the Logos and kingdom.

27. For a perspective that reinforces how critical it is to avoid false dichotomies concerning the question of Christian influence on the American experiment, see the following: Mark David Hall, "Did America Have a Christian Founding?" The Heritage Foundation, June 7, 2011, accessed June 26, 2019, https://www.heritage.org/political-process/report/did-america-have-christian-founding;

Novak, *Founders*, cited throughout this work; and see the extensive documentation in Federer's *God and Country*, also cited throughout this work.

28. Beckwith and Koukl helpfully refer to the present cultural context as "feet firmly planted in mid-air." Francis J. Beckwith and Gregory Koukl, *Relativism: Feet Firmly Planted in Mid-Air* (Grand Rapids, MI: Baker Books, 1998).

29. For a popular and somewhat sensationalistic version of this argument, see Bill Federer, "The Ten Commandments, and the Importance of Educated and Moral Citizens," accessed January 23, 2019, https://myemail.constantcontact.com/The-Ten-Commandments--and-the-importance-of-educated---moral-citizens.html?soid=1108762609255&aid=XYm7YsOdCqI.

30. The postmodern "story" that all stories are personal or cultural preferences is self-refuting if it is true, and irrelevant if it is false. If the postmodern story is the Story, then there is at least one story that is more than a story, and therefore some normative truth exists. If the postmodern story is just another story, then it can be ignored. As many have noted, most relativistic variations of postmodernity, which deny the existence of normative metanarratives, subtly try to sneak in normative truth through the back door. In other words, postmodernism is a meta-narrative, the very thing postmodernists claim to reject and despise.

31. Apologetics refers to making the case for the Christian faith (1 Peter 3:15).

32. I define worldview as a major perspective and passion that consistently or inconsistently clusters together key convictions and commitments concerning the primary or fundamental questions of life, the after-life, existence, values, ethics, and our common life together.

33. *Sophos* means wisdom and *philos* means love.

34. See Carmin Chappel, "Alexandria Ocasio-Cortez: A System That Allows Billionaires to Exist Alongside Extreme Poverty Is Immoral," CNBC Politics, January 22, 2019, accessed January 23, 2019, https://www.cnbc.com/2019/01/22/alexandria-ocasio-cortez-a-system-that-allows-billionaires-to-exist-is-immoral.html. See also Morgan Gstalter, "Holocaust Remembrance Group Invites Ocasio-Cortez to Tour Auschwitz with Survivor," The Hill.Com, June 22, 2019, accessed June 24, 2019, https://thehill.com/homenews/house/449833-holocaust-commemoration-group-invites-ocasio-cortez-to-tour-auschwitz-with; and Joel B. Pollak, "Alexandria Ocasio-Cortez Refuses Invitation to Visit Auschwitz Concentration Camp," Breitbart, June 23, 2019, accessed August 27, 2019, https://www.breitbart.com/politics/2019/06/23/alexandria-ocasio-cortez-refuses-invitation-to-visit-auschwitz-concentration-camp/.

35. See Daniel Funke, "How The Washington Post Tallied more than 10,000 Trump Falsehoods in less than Three Years," *Poynter,* May 7, 2019, accessed June 25, 2019, https://www.poynter.org/fact-checking/2019/how-the-washington-post-tallied-more-than-10000-trump-falsehoods-in-less-than-three-years/; FactCheck.org: A Project of The Annenberg Public Policy Center, accessed June 25, 2019, https://www.factcheck.org/person/donald-trump/; Glenn Kessler, "Obama's Biggest Whoppers," *The Washington Post*, January 19, 2017, accessed June 25, 2019, https://www.washingtonpost.com/news/fact-checker/wp/2017/01/19/obamas-biggest-whoppers/?utm_term=.b348065fb03d; Brett Stephens, "Sex, Lies and Presidents: Trump's Defenders are Reading from the Clinton Playbook," *The New York Times*, August 24, 2018, accessed June 25, 2019, https://www.nytimes.com/2018/08/24/opinion/impeachment-trump-clinton.html; James Bovard, "How Quickly NY Times Forgets Obama's Lies and Frauds," Mises Institute, December 19, 2017, accessed June 25, 2019, https://mises.org/power-market/bovard-how-quickly-ny-times-forgets-obamas-lies-and-frauds.

36. This image is from Google's public image file: "Free to Use, Share or Modify, Even Commercially," accessed June 25, 2019, https://www.google.com/

search?as_st=y&tbm=isch&as_q=pro+choice+pro+-faith+pro+family&as_epq=&as_oq=&as_eq=&cr=&as_site-search=&safe=active&tbs=sur:fmc#imgrc=OHKID7uEaqtgUM:.

37. Tim Stafford, "The Abortion Wars," *Christianity Today* (January 1, 2003), accessed January 22, 2019, https://www.christianitytoday.com/ct/2003/januaryweb-only/abortion-wars-history-prolife-christians.html.

38. Guttmacher Institute, "United States Abortion," accessed November 26, 2019, https://www.guttmacher.org/united-states/abortion.

39. This image is from Google's public image file: "Free to Use, Share or Modify, Even Commercially," accessed June 25, 2019, https://www.google.com/search?safe=active&as_st=y&tbs=sur%3Afmc&tbm=isch&sa=1&ei=RT2ZXInPI4Tl-5gLTqoqgCg&q=BAPHOMET&oq=BAPHOMET&gs_l=img.3..35i39l2j0l8.16775.17756..18204...0.0..0.90.644.9......1....1..gws-wiz-img.......0i8i30j0i24j0i5i30.Wze5UV3MFEk#imgrc=Z6HWAaelwGLXZM. See this link for the "Knowledge is the Greatest Gift" image placed in the Illinois State Capitol, accessed June 25, 2019, https://www.nbcnews.com/news/us-news/satanic-statue-erected-illinois-state-capitol-other-holiday-decorations-n944706. Elisha Fieldstadt, "Satanic Statue Erected in Illinois State Capitol with Other Holiday Decorations: The Resin Sculpture, Dubbed a 'Snaketivity,' Depicts a Hand Holding an Apple, with a Snake Wrapped round It," NBC News, December 6, 2018, accessed June 25, 2019, https://www.nbcnews.com/news/us-news/satanic-statue-erected-illinois-state-capitol-other-holiday-decorations-n944706. The defenders of the satanists will likely argue that they are not affirming a personified conception of evil, but freedom of thought and speech. This rejoinder missed the point of this book entirely. The issue with the "Snaketivity" is the semantic seduction that attempts to eradicate the Judeo-Christian influence and redefine foundational Christian terms and concepts that largely birthed the very freedom of thought

that allows for the public display of the "Snaketivity." The satanists, whether they believe in a personalized, supernatural, devil or not, are seductive parasites on the very Judeo-Christian values they seek to invert. It is irrelevant to the present discussion whether they affirm a personal devil and are merely "demythologizing" Judeo-Christian beliefs and terms.

40. "What About Ulysses S. Grant?" *Christianity Today*, Christian History, accessed June 28, 2019, https://www.christianitytoday.com/history/issues/issue-33/what-about-ulysses-s-grant.html.

41. Peyton Dillberg, "Socialist Students Bawk to Ban 'White Supremacist' 'Capitalist Cult' Chick-fil-A," Campus Reform, January 22, 2019, accessed January 25, 2019, https://www.campusreform.org/?ID=11777.

42. The Chick-Fil-A photo, taken on Wednesday, April 24, 2019 by the author, is of a sign in Florida.

43. Tim Fitzsimmons, "FAA Investigating Chic-fil-A's Exclusion at U.S. Airports," NBC News, May 28, 2019, accessed June 25, 2019, https://www.nbcnews.com/feature/nbc-out/faa-investigating-chick-fil-s-exclusion-u-s-airports-n1010841.

44. Matthew Lee Anderson, "Infanticide Debate Reflects a New Era for Abortion Politics," Christianity Today, February 5, 2019, accessed February 22, 2019, https://www.christianitytoday.com/ct/2019/february-web-only/infanticide-abortion-law-new-york-virginia-pro-life-future.html.

45. Devan Cole, "Virginia Governor faces Backlash over Comments Supporting Late-term Abortion Bill," CNN [Politics], January 31, 2019, accessed June 25, 2019, https://www.cnn.com/2019/01/31/politics/ralph-northam-third-trimester-abortion/index.html.

46. Marvin Olaskey, *The Tragedy of American Compassion* (Washington, DC: Regnery Publishing, 1992).

47. See Etienne Balibar and Immanuel Wallerstein, *Race, Nation, Class: Ambiguous Identities*, Balibar translated by Chris Turner (London/New York: Verso Publications, 1988). Balibar's argument is informed by postmodern thought, and is somewhat esoteric, with the key point seeming to be that some approaches to addressing racism actually foster a new kind of racism or neo-racism. Hence, Balibar asks in chapter 1, "Is there a 'Neo-Racism'?" I am using the concepts such as neo-racism and neo-sexism to suggest that many of the leaders in the fight against various "isms" are actually engaging in the very "isms" they seek to counter.

48. Noah Rothman, "Social Justice Has Become a New Excuse for Prejudice," *New York Post*, February 2, 2019, accessed February 3, 2019, https://nypost.com/2019/02/02/social-justice-has-become-a-new-excuse-for-prejudice/. Rothman argues that social justice used to drive us toward objective thinking and fair play. He argues that increasingly "social justice" is becoming the antithesis of "blind, objective justice." If that is true, even in part, it would evidence the thesis of this book that many are being seduced by semantic theft.

49. RT, "Get Woke, Go Broke: Oberlin College hit with $44 MILLION Penalty for Accusing Local Bakery of Racism" June 14, 2019, accessed June 24, 2019, https://www.rt.com/usa/461913-oberlin-bakery-racism-fine/. This source, formerly Russian TV, was chosen to avoid relying on American networks for an approach to this story. Virtually every major American news outlet, and many local news outlets, covered this story. The "get woke" reference is to how politically correct business plans can backfire.

50. Religious leaders, relative to applying their faith to culture and politics, "are even more politically divided than the rest of us [or their own congregants], according to a new data set representing the largest compilation of American religious leaders ever

assembled." Indeed, "religious leaders have sharply divided themselves along political lines." Some religious leaders are clearly being seduced and then seducing their congregations, so if this work resonates with the reader, the hope is that some teachable religious leaders might be reached through placing this book in their hands. See Kevin Quealy, "Your Rabbi? Probably a Democrat. Your Baptist Pastor? Probably a Republican. Your Priest? Who Knows," *New York Times*, June 12, 2017, https://www.nytimes.com/interactive/2017/06/12/upshot/the-politics-of-americas-religious-leaders.html.

51. Emphasis added. All Scripture references are from the NASB unless otherwise designated.

52. Cam Smith, "Connecticut Parents Petition to Ban Transgender Track Athletes," *USA Today*, High School Sports, June 6, 2018, accessed July 9, 2018, http://usatodayhss.com/2018/connecticut-parents-ban-transgender-track-athletes.

53. Cam Smith, "Connecticut."

54. Martyn Zielger, "Martina Navratilova Softens Her Transgender View," *The Times*, June 26, 2019, accessed June 28, 2019, https://www.thetimes.co.uk/article/martina-navratilova-softens-her-transgender-view-w9z8wn062.

55. I am writing this work mostly from the perspective and context of American evangelicalism, Christian orthodoxy, and Wesleyan influenced evangelicalism. The broader context, however, of this work, and the broader appeal is that of contending for orthodox and biblical Judeo-Christian influence in church and state. Hence, the appeal is to all who seek to maximize Judeo-Christian influence, regardless of their faith tradition (Roman Catholics; Orthodox; Judaism; religious traditions that resonate with the message of the book). For simplicity, sometimes evangelical influence will be referenced, but not in an exclusive fashion. Evangelical Christianity was a significant actor relative to Judeo-Christian

influence, and is the context of this work, but this project is biblically ecumenical.

56. Ray Gronberg, "How will Duke Divinity Respond to Recent LGBT protest? Task force sets out to decide," *The Herald Sun,* March 9, 2018, accessed July 9, 2018, https://www.heraldsun.com/latest-news/article204350619.html.

57. Kashmira Gander, "Why We Should Reconsider Assigning Babies as 'Boys or Girls' at Birth," *Independent,* September 7, 2017, accessed July 9, 2018, https://www.independent.co.uk/life-style/health-and-families/baby-gender-why-not-boys-girls-trans-assign-birth-non-binary-reveal-party-gendered-intelligence-a7933871.html.

58. Sarah Brown, "Harvard Cracks Down on All-Male Clubs. But It's Women's Groups That Have Vanished," *The Chronicle of Higher Education*, January 9, 2019, accessed January 11, 2019, https://www.chronicle.com/article/Harvard-Cracks-Down-on/245436.

59. Supreme Court of the United States, Opinions, October Term, 2014, "OBERGEFELL ET AL. v. HODGES, DIRECTOR, OHIO DEPARTMENT OF HEALTH, ET AL.," accessed July 11, 2018, https://www.supremecourt.gov/opinions/14pdf/14-556_3204.pdf. Emphasis added to draw attention to the semantic analysis in this argument.

60. Kate Shellnutt, "Going Dutch: Netherlands Imports Nashville Statement Controversy," *Christianity Today*, January 10, 2019, accessed January 14, 2019, https://www.christianitytoday.com/news/2019/january/nashville-statement-netherlands-lgbt-cb-mw-dutch-christians.html?utm_source=ctweekly-html&utm_medium=Newsletter&utm_term=11818316&utm_content=629134097&utm_campaign=email.

61. Historical Marker Project, Soldiers' Reaction to Lincoln's Emancipation," accessed July 30, 2018, https://www.

historicalmarkerproject.com/markers/HMV7D_soldiers-reaction-to-lincolns-emancipation_Perryville-KY.html. Also, I personally read this marker at the historic Perryville battle site on July 29, 2018. Emphasis added to the terms "odious despotism."

62. Lily Rothman, "75 Years Ago: Hitler's Phony Plea for Peace." *Time*, October 6, 2014, accessed July 9, 2018, http://time.com/3461961/hitler-peace-speech/.

63. Matt Stout, "Elizabeth Warren Calls on Democrats to 'Save this Democracy' at State Convention," *The Boston Globe*, June 2, 2018, accessed July 16, 2018, https://www.bostonglobe.com/metro/2018/06/01/warren/bSe2zyBinuhVtwLkT2WOIM/story.html.

64. 2 Timothy 3:16, *theopnustos*.

65. John 14:6.

66. Public education here refers to primary, secondary, collegiate, and graduate school education. See Chapter 2 concerning the Christian influence on the birth of public education.

67. Sean Coughlan, "'Intolerance' Threat to University Free Speech," BBC News, March 27, 2018, accessed July 11, 2018, https://www.bbc.com/news/education-43544546. Matthew Reisz, "How Far Should Universities Restrict Freedom of Speech?" The Times Higher Education, September 12, 2015, accessed July 11, 2108, https://www.timeshighereducation.com/news/how-far-should-universities-restrict-freedom-speech.

68. Scott Jaschik, "Professors and Politics: What the Research Says," *Inside Higher Ed,* February 27, 2017, accessed June 24, 2019, https://www.insidehighered.com/news/2017/02/27/research-confirms-professors-lean-left-questions-assumptions-about-what-means. This is a helpful review of some research, yet the argument of the article simply and naively runs roughshod over the realities

of human nature and the extremely powerful culture of influence at colleges and universities—not to mention legion anecdotal stories from families, possible bias and prejudice in reading lists, assignments, grading, lectures, curriculum, out-of-class learning experiences, mandated ethical norms, peer pressure, and countless other influencers. One has to wonder, have some of these defenders of the status quo bias and prejudice actually been to college or seriously reflected on the college experience and how it interfaces with human nature? Do they seriously think that most major power centers of culture today would lean politically left apart from generations of university influence? Have they failed to notice the ideological morphing of the colonial nurseries of piety (as Edwin Guastad put it) into sometimes post-Christian, anti-Christian, secularized or relativized institutions?

69. The context of this passage suggests that Lewis is using the term "civilization" in the first sense (from the *Oxford Dictionary*): 1. "The stage of human social development and organization which is considered most advanced.... *'the Victorians equated the railways with progress and civilization....'* 1.1. The process by which a society or place reaches an advanced stage of social development and organization. 1.2. The society, culture, and way of life of a particular area ... *'the great books of Western civilization'* ... *'the early civilizations of Mesopotamia and Egypt'* ... Civilization." English Oxford Living Dictionaries, "Civilization," accessed February 5 and July 5, 2018, https://en.oxforddictionaries.com/definition/civilization. Lewis also seems to be saying that "civilization" implies being civilized ("a relatively high level of cultural and technological development ... characterized by taste, refinement, or restraint"), as opposed to barbaric (i.e., less civilized, unrefined, mercilessly harsh, and broadly unjust) as in the following: "A *civilized* society must respond to crime with fairness and justice." "Stop yelling. We have to be more *civilized* about this." "Try to act like a *civilized* human being!" "a *civilized* way to spend the evening." See: *Merriam-Webster*, and *Merriam Webster*, and *Merriam-Webster Learner's Dictionary*, "Civilization," https://www.merriam-webster.com/dictionary/civilization; http://www.

learnersdictionary.com/definition/civilized. For Lewis (see *Mere Christianity*, Book 1), sustained civilization requires a solid moral foundation. C. S. Lewis, *Mere Christianity,* rev. and amp. ed. (San Francisco, CA: HarperSanFransciso, 2001). Concerning the objection that this entire discussion seems to be an antiquated defense of Anglo-colonialism and Western civilization, please see Chapters 2, 3, 6, 9 and Appendix B. The rejection of the ideal of civilization, or the uncritical rejection of the whole of Western civilization, is arguably a dated and unreflective contemporary fallacy.

70. "One of the most dangerous errors instilled into us by nineteenth-century progressive optimism is the idea that civilization is automatically bound to increase and spread. The lesson of history is the opposite; civilization is a rarity, attained with difficulty and easily lost." C. S. Lewis, "Our English Syllabus," in *Rehabilitations and Other Essays* (Oxford, England: Oxford University Press, 1939), 82.

71. "Semantic" is used here primarily in the general and informal sense of the analysis of the presuppositions and logic of word usages, word meanings, and word relationships. See Alan Cruse, *Meaning in Language: An Introduction to Semantics and Pragmatics*, 3rd ed., Oxford Textbooks in Linguistics (Oxford, England: Oxford University Press, 2011).

72. The following discussion should confirm the appropriateness of the *war* analogy, but for now the point of this analogy is not to suggest actual, physical military conflict or evoke militancy, but to emphasize how much is at stake; the intensity and global nature of the conflict; the impact on nations, lives, and communities; and, the close connection among semantics, power, and the battle for conceptual and geographical territory. The proper tone of apologetics will be addressed in the immediate pages that follow. It is not clear that the evangelical church has learned how epic these verbal battles are relative to our future and the future of civilization, not to mention the future of the church. This work will argue

that the abuse of language is often a greater threat to civilization than terrorism.

73. Donald T. Williams, "Discerning the Times: Why We Lost the Culture War and How to Make a Comeback," *Journal of International Society of Christian Apologetics* 9 (2016): 4–11, http://www.isca-apologetics.org/sites/default/files/JISCA-2016-v9. pdf. Barton Swaim, "The Left Won the Culture War. Will They be Merciful?" *The Washington Post*, 27 May 2016, https://www. washingtonpost.com/opinions/the-left-won-the-culture-war-will-they-be-merciful/2016/05/27/5c5014c2-2024-11e6-8690-f14ca9de2972_story.html?utm_term=.86a113384093. The role of semantic polemics and apologetics after the alleged loss of the culture war is the subject of this entire work. Regardless of the status of the war, the semantic conflicts and posturing continue across the globe.

74. Maura Lerner, "He, She, or Ze? Pronouns Could Pose Trouble under University of Minnesota Campus Policy," *Startribune*, July 14, 2018, accessed July 20, 2019, http://www. startribune.com/he-she-or-ze-pronouns-could-pose-trouble-under-u-campus-policy/488197021/.

75 Norman Geisler refers to the apologetic task as "pre-evangelism. Norman Geisler, *Christian Apologetics*, 2nd ed. (Grand Rapids, MI: Baker Academic, 2013).

76. 1 Peter 3:15; Ephesians 4:15. Denial of the harsh reality of war is futile and dangerous and fails to grasp the urgency of the moment. Denial is also incapable of motivating evangelicals to prepare, engage, and devise appropriate tactics to respond to the present conflict in the church, law, politics, media, education, and entertainment.

77. Polemics is used in this book as persuasion directed toward issues within the church, such as Luther's Ninety-Five Theses, or Augustine's critique of Pelagianism. "Polemics is that department of

theology which is concerned with the history of controversies maintained within or by the Christian Church, and with the conducting of such controversies in defense of doctrines held to be essential to Christian truth or in support of distinctive denominational tenets." C.A. Beckwith, The New Schaff-Herzog Encyclopedia of Religious Knowledge, Vol. 9, Petri–Reuchlin (Grand Rapids, MI: Baker Book House, 1954), https://www.ccel.org/s/schaff/encyc/encyc09/htm/iv.iii.x.htm. In contrast, apologetics is directed largely to critics or inquirers outside of the church—apologetics is the persuasive defense of the faith.

78. It is more than common knowledge that the definition of evangelicalism or American evangelicalism is fraught with challenges. See Darren Dochuk, Thomas S. Kidd, and Kurt W. Peterson, eds., *American Evangelicalism: George Marsden and the State of American Religious History* (Notre Dame, IN: University of Notre Dame Press, 2014).

79. Especially during the nineteenth and early twentieth centuries.

80. Many warned that liberal or modernist theology was essentially a new religion (e.g., Machen in *Christianity and Liberalism*, or Barth in *Der **Römerbrief*** and throughout his writings, or even the liberal Schweitzer's alarm concerning classical liberal Christology). What seems somewhat deficient in response to both modernist and postmodernist or ultramodernist challenges to orthodoxy is an emphasis on semantic apologetics and polemics that equip pastors, priests, and laity with concise and comprehensive semantic tools that expose these momentously consequential language games. Machen seems to have been the most intentional major response to such semantic distortions in the age of modernity, but this historical question would be a worthy research project of its own. H. Wayne House did some of this in his *Charts of Christian Theology and Doctrine*, but a half-century after the demise of classical liberalism.

81 D. K. Matthews, *A Theology of Cross and Kingdom: Theologia Crucis after the Reformation, Modernity, and Ultramodern Tribalistic Syncretism* (Eugene, OR: Pickwick Publishers, 2019), 213.

82. "31% Think U.S. Civil War Likely Soon," Rasmussen Reports, Wednesday, June 27, 2018, accessed July 2, 2018, http://www.rasmussenreports.com/public_content/politics/general_politics/june_2018/31_think_u_s_civil_war_likely_soon.

83. This image is from Google's public image file: "Free to use, share or modify, even commercially," accessed June 25, 2019, https://www.google.com/search?as_st=y&tbm=is-ch&as_q=ninotchka&as_epq=&as_oq=&as_eq=&cr=&as_site-search=&safe=active&tbs=sur:fmc#imgrc=Jot-tctaLp28-M:.

84. See Chapters 1, 2, and footnote 77 concerning the endless debate concerning the definition of evangelicalism or American evangelicalism.

85. Laurie Goldstein, "Outraged by Glenn Beck's Salvo, Christians Fire Back," *The New York Times*, March 11, 2010, http://www.nytimes.com/2010/03/12/us/12justice.html.

86. 2017 to the present, meaning since Donald Trump was elected.

87. See Lori Brandt Hale and Reggie L. Williams, "Is This a Bonhoeffer Moment? Lessons for American Christians from the Confessing Church in Germany," *Sojourners*, February 2018, accessed February 27, 2018, https://sojo.net/magazine/february-2018/this-bonhoeffer-moment-American-Christians Sojourners.

88. The argument that the pursuit of "civilization" is or has been simply a smokescreen for Western oppression or Christian "hegemony" will be addressed beginning in Chapter 1. Additionally,

this work is written in and assumes a Western context, but that does not in itself invalidate the arguments, or all aspects of Western Civilization, or the need for Christian scholars in the West to address their own context, or the potential global relevance and value of the arguments in this work.

89. Noah Rothman, *Unjust: Social Justice and the Unmaking of America* (Washington, DC: Regnery Publishing, 2019).

90. Rothman, *Unjust*, xvi.

91. Rothman, *Unjust*, 232.

92. Rothman, *Unjust*, 232–33.

93. Rothman, *Unjust*, 233.

94. Rothman, *Unjust*, 234–35.

95. Graham Hillard, "The Social-Justice Movement's Unjust Crusade," *National Review*, March 7, 2019, accessed July 2, 2019, https://www.nationalreview.com/magazine/2019/03/25/the-social-justice-movements-unjust-crusade/.

96. Henry was best known for using this phrase, the "crisis of truth and word." See Carl F. H. Henry, *God, Revelation and Authority*, 6 vols. (Wheaton, IL: Crossway Books, 1999).

97. Carl F. H. Henry, *Twilight of a Great Civilization: The Drift Toward New Paganism* (Westchester, IL: Crossway Books, 1988), 15.

98. Josh McDowell and Bob Hostetler, *Right from Wrong: What You Need to Know to Help Youth Make Right Choices* (Nashville, TN: Thomas Nelson Publishers, 1994).

99. Douglas Groothuis, *Truth Decay: Defending Christianity against the Challenges of Postmodernism* (Downers Grove, IL: InterVarsity, 2000). Nancy Pearcey, *Total Truth: Liberating Christianity from its Cultural Captivity* (Wheaton, IL: Crossway, 2004).

100. See James K. A. Smith, *Who's Afraid of Postmodernism: Taking Derrida, Lyotard, and Foucault to Church* (Grand Rapids, MI: Baker Academic, 2006).

101. That is, the preserving of biblical and Judeo-Christian orthodoxy in faith communities. One example of polemics would be how the church resisted, inside of the church, attempts to deny or diminish the humanity of Christ.

102. The respectful, loving and persuasive advocacy for and defense of core biblical and Christian beliefs, practices and allegiances or passions.

103. There were clearly other factors, such as the collapse of Enlightenment optimism, rationalism, faith in science, faith in reason, or sociological factors, but this general "death of God" drift in Western Civilization was not atomistic but organic, and it was animated by underlying beliefs and values. Judeo-Christian influence was replaced with legion alternative and sometimes anti-Christian and anti-biblical postures that fueled the rush toward the cultural death, or at least marginalization, of the heart orientation and core concept of God. This was a seismic shift still not fully comprehended, though perhaps well illustrated in Neitzsche's parables.

104. Francis A. Schaeffer, *How Should We Then Live: The Rise and Decline of Western Thought and Culture* (Wheaton, IL: Crossway Books, 1976), 19.

105. Schaeffer, *How Should We Then Live*, 227.

106. Schaeffer, *How Then Should We Live*, 227–28.

107. See works by James K. A. Smith in the Cultural Liturgy series such as volume 1, *Desiring the Kingdom: Worship, Worldview, and Cultural Formation* (Grand Rapids, MI: Baker Academic, 2009).

108. Schaeffer, *How Then Should We Live*, 212.

109. Charles L. Kesler, "America's Cold Civil War," *Imprimis*, 47, no. 10 (October 2018), accessed January 16, 2019, https://imprimis.hillsdale.edu/americas-cold-civil-war/.

110. Griffin Paul Jackson, "No Matter Where You Are, Religious Freedom Is Getting Worse," *Christianity Today*, accessed October 18, 2019, https://www.christianitytoday.com/news/2019/july/religious-freedom-getting-worse-pew-ministerial.html.

111. Stage one and two could be reversed, or simply viewed as coterminous.

112. Though the application of this law was less than ideal at times, it reflected the passion and conviction that normative truth was essential for civilization. See New England Historical Society, "How the Old Deluder Satan Act Made Sure Puritan Children Got Educated," accessed July 3, 2018, http://www.newenglandhistoricalsociety.com/old-deluder-satan-act-made-sure-puritan-children-got-educated/.

113. Jack Grove, "US Watchdogs Face 'Crisis' in Post-Truth Age: Increased Scrutiny of US sector and Distrust of Academics Puts Traditional Quality Assurance Models in Question," *CHEA Accreditation in the News*, from *The Times Higher Education Word University Rankings*, May 10, 2017, https://www.timeshighereducation.com/news/us-watchdogs-face-crisis-post-truth-age#survey-answer.

114. Dennis McCallum, ed., *The Death of Truth: What's Wrong with Multiculturalism, the Rejection of Reason and the*

New Postmodern Diversity? (Minneapolis, MN: Bethany House Publishers, 1996).

115. Garth Kant, "Obama Mourns Loss of 'Objective Truth,' Twitter Reminds Him of a Few Things," *Daily Caller*, July 17, 2018, accessed July 23, 2018, http://dailycaller.com/2018/07/17/obama-mourns-loss-of-objective-truth-twitter/.

116. Thomas Oden famously referred to historic orthodox Christianity as at least encompassing (1) five centuries, (2) four Councils, (3) three creeds, (4) two Testaments, and (5) one Bible.

117. See the Introduction and Chapter 1 for further explanation of the definition and usage on this work of polemics and apologetics.

118. See the Introduction concerning an appropriate response to the status of the culture wars in America.

119. Supreme Court of the United States, Opinions, October Term, 2017, "MASTERPIECE CAKESHOP, LTD., ET AL. v. COLORADO CIVIL RIGHTS COMMISSION ET AL.," accessed July 5, 2018, https://www.supremecourt.gov/opinions/17pdf/16-111_j4el.pdf.

120. Supreme Court, Opinions.

121. See Chapter 9.

122. The self is the prime or only reality, or the only reality that can be known to exist.

123. See Timothy Smith, *Revivalism and Social Reform: American Protestantism on the Eve of the Civil War* (Eugene, OR: Wipf and Stock Publishers, 2004). This work was first published in 1957. Also see Donald W. Dayton, *Discovering an Evangelical Heritage* (Grand Rapids, MI: Baker Academic, 1976).

124. Barna Group, "The End of Absolutes: America's New Moral Code," accessed July 5, 2018, https://www.barna.com/research/the-end-of-absolutes-americas-new-moral-code/.

125. Williams, "Discerning the Times," 4.

126. Justin Martyr, "The Defence and Explanation of Christian Faith and Practice," *Apologies*, A. W. F. Blunt (Cambridge: Cambridge Patristic Texts, 1911), in *The Early Christian Fathers: A Selection from the Writings of the Fathers from St. Clement of Rome to St. Athanasius*, ed. and trans. Henry Bettenson (Oxford, England: Oxford University Press, 1956), 58.

127. Andrew McGowan, "Eating People: Accusations of Cannibalism against Christians in the Second Century," *Journal of Early Christian Studies* 2 (1994): 413–42. Dr. McGowan is Dean and President of Berkeley Divinity School at Yale University and the McFaddin Professor of Anglican Studies and Pastoral Theology.

128. This thesis will be discussed and explored in much greater detail in Chapters 5, 6 and 10. Especially see the discussion concerning *polybabble* in Chapter 5.

129. "I don't believe the arc of the universe bends towards justice. I don't even believe in an arc. I believe in chaos. I believe powerful people who think they can make Utopia out of chaos should be watched closely. I don't know that it all ends badly. But I think it probably does." "But history is a brawny refutation for [the idea] that religion brings morality." Note the semantic ambiguity in how Coates used the term "religion," which makes him, at this point, a scholar on the level of John Lennon in *Imagine*. Ta-Nehisi Coates, "The Myth of Western Civilization," *The Atlantic* (Dec. 2013), https://www.theatlantic.com/international/archive/2013/12/the-myth-of-western-civilization/282704/.

130. Ultramodernism is syncretistic modernism. Modernism had faith in science, reason, technology, Western civilization,

and rational toleration as means toward achieving a bright future. Syncretistic modernism (called postmodernism by some) refers to modernism's current lingering meltdown where there is a loss of faith in the dream of modernist civilization, along with an inability to abandon many of the assumptions of modernism, much less to provide an ethical foundation capable of sustaining an aspirational civilization. The solution is a syncretistic (incoherent mixing) of beliefs, values, and practices from many sources and even a mixing of modern and anti-modern sentiments and values. For example, the syncretistic modernist, while flying first class on a plane and using a tablet to connect to the World Wide Web blogs about the evils of Western civilization. This is more than hypocrisy; this is extreme syncretism without apology, for there is no real need or even possibility of justifying beliefs after the death of any meaningful definition of truth and reason.

131. Coates, "Myth of Western Civilization."

132. Influenced by pop philosopher Francis Schaeffer, now allegedly "fallen from favor" or unknown by evangelical millennials. Mark Tooley, "Falwell, Trump, Christianity and Nationalism," *The Christian Post*, January 28, 2016, http://www.christianpost.com/news/falwell-trump-christianity-nationalism-156066/.

133. See Coates, "Myth of Western Civilization."

134. See again Tooley, "Falwell, Trump, Christianity and Nationalism." This blog by Mark Tooley presents the many nuances of *nationalism*, which well supports the thesis of this book. See also Norman Horn, "Christians Cannot Be Nationalists," Libertarian Christian Institute, September 1, 2011, http://libertarianchristians.com/2011/09/01/christians-cannot-be-nationalists/.

135. See *Resident Aliens: Life in the Christian Colony*, which makes the claim and extended argument that H. R. Niebuhr's *Christ and Culture* may well be the most destructive twentieth century work on faith and culture. Time and space disallow an analysis of

this allegation, but it is hoped that someday an argument will be advanced that *Resident Aliens* may well deserve such a dubious honor, and that a more appropriate sub-title for this work would be *Life in the Christian Ghetto*, objections notwithstanding. Stanley Hauerwas and William H. Willimon. *Resident Aliens: Life in the Christian Colony: A Provocative Christian Assessment of Culture and Ministry for People Who Know That Something Is Wrong*, exp. 25th anniv. ed. (Nashville, TN: Abingdon Press, 2014).

136. See CT Editors, "Is it Time for Evangelicals to Strategically Withdraw from the Culture: Four Evangelical Thinkers Consider What Rod Dreher's Benedict Option Means for the Church," *Christianity Today*, February 27, 2017, http://www.christianity-today.com/ct/2017/february-web-only/benedict-option-evangeli-cals-strategically-withdraw-culture.html; Rod Dreher, *The Benedict Option: A Strategy for Christians in a Post-Christian Nation* (New York, NY: Penguin Random House, 2017).

137. Eric Zorn, "'Hands Up, Don't Shoot' is a Lie Obscuring a Bigger Truth," *Chicago Tribune*, March 19, 2015, accessed July 5, 2019, https://www.chicagotribune.com/columns/eric-zorn/ct-fer-guson-brown-wilson-hands-up-shoot-holder-usdoj-perspec-0320-jm-20150319-column.html.

138. Mark Labberton, "Political Dealing: The Crisis of Evangelicalism," Fuller Theological Seminary, Fuller Studio, April 20, 2018, accessed June 26, 2019, https://www.fuller.edu/posts/political-dealing-the-crisis-of-evangelicalism/. "This speech was given by Fuller Seminary President Dr. Mark Labberton at a private meeting of evangelical leaders held at Wheaton College in Chicago, Illinois, on April 16, 2018. The following has been edited from his notes for clarity and to give context to excerpts that have been disseminated elsewhere."

139. Mark Labberton, "Introduction," in *Still Evangelical? Insiders Reconsider Political, Social, and Theological Meaning*,

Mark Labberton, ed. (Downers Grove, IL: InterVarsity Press, 2018), 1–17.

140. Stephen Young, "Robert Jeffress: Christians Who Don't Back Trump Are Morons, Like Christians in Nazi Germany," February 13, 2019, accessed June 26, 2019, https://www.dallasobserver.com/news/probation-system-traps-some-for-decades-11685068.

141. Michael Massing, "Making Sense of Evangelical's Support of Trump," *The Guardian*, June 7, 2019, accessed June 26, 2019, https://www.theguardian.com/commentisfree/2019/jun/07/evangelical-americans-trump-supporters-progressives.

142. Daniel Strand, "Religious Left Misdiagnoses Crisis of Evangelicalism," *Providence: A Journal of Christianity and American Foreign Policy*, May 1, 2018, accessed June 26, 2019, https://providencemag.com/2018/05/religious-left-misdiagnoses-crisis-evangelicalism-power-donald-trump/.

143. Ed Stetzer, *Christians in the Age of Outrage: How to Bring our Best when the World is at its Worst* (Carol Stream, IL: Tyndale House Publishers, 2018); David Kinnaman and Mark Matlock, with Amy Hawkins, *Faith for Exiles: 5 Ways for a New Generation to Follow Jesus in Digital Babylon* (Grand Rapids: Baker Books, 2019); Glenn T. Stanton, *The Myth of the Dying Church: How Christianity is Actually Thriving in America and in the World* (New York, New York: Hachette Book Group, 2019).

144. Kinnaman, *Exiles*, 33.

145. Usefulness, social value, or contribution to a better world.

146. Barack Obama, "'Call to Renewal' Keynote Address," *New York Times*, 28 June 2006, http://www.nytimes.com/2006/06/28/us/politics/2006obamaspeech.html. The President's actual delivery of the speech strayed a bit from the prepared text and diminished the importance of "no longer *just* a Christian nation," and was

heard as "no longer a Christian nation," which of course led to the firestorm that followed. See the actual video of the speech at Barack Obama, "'Call to Renewal' Keynote Address." *YouTube*, 28 June 2006, https://www.youtube.com/watch?v=BFeGY5gbpCM.

147. William J. Federer, *America's God and Country: Encyclopedia of Quotations* (St. Louis, MO: Amerisearch, 2000), 378–79. Also see this University of California (Santa Barbara) resource for the full text of Abraham Lincoln's proclamation, Abraham Lincoln, "Proclamation 85 — Proclaiming a Day of National Humiliation, Prayer, and Fasting," August 12, 1861, online by Gerhard Peters and John T. Woolley, *The American Presidency Project*, http://www.presidency.ucsb.edu/ws/?pid=69979. The full text only enhances the argument of this present book:

By the President of the United States of America
A Proclamation

Whereas a joint committee of both Houses of Congress has waited on the President of the United States and requested him to "recommend a day of public humiliation, prayer, and fasting to be observed by the people of the United States with religious solemnities and the offering of fervent supplications to Almighty God for the safety and welfare of these States, His blessings on their arms, and a speedy restoration of peace;" and

Whereas it is fit and becoming in all people at all times to acknowledge and revere the supreme government of God, to bow in humble submission to His chastisements, to confess and deplore their sins and transgressions in the full conviction that the fear of the Lord is the beginning of wisdom, and to pray with all fervency and contrition for the pardon of their past offenses and for a blessing upon their present and prospective action; and

Whereas when our own beloved country, once, by the blessing of God, united, prosperous, and happy, is now afflicted with faction and civil war, it is peculiarly fit for us to recognize the hand of God in this terrible visitation, and in sorrowful remembrance of our own faults and crimes as a nation and as individuals to humble ourselves before Him and to pray for His mercy—to pray that we may be spared further punishment, though most justly deserved; that our arms may be blessed and made effectual for the reestablishment of law, order, and peace throughout the wide extent of our country; and that the inestimable boon of civil and religious liberty, earned under His guidance and blessing by the labors and sufferings of our fathers, may be restored in all its original excellence:

Therefore I, Abraham Lincoln, President of the United States, do appoint the last Thursday in September next as a day of humiliation, prayer, and fasting for all the people of the nation. And I do earnestly recommend to all the people, and especially to all ministers and teachers of religion of all denominations and to all heads of families, to observe and keep that day according to their several creeds and modes of worship in all humility and with all religious solemnity, to the end that the united prayer of the nation may ascend to the Throne of Grace and bring down plentiful blessings upon our country.

In testimony whereof I have hereunto set my hand and caused the seal of the United States to be affixed, this 12th day of August, A.D. 1861, and of the Independence of the United States of America the eighty-sixth.

ABRAHAM LINCOLIN.
By the President:
WILLIAM H. SEWARD, *Secretary of State.*

148. Federer, *America's God and Country*, 383–84. Also see the University of California (Santa Barbara) collection of primary sources: Abraham Lincoln: "Proclamation 97."

149. Federer, *America's God and Country*, 180.

150. Barna Group, "The State of the Church 2016," accessed January 19, 2019, https://www.barna.com/research/state-church-2016/.

151. Frank Newport, "2017 Update on Americans and Religion," accessed January 19, 2019, https://news.gallup.com/poll/224642/2017-update-americans-religion.aspx.

152. This table in the Appendix is illustrative and not exhaustive.

153. John Ankerberg, "Homosexuality and Sexual Ethics–Program 1," *The John Ankerberg Show*, 1989, https://www.jashow.org/articles/general/homosexuality-and-sexual-ethics-program-1/.

154. This is only an illustrative mini-lexicon from Pauline polemics and apologetics.

155. See Galatians concerning legalism. See 1 Corinthians 5 and countless other Pauline passages concerning antinomianism.

156. Friedrich Schleiermacher, *On Religion: Speeches to Its Cultured Despisers,* trans. John Oman (New York, NY: Harper and Row, Publishers, 1968), 15.

157. If these progressives had simply left their orthodox denominations and started new religious movements or joined the Unitarian church, which dates back to the sixteenth century, or early nineteenth-century Transcendentalism, they could have preserved their ethical integrity. The wholesale and often covert redefinition of Christianity, however, simply lacked transparency and ethical integrity.

158. See Schleiermacher, *On Religion*, and especially see his discussion of feeling throughout the text, with a critical introduction to feeling in Speech Two. Also see his classic *The Christian Faith*, and his discussion of feeling, religious consciousness, and Christology throughout the entire work.

159. Rudolf Bultmann, *New Testament and Mythology and Other Basic Writings*, selected, ed. and tran. Schubert M. Ogden (Minneapolis, MN: Fortress Press, 1984).

160. Originally called *The Christian Oracle* (1884) and dedicated to mainline and progressive Christianity on the eve of the twentieth century, it affirmed that these progressive Christian values could issue forth in a "Christian Century." *Christianity Today*, founded in 1956 by Billy Graham and others, sought to provide an American evangelical alternative and has arguably eclipsed the former magazine's influence.

161. This is only an illustrative and comparative mini-lexicon to assist with the purpose of this book. The classical liberal variations were more varied and complex than what is provided here. These types of comparisons are also possible with other theological traditions (e.g., liberation theology, neo-orthodoxy), a task that exceeds the purpose of this book.

162. While it is true that there was often much controversy concerning what was or was not essential (e.g., Baptism), normative truth was affirmed, and a broad theological consensus (Nicene, Trinitarian, revelatory, supernaturalistic) is identifiable across the many streams of orthodox Christian theology.

163. Pew Research Center, "The U.S. as 100 people: Two Jews, one Muslim and 71 Christians," November 7, 2016, accessed October 19, 2019, https://www.pewresearch.org/fact-tank/2016/11/14/if-the-u-s-had-100-people-charting-americans-religious-affiliations/ft_16-10-13_100religious_affiliation420px/.

164. Pew Research Center, "In U.S., Decline of Christianity Continues at Rapid Pace: An Update on America's Changing Religious Landscape," October 17, 2019, accessed October 23, 2019, https://www.pewforum.org/2019/10/17/in-u-s-decline-of-christianity-continues-at-rapid-pace/.

165. Address delivered on September 20, 1912, at the opening of the 101st session of Princeton Theological Seminary. See the full speech within Machen, *What is Christianity*, 162.

166. Colossians 1:22, emphasis added.

167. Illustrative views: perspectival, empirical, correspondence, or the Nietzschean rejection of modernist, Christian, and disembodied truth, if not truth all together. Of course Kant's epistemology forever separated us from reality, and Nietzsche's epistemology forever separated us from anything that remotely resembled transcendent truth, which is far more extreme than a rejection of modernistic or rationalistic truth and reason.

168. Sometimes referred to as archetypal knowledge: "Alongside of the archetypal knowledge of God, found in himself, there is also an ectypal knowledge of Him, given to man by revelation. The latter is related to the former as a copy to the original, and therefore does not possess the same measure of clearness and perfection. All our knowledge of God is derived from His self-revelation in nature and in Scripture. Consequently, our knowledge of God is on the one hand ectypal and analogical, but on the other hand also true and accurate, since it is a copy of the archetypal knowledge which God has of himself." Louis Berkhof, *Systematic Theology*, new comb. ed. (Grand Rapids, MI: Eerdmans, 1996), 35. Unfortunately, this important distinction has not always been applied to knowledge in general and has focused on the knowledge of God or theology proper. Certainly if our knowledge of God is something like ectypal, then our knowledge of the world or reality generally (Truth) would also have to be distinguished from God's knowledge of reality and the world (TRUTH), and even our knowledge of reality and the world would not be ultimately autonomous but revelation dependent. I opt for a revelation-dependent (including via the *imago Dei*) and something close to a critical realist epistemology.

169. Not just used in a modernistic sense of objective modernist knowledge versus the alternative but referring more to non-normative truth (and ethics) in view of the increasing loss of Truth in contemporary civilization.

170. See the Preface and prior chapters concerning Carl F. H. Henry and the crisis of truth and word.

171. In the sense of the death of a stable foundation for conscience and empathy.

172. Edwin Gaustad and Mark Noll, *A Documentary History of Religion in America to 1877*, 3rd ed. (Grand Rapids, MI: Eerdmans, 2003). Harvard, William and Mary, Yale, the College of Philadelphia (Princeton), Columbia, Brown, Rutgers, and Dartmouth. This is not to say that occasional sightings of orthodoxy have been nonexistent in recent decades at these schools.

173. See chapter 2 of Gaustad and Noll, *A Documentary History*.

174. Harvard University, Harvard at a Glance, History, the "Harvard Shield," accessed July 6, 2018, http://www.harvard.edu/about-harvard/harvard-glance/history. The sketch is used with the written permission of the artist, Marcia J. Crots, and the original logo is a public domain item.

175. This is not to contend that the perspectival or even the passionate, emotional, embodied, biased, and prejudiced dimensions of the quest for knowledge are to be ignored. In addition, Christian theology has, for centuries, including Augustine, also referenced the noetic or mental dimension of the fall relative to this quest. Contemporary epistemology needs to take Kant and Nietzsche (and many others) into account while also recognizing their fallacious and often self-contradictory and self-stultifying conclusions and applications.

176. Emphasis added. See Gaustad and Noll, *Documentary History*.

177. Concerning Logocentric language and the contemporary crisis, see volume one and especially volume two (*God who Speaks and Shows*) of the massive six-volume work by Carl F. H. Henry,

God, Revelation and Authority, 6 vols. (Wheaton, IL: Crossway Books, 1999).

178. The context of the full quote is important for understanding Nietzsche: "There are many kinds of eyes. Even the Sphinx has eyes—and consequently there are many kinds of 'truths,' and consequently there is no truth." Friedrich Nietzsche, *Book Three: Principles of a New Evaluation of the Will to Power*, ed. Walter Kaufmann, trans. Walter Kaufmann and R. J. Hollingdale (New York, NY: Random House, 1967), 291. Nietzsche's argument about language contains some Truth, at least valid deductive reasoning. If the nonexistence of God obtains, and if the modernistic project has failed, especially regarding Truth and reason, then truth may be described (though not True) as embodied, evolutionary correspondent will-to-power. Infinite interpretations obtain and the only facts are interprefacts. "What therefore is truth? A mobile army of metaphors, metonymies, anthropomorphisms: in short a sum of human relations which became poetically and rhetorically intensified, metamorphosed, adorned, and after long usage seem to a nation fixed, canonic and binding; truths are illusions of which one has forgotten that they are illusions; worn-out metaphors which have become powerless to affect the senses; coins which have their obverse effaced and now are no longer of account as coins but merely as metal." Friedrich Nietzsche, "On Truth and Falsity in Their Extramoral Sense (1873)," in *Philosophical Writings*, ed. Reinhold Grimm and Caroline Molina y Vedia (New York, NY: Continuum, 1997), 92. An analysis of truth, absolute truth, perspectivalism, or Nietzsche's nuanced view of truth far exceeds the purpose, thesis, and necessary limitations of this book. Suffice it to say that while Nietzsche properly identified the volitional and emotional influences on the philosophical quest and modernist claims to objectivity (see the following quote), his utter theological failure relative to the epistemological implications of the existence of a Triune, personal, transcendent, revelatory and immanent Creator who created humanity *imago Dei* undermined all of his affirmations concerning the nature and attainability of Truth. It is critical for evangelicals to affirm that the rejection of modernism

does not require the rejection of some measure of normative Truth. Normative Truth can be maintained and even given passion and life or desire or longing without accommodating either to modernism or postmodernism, and the future of church and civilization may well depend on this important semantic distinction. Nietzsche observes, "To eliminate the will, to suspend the emotions altogether, provided it could be done—surely this would be to castrate the intellect, would it not?" Friedrich Nietzsche, *On the Genealogy of Morals*, trans. Francis Golffing (New York: Doubleday, 1956), 256.

179. Merely a matter of perspective, such as food preferences.

180. See the following Barna data: Barna Group, "Christians React to the Legalization of Same-Sex Marriage: 9 Key Findings," 1 July 2015, https://www.barna.org/barna-update/culture/723-christians-react-to-the-legalization-of-same-sex-marriage-9-key-findings#.VlNO8XarRD8; Barna Group, "5 Reasons Millennials Stay Connected to Church," 17 September 2013, https://www.barna.org/barna-update/millennials/635-5-reasons-millennials-stay-connected-to-church#.VlNFVXarRD8; Barna Group, "Scotland: Lessons for Effective Ministry in a Post-Christian Context," August 27, 2015, https://www.barna.org/barna-update/culture/730-scotland-lessons-for-effective-ministry-in-a-post-christian-context#.VlNMXnarRD8. Also see the Gallup data, such as, Gallup, "In Depth: Topics A to Z—Religion," accessed July 6, 2018, http://www.gallup.com/poll/1690/religion.aspx.

181. "The Declaration of Independence: The Want, Will, and Hopes of the People," July 4, 1776, UShistory.org, accessed July 23, 2018, http://www.ushistory.org/DECLARATION/document/.

182. Samuel Rutherford, *Lex, Rex, or the Law and the Prince: A Dispute for the Just Prerogative of King and People* (Seattle, WA: CreateSpace Independent Publishing Platform, 2012).

183. John Paul Sartre, *Being and Nothingness* (New York, NY: Washington Square, 1966), 762, 766. Note that some who

misunderstand *Being and Nothingness* would argue that Sartre rejects the project of being God, but these critics fail to see that Sartre references the project to become God in two senses or nuances. One is the flawed human desire to transcend human existence by positing or aspiring (Feuerbach) to be a transcendent personal God. Sartre, of course, rejects this human project for transcendence since his entire philosophy is the outworking of atheism. Yet the absence of God also creates, for Sartre, a second sense of becoming God, and that is that humanity now must *function* as God relative to truth, ethics, and personal meaning. This is quite an *angst*-ridden project, but it is the human situation in the shadow of *The Wall*.

184. While not endorsing everything in Schaeffer's popular level philosophy, his argument concerning how the breakdown in civilization leads to anarchy and/or a "strong man" is compelling, rooted in historical experience and evidence and rather applicable to contemporary world events. However, as noted in the introduction, history is fluid and the "strong man" trajectory is only one of many historical possibilities. Schaeffer, *How Should We Then Live*.

185. Brian Duigman, "Postmodernism," *Encyclopedia Britannica*, 2014, accessed July 23, 2018, https://www.britannica.com/topic/postmodernism-philosophy.

186. Gary Aylesworth, "Postmodernism," *Stanford Encyclopedia of Philosophy*, revised 2015, accessed July 23, 2018, https://plato.stanford.edu/entries/postmodernism/.

187. Jean-François, Lyotard. *The Postmodern Condition: A Report on Knowledge*, trans. Geoff Bennington and Brian Massumi (1997; repr., Minneapolis, MN: U of Minnesota Press, 1984).

188. Kelley with (and) Dew provide a helpful summary chart on key postmodern affirmations, as well as more extended narrative material on these key beliefs. The ten commandments of postmodernism are adapted directly from this material. See: Stewart

E. Kelley with James K. Dew Jr., *Understanding Postmodernism: A Christian Perspective* (Downers Grove, IL: IVP Academic, Intervarsity Press, 2017), 269, 5-8. This work may be the best and recent evangelical summary of a mature postmodernism. However, Kelly and Dew may not fully distinguish between cultural and civilizational postmodernism and the diverse and more nuanced perspectives of postmodern scholars. *Who's Afraid of Postmodernism?* Certainly not the author of the book and question, James Smith, or the author of this work, *Seduced*. No one should be afraid of modernism or postmodernism, but critically evaluate both movements, their cultural impact, and discern and distinguish the difference between their half-truths, whole truths, and hidden deceptions. Additionally, the cultural toxicity of cultural postmodernism must be affirmed along with the need to dialog constructively and empathetically with postmodern scholars. It is fine to dialog constructively with the academic community, but equally needful are clear statements on the adverse impact of most varieties of postmodernism on the church and culture. Yes, modernism had a negative impact on faith communities and civilization as well, along with its benefits.

189. Jim Dennison, "The Ten Commandments of Postmodernism," Stephanie, Engaging College Students [blog], no date, accessed November 25, 2019, https://stephaniemgates. com/resources/engaging-college-students.

190. Thomas C. Oden, *After Modernity ... What? Agenda for Theology* (Grand Rapids, MI: Zondervan, 1990).

191. Kelly (with Dew), *Understanding Postmodernism*, 75.

192. Saul D. Alinsky, *Rules for Radicals: A Practical Primer for Realist Radicals* (New York, NY: Vintage Books, Random House, 1971), ix.

193. E.g., see American Humanist Association: Good without a God, Press Release, February 25, 2016, "AHA Affirms Commitment

to Social Justice Advocacy," accessed July 23, 2018, https://amer-icanhumanist.org/press-releases/2016-02-humanists-affirm-com-mitment-to-social-justice-advoca/.

194. See Brian Barry, *Why Social Justice Matters* (Cambridge, England: Polity Press, 2005).

195. Olaskey, *The Tragedy*.

196. Michael Novak, *The Spirit of Democratic Capitalism*, rev. ed. (Lanham, MD: Madison Books, 1990).

197. Ben Johnson, "Unitarian Leftist: Socialism is Not Ethically Superior to Capitalism," Acton Institute, April 26, 2019, accessed June 24, 2019, https://acton.org/publications/transatlantic/2019/04/26/unitarian-leftist-socialism-not-ethically-superior-capitalism.

198. For a less academic summary of the socialistic backfire, see Michael Novak, *Writing from Left to Right: My Journey from Liberal to Conservative* (New York, NY: Image, 2013).

199. Olaskey, *Tragedy*.

200. Lewis, "Our English Syllabus," 82.

201. The idea that a utopian world simply is not possible. For Christian theology, utopia is possible but Parousia dependent.

202. Foundationless not in the sense of a Cartesian or phil-osophical foundationalism, which is certainly *passé*, but simply lacking any norm for truth or morality that can serve as a plumb line to assess the development of countless and rival civiliza-tional projects.

203. It should be noted that advocacy for secular, post-Chris-tian, politically liberal (evangelical and nonevangelical) civili-zational semantics has received plenty of press and will not be

rehearsed here. E.g., Pierre Wilbert Orelus, *Social Justice for the Oppressed: Critical Educators Speak Out* (Lanham, MD: Rowman and Littlefield, 2017); Barry, *Why Social Justice Matters*.

204. Emma Pettit, "'My Merit and My Blackness Are Fused to Each Other,'" *The Chronicle of Higher Education*, January 11, 2019, accessed July 14, 2019, https://www.chronicle.com/article/My-MeritMy-Blackness/245462?cid=db&elqTrackId=5f28ddb7d44546aab14a97c70194e31f&elq=b98e8e9cd76042a2b6ecaec27df71508&elqaid=21946&elqat=1&elqCampaignId=10724.

205. See, for example, the *Occupy Wall Street* article by Gina Crosley-Corcoran, "Explaining White Privilege to a Broke White Person…," accessed July 6, 2018, http://occupywallstreet.net/story/explaining-white-privilege-broke-white-person.

206. Paul James, *Globalism, Nationalism, Tribalism: Bringing Theory Back In* (London, England: Sage Publications, 2006); Barrie Axford, *Theories of Globalization* (Cambridge, England: Polity Press, 2013).

207. See chapter 8 of Donald W. Dayton, *Discovering*.

208. Theological anthropology refers to one's view or theology of human nature.

209. See Washington State University's Tim Kohler, writing in the journal *American Antiquity*. Science 2.0, News Staff, "The Most Violent Era in America Was Before Europeans Arrived," August 3, 2014, accessed July 23, 2018, https://www.science20.com/news_articles/the_most_violent_era_in_america_was_before_europeans_arrived-141847.

210. Kate Shellnut, "Americans Warm Up to Every Religious Group Except Evangelicals," *Christianity Today*, February 15, 2017, http://www.christianitytoday.com/gleanings/2017/february/americans-warm-feelings-religious-groups-evangelicals-pew.html.

See also this online article: "Americans Express Increasingly Warm Feelings toward Religious Groups," Pew Research Center, February 15, 2017, http://www.pewforum.org/2017/02/15/americans-express-increasingly-warm-feelings-toward-religious-groups/.

211. Paul G. Hiebert, "Beyond Anti-Colonialism to Globalism," *Missiology: An International Review* 19, no. 3 (1991): 263.

212. See Smith, *Revivalism*.

213. See the Benedict option referenced in Chapter 3.

214. Beckwith and Koukl, *Relativism*.

215. E.g., see Patrick Buchanan's blogs, "Patrick J. Buchanan— Official Website," accessed July 23, 2018, http://buchanan.org/blog/, especially those addressing America First, http://buchanan.org/blog/?s=america+first.

216. Long-time professor of Baylor University (over 50 years). These comments were made in class discussions during my PhD program (1992), long before *postmodernism* was a common buzz word.

217 Ludwig Wittgenstein, *Philosophical Investigations*, trans. G. E. M. Anscombe (London: Pearson, 1973).

218. This is an intentional reference to a magazine founded with somewhat utopian and progressive ideas for the twentieth century.

219. Paul G. Hiebert, "Beyond Anti-Colonialism to Globalism," *Missiology: An International Review* 19, no. 3 (1991): 263.

220. The italicized words in the biblical passages were in the original of the NASB version utilized.

221. Matthew W. Bates argues recently that the essence of faith is "salvation by allegiance alone." Fortunately, he better nuances the thesis and the nature of faith throughout the book, yet the title and the foci of the book do seem to give insufficient attention to the transformational open heart surgery and new covenant that makes allegiance and faith with works possible. I remember once having a conversation with a bright young Islamic scholar from Iran. He struggled with the cheap grace of faith, but seemed to also resist a reductionistic view of salvation in Islam. For him, "submission" to Allah must include grace, and allegiance seemed like what he was communicating concerning the true nature of salvation. He simply could not grasp how cheap grace and faith without works was transcended by radical, transforming grace-based faith that birthed allegiant faith with works. My preference in view of the biblical mega-theme of the new covenant is to nuance faith as a trust that includes and engenders allegiance rather than nuancing allegiance to include new covenant faith. See: Matthew W. Bates, Salvation by Grace Alone: Rethinking Faith, Works, and the Gospel of Jesus the King (Grand Rapids: Baker Academic, 2017). Bates also has a related work that will appear sometime in 2019 (*Gospel Allegiance*, Brazos Press) that perhaps will refine the thesis which seems to be endorsed by Scot Mcknight.

222. See Edwin S. Gaustad, *Faith of the Founders: Religion and the New Nation, 1776-1826* (Waco, TX: Baylor University Press, 2004); Joe Carter, "Founding Believers," *First Things*, September 22, 2010, https://www.firstthings.com/web-exclusives/2010/09/founding-believers. Carter's article is a helpful assessment and summary of David L. Holmes's *The Faiths of the Founding Fathers*. Also see Mark David Hall, "Did America Have a Christian Founding?" May 13, 2011 (Heritage Lectures, Washington, DC: Heritage Foundation, June 7, 2011). The numerous works on this topic should be read critically, including the works of evangelical author David Barton, but the net impact of Barton's many works irrefutably establishes the argument associated with this endnote. See, for example, these works by Barton: *The Jefferson Lies: Exposing the Myths You've Always Believed About Thomas*

Jefferson (2016); *Separation of Church & State: What the Founders Meant* (2007); *America's Godly Heritage* (2009); *Original Intent: The Courts, the Constitution, & Religion* (2010). It is fair to say that Barton is despised by those believing he is falsely imposing an evangelical revisionism on American history, just as Barton and many evangelicals have little patience with progressive revisionists who seek to gut entirely the reality and significance of Judeo-Christian influence on the American experiment. This debate will not be settled here, and the writings on this are many, perhaps too many, but what Barton does present is documented evidence based on actions, direct quotes, and historical artifacts that clearly make the point that the Founding Fathers were not in sync with contemporary notions of a secular or post-Christian-influenced America—and the attendant distortions and abuses of the concept of freedom of speech.

223. For extensive and detailed documentation of these references, see Tara Ross and Joseph C. Smith, Jr., *Under God: George Washington and the Question of Church and State* (Dallas, TX: Spence Publishing, 2008), xx, 3, 17, 27, 69, 92, 126. Emphasis added.

224. Federer, *America's God and Country*, 23–24. Emphasis added.

225. Alexander Hamilton, James Madison, and John Jay, *The Federalist*, ed. Benjamin Fletcher Wright (New York, NY: Barnes and Noble Books), 1961.

226. Federer, *America's God and Country*.

227. *The Founders on God and Government*, ed. Daniel L. Dreisbach, Mark D. Hall, and Jeffrey H. Morrison (Lanham, MD: Rowman and Littlefield, 2004).

228. Novak, "Foreword: Religious Liberty," *The Founders on God*, ix.

229. Novak, "Foreword," x.

230. Novak, "Foreword," x–xi.

231. Cited in Federer, *America's God and Country,* 247.

232. Cited in Federer, *America's God and Country,* 246.

233. Novak, "Foreword," xi.

234. Novak, "Foreword," xii.

235. Novak, "Foreword," xiv.

236. Novak, "Foreword," xii–xiii.

237. Novak, "Foreword," xiii.

238. Novak, "Foreword," xiii–xiv.

239. Novak, "Foreword," xiv.

240. Novak, "Foreword," 15.

241. See Ruth Ben-Ghiat, "Liberals are Reclaiming Patriotism from the Right," CNN Opinion, (Updated) July 2, 2017, accessed July 23, 2018, http://www.cnn.com/2017/07/02/opinions/liberal-patriotism-rise-opinion-ben-ghiat/index.htm.

242. E.g., Neo-Nazis or white supremacists.

243. George Washington, "Farewell Address," September 19, 1796, in Federer, *God and Country*, 661. See also Ross and Smith, *Under God*, xx, for additional documentation.

244. James C. Livingston, *Modern Christian Thought: From the Enlightenment to Vatican II* (New York, NY: MacMillan Publishing, 1971), 17–20.

245. This research is well-known, but see Bradford Richardson, "Liberal Professors Outnumber Conservatives Nearly 12 to 1, Study Finds," *The Washington Times*, October 6, 2016; Scott Jaschik, "Professors and Politics: What the Research Says," *Inside Higher Education*, February 27, 2017. Jascchik's meta-analysis is interesting but contains so many logical flaws, false dichotomies, and reliance upon student and faculty perceptions in environments where conformity may be required to succeed that it is hard to assess, but Jaschik's argument is that the problem of liberal bias is overstated and nuanced (e.g., different regions have different data, different majors have different data). There is some truth to his argument, but the real issue here is what is being taught in the classroom, which inevitably influences and shapes culture, not whether a student had a good experience at the university. The implied suggestion that what is being taught in the classroom is not greatly framed by the orientation of the professor and not influential on students seems to lack credibility and defy common sense. In addition, college and university learning is not limited to the classroom, so the general culture of such institutions must also be assessed.

246. See John West's article, "Are Young People Losing Their Faith Because of Science," http://www.discovery.org/scripts/viewDB/filesDB-download.php?command=download&id=9791, for a helpful overview of the debate.

247. These are but a few illustrations of harsh and appropriate biblical judgments. See Matthew 23 or Galatians 1.

248. Brett McCracken, *Gray Matters: Navigating the Space between Legalism and Liberty* (Grand Rapids, MI: Baker, 2013).

249. Michael Novak, "Social Justice: Not What You Think It Is," *The Heritage Foundation. Report: Poverty and Inequality,*

December 29, 2009, accessed December 19, 2019, http://www. heritage.org/poverty-and-inequality/report/social-justice-not-what-you-think-it. Emphasis added.

250. Michael Novak, "Defining Social Justice," *First Things,* December 2000, accessed January 23, 2019, https://www.firstthings.com/article/2000/12/defining-social-justice.

251. See their home page at https://sojo.net/, accessed July 23, 2018.

252. This is well-known and researched, but see http://www.cnn.com/2017/04/28/politics/pew-analysis-white-evangelicals-trump/. See also http://www.pewresearch.org/fact-tank/2017/04/26/among-white-evangelicals-regular-church-goers-are-the-most-supportive-of-trump/?utm_source=Pew+Research+Center&utm_campaign=f01dd8b2e6-EMAIL_CAMPAIGN_2017_04_26&utm_medium=email&utm_term=0_3e953b9b70-f01dd8b2e6-400296741; http://www.pewresearch.org/fact-tank/2016/03/14/exit-polls-and-the-evangelical-vote-a-closer-look/; and, http://www.pewresearch.org/fact-tank/2016/11/09/behind-trumps-victory-divisions-by-race-gender-education/.

253. Vox, "Poll: White Evangelical Support for Trump Is at an All-Time High," accessed July 6, 2018, https://www.vox.com/identities/2018/4/20/17261726/poll-prri-white-evangelical-support-for-trump-is-at-an-all-time-high.

254. King James Version is used here due to its common usage. Mark 16:15.

255. Bruce Thornton, "The Truth About Western 'Colonialism,'" Hoover Institution, July 21, 2015, accessed November 26, 2019, https://www.hoover.org/research/truth-about-western-colonialism.

256. Thornton, "The Truth."

257. See Acts 17 and 1 Peter 3:15.

258. Brooke Noel Moore and Kenneth Bruder, *Philosophy: The Power of Ideas* (New York, NY: McGraw-Hill, 2014).

259. And practice loving our neighbor.

260. John D. Inazu, *Confident Pluralism: Surviving and Thriving through Deep Difference* (Chicago, IL: University of Chicago Press, 2016).

261. Henry, *God, Revelation and Authority*, 17–31.

262. This table is illustrative in order to cluster related topics (semantic clusters) relative to the discussion. This table is preliminary for the purpose of dialog, not exhaustive or comprehensive, and narrative in nature rather than *bumper sticker style* simplistic definitions in order to connect to the previous discussion and clarify the contemporary context (semantic tapestry) of the terms. The primary purpose of the table is to serve as a tool for Christian leaders who resonate with these semantic distinctions. The contemporary sound bite culture fits well in a post-Truth culture where the genuine pursuit of Truth, understanding, and collegial dialog is abandoned in favor of pure advocacy. This table and work hope to move beyond some of the semantic ambiguity in the contemporary conversation via more narrative-oriented definitions and contrasts.

263. *Oxford Learner's Dictionaries.*

264. *Oxford English Dictionary: The Definitive Record of the English Language* (Oxford, England: Oxford University Press, 2016), http://www.oed.com/. "The *Oxford English Dictionary* (*OED*) is widely regarded as the accepted authority on the English language. It is an unsurpassed guide to the meaning, history, and pronunciation of 600,000 words—past and present—from across the English-speaking world. As a historical dictionary, the *OED* is very different from Dictionaries of current English, in which

the focus is on present-day meanings. You'll still find present-day meanings in the *OED*, but you'll also find the history of individual words, and of the language—traced through 3 million quotations, from classic literature and specialist periodicals to film scripts and cookery books." http://public.oed.com/about/

265. See http://www.telegraph.co.uk/culture/books/book-news/7970391/Oxford-English-Dictionary-will-not-be-printed-again.html. Alastair Jamieson, "Oxford English Dictionary 'Will Not be Printed Again,'" *The Telegraph*, August 29, 2010.

266. *Merriam Webster's Dictionary for Learners* (2017), defines "Lexicon" as "the words used in a language or by a person or group of people.'" http://www.learnersdictionary.com/definition/lexicon. *The Oxford Learner's Dictionaries* (2017) defines "Lexicon" as "the vocabulary of a person, language, or branch of knowledge." https://en.oxforddictionaries.com/definition/lexicon. All material in Table 5 is directly quoted from the respective sources; hence, quotation marks are not included for ease of reading and usage.

267. The definition is not available (NA) in referenced source.

268. The pro-environment/creation care debate and semantic positioning are well-known and have received almost *ad nauseam* attention elsewhere. Consistent with the methodology of this work and how other terms have been handled, the definition of a legitimate biblical concern (e.g., creation care or stewardship) should be distinguished from an alleged political means of caring for the creation. In other words, evangelicals with different views on the *how* of creation care or stewardship, which should continue to be vigorously debated, should not be viewed *a priori* or presumptively as for or against genuine creation care. Indeed, political solutions and tactics claiming to be biblical may well undercut the very creation care claimed by the respective movement.

269. See their home page at https://acton.org/.

270. See Table 5 for the full quotation concerning ethnocentrism.

271. Michael Novak, "Social Justice: Not What You Think It Is," *The Heritage Foundation. Report: Poverty and Inequality*, December 29, 2009, http://www.heritage.org/poverty-and-inequality/report/social-justice-not-what-you-think-it.

272. Sarah Pulliam Bailey, "Russell Moore Wants to Keep Christianity Weird," *Christianity Today*, September 8, 2015, http://www.christianitytoday.com/ct/2015/september/russell-moore-wants-to-keep-christianity-weird.html. To be fair, Moore is not calling for cultural disengagement or abandonment of the fight for religious liberty. However, in view of his embrace of "cultural margins," his nonnuanced emphasis on biblical teachings on aliens and exiles, his warnings not to pursue a "Christian America" (note the semantic ambiguity and false dichotomy here), and his salient Baptist or Anabaptist tendencies defining the goal of the gospel as gathering the redeemed in juxtaposition to civilizational influence, he did almost seem energized that the loss of cultural power was, as Bailey writes, "the best thing that ever happened" to evangelicals. This giddiness is just as troubling as the triumphalist, corporate American prosperity gospel he rightly criticizes that was characteristic of some wings of prior evangelical generations. As argued previously, the evangelical church needs to move beyond Americentric and Eurocentric conceptualizations of evangelical polemics, apologetics, and civilizational influence. We not only want to redeem from every tribe and tongue and nation, but we want truly to redeem and seek to be the church, salt, and light across the globe. We are not merely, as D. L. Moody put it, grabbing survivors in a lifeboat from the sinking vessel called planet earth. We are holistically redeeming co-travelers on the journey and not only preparing them for time and eternity but repairing the ship and influencing its course. Regardless of the future of America or Europe, the future journey of the church and civilization(s) will be greatly impacted by intentional semantic polemics and apologetics and unrelenting tactful, loving cultural engagement as we seek to prepare for and approximate the New Creation.

273. "Victory Reports," ACLJ, https://aclj.org/victory-reports, accessed July 25, 2019. While not embracing all of the activities of any organization, including groups with very different agendas than the ACLJ such as *Sojourners,* the point here is that countless faith based organizations are sacrificing much in very difficult trenches to secure freedoms for all, including the freedoms of the critics of such cultural engagement who parasite off of their herculean labors.

274. See Ed Stetzer, "Religious Liberty and the 'Culture War,'" accessed October 2, 2019, http://www.christianitytoday.com/edstetzer/2014/february/religious-liberty.html. In this survey most Protestant pastors prefer to speak of "losing" rather than "lost," but this survey was prior to a number of key events such as the 2015 U.S. Supreme Court ruling on the redefinition of marriage.

275. E.g., by the political correctness movement, progressive theology, or the New Atheism.

276. For those assuming a more politically liberal posture and desiring more criticisms of conservative evangelical and fundamentalist semantics it should be noted that Jim Wallis's more politically liberal critique of Glenn Beck's alleged distortion of social justice was referenced in the introduction. The volume of terms and issues makes it impossible to counter every possible perspective in this present work.

277. See Robert Epstein, "What's Going On with Donald Trump? Psychologist Explains the President's Lies, Reversals," *USA Today*, July 30, 2018, accessed July 30, 2018, https://www.usatoday.com/story/opinion/2018/07/30/trump-lies-reversals-rudderless-unprincipled-leader-psychologist-column/848728002/.

Yet this [public] theology [of engagement] does not rest in sheer accomplishment. [Messiah's or] Christ's "coming" is the Son's unitary mission across all time, and so Christ's [or Messiah's] saving work has both always and not yet been completed. During the [present age of the] world, we should live adventally, celebrating the inauguration of our redemption, in and through our participation in Christ's [or Messiah's] mission.

The . . . engagement proposed here is a form of participating in God's kenotic [self-emptying, sacrificial, and *agape*] engagement with the world. By engaging in public interactions with others and enduring the risks those engagements entail, we come better to see and participate in God *pro nobis* [for us or on our behalf].

[This] thoroughly theological and eschatological [future vision] account of human life during the [present age of the] world helps us develop a political theology based on a dynamic engagement in the world.

[This proposal] sees the human's basic desire to be one of ever deepening communion with God, a communion that is realized, in this world, not through a sinful detachment from the world, but rather through a proper engagement with it.

God is most fundamentally found not by escaping the self, the world, or other people, but by engaging them; such engagement shapes us in ways good for our souls and the souls of our interlocutors [those with whom we engage, dialog, and debate].

More fundamentally still, secular thinkers will be uncomfortable about [the Judeo-Christian] . . . understanding of the destiny of public life itself. [This goes against] the too easy refusals of much contemporary secular political thought, for [Judeo-]Christian public life should be properly, ultimately, one more form of love, of seeking communion, of seeking the Beloved Community. Hence, [Judeo-Christian believers] . . . affirm that politics turns out to be theology, a way of seeking God. Here is the deepest tension, on this . . . proposal, between [Judeo-]Christian engagement in public life and that public life's professed self-understanding.

—Charles Matthewes, *A Theology of Public Life*,
Cambridge University Press.

CPSIA information can be obtained
at www.ICGtesting.com
Printed in the USA
LVHW072348170720
661007LV00006B/190